EARLY MODERN SPECTATORSHIP

EARLY MODERN SPECTATORSHIP

Interpreting English Culture, 1500–1780

Edited by
RONALD HUEBERT
and
DAVID McNEIL

McGILL-QUEEN'S UNIVERSITY PRESS
Montreal & Kingston • London • Chicago

ISBN 978-0-7735-5676-8 (cloth)
ISBN 978-0-7735-5677-5 (paper)
ISBN 978-0-7735-5791-8 (ePDF)
ISBN 978-0-7735-5792-5 (ePUB)

Legal deposit second quarter 2019
Bibliothèque nationale du Québec

Printed in Canada on acid-free paper that is 100% ancient forest free (100% post-consumer recycled), processed chlorine free

This book has been published with the help of a grant from the Canadian Federation for the Humanities and Social Sciences, through the Awards to Scholarly Publications Program, using funds provided by the Social Sciences and Humanities Research Council of Canada.

Funded by the Government of Canada | Financé par le gouvernement du Canada | Canada

Conseil des arts du Canada | Canada Council for the Arts

We acknowledge the support of the Canada Council for the Arts, which last year invested $153 million to bring the arts to Canadians throughout the country.

Nous remercions le Conseil des arts du Canada de son soutien. L'an dernier, le Conseil a investi 153 millions de dollars pour mettre de l'art dans la vie des Canadiennes et des Canadiens de tout le pays.

Library and Archives Canada Cataloguing in Publication

Title: Early modern spectatorship : interpreting English culture, 1500–1780 / edited by Ronald Huebert and David McNeil.
Names: Huebert, Ronald, editor. | McNeil, David, 1955– editor.
Description: Includes bibliographical references and index.
Identifiers: Canadiana (print) 20190067861 | Canadiana (ebook) 20190067918 | ISBN 9780773556775 (softcover) | ISBN 9780773556768 (hardcover) | ISBN 9780773557918 (ePDF) | ISBN 9780773557925 (ePUB)
Subjects: LCSH: Performing arts—Audiences—England—History. | LCSH: Arts audiences—England—History. | LCSH: England—Civilization.
Classification: LCC PN1590.A9 E27 2019 | DDC 791.0942—dc23

To our students at Dalhousie University and the University of King's College (1974–2018), whose observations taught us much, and whose accomplishments we continue to watch with enjoyment.

Contents

Bibliographical Note

Whenever quotations are drawn from old-spelling texts, whether in print or in manuscript, usage of *i/j*, *u/v*, and long *s* has been silently modernized, obvious typographical errors have been corrected, and a few archaic abbreviations have been expanded. The official reckoning of dates in the sixteenth and seventeenth centuries was still governed by the Julian calendar, which designates 25 March as the first day of the year. To avoid confusion, therefore, dates between 1 January and 24 March are usually cited as follows: 30 January 1648/49. The slash separates the Julian (old style) reckoning from the Gregorian (new style) adopted by England in 1752 and now adhered to in most jurisdictions.

Preface

The plan on which this book is based came into being in December 2011 when the co-editors were celebrating the end of a busy academic term with a collegial lunch. The conversation drifted as widely as it does on occasions like this, but it seemed to return as if driven by a will of its own to an idea that had been emerging in the research and teaching that each of us had been doing separately. That idea of course is the keyword in the title of this volume: *spectatorship*. Once we had identified this idea as a shared preoccupation, we were able to ask ourselves if there might not be special advantages (and pleasures) to be found in collaboration. By the time lunch had ended we had developed a tentative interest in working as a team.

Our next step was to speak informally about this topic to our colleagues and advanced students at a Friday afternoon colloquium in the Department of English, Dalhousie University, in early 2012. This led to a slightly more formal presentation, "The Public Execution as a Theatrical Event," at the European Studies Conference, Dalhousie (2012), a very early iteration of what we present now as chapter 6. We team-taught a graduate seminar, English 5276: Early Modern Spectatorship, in the fall term of 2012 and again in 2014. Having by this time discovered that ours was a promising inquiry, we began a conversation with McGill-Queen's University Press about the prospect of creating a volume of essays like the one you now hold in your hands. We were lucky indeed to enjoy the support of two successive editors at McGill-Queen's: Mark Abley, who encouraged us from the outset and secured for us an advance contract to publish this collection, and Richard Ratzlaff, who took over our file at a sensitive stage and guided us with great skill to the desired objectives known as final approval and financial support.

The stable relationship with McGill-Queen's made our task of recruiting contributions from first-rate scholars relatively easy. Early on we used the indirect method of inviting conference papers in the hope that some of these would develop into mature essays. We organized two panels on spectatorship at the meetings of the Canadian Society for Renaissance Studies in 2013, and a third at the annual conference of the Canadian Society for Eighteenth-Century Studies in 2014. These events included presentations by Rick Bowers, John Lepage, and Allison Muri which led to the creation of chapters 8, 11, and 12 in our volume. Ronald Huebert's chapter 7 was drafted first as a plenary lecture for the Canadian Society for Renaissance Studies (2014), and supplemented with material presented to the John Donne Society (2014) and the Renaissance Society of America (2015). David McNeil's treatment of Ned Ward's *The London Spy* in chapter 9 was first ventured at meetings of the Association of Canadian College and University Teachers of English and of the International Society for Eighteenth-Century Studies (2015). In addition to the authors already mentioned, we were able to secure commitments from scholars in Canada (William W.E. Slights, Ian McAdam, Emily M. West, Frans De Bruyn), the United States (Nova Myhill), and Great Britain (Lydia Hamlett) for the creation of chapters 3, 4, 5, 10, 2, and 13 respectively. It is with some pleasure and pride that we are able to say that the list of authors with which we began in our first proposal to the press is now the list of authors in our table of contents.

What we offer here is a wide-ranging treatment of a topic that turns out to have been of great interest to early modern thinkers, whether they were preoccupied with theatrical spectacle, or map-making, or exemplary punishment, or virtually any other aspect of their culture. The diversified interests of our authors have enabled us to venture well beyond what we could have attempted as individuals, or even as a collaborative team. Still, we are aware that not every aspect of spectatorship gets a full treatment here. The history of science does indeed create the context for Emily M.

West's discussion of optical technologies (chapter 5), but there could have been more detailed treatment of scientific observation; Sir Francis Bacon and Sir Thomas Browne are names that, for very different reasons, come to mind. But no single volume can deal comprehensively with everything, and we are satisfied that the materials available here will offer sufficient variety for a reader who wants to explore.

All that remains now is to offer words of thanks both to the institutions that have fostered our work and to individuals who have supported or encouraged it. The Department of English at Dalhousie University has given us the opportunity to develop this project, and many of our colleagues have given it their thoughtful attention. The scholarly societies most receptive to our project have already been identified. Practical support has come to us from the Research Development Fund at Dalhousie University and from the Research and Travel Fund at the University of King's College. This book has been published with the help of a grant from the Federation for the Humanities and Social Sciences, through the Awards to Scholarly Publications Program, using funds provided by the Social Sciences and Humanities Research Council of Canada.

Securing illustrations for a book of this kind, along with permissions to print them, is a complicated and time-consuming task. Under this heading we are happy to record here the assistance of Mai Pham (Bridgeman Images), Phoebe Coleman (The Globe Theatre), Princess Pratt (Alamy), Allison Muri (The Grub Street Project), Wayne Franits, and Jack Kilgore. We acknowledge also the contributions of two student assistants, Jeremy Foote and Katy Weatherly. In addition to our two editors, several staff members at McGill-Queen's have worked on our behalf: this list includes Jacqueline Michelle Davis, Filomena Falocco, Kathleen Fraser, Finn Purcell, and Ryan Van Huijstee. Our copy editor, Catherine Marjoribanks, deserves special thanks for the care and intelligence with which she has corrected numerous errors and improved our prose. A further list of persons who have given us invaluable support and expert knowledge would include Patricia Chalmers, Kala Hirtle, Krista Kesselring, Joseph Khoury, Keith Lawson, Mary Beth McIsaac, Karen Smith, and Ian Stewart.

If we return now to the lunch with which these remarks began, we will need to admit that, during the life of this project, there were many more meetings; it would hardly be an exaggeration to say that we came to depend on a weekly meeting to ensure that our project was moving forward. We were fortunate indeed that our wives, Elizabeth Edwards and Erin McNeil, came to see these meetings not as nuisances to be tolerated, but as occasions of great value to both of us. That, indeed, is what they were.

R.H. and D.M.
4 August 2018

EARLY MODERN SPECTATORSHIP

I

Early Modern Spectatorship: An Overview

RONALD HUEBERT AND DAVID McNEIL

The keyword around which we have arranged the essays in this volume was a newcomer in the early modern period. The first edition of Johnson's *Dictionary* (1755) has an entry for "spectatorship," which it glosses as the "Act of beholding," before calling upon the authority of Shakespeare by citing his only recorded use of the word, in *Coriolanus*. Menenius, furious with the First Watchman for barring his access to Coriolanus, warns him of the consequences to come: "Guess but by my entertainment with him if thou stand'st not i'th' state of hanging, or of some death more long in spectatorship and crueller in suffering."[1] For our purposes it is worth noting that Shakespeare uses the word to refer not to the daily performances of his own professional life but to the stamina required to watch a public execution. Perhaps this is why the editors of the *Oxford English Dictionary* (*OED*), while repeating the citation from *Coriolanus*, change the gloss to "Presentation to the eyes of spectators" and declare this meaning obsolete. We are inclined to the view that Johnson was closer to the truth, partly because the act of beholding is exactly the meaning implied in subsequent usage. Just one example will have to suffice, a somewhat painful self-description by Dudley, 3rd Baron North, in the preface to *A Forest of Varieties*. North laments that "the direful extremeties" of recent years have "caryed me to an affectation of dissolution rather then to endure the spectatorship of the growing miseries & approaching tragedies."[2] As a royalist writing in 1645, North had a lot to be nervous about, as our own account of the execution of Charles I (see chapter 6) will attest. For the moment it is enough to observe that the word "spectatorship" is doing important work for early modern users of the English language.

The word "spectator" had of course already entered the language, having arrived by way of Latin, without a *ship*, to designate "A looker on; a beholder" (Johnson), or "A person who sees, or looks on at, some scene or occurrence; a beholder, onlooker, observer" (*OED* Online 1a). Both dictionaries again cite examples from Shakespeare, including the appeal by Time in *The Winter's Tale* to the permissive patience of the "Gentle spectators" (4.1.20). But the spectator is a living presence in the language well before Shakespeare; Thomas Becon, in a prefatory letter to *The new pollecye of warre* addressed to Sir Thomas Wyatt, worries about having been "but a vayne gazer and ydle spectator"[3] rather than an active player in the events of his time. And, as various elements in the *OED* entry remind us, the spectator lives on long after Shakespeare, now as the title of a celebrated eighteenth-century periodical, or again as partner in the compound noun "spectator sport."[4]

More than just a word, spectatorship is an idea with rapidly growing momentum in the critical vocabulary, as our collection of essays will reflect. An initial "document title" ProQuest Dissertations & Theses search turned up 129 items for "spectatorship" with the bulk coming in the last three decades.[5] Then there are the numerous articles and monographs with the related terms "spectator" or "spectacle" in the title, some of which we will soon be citing here. Researching the subject without guidance is a bit like trying to drink from a firehose; we were therefore grateful to discover Dennis Kennedy's book *The Spectator and the Spectacle: Audiences in Modernity and Postmodernity*, a comprehensive, academic, and accessible introduction to our topic by a senior drama scholar.[6] While Kennedy's work concentrates on contemporary and twentieth-century examples ranging from Shakespearean production to sports and popular culture, he has great insight into numerous aspects of spectatorship, is able to link his commentary to much of the related theoretical framework (e.g., Debord on the spectacle, Baudrillard on the simulacrum, etc.), and displays the merit of not attempting to force his insights or commentary into one overall scheme or agenda. What the reader gets in *The Spectator and the Spectacle* is a wealth of accurate observations documented with concrete evidence and informed research. Similarly, our collection offers a wide range of approaches and topics, and, while they do form a coherent whole, they have not been selected because they happen to conform to a single theory of spectatorship.

In practical terms, spectatorship is an essential component in theatre and film studies, since both depend explicitly on the presence of the spectator. However, a glance at the list of critical works in our bibliography will indicate that the concept may be easily represented in poetry, fiction, and critical prose. If we think generally for a moment and consider all the philosophical commentary that draws on the metaphor of seeing as knowing, which we can trace from Plato's cave to twentieth-century phenomenology and beyond, our subject is in danger of exploding into a blinding light. If spectatorship is everything, and everything spectatorship, there is nothing else to say. However, the essays collected here focus on specific early modern topics rather than broad theoretical ideas. The light they shed resembles that which emanates from a crack in the wall rather than a full stream that blinds. In short, we have tried to capture some of the energy of the broad intellectual frisson, and to direct it into more manageable channels, where critical analysis can be productively carried out. Perhaps the most important step in our management of spectatorship has been to historicize it. We are dealing here not with spectators from all cultures and all historical periods; instead, we restrict ourselves to what can be discovered about the practices of spectatorship within English culture between 1500 and 1780. Whenever we overstep these boundaries (and there are many such occasions) it is because one of our authors needs to allude to Dutch painting or medieval piety or French theatre in order to solve a particular question of interpretation about early modern English cultural practice. We are confident that readers will allow us this indulgence, and we hope there are times in which digression will enhance enjoyment.

As a way of bringing together these preliminary observations, we now offer a provisional definition of the historical subject and the set of practices around which these essays are organized. For the purposes of this collection, spectatorship denotes the natural act of human observation in all its diversity, and with all that is implied therein – the will to see (or witness), overcoming the challenges that arise, possibly overstepping moral boundaries, carrying subsequent impressions with all their fallibility into the future, and finally representing this act or aspect thereof in an engaging literary, visual, or dramatic work. Our ocular curiosity may itself not have changed all that much from the early modern period (this remains an open question), but our methods of seeing and being seen certainly have. What these essays offer readers is insight into a familiar condition seen from a distance.

And we propose a supplement to the definition, which can be explained by means of a scientific analogy. In quantum physics, Heisenberg based his uncertainty principle on the awareness that "the act of observation affects the particle being observed."[7] Early modern spectatorship offers many examples of remarkably similar phenomena. Awareness of the spectatorship effect, as we might call it, was readily available in early modern culture, to judge by Casanova's account of his encounters with the nun known as M—M—; he meets her secretly at a Muran casino while her friend, the French ambassador, watches them from a peephole. Casanova's knowledge that he will be watched makes him take special preparations to serve up a "spectacle worthy of Paphos and Amathos," and, while he is quite satisfied with the strength of his performance and that of his partner, he ironically chooses not to describe it for the reader.[8] It hardly needs to be said that the presence of spectators in early modern theatres altered the behaviour of the actors who entertained them. But it is just as likely that the mood of the crowd at a public execution had a bearing on how the condemned person spoke and on how the executioner carried out his task. At the funeral of Sir Philip Sidney (see chapter 8), the protracted spectatorship of a procession changed the meaning of the event. We can't do a full inventory of the pattern here, but we do serve notice that there will be many more examples.

So far we have been writing what could be thought of as an invitation to read the essays in this volume. An open-ended gesture of this kind has its place, but it now needs to be supplemented with particular commentary about the topics addressed in the pages that follow. We have chosen to organize our discussion topic by topic, even if this means that some of our essays will be mentioned under more than one heading. To proceed in this way will allow each contribution to stand on its own, but it will also suggest some of the ways in which the various essays interact with one another and with the idea of our project as a whole.

Fig. 1.1 Frontispiece, Francis Kirkman's *The Wits* (1662).

Theatrical Spectatorship

As the rich and much studied theatrical archive would affirm, much early modern spectatorship occurred in the playhouses, the pleasures of which are celebrated in the engraved frontispiece to Francis Kirkman's *The Wits* (see fig. 1.1). Theatrical spectatorship is discussed at length in the contributions of Nova Myhill and Emily M. West (chapters 2 and 5 respectively). The shared, but sometimes contested, space between the players and the audience is Myhill's concern in her broad history of spectatorship in London's professional theatres from the late sixteenth century to the Restoration.[9] First, she examines a wide selection of texts (e.g., treatises, pamphlets, and guidebooks) that deal with the subject of the audience and how it might be affected by what it sees, or how it might ignore what passes on the stage. Then, she turns to the descriptions of audience behaviour in plays such as *A Midsummer Night's Dream*, *The Knight of the Burning Pestle*, and *A True Widow*, and points to the spectacle potential of Dorset Garden Theatre, which opened in 1671 on the Thames with elaborate stage machinery and changeable scenery. The latter was put to good use in the 1687 production of Aphra Behn's *The Emperor of the Moon*, the subject of Emily M. West's essay, which examines how the play satirizes the new science with its ocular instruments like the microscope and the telescope. These devices, of course, would give access to what the naked eye had been denied: a view of a sub-particle world and of the cosmos. West, however, marks how the English theatre of the late seventeenth and early eighteenth centuries entertained critiques of the new science and its instruments with characters like Shadwell's virtuoso, Sir Nicholas Gimcrack, and Aphra Behn's Dr Baliardo. The history of science bears out this resistance to new technologies.[10] Nevertheless, spectatorship remained important in the development of the new science insofar as it was a way of finding public support and raising research money.[11]

The most famous performances in the early modern playhouses were of plays by Shakespeare, and several of these are given detailed attention in chapters 3 and 4. William W.E. Slights anticipates our next topic, surveillance, as he explores the representations of shame in several texts by Shakespeare (chapter 3). The first of these is *Othello*, in which Iago orchestrates a strategy of surveillance that leads with deadly accuracy to Desdemona's public shaming and murder. All of the evidence is fabricated, as we know, but that doesn't change the outcome. A similar abuse of sexual surveillance in *Much Ado About Nothing* is disarmed because three people at least (Beatrice, Benedick, and the Friar) approach Hero's public shaming with skepticism and are able to reinterpret her blush. No such support is available to the heroine of *The Rape of Lucrece*, of course. In her case, surveillance has been so profoundly internalized that she has no way to escape. We should acknowledge here that in our own day, as in Shakespeare's, a young woman is likely to experience anxiety about her inability to control how she is being looked at. If this has become a question of Internet voyeurism only in our century, it is all the more remarkable that Shakespeare saw the problem as clearly and compellingly as he did.

The focus of attention in much of Ian McAdam's essay, chapter 4, is on Malvolio from *Twelfth Night*. McAdam argues that, in Malvolio's scenes and elsewhere in the play, spectatorship is a form of manipulation that leads to undesirable results: repression, self-deception, humiliation. This mode of argument allows him to illuminate both the unforgivable arrogance of Malvolio's character and the inescapable pathos of his position. Perhaps more surprisingly, McAdam is able to use a similar critical approach to make sense of Antonio, the most enigmatic character in the play. We will not repeat McAdam's interpretation here; instead, we will recommend his essay as one in which the implicit connection between spectatorship and surveillance enhances the experience of watching the plays performed.

Surveillance

This might be the place to make the claim that, were it not for the cultural interpretations of Michel Foucault, the question of spectatorship would not have its present standing. We are thinking specifically of *Discipline and Punish*, a work we acknowledge by citing "The Spectacle of the Scaffold" in our own treatment of public executions (see chapter 6, n1). But Foucault's influence deserves more comprehensive recognition than this. The degree to which he has raised awareness of surveillance in early modern culture, for example, is quite remarkable. One thinks immediately (and quite rightly) of the essay on "Panopticism," also from *Discipline and Punish* – panopticism being a concept that takes on growing importance in a world increasingly monitored by CCTV cameras and interlinked security organizations. But a reminder is in order, perhaps, that this famous discussion begins with a detailed account of the strict procedures for quarantine and daily inspection that governed the life of a French city in the event of an outbreak of bubonic plague in the seventeenth century, and ends with a brief but telling allusion to the Inquisition.[12] Clearly Foucault is implying that the relentless surveillance made possible by Bentham's architectural machine was the culmination of early modern prototypes. One of these would be the ever-watchful eye of Providence pictured at the top of the title-page engraving in Sir Walter Ralegh's *History of the World* (see fig. 1.2). Several of the essays in our collection would support this implicit Foucauldian claim.

In early modern England, surveillance was not yet entrusted to a well-organized police force, since no such institution had yet come into being. The evidence at our disposal would suggest that policing was done in ways that most of us would find either laughable or completely unacceptable, or both. Shakespeare's comedies furnish plenty of examples. Dogberry (as Constable) and Verges (as Headborough) are nominally in charge of the Watch in *Much Ado About Nothing*; that is, they are selected for unpaid police duty, for which they show ineptitude of an order that doubtless made Shakespeare's spectators laugh as loudly as we do. In *Twelfth Night*, policing is both more sinister and less amusing. The Officers who arrest Antonio do so in the name of Duke Orsino. Similarly, when Malvolio is put under house arrest, it is Countess Olivia's retainers who are in charge. The tragedies are full of evidence that the branch of police work we are calling surveillance was carried out by the servants of those in power. Macbeth admits that he "keep[s] a servant fee'd" (3.4.133) in every house to ensure that he'll be informed of any insubordination before it happens; Claudius employs Rosencrantz and Guildenstern to spy on Hamlet, and shares with Polonius the position of voyeur ("seeing unseen"[13]) at the nunnery scene. These are fictional examples, to be sure, but evidence from lived experience would not be hard to find. When the Privy Council intervened so as to ensure that Christopher Marlowe would be awarded his master of arts degree from Cambridge University on the grounds that he "had done her Majesty good service, and deserved to be rewarded for his faithful dealing,"[14] the service alluded to is probably some form of espionage connected to his residence in the Low Countries (in the city of Flushing, in particular) during the time in question. Whether or not Marlowe was a spy, it's clear that many of his contemporaries might have been nervous about who exactly was watching them and why.

What all of this means is that the spectator may occupy a precarious position, depending on what kind of spectacle he or she is observing. If it's a public execution, for example, the spectator may feel that he himself is being watched. We believe this to have been true of John Louthe, who

Fig. 1.2 Title page to Sir Walter Ralegh's *The History of the World* (1614).

claimed that he couldn't endure watching Anne Askew's burning without denouncing those who tormented her, even though his words made him the object of suspicion and retaliation (see chapter 6). At the opposite end of the Christian continuum stands Myles Huggarde, quite probably an eyewitness of Askew's burning, certainly a hostile narrator of the event, and perhaps an informer whose testimony had helped to convict her.

The staging of public executions is already a copiously studied topic, as our notes will make clear; our innovation has been to look at the question not primarily from the point of view of the regime that is asserting its power, or from the point of view of the putative criminal who must pay a heavy price, or of the various officers to whom parts are strictly assigned, but rather from that of the spectators who came by the thousands, and sometimes travelled many miles, to witness the savage spectacle. The abhorrence that we as postmodern readers may feel for electronic displays of politically motivated executions may mark an important difference between our culture and that of early modern Europe. But we should remind ourselves that the transition has been a fairly recent one. In the city of Halifax, Nova Scotia, one of the busiest intersections is still called the Willow Tree, as if to maintain a ghostly memory of the gibbet that, legend has it, once stood there.

The English Reformation, the Catholic response to the Reformation, and the many years of religious tension, suspicion, and outright conflict that followed made it clear to everyone that choosing or affirming a religious allegiance was a matter of critical importance and consequence. The career of John Donne makes this point inescapable. Chapter 7 asks readers to appreciate a negotiation between Catholic tradition and Reformation zeal that was often painful for Donne. And sometimes, as powerful texts in both verse and prose reveal, Donne's pain included the awareness of being watched, not only by God but by demanding patrons or curious parishoners or well-meaning friends. How Donne looks at God becomes, in this chapter, a special opportunity for others, even readers separated from him by four hundred years of history, to make him the object of their surveillance.

Perambulation

While it can be said that a European backdrop is present in this volume, most of the content is decidedly English, and within that compass it is also accurate to recognize a London-centricity. From Sidney's funeral march to the popular amusements recorded by Ned Ward, we are largely tracing London entrancement. From that vantage point, the "prospect poem," discussed in chapter 10, then takes us, by design, outside the urban environment and invites us to adopt a panoramic point of view. In chapter 8, Rick Bowers reminds us that the moving picture is not restricted to the cinema but was made possible by certain mechanical devices like the one John Aubrey saw in 1635 – a succession of illustrations taken from Lant's book on Sidney's funeral that were pulled forward on a roller and gave the impression that the figures were indeed in motion. Not only did the moving pictures mesmerize Aubrey in 1635, but an imitation of this mechanism has been rendered in digital form for today's Internet spectators, and so it might be said that Sidney's funeral display, which, according to Bowers, constituted a new form of public national heroism, is reborn as a simulacrum. It is not surprising that London, the urban centre, would offer the most diverse form of entertainments for the eye. If this idea can be said to prefigure today's London Eye experience, it can also be situated historically by consulting the maps of London by Norden (1593), Strype (1720), and Rocque (1749) reproduced in this volume (see figs. 8.1, 12.1, 12.2, 9.1, 9.3, 9.4, and 9.5).

Diversity arising from amusement beyond the ocular is perhaps most evident in McNeil's examination of Ned Ward's *London Spy* (chapter 9). Unlike the highlighting of visual material in Lant's publication, Ward's work is simple in design insofar as it consists of eighteen monthly instalments or essays that represent in text the material experiences of the street and its low-life establishments. Ward's readers must use their imaginations to see what London has to offer a young man seeking novelty, and all they have to go on are the colourful, detailed, and sometimes predictable "characters" that Ward draws with his words. McNeil recognizes that the reader is not just imagining Ward's London in the geographic sense, as the Spy and his companion make their way from the east end to the west and then back east, but sharing with the pair a full calendar of entertainments, beginning with Bartholomew Fair, the Mayor's Procession, etc. Critics have long associated Ward with the emergence of the popular periodical, and *The Spectator*, of course, is at the centre of the future development of this genre. However, we might also note how the term and genre spill over into French culture, as the idea of a "*spectacle*" takes on the meaning of the *business* of showing, of creating allure.

We get well beyond London in chapter 10 with Frans De Bruyn's analysis of topographical poetry, which has delighted readers of all ages with its bird's-eye representations of, again, not just the physical landscape but of the history that is written into that landscape (if only, at times, in the historical imagination). De Bruyn traces "how a literary convention that began by insisting on the actual ocular experience of looking at a landscape from a specific vantage point (in John Denham's *Coopers Hill*, James Thomson's *The Seasons*, and John Dyer's *Grongar Hill*, for instance) evolved over the eighteenth century in ways that transformed actual sight into imagined sight and eventually abandoned sight altogether" (243). In the words of De Bruyn, the reason for this evolution is that "the nascent science of statistics supplanted the ocular reach of the poetic prospect" (243). And so it is with Edmund Burke's rejection of Richard Price's characterization of the events in France in 1789, or Burke's earlier vision of the events in America, and earlier still, the prospect of Milton's Archangel Michael as he unveils it to Adam from the highest point in Paradise.

The Iconography of Watching

Three of the chapters in this collection deal with spectatorship and the visual arts. First, in chapter 11, John Lepage considers depictions of a pair of philosophers who represent opposite positions in the cultural history of the West: Democritus, the laughing philosopher, and Heraclitus, the weeping philosopher. That these two figures were understood to be in constant dialogue is an important part of their cultural function, as is the presence of the *theatrum mundi* topos in all the arts. One of the most engaging uses of the latter insofar as spectatorship is concerned comes in a novel, specifically Henry Fielding's *Tom Jones*, just after the reader is led to condemn the behaviour of Black George, who slips Tom's £500 note into his own pocket (see book 7, chap. 1). The narrator performs an anatomy of the audience as per society's classes and concludes that "the Man of Candour, and of true Understanding, is never hasty to condemn."[15] While humanity, with all its levels and fallibility, may not have any right to condemn, the same would not be true of the divine, sometimes represented by the providential eye alluded to already (see fig. 1.2). In any case, Lepage accepts the Leonard Barkan notion that the Horatian *ut pictura poesis* motto should be understood as giving primacy to mute poetry over speaking pictures, and that the visual image is always in service of literary art. Hence, the central image for Lepage is the dramatic portrait of the laughing philosopher as the frontispiece to Robert Burton's *The Anatomy of Melancholy*, which epitomizes the sense of spectatorship that prevails from beginning to end in the dialogue between Democritus and Heraclitus.

After this broad account, we turn to a reconsideration of William Hogarth's *A Harlot's Progress* (1731). Technological developments in the digital humanities have enhanced our knowledge of spectatorship in the early modern period, including the literary culture of London. Easy Internet access to annotated high-resolution maps, provided by research initiatives like The Grub Street Project, now allows the curious everywhere to examine detailed representations of the streets and alleys of seventeenth- and eighteenth-century London. Thus, Allison Muri's contribution (chapter 12) is both a study in iconography and another London perambulation. Muri, who has led The Grub Street Project,[16] calls our attention to the historical detail behind Hogarth's *A Harlot's Progress* in an effort to demonstrate how Bakhtin's idea of the chronotope might be employed to illuminate the print series.[17] According to Muri, "the paths Moll Hackabout follows through and around the spaces of London reflect a temporal progress of spectacle in the papers, and similarly serve to ironically undermine the redemptive possibility that the prints might at first seem to suggest" (299). This folding of the spatial and temporal resembles McNeil's comments on the contents of *The London Spy*, which is not just a perambulation of London and environs but one that is tied to a calendar of events, some annual, others unique.

Iconographic interpretation needs to proceed with great subtlety when the object of study is the specific practice of decorative art, as in Lydia Hamlett's examination of the early eighteenth-century murals by Louis Laguerre (chapter 13). Hamlett focuses on Laguerre's work at Marlborough House, Blenheim Palace, and Petworth House and how it "tell[s] us something not only about the intended functions of these murals and how they were to be viewed but also about post-Restoration spectatorship in general" (331). A visitor to Marlborough House might be said to walk into a visual re-enactment of the War of the Spanish Succession as its famous battles and not-so-famous scenes of pillage and horror cover the walls. Directed by the Duchess of Marlborough, Laguerre was paying tribute to the Duke's great military accomplishments. Something a little different was called for in the saloon at Blenheim. In a kind of imitation of the Grand Couvert at Versailles, where the monarch dining was a public spectacle for court viewers, the walls here were painted to depict representatives from four continents, peering inwards as if into a pavilion, making a dinner guest feel their simulated gaze. Finally, at Petworth the spectator is enticed to witness female transformation in the mythic scenes (e.g., those of Pandora and Epimetheus) and to associate them with the Duchess of Somerset.

Rethinking the Rules

We are of course aware that most of our readers will be *selecting* what they want from this volume: a reader doing research on mural paintings may select chapter 13 only; a Shakespeare scholar may turn to chapter 3 or 4, or perhaps to both. Very few will read our book, as we have done repeatedly, from beginning to end. And this recognition of our own special relationship to the project as a whole prompts us to conclude with some general observations about early modern spectatorship. These observations will suggest that, far from remaining constant over the *longue durée* we have chosen to study (1500–1780), the game of spectatorship changed many of its rules between the time of Sir Thomas More and that of Samuel Johnson. We cannot here give a full inventory of these changes, but we can outline revisions that, we believe, occurred on three fronts: the spectator's authority, the reflexivity of spectatorship, and the angle of vision.

The Spectator is a name to reckon with in the history of British periodical literature. Created by Joseph Addison and Richard Steele, it began its highly influential run of daily publication on 1 March 1711. The title of this work by itself would be enough to suggest that spectatorship had become, in the eighteenth century, a highly regarded activity. The invention of a fictional spokesperson, "Mr Spectator," who in effect sets the cultural standards for his milieu, is a further endorsement of this authority. No such publication would have been possible in 1511 or even 1611, when the spectator would have been too abjectly convinced of his or her marginal status, or too preoccupied with evading the spy network, to be confident of an authoritative voice. A small cultural change, you may say, but a noticeable one. And a change that works in tandem with two further revisions we will now identify.

Spectatorship, during the extended early modern period that we have chosen to study, gradually took on qualities that we will describe as reflexivity. We borrow this term from grammatical practice in some European languages other than English. The phrase "*je me souviens*" will be familiar to every speaker of French, and to most anglophone Canadians with even a modest appreciation of the other official language. Similarly, "*ich erinnere mich*" will be perfectly recognizable to any speaker of German. In both cases the action of the verb is transmitted to the subject, as the somewhat cumbersome English translation "I remind myself" would suggest.

We believe that, by analogy, it is possible to observe increasing reflexivity within early modern acts of spectatorship. What we mean here is that spectators become increasingly aware that, while watching others, they are themselves being watched. It is difficult to explain this paradigm convincingly in the abstract, but easy to identify it in those instances where it happens. We will point to just two such occasions, and let the reader add others at will. The first case is the opening moments of Francis Beaumont's play *The Knight of the Burning Pestle*, discussed at some length by Nova Myhill in chapter 2, during which the citizen playgoers George and Nell refuse to accept passive spectatorship, demand sitting positions on the stage, and then insist on rewriting the script to suit their own requirements.[18] Our second example is Louis Laguerre's murals for the saloon at Blenheim Palace in which, as Lydia Hamlett argues in chapter 13, "the realm and gaze of the painted spectators" (338) is surely itself the object of spectation. The historical positioning of these two examples (1607 and c. 1719) would suggest that reflexive spectatorship is a category still coming into its own.

And finally, the angle of vision. After Marlowe's Doctor Faustus signs his pact with the devil, he quickly lapses into the proper angle of vision for a spectator inhabiting traditional culture: "When I behold the heavens then I repent / And curse thee, wicked Mephastophilis, / Because thou hast depriv'd me of those joys."[19] But this is only a lapse. Faustus aspires to fly, just as Icarus did before him, and with demonic assistance he is able to do so: while riding in a chariot drawn by a team of dragons, Faustus can take the much coveted bird's-eye view of Germany, France, and Italy, including Venice, "In mid'st of which a sumptuous temple stands / That threats the stars with her aspiring top" (3.1.17–18). Everything Faustus says makes it clear that he will never be content as the little man looking upward. And there is a sense in which his restlessness is carried forward into the future of early modern culture. As spectators gain authority, at times even taking control of the script, they come to think of themselves as looking down on a world spread out beneath them. This is certainly the whole point of ascending the highest available peak, as De Bruyn's topographical poets do, in order to represent for us our own world, perhaps, but seen from above. In 1783, a few years after our closing date (1780), the invention of the hot-air balloon by the brothers Montgolfier would make the bird's-eye view technically available, if not yet widely accessible.[20] The spectator is no longer being hurled back into the sea, as Icarus was, but has begun an ascent that will eventually show us what our earth looks like from a space station on the moon.

NOTES

1 Shakespeare, *The Tragedy of Coriolanus*, 5.2.62–5. Unless noted otherwise, Shakespeare references are to individual volumes in the Oxford Shakespeare, as identified under Primary Sources in the Bibliography. References are to act, scene, and line.

2 North, *A Forest of Varieties*, A2.

3 Becon, *The new pollecye of warre*, B4.

4 For further comment about the history of the word "spectator," see Porter, *Making and Unmaking in Early Modern English Drama*, 32–3.

5 ProQuest Dissertations & Theses Global, "Document Title" search for "Spectatorship" done on 11 January 2017, by David McNeil.

6 Kennedy, *The Spectator and the Spectacle*.

7 Jha, "What Is Heisenberg's Uncertainty Principle?"

8 Casanova, *The Memoirs of Casanova*, Episode 8, "Convent Affairs," chap. 18. Location 17000–17980.

9 Jim Davis moves the discussion historically a step forward in "Spectatorship," *The Cambridge Companion to British Theatre, 1730–1830*, 57–69.

10 For instance, see Coppola, *The Theatre of Experiment*.

11 Larry Stewart has demonstrated this trend with respect to physics in the latter half of the eighteenth century. See his chapter "Physics on Show: Entertainment, Demonstration, and Research in the Long Eighteenth Century" in *The Oxford Handbook of the History of Physics*, 300–25.

12 Foucault, "Panopticism," in *Discipline and Punish: The Birth of the Prison*, 195–200, 227. For a discussion of the influence of Foucault's work on twentieth-century theorists, see Jay, "In the Empire of the Gaze: Foucault and the Denigration of Vision in Twentieth-Century French Thought," in *Foucault: A Critical Reader*, 175–203.

13 Shakespeare, *Hamlet*, 3.1.32.

14 See Riggs, *The World of Christopher Marlowe*, 180.

15 Fielding, *The History of Tom Jones*, 329.

16 See Muri, "The Technology and Future of the Book," 235–50; "Graphs, Maps, and Digital Topographies," 79–98; "Beyond GIS"; and "Alexander Pope's Dunciad (1728–9)."

17 Mikhail Bakhtin defined the "chronotope" as "the intrinsic connectedness of temporal and spatial relationships that are artistically expressed" in which "spatial and temporal indicators are fused into one carefully thought-out, concrete whole.... [Time] becomes artistically visible; likewise, space becomes charged and responsive to the movements of time, plot and history." See *The Dialogic Imagination*.

18 For a thoughtful and persuasive approach to this topic, see Pangallo, "'Mayn't a Spectator Write a Comedy?'" 39–59.

19 Marlowe, *Doctor Faustus: A 1604-Version Edition*, 2.3.1–3. Subsequent references are to this edition. References are to act, scene, and line.

20 See Jackson, *Airships*, 15–17, and Holmes, *Falling Upwards*.

2

Making Spectacles: Spectatorship and Authority on the Early Modern Stage

NOVA MYHILL

Beginning with the construction in 1567 of the Red Lion, the first purpose-built professional theatre in London, theatrical spectatorship became a social activity predicated on the regular, rather than the occasional, availability of access to theatrical performances, and one that occurred in venues specifically designed to create a particular set of relations between spectators and the plays that they came to see. While nominally and legally under the patronage of nobility and, after the accession of James I in 1603, members of the royal family, theatrical companies from 1567 to 1642 depended on attracting a paying audience to public theatres for the vast majority of their revenue, a circumstance that still obtained, although under some significantly different circumstances, after the restoration of the monarchy in 1660. The professional theatre in early modern England therefore operated under two very distinct forms of patronage: the political patronage of the court and the economic patronage of the more socially mixed audience.

When David Garrick proclaimed that "The Drama's Laws the Drama's Patrons give / For we that live to please, must please to live,"[1] he was quite clear about which form of patronage obtained at the Theatre in Drury Lane in 1747: "The Stage but echoes back the publick Voice." This position stands in stark contrast to the anxiety, expressed in an antitheatrical tract from 1612, that "Players assume an unlawfull office to themselves of instruction and correction,"[2] with its implication that the audience would echo what it heard and saw on the stage, not the other way round. A history of theatrical spectatorship in early modern England can be productively framed in terms of the negotiation between these two positions and their underlying assumptions about the relative authority of spectator and spectacle, and the flexibility of those positions, in the social and physical environments of London's public theatres.

Beginning with the antitheatrical writings of Stephen Gosson and Antony Munday in the 1570s and '80s and ending with the performance of Thomas Shadwell's *A True Widow* in Dorset Garden by the Duke's Company a century later, this essay considers the period from the beginnings of the professional theatre in England to the late seventeenth century in terms of continuity as well as change. The closing of the theatres between 1642 and 1660 is quite justifiably treated as marking an epochal division in the history of theatre in England; the claim that "the revolutionary nature of the changes effected in the Restoration theatre cannot be too strongly emphasized"[3] is certainly the dominant view.[4] While not disputing the significance of these differences, I think it is quite possible to overstate them, particularly as they pertain to the relations between spectators and performance in the first twenty years after the Restoration. The introduction of perspective scenery did not remove significant portions of the theatre audience from their position behind the forestage, and it certainly did not make the Restoration theatre less a place to see and be seen than its Caroline predecessors. *A True Widow* relies on the same competition between the performers and the onstage audience for attention and asks the same questions of what the price of admission really buys as do Ben Jonson's plays, written for the Blackfriars forty or fifty years earlier. With this continuity in the visibility of the theatre audience in mind, let us consider how it might shape considerations of theatrical spectatorship in the period.

Contesting Priority

Importantly, the theatre in sixteenth- and seventeenth-century London, regardless of its physical form, was a social environment, in which the spectators and actors shared the same light and frequently the same physical spaces. Accounts of playgoing in Elizabethan England offer accounts of both "the audience's mute wonder"[5] and the diversity and the activity of the crowd of spectators; the first of these prioritizes the spectacle of the dramatic performance, while the second emphasizes the extent to which the audience itself functioned as a spectacle that competed with the actors for both space and attention.[6] This tension between the theatre as a space of imaginative engagement in which the bones of Talbot might be "new embalmed with the teares of ten thousand spectators"[7] weeping over his death in Shakespeare's *Henry VI, Part 2*, and as a social locus in which audience members "come to see and be seen"[8] with relatively little interest in the play itself, animates considerations of the types of spectatorship available to the early modern theatregoer. The range of possibilities both shapes and is shaped by the differing types of audience visibility that might be purchased at outdoor amphitheatres such as the Theatre (1576), the Rose (1587), the Globe (1599), and the Red Bull (1604); the indoor hall playhouses of the Tudor/Stuart period, particularly the second Blackfriars (1596); and Restoration theatres that employed changeable scenery such as the Dorset Garden Theatre (1671).

Only when the early modern spectator becomes an object of spectatorship does he or she leave textual traces, and such traces are infrequent in the surviving external evidence.[9] In the absence of such documentation, the representation of audience behaviour within plays and inductions provides an important means of considering the shifting assumptions and anxieties about theatrical spectatorship in early modern London. While such representations are almost inevitably satirical and cannot be taken as accurate representations of audience behaviour, "satire needs something real to attack or it is not satire."[10] The dramatic representation of audiences presents possible modes of reception for scrutiny in the same way that inset spectacles such as plays within plays present modes of performance, and invites similar forms of analysis on the part of both contemporary audiences and modern scholars. Scholars of both Shakespearean and Restoration drama agree that representations of disruptive and incompetent audiences serve "to dissuade potential troublemakers by presenting them with an intensified image of certain kinds of undesirable behaviour and encouraging the rest of the audience to reinforce its unattractiveness by laughter."[11] But we can also read these representations of spectatorship as having more specific goals than simply discouraging disruptive behaviour

– goals that shifted as expectations of theatrical spectatorship became increasingly specific to particular theatres and to particular areas within individual theatres.[12]

As the period goes on, it is possible to trace certain patterns in the forms of spectatorship presented for correction. In the 1580s and even the 1590s, the demands made on spectators were relatively simple. The professional theatre was a new commercial, social, and artistic institution, and the conventions of both performance and reception were being worked out, defining a form of spectatorship that went beyond "the most basic form of theatrical competence – the ability to recognize the play as such"[13] to include certain habits of thought and reception. Despite Peter Quince's anxiety in *A Midsummer Night's Dream* that Bottom's excessively terrifying performance as the lion "would fright the Duchess and the ladies that they would shriek; and that were enough to hang us all,"[14] audiences in the Elizabethan period are never represented as unable to distinguish between fiction and reality; at issue instead is the question of to what extent theatrical spectators might engage with the theatrical spectacle, and how judgment might be applied.

Early representations of theatrical audiences overwhelmingly represent the practice of theatrical spectatorship as watching occasional drama in the courts of royalty, as in the case of the mechanicals performing for Theseus's wedding in *A Midsummer Night's Dream*. To watch these instances is to see a literalization of the position of players as servants to a great lord or monarch, to imagine that theatrical spectatorship is primarily a matter of interpretive authority, that the audience is composed of "gentles all,"[15] and that the spectatorial relationship that matters is a one-way gaze from playgoer to performance. But the existence of all early modern playhouses depends on thousands of people regularly choosing to attend the theatre and being willing to pay for the privilege, and the experience of watching the play was only part of what attending the theatre might entail. As the seventeenth century wore on, representations of theatrical spectatorship included scenes set in the playhouses themselves and became increasingly focused on how the financial aspect of the public theatre – an issue entirely undiscussed in earlier drama – might restructure the relation between spectator and spectacle. In *The Magnetic Lady*, performed at the Blackfriars in 1633, Ben Jonson's audience surrogate, Damplay, proclaims, "I care not for marking the play: I'll damn it, talk, and do that I come for" because he has "give[n] my eighteen pence or two shillings for my seat."[16]

Damplay's insistence that "I will not have *Gentlemen* lose their priviledge, nor I my selfe my prerogative, for neere an overgrowne, or superannuated Poët of 'hem all. Hee shall not give me the Law; I will censure, and be witty, and take my Tobacco, and enjoy my *Magna Charta* of reprehension, as my Predecessors have done before me" (3 Chor. 22–5) frames his position as an audience member as being in direct competition with the playwright as the creator of theatrical spectacle. This echoes concerns about the fluidity of the positions of spectator and spectacle clearly visible in the rush of early antitheatrical pamphlets in the late 1570s and early 1580s. Antony Munday claims that "none delight in these spectacles, but such as would be made spectacles," bitterly complaining of the "yong ruffins [and] harlots, utterlie past all shame: who presse to the fore-frunt of the scaffoldes, to the end to showe their impudencie, and to be as an object to al mens eies."[17] There they "commit that filthines openlie, which is horrible to be done in secret." The exact nature of this "filthines," and whether Munday's description has any basis in actual audience behaviour, is unknowable; Elizabethan antitheatrical writings are even less reliable indices of theatrical practice than later pamphlets because their arguments are drawn primarily from the Church fathers rather than contemporary practice. But this limited connection to actual theatregoing makes these documents particularly revealing in their specific anxieties about theatrical spectatorship: here, the potential for the ruffian and the harlot to use the theatre space to make themselves the centre of the audience's attention, and the possibility that they might attract at least as much attention as the play itself and serve as a quite different form of example.

Munday's anxiety about the relation between spectacle and spectator stems from the fact that humanist theories of education, which are substantially formulated as the imitation of models, rely upon the authority of the spectacle over the spectator as a necessary component of all education.[18] The theatre therefore poses two entirely distinct threats – first, that spectators will be re-formed to resemble the performance that they see, taking "those impressions of mind … which the players do counterfeit on the stage,"[19] and second, that they might, like Munday's harlots and ruffians, make spectacles of themselves and thus assume the unlawful authority of example that he fears in the players. Theatrical representations of audience behaviour, however, reject both of these models that locate authority exclusively in either spectacle or spectator, and request instead for the playgoers "gently to hear, kindly to judge our play" (*Henry V*, Prologue, 34). In its emphasis on the audience's capacity for judgment, the Prologue to Shakespeare's *Henry V* stresses the need for active engagement and interpretation on the part of the spectators, asking them to "piece out our imperfections with your thoughts" (23), a model of collaborative creation.

When Theseus, in *A Midsummer Night's Dream,* chooses the mechanicals' play because of, rather than despite, Philostrate's insistence that "it is nothing, nothing in the world / Unless you can find sport in their intents ... To do you service" (5.1.78–81), he attempts to avoid the power of spectacle that the antitheatrical writers fear. The anxieties about the "shaping fantasies" of the lunatic, the lover, and the poet are put to rest by the certainty that the mechanicals are "nothing," and can produce no effect except the one Theseus himself shapes. The spectacle is thus not the mechanicals' "mistaking" but the court's "tak[ing] what they mistake" (5.1.90): the spectacle of the magnanimity of "giv[ing] thanks for nothing" (5.1.89). Reversing the antitheatrical anxiety about the shaping power of the spectacle, Theseus desires the shaping powers of the spectator in a similarly absolute manner. His reading of the spectacle denies any possibility of being part of a transaction; the mechanicals' play will be a product of his "imagination ... and not theirs" (5.1.207), as Hippolyta reminds him.

The comments Theseus, Demetrius, and Lysander make on the mechanicals' play are exceptionally literal. Refusing to engage with the fictive world or the narrative before them, they comment on talking walls and interrupt Starveling's Moonshine until he loses patience and explains himself to them. Certain of the stability of their own position, and their new marriages, the courtiers vanquish fancy with reason, rigidly control their eyes, and see only their social inferiors striving "to do [Theseus] service" (5.1.81). The limitations of this view are fairly obvious, particularly in its implicit denial of the experiences of the lovers in the forest and its distance from Bottom's "most rare vision" (4.1.200). In seeing the mechanicals as having "nothing" to contribute to the evening's entertainment except an opportunity for their audience to show their ability to do all of the work of interpreting, the courtly spectators lose the ability to see themselves. The return of the fairies to the stage to bless the marriage beds insists on the errors of this view and subjects the three couples to the spectacular powers that Theseus's reason refuses: powers that are used to preserve the marriages and assure that their "issue … Ever shall be fortunate" (5.1. 383–4).

Theseus's viewing of "Pyramus and Thisbe" precisely refutes all of the anxieties of viewing presented in the antitheatrical tracts discussed above. If all spectators might provide the shaping force of imagination, rather than being shaped by that of the players, then the theatre would only confirm rather than transform. If spectacles are "nothing," and spectators are everything, no transaction, no transformation, can take place. But, unlike Heywood's *Apology for Actors*, which claims that "Plays are in use as they are understood / Spectators' eyes may make them bad or good,"[20] *A Midsummer Night's Dream* does not suggest this reversal of authority as a viable alternative, insisting instead on a transactional model of vision in which the position of spectator involves both seeing and being seen, judging and being judged.

Competing Spaces

Consideration of the physical spaces of these performances invites us to locate the position of the spectator in more literal terms; even as the represented audiences on the Elizabethan stage embodied the fiction of a socially and intellectually unified group composed of "gentles all," the physical configuration of the amphitheatres and the associated price structure ensured that the theatre was as hierarchical a space as any in England, and that a shared spectacle did not mean a unified audience. The process of moving to better seats in the amphitheatres such as the Theatre, Globe, Rose, and Red Bull involved literally buying access to the next social level; Thomas Platter visited the Globe in 1599, reporting that "whoever cares to stand below pays only one English penny" but that a seat costs another penny, and "if he desire to sit in the most comfortable seats … where he not only sees everything well, but can also be seen, then he pays yet another English penny at another door."[21] As the number of London theatres increased in the early seventeenth century and both the theatres and their clientele diversified, the vision of a unified audience became less tenable even as a fantasy.

In 1596, James Burbage purchased the Great Hall of the Upper Frater in the liberty of Blackfriars and began work to transform it into a public theatre as a replacement for the aging Theatre, where he was in danger of losing his lease.[22] The decision to build a dedicated theatrical space based on the smaller occasional indoor theatre spaces such as the Chapel at St Paul's Cathedral was an important moment in the development of the English stage in both social and architectural terms. The new theatre that Burbage and his associates constructed for the Lord Chamberlain's Men was significantly smaller than the Theatre, which had held between two and three thousand spectators; the Blackfriars playhouse had a capacity of about six hundred, and presumably planned to charge much higher prices. It was located within the walls of the city rather than on its disreputable outskirts, close to the Inns of Court and other locations populated by fashionable young men interested in making their mark, and ultimately became the first indoor professional theatre where the actors were adult professionals rather than the highly trained boy companies of St Paul's and the Children of the Chapel (see fig. 2.1).

But it would be over twenty years before that happened, because the residents of Blackfriars, including the company's own patron, protested Burbage's planned use of the theatre, which, they claimed, "will grow to be a very great annoyance and trouble ... to all the inhabitants of the [Blackfriars] precinct ... by reason of the great resort and gathering together of all manner of vagrant and lewd persons that, under colour of resorting to the plays, will come hither and work all manner of mischief."[23] The Privy Council refused Burbage permission to use his new theatrical space, and the Lord Chamberlain's Men instead solved their tenancy problem by disassembling the Theatre, sliding it across the frozen Thames, and reconstructing it as the Globe on the south bank in 1599. The theatre at Blackfriars, unavailable to the adult company, was leased to the Children of the Queen's Revels from 1600 to 1609, when changes in the political climate allowed the Lord Chamberlain's Men, now the King's Men, to finally take occupancy of their theatre.

When they did so, they moved into a space that was fully enclosed against the weather, lit with candles and at least some windows. The space provided seating for all audience members and "most significantly, it reversed the open air playhouse's prioritization of the poorest people, who

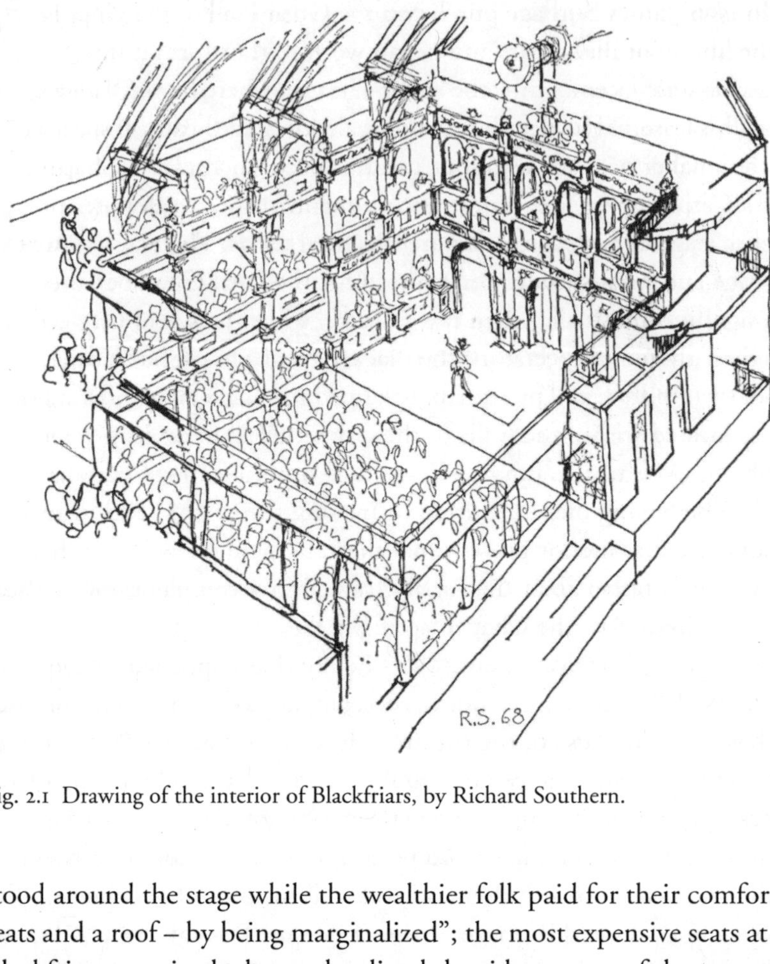

Fig. 2.1 Drawing of the interior of Blackfriars, by Richard Southern.

stood around the stage while the wealthier folk paid for their comforts – seats and a roof – by being marginalized"; the most expensive seats at the Blackfriars were in the boxes that lined the sides or rear of the stage, and the second most expensive were on the stage itself.[24] The Blackfriars drew a significantly different and more socially homogeneous audience than the Globe, particularly during its years as a boys' company playhouse; its minimum admission price of sixpence for the seats in the pit made it a vastly more expensive alternative to the outdoor amphitheatres, where admission started at a penny, and while its repertory may or may not have differed from the Globe's once the King's Men were operating both theatres, it certainly did while it was the home of the Children of the Queen's Revels. Satirical representations of the Blackfriars audience offer us an important model of theatrical spectatorship as the professional theatre became both more entrenched and more diversified around the time that James I assumed the throne in 1603.

In *The guls horne-booke* (1609), Thomas Dekker, a successful playwright as well as a prolific pamphleteer, mocks the ostentatious behaviour of the London would-be gallants, who have "a poore and silly ambition to be thought you inherit the revenues of extrordinary wit";[25] his chapter on "How a Gallant should behave himselfe in a Playhouse" advises his would-be gallant to "presently advance himselfe up to the Throne of the Stage ... on the very Rushes where the Commedy is to daunce, yea ... under the state of Cambises himselfe," a location vastly superior to the lord's rooms, the boxes that "by the inquity of custome, conspiracy of waiting-women and Gentlemen-Ushers ... and the covetousnes of Sharers, are contemptibly thrust into the reare," where "much new Satten is there damnd by being smothred to death in darknesse" (C2–2^{v}). The occupation of the stage, "whether ... [of] the publique or the private Playhouse," grants the gallant a solid advantage over "your Groundling and Gallery Commoner, [who] ... buyes his sport by the penny" (C2^{v}), because the space of the stage gives the would-be gallant a level of visibility equal to that of the actors and far surpassing that of the occupants of the boxes.

Where Shakespeare's audience in *A Midsummer Night's Dream* is represented as understanding the play as presented for their convenience, it is at least actually watching the play; Dekker's gallant understands the play as entirely incidental to the main function of the theatre – a venue that gives him the opportunity to display "the best and most essencial parts of a Gallant (good cloathes, a proportionable legge, white hand, the Persian lock, and a tollerable beard)" (C2^{v}). Dekker's satire, while presumably not a literal description of the Jacobean playhouse and certainly not exclusive to the Blackfriars, emphasizes the overwhelmingly social function of the theatre, and the extent to which spectatorship is focused on other audience members. While the stage gives the gallant a visible place from which to "laugh alowd in the middest of the most serious and saddest scene of the terriblest Tragedy: and to let that clapper (your tongue) be tost so high that all the house may ring of it" (C3^{v}), and thus bring his name to every man's lips, it also exposes him to censure: "whether you be a foole or a Justice of peace, a Cuckold or a Captein, a Lord Maiors sonne or a dawcock, a knave or an under Shreife, of what stamp soever you be, currant or counterfeit, the Stagelike time will bring you to most perfect light, and lay you open" (C3). Acknowledging the public nature of theatrical space, rather than fictionalizing it as the court with its restricted access, Dekker's satire emphasizes its potential to afford spectators the otherwise socially unavailable position of spectacle. Princes (like Theseus) may be "as it were set … on a stage, in the sight of all the people,"[26] but the striving gallant has fewer opportunities to make a spectacle of himself; Gurr suggests that "the social advantage of parading oneself at the Blackfriars or the Cockpit came second only to an appearance at the court itself."[27]

Henry Fitzgeffrey's satirical "Notes from Black-Fryers" (1617) similarly suggests that the most important reasons for attending the theatre all involve displaying a carefully curated version of oneself to the rest of the audience; the play is, at best, incidental. But where Dekker's pamphlet focuses on the gallant making a spectacle of himself, Fitzgeffrey's poem places his narrator, an Inns of Court student killing time before watching a play he is certain will bore him, in the position of an invisible spectator not to the play but to the other audience members, who represent a broad range of social types each with its own location in the theatre, including the braggart soldier who "in the middle region doth stand,"[28] a "*Cheapside* Dame" who is "bespoken for a box" (F1, F1^{v}), and the "*Tissue slop*" who enters the stage with "Stoole and Cushion" (F2^{v}), busily spending his entire revenue. The satire associates particular social types with particular physical locations, a trend also apparent in Restoration accounts of playgoing, but all are part of the spectacle that allows the narrator to assert his own authority as judge. As the members of the audience place themselves on display, Fitzgeffrey's narrator evaluates them all, anatomizes their abuses, and, according to the commendatory poem that follows the "Notes," will thus save the stage by refining its audience, educating it not to hiss "true Verse" (F8^{v}) – that is, to prefer its own pretentions of judgment to the narrator's.

Competing Judgments

In some sense, the position of an audience member in Blackfriars is always that of judgment; to enter the space is to claim the right to "judge for [one's] sixpence"[29] – a claim that can be made by anyone with sixpence to spend, and a claim that various playwrights in the early seventeenth century sought to shift from economic to critical terms. It is in this context that I wish to consider the effect of George and Nell, the "citizen" characters who join the gallants seated on the stage, on the various parts of the Blackfriars audience in Francis Beaumont's *The Knight of the Burning Pestle* (1608).

The printer Walter Burre's description of *The Knight of the Burning Pestle* as "unlike his brethren" seems apposite in a number of ways; it is the first play to take playgoing in the commercial theatres of early modern London as its explicit subject, and to take effective advantage of the physical configuration of the seating arrangements that allowed actors to join the audience members seated on the stage. The play depends on the collapse of the physical and social boundaries between player and spectator; three lines into the prologue of the play, George, a "member of the noble city,"[30] interrupts the player and demands the company replace its planned citizen comedy, "The London Merchant," with a new play "to the honor of the commons of the city" (25), starring his apprentice, Rafe. George and his wife Nell then join the stage-sitters for the duration of the play, making frequent comments on and occasional interventions in what they see performed.

With its almost continuous presentation of George and Nell's spectatorial practice, *The Knight of the Burning Pestle* focuses attention on both the social homogeneity of the Blackfriars audience (no matter who they are or where they sit, the audience is positioned to see George and Nell as outsiders, unaware of or resistant to the conventions of watching a Blackfriars play) and the potential heterogeneity that economic forces might introduce. The part of the audience most directly affected by *The Knight of the Burning Pestle* would be the stage-sitters like Fitzgeffrey's "*Tissue slop*" or the gallant Dekker satirizes taking a place on "the Throne of the stage." When George and Nell take their own seats on the stage, they enter the social space of the gallants seated on stage who display their status as both models of fashion and arbiters of taste.

George and Nell's presence fundamentally alters the dynamics of the Blackfriars, framing the onstage spectators as incidental to the play rather than the other way round, and emphasizing their vulnerability to judgment from the rest of the audience. While George's proclaimed status as a citizen marks him as coming from a lower social position than most of the habitual stage-sitters, he is not a completely incompetent spectator, just one who goes a few steps further than behaviour satirized in other places.[31] Rather than merely complaining loudly about the play to his friends, he complains to the players; rather than conspicuously absenting himself, "drawing what troupe he can from the stage,"[32] he asks for a different play. As various satires attest, the strictly economic terms that define who can sit where in the Blackfriars open the possibility of any man with the money to spend taking a visible place of judgment on the stage. George and his ilk are, at least according to the satires, an occupational hazard for would-be gallants, but also potentially a foil against which their clothing and their wit may shine the brighter.

While George's behaviour may be an exaggerated version of an established form of spectatorship, his wife Nell's is something else again. Not only does she enter from the pit, which both external and internal evidence suggests was not common practice, but the play makes much of the disruption this creates among the stage-sitters: "Pray gentlemen, make her a little room, I pray you, sir, lend me your hand to help up my wife" (Induction 46–8). In order for the play to progress, one of the "gentlemen" must obey George's directive, despite both the character of George and the boy who plays him being his social inferior, and must yield at least some of his hard-won onstage display space to a figure playing by an entirely different set of rules.

Nell's gender, far more than her class, marks her as distinct from the "gentlemen" seated on the stage. Her demonstrated theatrical incompetence – she has never been to a play, and the plays she wants to see are not ones that this venue would produce – extends to her unawareness of the conventions of stage-sitting, and this, despite her initially apologetic position, allows her to assert her authority over the space in two ways: both through her husband's largely financial authority (over the course of the play, he spends nearly a pound to influence the action of the play, largely at her urging) and through her own sense of parental authority over the boy players, whom she sees as being fundamentally like her apprentice Rafe. Nell, not George, is the one who most frequently addresses the "gentlemen" with whom she shares the stage, asking them to experience the play as she does, both morally and aesthetically. Nell cares nothing for the play, but she cares a great deal for the boys, whom she views as bodies to be fixed, not performers to be judged: "Faith the child hath a sweet breath George, but I think it be troubled with the worms. *Carduus benedictus* and mare's milk were the only thing in the world for't" (3.303–6).

The final limitation that the play places on the gallants is the extent to which it usurps the intervals.[33] Given the need to tend the candles regularly, performances in the indoor theatres observed act breaks during which the action of the play stopped and was replaced by some entr'acte of the type exhibited in *The Knight of the Burning Pestle* – music or a dance – during which the audience, particularly the part of it that sat on the stage, moved around and commented with greater freedom than when the play was being performed. But the intervals are dominated instead by George and Nell, in ways that again assert their control over both the performers and the stage-sitters. In the third interval, for instance, Nell assumes the position of hostess, providing drinks for the gentlemen and then regulating their theatrical experience; the entertainment is to be a boy dancing, but as soon as the dance begins, Nell decides to correct it: "George, I will have him dance 'Fading'. – 'Fading' is a fine jig I'll assure you, gentlemen. – Begin, brother. – Now 'a capers, sweetheart. – Now a turn o'th'toe, and then tumble. Cannot you tumble youth?" (9–12). Nell's judgment that "'Fading' is a fine jig" may or may not produce the jig – certainly it is not sufficient to make the boy tumble or eat fire, as she also requests – but it allows her, rather than the paying stage-sitters, to set the standards for entertainment.

Competing Classes

While *The Knight of the Burning Pestle* offers a fascinating opportunity to view fantasies of spectatorship in the Jacobean private theatre, it was also a commercial failure. The critical consensus is that the original audience rejected something related to the intervention of George and Nell, but beyond that opinion diverges, with critics variously claiming the problem was that Beaumont satirized citizen tastes too much, not enough, too exclusively, too inclusively.[34] Whatever the reason for the play's initial failure, it seems clear that Beaumont misjudged his audience's tastes, which we might take as a sign not of Beaumont's lack of awareness but of the difficulty in conceiving of the Blackfriars audience as a single social unit.

In the drama of the 1620s and '30s, representations of the audience increasingly emphasize segmentation both between and within social classes. Where *The Knight of the Burning Pestle* substantially restricts itself to two forms of spectatorship, embodied in George and Nell separately, the Caroline theatre routinely presents a significantly broader range of possible positions for spectators to define themselves with or against. Where Elizabethan dramatists tend to present an audience that functions as a unified group, with any variation from this consensus clearly marked as aberrant, Caroline playwrights are more likely to represent spectatorial practice as varying depending on class, gender, and level of theatrical experience, and to suggest the stage's vulnerability to the censure of its audience.[35]

Michael Neill argues that "it was only with the rise of the relatively exclusive private houses of the second decade of the seventeenth century that the playgoing (and play reading) public began to develop a general connoisseurship in any way analogous to the patrons of painting," claiming that the tastes of the Caroline audience were relatively uniform, set by "aristocrats who, in a deferential society, exercised an influence out of all proportion with their actual numbers."[36] But dramatic material such as inductions suggests that the uniformity of taste and experience that Neill envisions was not universal, even in the private theatres.

Ben Jonson's inductions to *The Staple of News* (1626) and *The Magnetic Lady* (1633), both performed at the Blackfriars by the King's Men, focus on issues of gender and class respectively in their represented audiences. Both inductions present a range of responses within these categories; despite all being labelled as "gossips," the represented onstage audience members watching *Staple* differ significantly in their theatrical expectations and methods of spectatorship, and Probee and Damplay, both representatives of the class that pays for the most expensive and visible seats in the theatre, bring almost entirely opposed expectations of theatregoing to *The Magnetic Lady*.[37] Where *A Midsummer Night's Dream* treated all audience members as needing the same lesson in how to watch and *The Knight of the Burning Pestle* drew extremely broad distinctions between classes, Caroline drama makes distinctions within categories. Theatrical spectatorship was being reconfigured from the involuntary mob reaction imagined by early antitheatrical writers, in which spectators respond "with one voyce" and "runne together by heapes, they know not whither; and lay about with their clubbes, they see not why,"[38] to a specialized technique that could be learned. If in *The guls horne-booke* the ostentatious stage-sitter was characterized as a "gull" in his deliberate setting of himself against the play in order to "laugh alowd in the middest of the most serious and saddest scene of the terriblest Tragedy" (C3^v), regardless of his social status, by the 1630s, the theatre audience was recognized as bringing a variety of desires to the play.

The tension between finance and judgment is most explicit in Richard Brome's induction to *The Careles Shepherdess*, in which representatives of four significantly different segments of the private theatre audience share the onstage seating at the private theatre at Salisbury Court because all have paid for their places. Spruce, the courtier, and Spark, the Inns of Court man, attempt, largely successfully, to defend the "Prerogative of the wits in Town" to "censure Poetry"[39] against the social pretensions of Landlord, the country gentleman, and Thrift, the citizen. Thrift, with his obsessive concern with cost and his repeated efforts to bargain with the doorkeeper for a reduced admission price, cannot be prevented from taking the stage, but ultimately takes his business to the Red Bull or Fortune, public amphitheatres where he can "see / A play for two pence, with a Jig to boot" (B4^v); in his choice to exclude himself from the private theatre, he seems to ratify the suggestion from the coterie audience members that purchasing a physical place of judgment is not enough to buy the social authority that comes with it. But the induction ultimately gives the last word to Landlord, who observes that Spruce and Spark withdraw from their seats on the stage to less conspicuous seating in a box "lest some creditor should spy them" (B4^v); despite the suggestion that the stage is simply a social venue, social forces are precisely those that clear away this represented audience so that the stage is ultimately left to the play. While Spruce and Spark attempt to proclaim a non-economic basis for spectatorship, insisting that the ability of their social inferiors to purchase seats in their section of the stage does not, as Dekker suggests, grant them "a signed patent to engrosse the whole commodity of Censure" (C2^v), their eventual need to stop making spectacles of themselves for fear of the consequences of their economic behaviour (being arrested for debt) suggests that whatever authority over the play their connoisseurship might give them is ultimately subservient to socio-economic forces outside the theatre, a circumstance brought vastly more sharply into relief with the closure of the theatres in 1642.

The "Order for Stage Plays to cease" justified the closure of the public theatres because "Public Sports do not well agree with Public Calamities, nor Public Stage-plays with the Seasons of Humiliation ... instead of which are recommended to the People of this Land the profitable and seasonable considerations of Repentance, Reconciliation, and Peace with God."[40] The closure of the theatres was thus part of a response to the political and military crisis of the Civil War, rather than the culmination of a systematic parliamentary campaign against them, and seems to have been originally envisioned as a temporary measure, on the same logic as the repeated plague closures throughout the early modern period.[41] But the theatre also held a special symbolic place, identified by both royalists and parliamentarians with the court of Charles I and a form of display that the Commonwealth government defined itself against; Wiseman suggests that "the edict of 1642 *turned into* a campaign [against the theatres] as the war went on."[42] Parliamentary orders of 1647–48 specifically targeted players for punishment and ordered the playhouses torn down; in March of 1649, the interiors of the Fortune, Cockpit, and Salisbury Court playhouses were dismantled.[43] But despite this active suppression of professional theatre, both the Cockpit and Salisbury Court were later refurbished as theatres, and the Red Bull remained in intermittent use throughout the Commonwealth period.

When the monarchy was restored in May of 1660, Charles II almost immediately restored the theatre as well, granting a warrant in August of that year giving Thomas Killigrew and William Davenant "the power and authority to erect two companies of players,"[44] effectively bringing the only theatre permitted in London under the direct control of the monarch. While new plays were commissioned, the initial repertory was drawn substantially from what had come before, and surviving pre-Commonwealth private theatres, including the Cockpit and Salisbury Court, were the first homes for Davenant and Killigrew's companies before being replaced by new theatres created by the conversion of Lisle's and Gibbons's Tennis Courts; these spaces were ultimately replaced by Dorset Garden in 1671 and the Theatre Royal in Drury Lane in 1663.

While the new theatres were slightly larger than the Cockpit, their seating capacity was similar; the extra space was used for perspective scenery. The addition of the scenic stage behind the forestage had less effect on the physical position of the theatre audience than might be supposed. While the size of the forestage was reduced (much to the consternation of older actors) until the audience was substantially separated from the stage by the proscenium at the turn of the century,[45] this was not the case when Dorset Garden, the theatre most responsible for the rise of the scenic stage, was initially constructed. As Joseph Donohue observes, "especially in the early years after Charles II's restoration, the substantial thrust of the forestage resulted in the actors being surrounded on three sides by that visible audience" both in boxes and, at least on occasion, on the stage itself. [46] This configuration, in combination with the equal lighting of stage and audience, consistently positioned the audience as being as much an object of spectatorship as the actors in both the Restoration and Shakespearean theatre. The major division in the early Restoration theatres that included provisions for changeable scenery, such as Dorset Garden, was not between the audience and the stage but between the forestage and the scenic stage: "the forestage and its acting area were … part of the auditorium and not part of the scenery [see fig. 2.2]. The lit actor was related to the spectator and the auditorium, not to the shadowy painting on the flats behind him." The configuration of box, pit, and gallery became standard, with boxes, including the Royal Box, located at stage level on the sides of the stage.

Losing the Pleasure of the Play

At its inception, the Restoration theatre was a court phenomenon; Donohue observes that "never had a monarch been associated so closely with the public theatre," with the king and his followers attending the Duke of York's theatre twenty-three times between November 1668 and June 1670.[47] But while the audience of the 1660s and '70s included members of the court and their supporters, it was also by no means socially uniform and was physically segregated on economic lines in much the same way as in the Jacobean and Caroline private theatres. The reduced number of

Fig. 2.2 Dorset Garden Theatre, interior.

authorized theatre companies after the Restoration and the fundamental similarities in their playing spaces had the effect of emphasizing social distinctions within the audience to an even greater extent than in the Caroline theatre.

The Country Gentleman's Vade Mecum (1699), like Fitzgeffrey's "Notes from Black-Fryers," divides the playhouse into areas characterized by socially distinct groups of spectators: "an Upper-Gallery for Footmen, Coachmen, Mendicants, etc. … the *Boxes* where there is one peculiar to the King and Royal Family, and the rest for Persons of Quality, and for the Ladies and Gentlemen of the highest Rank, unless some Fools that have more Wit than Money [*sic*], or perhaps more Impudence than both, crowd in among 'em. The second is call'd the *Pit*, where sit the Judges, *Wits* and *Censurers* or rather *the Censurer without either Wit or Judgment* … The third is distinguisht by the Title of the *Middle Gallery*, where the Citizens Wives and Daughters, together with the *Abigails*, Serving-men, Journey-men and Apprentices commonly take their Places."[48] But these distinctions were by no means absolute; Samuel Pepys's diary records him purchasing seats in all four of these areas at various times.[49]

Unlike Fitzgeffrey's account of the Jacobean private theatre, the *Vade Mecum* distinguishes sharply between "Persons of Quality" and the "Judges, *Wits*, and *Censurers*." The presence of the Royal Box, whether or not it was occupied by royalty at any given performance, provided a spectacle with which neither the performers nor the wits could effectively compete; the possibility of the monarch attending the same performances which any person in London with a shilling to spend might attend[50] re-framed the occasion into something more akin to the court masque, at which the monarch, not the performers, is always the centre of attention. In the *Vade Mecum*, condemnation of the "impudence" of those who were not "Persons of Quality" but "crowd among 'em" frames the significance of the place in terms of the audience, not the stage.

Charles II and his court created an environment of both sophistication and alternative spectacle. Samuel Pepys was simultaneously delighted and irritated by the apparently inescapable conversation of Sir Charles Sedley and two ladies at a revival of Beaumont and Fletcher's *The Maid's Tragedy* (c. 1610) at "the King's House" in 1667: "a more pleasant recontre I never heard. But by that means lost the pleasure of the play wholly, to which now and then Sir Ch. Sidlys exceptions against both words and pronouncing was very pretty."[51] Pepys's loss of the pleasure of the play is compensated by the gain of Sedley's "very pretty" complaints about the performance, and much of that pleasure is derived precisely from observing a specific and identifiable spectator rather than a social type.

Thomas Shadwell's introductory epistle to Sedley in the printed edition of *A True Widow* characterizes Sedley's position as a judging spectator in significantly different terms. The play was a commercial failure, but Shadwell emphasizes that "since my Comedies are approved and commended by you, and Men of your sort, the rest of the Audience must forgive me if I am much more exalted by the praise of such as you than I can ever be humbled by their censure."[52] Sedley, in his capacity as fellow playwright, offers Shadwell aesthetic success, which becomes a measure of the failure of the theatre audience's judgment. This distinction works in the opposite way to that of the *Vade Mecum*: Sedley, and other "Persons of Quality," are defined in terms of readership rather than spectatorship, and the commercial failure of *A True Widow* positions the theatrical spectator as the foolish lover of farce, not the wit or the person of quality.

Shadwell's consideration of the relative importance of theatrical spectatorship and readership in the prefatory material to the print edition is further complicated because the fourth act of *A True Widow*, like all of *The Knight of the Burning Pestle*, is set in "the Play-house" where most of the characters go to watch a play "bespoke" (3:330) by Carlos, the play's locus of male wit. In his note to the reader, Shadwell suggests that the inset play was an innovation that the theatre audience did not understand how to interpret: "For some, I believe, wish'd all the Play like that part of a Farce in it; others knew not my intention in it, which was to expose the Style and Plot of Farce writers, to the utter confusion of damnable Farce, and all its wicked and foolish adherants" (3:288). This condemnation of both farce and its adherents conflates play and playgoer, suggesting that the satiric nature of *A True Widow* functions to condemn rather than reform portions of its audience.

Shadwell's account of the theatre audience emphasizes the distinctions within this group and observes that "Satyr will always be unpleasant to those that deserve it. It was not my design in this play to please a Bawd of Quality, a vain Selfish, a senseless, noisie Prig, a methodical blockhead, having only a form of Wisdom, or a Coxcomb that's run stark mad after Wit, which uses him very unkindly, and will never be won by him; nor did I think to please the Widdows in the Name" (3:284). The epistle thus conflates the social types in the audience with the social types displayed in the play. The scene set in the playhouse, presumably to be identified as Dorset Garden, where *A True Widow* received its first and only production in December 1678, satirizes a great variety of social behaviours and pretensions, and as such offers a sense of both how the playhouse functioned socially and the forms of authority available to the spectators in this space.

Before the scene, Theodosia lays out her rules of playgoing to Carlos, forbidding him to see plays without her, to go behind the scenes, or to "talk with the Vizors in the Pit, though they look never so like women of quality" (3:330). Carlos agrees to her terms "for my own sake" – going behind the scenes is "grown the sign of a fop" – but protests that he does not see how he will acquire the "general Fame and Reputation" that she wants him to have with these restrictions: the "Men of vogue ... dive like Ducks at one end of the Pit, and rise at the other, then whisk into the Whore-Boxes, then into the Scenes, and always hurry up and down" (3:330). This constant movement of "men of vogue" functions as a way to assert control over theatrical space which the Lord Chamberlain attempted to regulate "at frequent intervals ... presumably to little or no effect."[53] The edict that "no person of what quality soever to presume to stand or sit on the stage, or to come within any part of the scenes"[54] emphasizes the frequency with which the behaviour satirized in *A True Widow* took place, and frames the contest for authority not as a contest between audience and actors but between audience members of varying "quality" and "our royal authority."[55]

Competing Prices

Within the inset play, however, control rests not with the "royal authority" but with the economic authority of Carlos. The scene involves actors occupying multiple audience locations, including at least one box that Carlos has reserved for Theodosia and "all the good company of the house." Carlos's economic control over the space gives him power over both the actors and some audience members not of his own party; very early in the scene a doorkeeper enters and informs him that "Ladies and several Gentlemen knock to get in" (3:333), and Carlos orders him to "let the Ladies in for nothing, but make the men pay." The ladies are "mask'd" and the men are "of several sorts." After establishing those sorts – the wits and the bulls – the scene introduces another set of men whose exclusive purpose is to quarrel with the doorkeepers about money, drawing attention to the practice of not paying for seeing less than one act,[56] and running up a tab to see the plays on credit "as familiarly as with their taylors" (3:334). These interactions emphasize the understanding of the play as commodity; admission is sold essentially by the act, and appearance at the theatre is part of displaying oneself as a member of a particular sort of group, just as having the correct tailor is. Until the inset begins, the play itself is almost never mentioned; unlike "Pyramus and Thisbe," which is introduced by both Philostrate and the players, or "The London Merchant," which is the specific target of George's indignation in *The Knight of the Burning Pestle*, this inset play is only the excuse for presenting the social venue of the theatre.

The inset play runs for about thirty lines before the represented audience begins to comment on it. Theodosia and Carlos, whom *A True Widow* holds up as the models of wit, are the first to speak, noting the "lewd" writing, which the fools praise. Other viewers complain about the lack of "Drums and Trumpets and much ranting and roaring" (3:336), sounding very much like Landlord and Thrift in the induction to *The Careles Shepherdess*. And Prig "raps people on the Backs and twirls their Hats, and then looks demurely, as if he did not do it" (3: 337). This ultimately leads to a brawl in the box at the conclusion of which Bellamore, Stanmore, and Carlos "beat the Bullies out of the House; the Actors run off; Ladies run out shrieking"; Carlos is unable to get the play to resume as one of the actresses has fallen into a fit for fear of the swords, and the play ends in disorder.

When the fight among the represented audience members breaks up the play, Carlos tells an actor, "I have prepared an Entertainment upon the Stage; we'll have an Entry, a Song, or some Musick; there is no loss of the Play" (3:339). Young Maggot also has an alternative to propose: "Be not so much troubled that the Play was interrupted by the Bullies; for I have a Poem about me which I'll entertain you with, that may be more agreeable" (3:341). The play is explicitly incidental to the theatregoing experience, which in turn suggests the extent to which royal patronage inheres in the spectacle of the court attendees at the theatre rather than in the performance of the plays themselves – Sedley's conversation, not *The Maid's Tragedy*. The fourth act of *A True Widow* stages the fantasy that the theatre is a space in which any box-holder might take on the position of the king; any box might function as the controlling spectacle of the social space of the theatre to which the play is a poor servant.

In the same way that *The Knight of the Burning Pestle* stages the disenfranchisement of the gallant stage-sitters, *A True Widow* essentially removes the Royal Box from consideration, as Carlos ultimately controls the entire theatrical space due to his financial power over it. This situation is fundamentally different from the Jacobean and Caroline private theatre models in which the king never enters the theatre and the theatre functions as a substitute for the royal court only by analogy. In the Restoration theatre, as the *Vade Mecum* warns, impudent gallants might upstage both the play and the party in the Royal Box. This is almost the obverse of the Elizabethan situation, where the spectator can pretend to be like the king only at the cost of ceding the authority of being a paying customer; by the end of the century, the economic authority of the spectators had firmly displaced the political authority that the spectacle of the stage had once been assumed to carry.

NOTES

1 Johnson, *Prologue and Epilogue spoken at the Opening of the Theatre in Drury-Lane, 1747*, 2.

2 I.G., *A Refutation of the Apology for Actors*, 58.

3 Thomas and Hare, *Restoration and Georgian England*, 2.

4 For a concise and representative account of the post-Restoration theatre as being shaped by major innovations imported from France by the court of Charles II far more significantly than it was by its Caroline predecessors, see Thomas and Hare, *Restoration and Georgian England*, 1–4.

5 Menzer, "Crowd Control," 26. Menzer's article provides numerous instances of this audience, united through its rapt attention to the actors' performances.

6 For discussions of audience behaviour focused on other audience members rather than the performers, see Thomson, "Playgoers," 3–44, and Stern, "Taking Part," 35–53.

7 Nashe, *Pierce Penniless his Supplication to the Divell*, H2.

8 Jonson, *The Staple of News*, 10.

9 Gurr has assembled most of the surviving documents on audience behaviour from 1567 to 1642 as an appendix to *Playgoing in Shakespeare's London*. The situation is a little better for Restoration drama, but scholars still must disproportionately rely on a relatively small number of sources such as Pepys's diary.

10 Thomson, "Playgoers," 6.

11 Love, "Who were the Restoration Audience?" 24. Alvin Kernan similarly argues that in the drama of Shakespeare and his contemporaries, "the [represented] audience plays its part badly and misinterprets the play" in ways that would encourage public theatre audiences to respond differently; see Kernan, "Shakespearean Comedy," 93.

12 The focus on market segmentation originates in the work of Andrew Gurr, particularly *Playgoing in Shakespeare's London.* Lucy Munro points out, however, that there is evidence that "adult and children's companies were at times competing for the same audience rather than attracting an entirely discrete clientele" (*Children of the Queen's Revels*, 62).

13 Elam, *The Semiotics of Theatre and Drama*, 87.

14 Shakespeare, *A Midsummer Night's Dream* 1.2.60–2. Further citations appear parenthetically.

15 Shakespeare, *Henry V*, Prologue 8. Further citations appear parenthetically.

16 Jonson, *The Magnetic Lady*, in *Ben Jonson*, vol. 6, 3 Chor. 19–22, 2 Chor. 60. Further citations appear parenthetically.

17 Munday, *A Third blast of retrait from plaies and Theaters*, E7v, G3.

18 The centrality of exemplarity in pedagogical treatises such as Roger Ascham's *The Schoolmaster* (1570) offers an important framework for considerations of the anxieties that surround theatrical spectatorship. For an account of humanist education as "the imaginary grasped as practice," see Halpern, *The Poetics of Primitive Accumulation*. Laura Levine extends this model more explicitly to the stage in *Men in Women's Clothing.*

19 Gosson, *Playes confuted in five actions*, G4. Halpern argues that Gosson's use of this language "figure[s] imitation as exact reproduction" (38). Levine goes further, arguing that in Gosson's formulation of the relationship between spectator and spectacle, taken to its logical end, "watching leads inevitably to 'being' – to [the audience member] assuming the identity of the actor" (13).

20 Heywood, *An Apology for Actors*, F2v.

21 Platter, *Thomas Platter's Travels in England, 1599*, 166.

22 Gurr, "London's Blackfriars Playhouse," 21–5.

23 Quoted in Gurr, "London's Blackfriars Playhouse," 23; E.K. Chambers, *The Elizabethan Stage*, 4:319–20.

24 Gurr, "London's Blackfriars Playhouse," 22. The most thorough accounts of the construction and layout of the Blackfriars remain Smith's *Shakespeare's Blackfriars*

Playhouse and Hosley's consideration of a large number of possible configurations for the space in "Blackfriars," *Revels History*, 3:197–226.

25 Dekker, *The guls horne-booke*, A1v. 16, 2015. Further citations appear parenthetically.

26 James I, *Basilikon*, 12.

27 Gurr, *The Shakespearean Stage*, 12.

28 Fitzgeffrey, *Satyres*, E7v. Further citations appear parenthetically.

29 Jonson, commendatory verses on *The Faithful Shepherdess*, reprinted in Gurr, *Playgoing in Shakespeare's London*, 223.

30 Beaumont, *The Knight of the Burning Pestle*, Induction 10. Further citations appear parenthetically.

31 Joshua S. Smith suggests that George and Nell are "exemplary representatives of an audience and are quite well-versed in the conventions of theatrical practice – not of the private theaters, but of the public"; see "Reading Between the Acts," 476.

32 Dekker, *The guls horne-book*, C4.

33 Smith, "Reading Between the Acts," offers the most thorough consideration of the intervals; his focus on the specific content of the interludes largely precludes consideration of the audience interactions implied therein.

34 Brent Whitted provides a helpful overview of the range of critical suggestions as to why the play might have failed to please the Blackfriars audience in its initial presentation; see "Staging Exchange," 112.

35 For an overview of relations between the Caroline theatre and its audience, see Neill, "Wits Most Accomplish'd Senate," 341–60. For a discussion of the potential to read the theatre audience either as a collection of individuals or as a corporate entity, see Yachnin and Dawson, *The Culture of Playgoing in Shakespeare's England*. For discussion of the assumptions about gendered spectatorship, or distinctions between the female and male viewers of plays, as being a key factor in the anti-theatrical debates of the late-seventeenth and early-eighteenth centuries, see Marsden, "Spectatorship," 877–98.

36 Neill, "Wits Most Accomplish'd Senate," 344, 342.

37 Myhill ("Taking the Stage," 37–54) discusses the differentiation of represented audience members in these plays in more detail.

38 Gosson, *Playes confuted*, D1v.

39 Brome, "Praeludium," B2. Further citations appear parenthetically.

40 "September 1642," 26–7.

41 Wiseman, *Drama and Politics*, 3.

42 Ibid., 5.

43 The fullest account of the fortunes of the playhouses during the 1640s and '50s remains Hotson's *The Commonwealth and Restoration Stage*, which discusses the dismantling of these interiors (43), and the position of playhouses and players in more general terms (3–58).

44 "Warrant granted by Charles II to Killigrew and Davenant, 21 August 1660," reprinted in Thomas and Hare, *Restoration and Georgian England*, 12. Killigrew and Davenant were granted individual patents in 1662.

45 Thomas and Hare, *Restoration and Georgian England*, 2, 72.

46 Donohue, "Theatres, Their Architecture and Their Audience," 2:293.

47 Donohue, "Introduction," 2:8.

48 *The Country Gentleman's Vade Mecum*, D4.

49 Donohue, "Introduction," 7–8. For further discussion of Pepys's theatre attendance as documented in his diary see Payne, "Theatrical Spectatorship in Pepys's Diary," 87–108.

50 The cheapest seats were one shilling; seats in the boxes cost four shillings (Thomas and Hare, *Restoration and Georgian England*, 176).

51 Pepys, *The Diary of Samuel Pepys*, 8:72.

52 Shadwell, *The Complete Works*, 3:284. Subsequent citations appear parenthetically.

53 Thomas and Hare, *Restoration and Georgian England*, 179.

54 This edict was published in 1673, and again in substantially the same language in 1708. See Thomas and Hare, *Restoration and Georgian England*, 179–80.

55 Thomas and Hare, *Restoration and Georgian England*, 180.

56 This is another area of contention between audience members and the Lord Chamberlain's office, which repeatedly forbade entry to the theatre "without paying the prices established for the respective plays … notwithstanding the pretended privilege by custom or forcing their entrance at the fourth or fifth act without payment." See Thomas and Hare, *Restoration and Georgian England*, 179.

3
"Shame's pure blush": Shakespeare and the Ethics of Spectatorship

WILLIAM W.E. SLIGHTS

The ubiquity of shame in literature and the graphic arts, not to mention everyday life, makes the concept extraordinarily difficult to delimit and define. Susanna, Lucretia, and Hero, for example, each face up to their shaming so differently that it would be nearly impossible to say just what the common shame-affect is in these cases. My concern, though, is not with the multiplicity of shame – what one noted psychiatrist has called "the many faces of shame"[1] – but with the conventional wisdom about its ethical import. Evidence for the presence of shame is generally held to be displayed on the blushing face, an assumption that needs to be questioned carefully. I propose to look at the face of "shame's pure blush" and to study this complex psychophysiological and ethical affect in Shakespeare's work and times.[2]

My thesis is that the early modern weapons system of shame is trained on Shakespeare's blushing victims in sexual and political situations as a way to externalize and displace the shame-affect triggered by the activity of spectatorship. That is, when Shakespeare's female characters are shamed in public, those who watch find themselves wishing to transfer elsewhere their responsibility for a complex ethical situation that reflects as much on their own engagement with the other as it does on the fictional aggression being staged. The audience is crucial to the theatrical transaction, then, and the playwright's challenge is to balance on- and offstage emotional responses so as to insist on the responsibility of any spectator for the well-being of others, as well as for the aesthetic gratification of the self.[3]

Much of what I have discovered about watching blushing faces and the sexual politics that emanate from them in early modern English poetry and drama falls into the category of misreading the other. Theatrical characters created by Marlowe, Middleton, and Shakespeare repeatedly, egregiously misread the faces of others in vain attempts to look into their hearts and anticipate their actions. No wonder, then, that spectators as well as actors are thrown into ethical dilemmas of interpretation. While modern philosophers such as Emmanuel Levinas and Martha Nussbaum can offer help with associated questions of ethical theory, and seventeenth-century commentators on the body, its controlling passions, and its social construction can guide us back in time to assumptions we no longer share, only careful attention to the poetic rhetoric of the passions can provide a reliable place from which to look into this body of theatrical literature.

Blushes: Seneca, Darwin, and the Exercise of Self-Attention

Duncan's warning in *Macbeth* that "There's no art / To find the mind's construction in the face" (1.4.11–12) is resolutely ignored in most early modern drama. Characters are forever trying to read someone's face for signs of their mental or emotional state, and their art is never more precarious than when they are after evidence on which to base some moral judgment or other. The notion that such states are "natural" and hence legible in the human body – the art of physiognomy – was solidly established in English writing by the fifteenth century.[4] No part of the body was more open to view than the face, and when it reddened in a blush, would-be moralizers, fully aware of the sanguineous links between the heart's secrets and the flush in the cheek, were quick to pounce.

The art of moralizing the human visage and its observable responses to stimulants, internal as well as external, was moving into a new phase in the late sixteenth century. Anatomists and poets were beginning to formulate a fresh set of dynamics in the relationship between material selves and the social-sexual politics of their changing communities. Behind this proto-scientific but still imperfectly calibrated set of observations lay an emerging ethics of reading – including reading the alterations of the body

– that revealed as much about readers themselves as about the objects of their scrutiny.[5] The dramatists of the period seized on these developments as a way to shape character conflict and audience response. Characters were defined not just by dramatic action but also by inward contemplation, a mental state frequently coloured by feelings of shame. In this state, they were thought to reveal their emotions via what Charles Darwin in his classic essay on the blush calls "self-attention."[6]

The exercise of self-attention in Shakespeare's plays – allowing characters to stand aside and judge their own motives and morals – has become a central critical concern in recent years, though little has been written about the blush.[7] Self-attention comes into play whenever the subject of blushing arises, creating at least the illusion of habitable moral space behind the flushed face. Seneca, a perennial Shakespeare influence, explains in the eleventh of his *Epistulae morales*, "On the Blush of Modesty," that blushing is a weakness, especially in the young, but one that reveals a good character capable of feeling modesty. Blushing may, however, have precisely the opposite moral valence in different people: "Some are most dangerous when they redden, as if they were letting all their sense of shame escape."[8] Without shame there are, presumably, no moral brakes on rage, licentiousness, or any other emotional excess. In Seneca's view, the feelings that cause the blush, whether indicative of modest restraint or wild abandon, are beyond human control: "We cannot forbid these feelings any more than we can summon them. Actors in the theatre, who imitate the emotions, who portray fear and nervousness, who depict sorrow, imitate bashfulness by hanging their heads, lowering their voices, and keeping their eyes fixed and rooted upon the ground. They cannot, however, muster a blush; for the blush cannot be prevented or acquired" (63).

He uses the theatre, in particular its limitations, to clarify a crucial point about human behaviour. Even the most consummate fakers of human affect, the "*artifices scaenici*," are physically incapable of conjuring up a blush to express their inner, moral condition. For Seneca the blush is, then, an authentic indicator of one's emotional life, and it arises from imagining oneself in a perpetual state of surveillance. While stage actors have an audience to provide an outside perspective on the self, the rest of us have to imagine discriminating onlookers. Seneca recommends that his friend Lucilius adopt Epicurus's advice and "Cherish some man of high character, and keep him ever before your eyes, living as if he were watching you, and ordering all your actions as if he beheld them" (Seneca 63–5). Early modern manuals of proper behaviour for women repeated this moral instruction *ad nauseam*, specifying fathers and husbands as the men of high character who were to be imagined as always watching for the blush of modesty.[9]

These self-appointed guardians of female virtue work by restricting female freedoms.[10] Though the gender roles in this scenario were designed to perpetuate a male-dominated hierarchy, Shakespeare repeatedly inverted them in his plays, thus casting doubt on the link then being forged between female physiological response and male moral judgments in the realm of human passions.

At times, however, Shakespeare invokes the moral valence of the shameful female blush without ironic inversion. In recognizably Senecan terms, his raging Venus lets "all [her] sense of shame escape" once she has enlisted Adonis's pity with her false swoon. Her face becomes, as it were, sexually engorged.

> Her face doth reek and smoke, her blood doth boil,
> And careless lust stirs up a desperate courage,
>   Planting oblivion, beating reason back,
>   Forgetting shame's pure blush and honor's wrack. (555–8)

Having forgotten "shame's pure blush" and the ruination of her female honour, Venus has lost the ability to stand aside and judge the morality of her own actions.[11] Flushed with desire, she has joined the ranks of those thought incapable of blushing: the blind, people of colour, and moral reprobates.

The blush was experienced and interpreted in the highly ambiguous space between body and mind, between unintended, uncontrollable physical action and a full-blown rhetoric of social intercourse. The generally accepted definition of the noun "blush" (*OED* sb. 4) includes both a physical effect ("the reddening of a face") and an emotional cause ("caused by shame, modesty, or other emotion"). At the moment a blush is acknowledged or attributed, the often incompatible discourses of physiology and morality begin to comment on one another in perplexing ways. Brian Cummings identifies precisely the kind of confusion caused by this overlap of discourses in the following passage from Thomas Wright's *The Passions of the Minde* (1601):

> they blush, because nature, being afrayde, lest in the face the fault should be discovered, sendeth the purest blood to be a defence and succor, the which effect, commonly, is judged to proceede from a good and virtuous nature, because no man can [but] allowe, that it is good to be ashamed of a fault.[12]

The concluding generalization about the benefits of feeling ashamed denies the need for the defence mechanism in the first place. We are left to wonder, is the blush the kind of thing that effectively keeps one in good standing in the world by offering a spontaneous apology for indiscretions, or is it an easily penetrated cover-up? Is the blush supposed to bespeak virtue or vice? Robert Burton appears to be equally confused about this point in his account of the immediate causes of melancholy. Having observed that the shame that occasions blushing (or "bashfulness") need not result from "*some fowle act committed*" but simply from the fear that someone might suspect a moral defect in us, Burton goes on to explain that "*The face labours and is troubled at his presence that sees our defects, and nature willing to helpe, sends thither heat, heat drawes the subtilest blood and so we blush.*"[13] But who or what is nature helping out, the outside observers of our shortcomings or our own attempts to disguise our emotional distress?

One point on which nearly all commentators on the blush agree is that the segment of society most susceptible to blushing is young women. One of the most colourful descriptions of the early modern female blush is Henry Hawkins's 1633 imaginary conversation between the heart and the blood about raising the alarm when a young virgin's virtue is under attack.

> The hart is put into a fright; the obsequious blood comes in anon, and asks: What ayle you, Sir? Goe, get you up, and mount to the turret of the cheeks … [T]he bloud obeyes, and makes the blush,

> that rayseth such alarmes, in tender Virgins most especially. What feares the Virgin, when she blushes so? The wrack of her honour.[14]

It is fear, according to the recusant emblematist, that initiates a visible sign of inner turmoil. His military vocabulary signals a male defence mounted on behalf of the tender, frightened virgin. The female of the species evidently requires aggressive protection, and the body responds with the appropriate physiological signs.

Ethical concerns about the psychic humiliation and physical abuse of women, often encapsulated in the term "abuse," are generally thought to be modern ones. Shakespeare's age is not held to the same purportedly high ethical standards as our own in this regard. Back then, the story goes, women were chaste, silent, and obedient, because of and in spite of their brutal treatment at the hands of the men closest to them. Anyone familiar with Renaissance drama knows that this is nonsense. Characters who raise their hands or the spectre of shame against their pure wives find themselves in severe ethical straits. But it is not at all clear just how the mechanisms of shaming and violence against women work in this drama, or how knowledge of these mechanisms might be reapplied in the lives of present-day spectators. To sort out these issues requires a careful and empathic response to the fictional others that inhabit the early modern stage.

Philosophies: Othello

Shakespeare was part of a pronounced shift in Jacobean tragedy that included Webster, Middleton, and Ford, one that moved the spectator's focus from the male heroics of overreaching superheroes and political nation-makers to women suffering brutal psychological attacks in the privacy of their own homes.[15] Along with these other playwrights, Shakespeare made his audiences into silent, nervous conspirators in the torment of his female characters as we are forced to share the voyeuristic perspective of his frantically possessive and fiercely judgmental male characters. This ethically disturbing spectatorial experience is nowhere more evident than in *Othello*.

In his book *Double Vision: Moral Philosophy and Shakespearean Drama*, Tzachi Zamir argues that Othello views his own life exclusively in terms of his usefulness to the state: maintaining order in Venice and its strategic outposts, responding to the urgent summons of his ruler, and smiting the turbaned Turk.[16] At the climax of the play he even murders his wife as a service to the state, "else she'll betray more men" (5.2.6). This is the "cause" in which he acts and for which he must die. He views himself as the instrument of the larger polity. Running counter to this conviction of instrumentality in Othello is Desdemona's reason for loving him. Although she was initially fascinated by his tales of privation and battle, there is something else in the narration of his life's "pilgrimage" (1.3.153) that touches her even more deeply, causing her to "pity" him (1.3.168) and triggering her intensely erotic response.[17] That story has a more powerful impact than Othello anticipated.

> My story being done,
> She gave me for my pains a world of sighs;
> She swore, in faith 'twas strange, 'twas passing strange;
> 'Twas pitiful, 'twas wondrous pitiful. (1.3.158–61)

She re-evaluates his life in terms that are foreign to him, responding to something intrinsic, not just instrumental, in his being. This unfamiliar ground for love is, according to Zamir, what throws Othello so far off balance once he has lost his sole "occupation" (3.3.345–57) that he comes to believe he must return to serving the state by killing his wife. The risk inherent in Desdemona's complete acceptance of Othello's otherness is that it leaves her unprotected and open to violence. It is she, according to Zamir, and not Othello, who "lov'd not wisely but too well" (5.2.344). The difficulty with this ingenious reading is that it comes very close to blaming the victim.

Martha Nussbaum, whose work has deeply influenced Zamir's, sets aside Desdemona's term "pity" as a description of the profound identification she feels with Othello: "'Pity' has come to have nuances of condescension and superiority to the sufferer that it did not have" in earlier times.[18] Instead, Nussbaum prefers the term "compassion," which would appear to capture both what Desdemona experiences and what audiences come to see is the true tragedy of her play. As Nussbaum puts it:

> [I]f we need a decent theory of value to guide us, compassion, as standardly exemplified and taught in tragic drama, has a pretty good theory to offer. The standard occasions for compassion, throughout the literary and philosophical tradition – and presumably in the popular thought on which the tradition draws – involve losses of truly basic goods, such as life, loved ones, freedom, nourishment, mobility, bodily integrity, citizenship, shelter. Compassion seems to be, as standardly experienced, a reasonably reliable guide to the presence of real value. (374)

It is hard to imagine someone observing Nussbaum's catalogue of losses and their attendant suffering, either in drama or in actuality, without sharing the pain of the sufferer. Still, we do well to heed Zamir's caution that "Understanding the suffering of another is neither a necessary nor a sufficient condition for moral action" (33). He cites, for example, the limiting case of the sadist who has a keen awareness of his victim's suffering and yet cannot be said to act morally. As Stephen Greenblatt has pointed out, Iago practises a deeply unethical form of empathy when he places himself so firmly in the shoes of his general as to allow Othello no place to stand in his familiar world of military service.[19] Such cases argue for a necessary refinement to the notion of ethical empathy. Unless the response to the other with whom one is inextricably interlocked forgoes the urge to judge and punish, no ethical standard can be achieved. The upshot of judging the other in the context of an honour-bound society will inevitably be disastrous.

If Zamir's analysis of the ethical crux of the play presents difficulties in the misconstruction of the victim, and Nussbaum's notion of compassion proves too blunt an instrument, where are we to turn for an ethical theory sufficiently sensitive and flexible to deal with the spectator's dilemma at the end of *Othello*? I would suggest an approach through the works of the twentieth-century French philosopher Emmanuel Levinas, but with modifications provided by his admirer in the world of ethical philosophy Seyla Benhabib. Levinas's thought has the distinct advantage of allowing for the element of wonder in an audience's ethical response to Shakespeare's tragedy.

The model of human interaction laid out in Levinas's *Totality and Infinity* maintains that the act of welcoming the other is the bedrock of ethical response.[20] Such a response provokes a profound interrogation of "the I" or "the same." As Levinas explains, "We call this calling into question by the presence of the other ethics" (43). The problem with ethical concepts like Nussbaum's compassion, he would say, is that they project ourselves onto the other, thus denying it its absolute otherness. Levinas's concept of the other insists on that difference and constrains the rampant imperialism of the power-seeking self, the Nietzschean will-to-power. I want to maintain that the choice to leave behind the solipsistic confines of the self in order to embrace the truth of the other is also essential to Shakespeare's dramatic actions, those of tragic isolation as well as those of comic entanglement. The full-face encounter with the other is as crucial to these actions as it is to what Levinas calls his ethical "first philosophy," and for many of the same reasons.[21] First, the narrow interests of the political can be expanded to embrace questions that are broadly ethical. Next, welcoming the other reveals the tenuousness of social cohesion as well as the selfishness of murder. Philosophically and theatrically, the other gains its fullest being as an opposed (but not necessarily hostile) face. Shakespeare's characters experience the ethical resistance presented by the face of the other when they are confronted by the intransigence of those they love and those they hate. In Levinasian terms, this "opens the dimension of infinity … [and] puts a stop to the irresistible imperialism of the same and the I."[22]

There are problems with using Levinas's thought to address the ethical situation of spectators at a play like *Othello*. For one thing, Levinas is notoriously difficult to understand. Even though the specialized vocabulary he develops for situating the ethical subject in relation to the other *seems* to be rather simple, those terms have only a tenuous and tendentious relationship to their widely accepted senses. Take the term "face." There is nothing physiological or anthropomorphic about this designation of the way we confront the infinite. For Levinas, the face does not alter its expression or serve to conceal (or reveal) some underlying motive. It is a purely abstract and highly generalized yet intensely immediate mode of confronting everything that is not us. It is ironic that at crucial turning points in his argument for the other as the trigger for all ethical activity Levinas relies on an image – the human face. Like Plato, he distrusts images, figures, and myths, though, also like Plato, he invokes them at precisely the point where he reaches the limits of the rational evidence available to him.

Another distinctive feature of Levinas's thought is his aversion not only to images of the kind that enrich literature but to examples of any kind. Aside from a few illustrative examples that he allows into his work on the Talmud, Levinas scrupulously avoids what he sees as the imprecision, the experiential messiness that accompanies appeals to exemplarity in philosophical discourse, which, by his lights, should develop only universal statements of ethical truths. He is particularly hostile to narrative examples, making him, as one Levinas scholar says, "a bad reader of literary texts."[23] We needn't exclude his ethical theory from literary studies on these grounds, however, particularly if we view it through the lens provided by one of Levinas's strong supporters, Seyla Benhabib. In her book *Situating the Self*, Benhabib recommends that we add to Levinas's generalized other the "concrete other" that "enjoins us to view every moral person as a unique individual, with a certain life history, disposition and endowment, as well as needs and limitations."[24] At this point in the debate, family and community emerge as crucial elements of ethical thought. "One cannot act within … ethical relationships," Benhabib insists, "without being able to think from the standpoint of our child, our spouse, our sister or brother, mother or father. To stand in such an ethical relationship means that we as concrete individuals know what is expected of us in virtue of the kind of social bonds which tie us to the other" (10). While this is not the language that Levinas chooses to employ, the conception of bonds to the other is compatible with Levinasian ethics and with the kind of domestic tragedy that Shakespeare writes in *Othello*.

Which brings us to those difficult moments in the play when Othello becomes most ethically active and when Shakespeare's spectators have most to lose – the scenes in which Othello the spy passes final judgment on Cassio (in 4.1) and Desdemona (in 5.2). We can approach these scenes now primed with Zamir's warning about the risk of welcoming the other, Nussbaum's recommendation of compassion or empathy, and Levinas's necessary confrontation with the face of the other that calls into question all we think we know about ethical judgment.

Leading up to these scenes, Iago maliciously demands of Othello, "Would you, the supervisor, grossly gape on? / Behold her top'd?" (3.3.395–6). The term "supervisor" implies not just slack-jawed gaping but actually doing something in a supervisory capacity, making the adulterous sex scene happen and feeling not just outraged but also "satisfied" (line 394) and empowered by becoming a morally active spectator.[25] In act 4 Iago urges Othello to "encave" himself (4.1.81) in order to gain evidence against Cassio. What he observes from his safe but limited vantage point is Cassio laughing scornfully and Bianca flourishing Desdemona's fatal handkerchief. Iago has primed Othello to supply the false soundtrack for the dumb show whose actual dialogue the offstage audience gets to hear. The discrepancy between what we hear and what Othello imagines creates what the aesthetic philosopher Edward Bullough calls "psychical distance," a kind of ironic space that encourages us to judge the character's error.[26] When the Cassio charade is finished, Iago is right there to help Othello interpret what he has just mis-seen. Othello is first crushed, then outraged.

> *Oth.* But yet the pity of it, Iago! O Iago, the pity of it Iago!
> *Iago.* If you are so fond of her iniquity, give her patent to offend, for if it touch not you, it comes near nobody.
> *Oth.* I will chop her into messes. Cuckold me! (4.1.195–200)

Othello's overwhelming sense of pity at first encourages us to defer any ethical judgment of him and to experience Nussbaum's "compassion" or empathy. But this is only part of our reaction to this ethically perplexing situation. The repeated clang of Iago's name in Othello's mouth and Iago's cynical suggestion to turn a blind eye to Desdemona's supposed infidelity push us away from empathic identification with the dupe. Othello's vicious and bloody conclusion and his moral outrage that *he*, commander of the Venetian forces on Cyprus, should be cuckolded force us to abandon our compassion for the moment. But in that instant, the face of the absolute other calls out to be welcomed, not reviled, by an act of ethical spectatorship. The old ethics of judgment and alienation must be transformed into

Fig. 3.1 Irène Jacob as Desdemona and Laurence Fishburne as Othello, in Oliver Parker's film *Othello* (1995).

positive engagement with (not pity for) the character we are actually seeing: the shattered, hateful Moorish general whose identity has been so utterly lost.

More than immediate, melodramatic consequences are at issue in Shakespeare's ethically expanded version of Geraldi Cinthio's narrative. Moments of this kind in the play cause not only Othello but also theatre audiences to "call into question," as Levinas says, what they believe they know about how ethical determinations are made. Indeed, "determination" is impossible as we watch these scenes unfold. Instead, questions and uncertainties keep our ethical faculty in play.

The last scene of ethical suspension, deferral, and continuation that I wish to look at is Othello's address to the sleeping Desdemona in act 5, scene 2. The uncanny calm of his opening line – "It is the cause, it is the cause, my soul" – is deeply upsetting to the audience who looks on, as it were, over his shoulder. The mesmerized gaze of Laurence Fishburne in the 1995 film (see fig. 3.1) guides the attention of the audience to the defenceless body of Desdemona (Irène Jacob).

But the cool detachment of the empowered voyeur does not last long. Desdemona's warm breath captivates Othello. Lynda Boose has noted in the scene strong parallels with pornographic snuff movies in which sexual climax coincides with the actual murder of a naked woman.[27] Desdemona faces, as Zamir argues, the ultimate risk of embracing the unpredictable other. But there is much more than sexual titillation and horror in this spectacle. As Kent Cartwright has argued, the audience's ethical uncertainty bears a strong resemblance to Othello's own bizarre confusion: "I'll kill thee / And love thee after" (5.2.18–19).[28] The audience has very nearly been lulled into thinking that its safe, "objective" distance of spectatorship permits it to judge the bewildered Othello. The stops and starts of the scene – is Desdemona dead or isn't she? – draw us back from the brink of that error. Instead, what Levinas calls "the dimension of infinity" opens up in the face of the other that must be welcomed, not condemned. The ethical complexity of this moment reminds us that voyeuristic smugness and titillation is the antithesis of what watching Shakespeare's tragedies is really about. The genuinely troubling questions of *Othello* remain to excite and engage our ethical and aesthetic consciences: What can possibly motivate an Iago? Is Othello the noble Moor or the enemy within? How *does* woe create wonder? The answers to these questions and others reside in the execution of ethically active spectatorship.

Shame: Much Ado About Nothing

In comedies where a society's sexual mores are on trial, correction is possible, and comic "evitability" – as opposed to tragic inevitability – rules the day. Thomas Heywood maintains in *An Apology for Actors* (1612) that dramatic impersonations of historical (or fictional) characters can have radically different effects on a theatre audience, "either animating men to noble attempts, or attaching the consciences of the spectators, finding themselues toucht in presenting the vices of others."[29] The process of suppressing "noble attempts" leads to "attaching" (arresting or attacking) the erring conscience of a character and also the doubting conscience of an engaged spectator. A character who opposes a villain like Don John or

Cloten can actively transform an audience. As Heywood puts it, "so bewitching a thing is lively and well spirited action, that it hath power to new mould the harts of the spectators and fashion them to the shape of any noble attempt" (B4). Heywood, in his eagerness to defend playgoing against the attacks of Puritan moralists imbued with what Jonas Barish calls an antitheatrical prejudice, presents a more positive account of spectatorship than do Shakespeare (whose onstage spectators are often dupes) or Ben Jonson (whose spectators are *always* dupes).[30] Shakespeare comes closest to a balanced view of the condemning and the forgiving spectator in *Much Ado About Nothing*, a play in which comic "evitability" is snatched from the jaws of tragic inevitability only with considerable strain on the language of community and a magical reversal of female shaming rituals. The play's interlocking intrigues are propelled by multiple acts of overseeing whose purposes range from poisoning love to promoting it, from shaming to celebration.

The subjection and abjection of the Italians by the Spanish and of women by men in *Much Ado* is largely a function of the language of shaming.[31] Claudio's repudiation of Hero in the church turns on interpreting her physical body as an aggregation of signs, like the printed text of a legal argument.

> There, Leonato, take her back again.
> Give not this rotten orange to your friend,
> She's but the sign and semblance of her honor.
> Behold how like a maid she blushes here!
> O, what authority and show of truth
> Can cunning sin cover itself withal!
> Comes not that blood as modest evidence
> To witness simple virtue? Would you not swear,
> All you that see her, that she were a maid,
> By these exterior shows? But she is none:
> She knows the heat of a luxurious bed;
> Her blush is guiltiness, not modesty. (4.1.31–42)[32]

Apart from the faulty ocular proof of witnessing Conrade conversing with Margaret at Hero's window, Claudio's only supporting evidence is his intended's blush. As we have seen, and as Claudio himself says, the blush is a notoriously ambiguous signifier, which he arbitrarily chooses to read as corroboration of her sexual guilt, not her maiden modesty. As in all scenes of shaming, the presence of an audience (here actually present on stage, not simply imagined) triggers the blush of shame (not, as we know, guilt) on Hero's face.

The audience consists, on one hand, of the accusing spectator (Claudio), whose judgment Hero may or may not respect, and, on the other, a more socially elevated audience (Don Pedro, Don John, and Leonato) that views her in a new and damaging relationship to the accuser. It is this higher-level audience whose construction of the situation she is unable to resist. Though innocent, Hero is genuinely ashamed in the face of her natal community and its Spanish overlords. The indirect accusation of unchastity that functions metonymically by associating Hero with a particular window, a strange ruffian seen conversing at that window, and a lustful bed is given credibility by the testimony of Don Pedro, Prince of Arragon, and his brother, Don John, deviser of the dissimulation. At this point Hero's mortified father, Leonato, cannot imagine contradicting the word of his Spanish superiors. Other members of the onstage audience – Beatrice, Benedick, and Friar Francis – though unconvinced by the denunciatory proceedings, are initially shocked into silence. We hear instead from Don Pedro ("I stand dishonor'd, that have gone about / To link my dear friend to a common stale" [64–5]), Don John ("There is not chastity enough in language / Without offense to utter" Hero's transgressions [97–8]), and Leonato ("why, doth not every earthly thing / Cry shame upon her? could she here deny / The story that is printed in her blood?" [120–2]). The calumny has achieved the status of a published narrative; it is said to be printed in the ink of Hero's infected blood upon her "foul tainted flesh" (143).

The consequences of the ritualistic shaming that Hero has undergone at the altar spread to infect Leonato, who wishes he had never fathered a child at all. The family name has been soiled, and even Hero's given name has been stripped from her. Claudio commands her to "answer truly to your name."

> *Hero*. Is it not Hero? Who can blot that name
> With any just reproach?

Claud. Marry, that can Hero,
Hero herself can blot out Hero's virtue. (80–2)

A Hero without virtue is no Hero at all but a nameless, worthless social outcast. But whether she herself experiences Claudio's denunciation as shameful depends on which part of the mixed onstage audience we regard as dominant. As the play is generally staged, the powerful Spaniards and their male Sicilian underlings dominate the scene, making Hero's blush and swoon appear to be motivated by her sense of externally inflicted shame. But other audience-agent dynamics are in play here. Some members of the onstage audience, notably Beatrice, Benedick, and the Friar, certainly do not share the mocking and condescending perspective of Hero's accusers, but their response is sufficiently delayed to allow the shaming moment its full force. The response of Hero herself may, it has been plausibly argued, be one not of shameful mortification but of furious outrage at the injustice of Claudio's charge. There is good reason, at least in interpretive retrospect, to see a flush of rage rather than a blush of maiden innocence on her cheek and to associate it with the vengeful rage of Beatrice's subsequent command, "Kill Claudio" (4.1.289), and not with the self-effacing retreat of a humiliated girl. The judgment that really counts, however, is that of the extra-fictional audience, the playgoers, and that judgment is artfully misdirected not once but twice to create the catharsis of comedy.[33]

At first we are led to believe that Don John's device has been successful and Hero thoroughly shamed in the eyes of her entire community. After her duped accusers have withdrawn and her father has adopted her apparent shame as his own, the Friar intervenes with a radical reinterpretation of Hero's blush, offered in the interest of deflecting the charge of unchastity. By careful "noting of the lady" (158) and rereading of the narrative said to be written in her face, the Friar turns her into the victim of a misunderstanding that is only later revealed as an elaborate hoax.

Friar. Hear me a little,
For I have only been silent so long,
And given way unto this course of fortune,
By noting of the lady. I have mark'd
A thousand blushing apparitions

> To start into her face, a thousand innocent shames
> In angel whiteness beat away those blushes,
> And in her eye there hath appear'd a fire
> To burn the errors that these princes hold
> Against her maiden truth. Call me a fool,
> Trust not my reading, nor my observations,
> Which with experimental seal doth warrant
> The tenure of my book; trust not my age,
> My reverence, calling, nor divinity,
> If this sweet lady lie not guiltless here
> Under some biting error. (155–70)

The speech is not easy to follow, perhaps the result of the Q compositor's having compressed it to fit at the bottom of G1^{v}, but the Friar's generous "reading" of Hero's physiognomy clearly corrects the earlier misreading. The story her body is telling changes over time, the angelic whiteness of "innocent shames" (perhaps the humiliation of being falsely accused?) replacing the array of blushes. There is also, he notes, a fire in her to turn away the heresy of her accusers, suggesting that her blushes betoken not embarrassment but fury. Still, the Friar's conciliatory, understanding tone starts a process of healing in the community that corrects "biting error" and replaces sexual humiliation with matrimonial celebration in act 5. Calamity is averted by a generous rereading of the colonized other and, eventually, by the magical re-creation of Hero in the person of her conveniently invented cousin. Family and community triumph over the spiteful shame-mongering of Don John and his cronies.

The audience plays a crucial part in the propagation and subsequent correction of the biting error played out in this scene. In any shaming situation, the person singled out for shaming is made to readjust downward her own estimate of her self-worth by observing herself through the eyes of a critical public and adopting that critique as valid. As the philosopher Gabriele Taylor puts it, "That it is the view of the public and public esteem which is all-important is reflected in the thought that shame requires an audience."[34] The pressure of the observing other can cause a radical revaluation of any particular action. In Taylor's words, "The crucial point is that only by seeing what he is doing through the other's eyes does he recognize the nature of his action, and so it is crucial, it seems, that there be some other through whose eyes he can look at his action."[35] Seeing the world, and particularly one's self, through the eyes of the other produces the kind of generosity but also the kind of cautions that are central to the ethics of social interaction. The playhouse audience, knowing Hero's innocence (as it knows Desdemona's), can be unbiased observers of both the mean-spirited and the generous responses of the onstage audience. That is, we see shame performed – its infliction and its emotional devastation – and we can appreciate both the personal pain it causes and the corrective effect it can have on a society teetering on the brink of a terrible error. As the feminist sociologist Elspeth Probyn says, shame is "felt on the skin, in the blush," but it also "organizes particular social relations."[36] "Shame," she goes on, can be "positive and productive" (34), because it warns the engaged audience of "the onset of the breakdown of humanity" (14), the interruption of "the affective investment we have in others" (13).[37] The shock waves of shame will always spread through the multi-layered audiences of the shaming action until everyone is implicated in one way or another.

And More Shame: The Rape of Lucrece

To be a spectator – as Shakespeare, the consummate man of the theatre, realized – unavoidably entails the experience of shame, but never more immediately than in his dramatically realized shame-narrative, *The Rape of Lucrece*. Only the biblical story of Susanna and the Elders (Daniel 13) was retold more often by early modern purveyors of erotic shame.[38] The tragicomic vindication of Susanna stands in sharp contrast to the unrelieved tragedy of the shamefully ravished Lucrece.

Shakespeare begins his story with Lucrece's nemesis, Tarquin, arriving at her home prepared to test the boasts of his fellow soldier, Collatine, about the unassailable purity of his wife.[39] After she repulses Tarquin's advances, he returns at night, turns a deaf ear to her pleas, rapes her, and slinks off into the darkness, leaving Lucrece to deal with the shame of her fallen state. She summons her husband and her father, who arrive with Junius Brutus and Publius Valerius, and, blushing deeply, she tells her sad story on condition that the men of her family take revenge on the house of Tarquin. Lucrece then stabs herself to re-establish her family's honour. Brutus spreads word of the treachery of King Tarquin's son among the citizens of Rome, who overthrow the tyrant. Shakespeare may have picked up the detail of Lucrece's blush from Ovid's retelling of Livy's history of Rome in the *Fasti* or from the tortured meditation on her rape and suicide in Augustine's *City of God*.[40] With her suicide, the narrative of shame is said to be written in Lucrece's blood on her defiled body, just as Leonato asserts that Hero's story is written on hers. A moralized symbolism of blood, gender, and honour is constructed in the aftermath of the rape, and an elaborate system of layered audiences eventually reveals the ethical inadequacy of that symbolism.

Lucrece's emotions are in a state of turbulence from the outset and her internal conflict is registered for all to see in the heraldic coloration of her face:

> Within [her] face beauty and virtue strived
> Which of them both should underprop her fame.
> When virtue bragg'd, beauty would blush for shame;
> When beauty boasted blushes, in despite
> Virtue would stain that o'er with silver white.
>
> But beauty, in that white entituled
> From Venus' doves, doth challenge that fair field;
> Then virtue claims from beauty beauty's red,
> Which virtue gave the golden age to gild
> Their silver cheeks, and call'd it then their shield,
> Teaching them thus to use it in the fight,
> When shame assail'd, the red should fence the white. (52–63)

This is the same contest of alluring beauty and shielding virtue, of red and white, that successively coloured Hero's face and "underprop[ped] her fame." It is not the female person but her reputation, boasted abroad by fiancé and husband, that requires underpropping and subtle readings of facial rubrication. Even the insensitive Tarquin realizes that the intensity of Lucrece's emotions, registered in her face, puts nature to shame, identifying the white with anger, the red with the flush of sexuality:

> Thus he replies: "The color in thy face,
> That even for anger makes the lily pale,
> And the red rose blush at her own disgrace,
> Shall plead for me and tell my loving tale." (477–80)

The fully articulate face speaks a language of moralized emotions which can be manipulated in the case of villains. Sinon, the most persuasive betrayer in classical history, who ushers in the Trojan horse, has been skilfully represented in Lucrece's painting so that his facial coloration will give away neither his guilt nor his fear:

> In him the painter labor'd with his skill
> To hide deceit, and give the harmless show
> An humble gait, calm looks, eyes wailing still,
> A brow unbent, that seem'd to welcome woe,
> Cheeks neither red nor pale, but mingled so
> That blushing red no guilty instance gave,
> Nor ashy pale the fear that false hearts have. (1506–12)

Despite Seneca's assertion that no one can artificially conjure up or suppress a blush, the "perjur'd Sinon" almost seems able to hide the emotions that would announce his dishonourable intentions in his face.

In an honour-based society such as Sinon's Greece or Tarquin's Rome the blush is a sign of blame, and the nature of that blame is rigidly gendered. The rape of Lucrece dishonours the house of Collatine as well as that of Tarquin, and in Lucrece's mind requires certain remedies. Chief among these remedies is the victim's suicide, which she willingly undertakes in order to bring forth honour out of shame, even though the men gathered round her insist she should feel no shame about her sexual violation.[41] As she explains:

> My honor I'll bequeath unto the knife
> That wounds my body so dishonored.

> Tis honor to deprive dishonor'd life,
> The one will live, the other being dead.
> So of shame's ashes shall my fame be bred,
> For in my death I murther shameful scorn:
> My shame so dead, mine honor is new born. (1184–90)

But her engagement to honour is contingent upon the new-found audience of her shame taking revenge on her despoiler: "My resolution, love, shall be thy boast, / By whose example thou reveng'd mayst be. / How Tarquin must be us'd, read it in me" (1193–5). The matter of the audience of shame is all-important, and we will come to it presently, but for the moment we need to focus on the performance of gender roles by women and men within the shame scenario.

In her own eyes, Lucrece must die, but there must be no mistake about where the blame for this disgrace and sacrifice comes to rest:

> O, let it not be hild
> Poor women's faults that they are so fulfill'd
> With men's abuses: those proud lords to blame
> Make weak-made women tenants to their shame. (1257–60)

Women are but tenants in a house of shame built of men's abuses. The real correction must be made between men, and this is where the exclusively male audience at the scene of Lucrece's shame comes into play.

Initially the scene of ravishment has no spectators, just the two actors, perpetrator and victim. When Tarquin creeps away under cover of night, Lucrece is left to grieve her fate in tragic isolation. She mourns that "now I have no one to blush with me" (792). It would seem, then, that it is possible to experience the crushing burden of shame without an audience, at least in a case where the rape victim imagines "that every eye can see / The same disgrace" that Lucrece has forever imprinted on her inward eye (750–1). Put succinctly by the narrator, "cloudy Lucrece shames herself to see" (1084).[42]

Even as Lucrece internalizes her outrage and Tarquin's spreading shame, she prepares a letter summoning Collatine to their "house of grief" (1308). She is no more explicit than this in the letter, preferring to enhance her narrative in a fully dramatized account with her husband as audience: "she would not blot the letter / With words, till action might become them better" (1322–3).[43] When Lucrece calls Collatine's "sour-fac'd groom" to carry her note (1334), the narrator tells us that this bashful servant appears "blushing on her" (1338–41). Racked with her own inner sense of shame, Lucrece misconstrues the groom's blush:

> But they whose guilt within their bosoms lie
> Imagine every eye beholds their blame,
> For Lucrece thought he blush'd to see her shame. (1342–4)

The two characters stand blushing furiously at one another, spreading their unease to the reader, who is incapable of doing anything to undo their miscommunication.[44]

> His kindled duty kindled her mistrust,
> That two red fires in both their faces blazed;
> She thought he blush'd, as knowing Tarquin's lust,
> And blushing with him, wistly on him gazed;
> Her earnest eye did make him more amazed.
> The more she saw the blood his cheeks replenish,
> The more she thought he spied in her some blemish. (1352–8)[45]

Shakespeare arrests the forward motion of his poem here (and elsewhere) to permit the dynamic of spectatorship to gain its own momentum.[46] He allows the misconstruction of the epistemology of the blush to sink in. The ethical perceptions of the multi-layered audience are seriously disrupted by this error and are unlikely to be clarified until other layers of audience perception are added. This can happen only when Collatine, Lucretius, Valerius, and Brutus see first-hand the aftermath of Tarquin's shameful assault and take the necessary public action, strictly enjoined by Lucrece, to avenge the private insult. As always in Shakespeare, revenge is a bloody political business, involving in this case the extermination of Tarquin and his entire tyrannical line. The upshot of judging the other in the context of an honour-bound society is tragic and entails what A.C. Bradley sees as the sacrifice of good along with the purgation of evil. Such moralizing of the natural body and its trials is an anti-ethical activity, substituting, as Marx argued, raw power for social justice.[47]

At the moment of Lucrece's suicide, Shakespeare slips into a rhetoric that moralizes the female body. Her self-mutilated body becomes an island encircled by two rivers of blood:

Some of her blood still pure and red remain'd,
And some look'd black, and that false Tarquin stain'd.

About the mourning and congealed face
Of that black blood a wat'ry rigol goes,
Which seems to weep upon the tainted place,
And ever since, as pitying Lucrece' woes,
Corrupted blood some watery token shows,
And blood untainted still doth red abide,
Blushing at that which is so putrefied. (1742–50)

The separation of the dark blood clot from the watery serum is physiologically correct; suggesting that her red blood is blushing at Lucrece's bodily putrefaction is pure, culturally constructed fantasy. It is, though, a fantasy that the onstage spectators readily embrace. As for the rest of us, we may well experience a profound unease at the spectacle of supposedly tainted female flesh being sacrificed to an ideal of male honour, as the result of yet another misreading of the blush.[48]

A Tentative Conclusion

If Emmanuel Levinas is right that bringing ourselves face to face with the other without rushing to judgment is the starting point for social justice, then the conclusion of *Othello, The Rape of Lucrece*, and other tragedies of male honour and revenge would seem an unfortunate end point. Perhaps Shakespeare came to a more just appraisal of the spectator's ambiguous blush later in his dramatic career. He came to dramatize not the "correct" interpretation of the blush but the need to suspend our judgments while we experience human calamity and folly far beyond our own narrow moral certainties.

An explicit moralizing of the face of the other occurs in *Venus and Adonis*, where blushing is fully eroticized. The ground of the moralized blush, supposed herald of shame across cultures, is provided in philosophical and scientific writing from Seneca to Thomas Wright and Robert Burton to Charles Darwin. The evasion of ethical responsibility that such thinking fosters becomes evident in works like *Othello* in which personal abuse is repeatedly excused in a habit of blaming the other, particularly the imagined demonic other. The tragic upshot of misreading and misjudging the other is the pursuit of revenge.

In *Othello* the spectator glimpses a possible alternative to revenge in what Tzachi Zamir calls "pity" and Martha Nussbaum calls "compassion." Running beneath this ethical aspect of the Othello-Desdemona marriage is an erotic undercurrent that terrifies the military hero, forcing him to retreat into the familiar comradeship of his ensign Iago and a certain outcome of violent revenge. The briefly shared compassion of the married couple and its defeat by an ethic of revenge stimulates what Thomas Heywood called "the consciences of the spectators." Appalled playgoers and readers watch as the opportunity to pull back from disaster is tragically lost.

On the other hand, the shaming rituals of *Much Ado About Nothing* afford the chance to avoid what Elspeth Probyn calls the "breakdown of humanity." What seemed at first a terminal case of blushing in Hero reveals itself instead as an angry denial of slander and is the harbinger of a second chance for marriage. The second chance in this comedy adumbrates an important pattern in the late romances, the tragicomedies of recurrent occasion. The trap that is averted in these plays is the temptation to rush to moral condemnation based on a misreading of the victim's body, the outraged facial flush (*not* the guilty blush) of a Hero or a Hermione. The ethical engagement of the audience, its opportunity to face the dramatized other with full acceptance, prevents the bitter judgments that result in acts of vengeance.

The ethical suspension of destructive judgments is often not available to Shakespeare's audiences or his characters. When the poet presses beyond the value system of the traditional *blason* in representing the colourful alternations of Lucrece's face, not even the growing distance of the spectators – maid, groom, family, citizenry of Rome, all students of classical literature

– can humanely resolve the ethical dilemmas that surround the rape. The "honourable" tragic outcome is inevitable. Since the true shame of the scene of rape and its aftermath must be borne by the spectators, it is little wonder that Shakespeare's most ambitious narrative poem has lacked admirers. Few readers have been willing to engage in what Emmanuel Levinas calls "the *direct* and *full face* welcome of the other."[49]

I have been arguing that the purest form of the blush in early modern literature is caused by the full-face encounter with the other, and that it is nothing to be ashamed of. The critical self-attention stimulated by becoming aware of another's judging presence in the scene can be immensely healthy and renovative. It draws one out of oneself and into a constructive ethical engagement with the social and political worlds of the fictional narratives. It also offers a sharp critique of the power mechanisms that drive those dramatic worlds, particularly from the vantage point of a twenty-first-century spectator.

NOTES

I wish to thank Heather Dubrow, Evelyn Gajowski, and Ronald Huebert for their comments on early drafts of this essay.

1 Nathanson, ed., *The Many Faces of Shame*. Nathanson is a pioneer in the study of the shame-affect.

2 My title phrase is from *Venus and Adonis*, line 558. Unlike Shakespeare's mortal characters, Venus is capable of *forgetting* shame and its consequences. Her face is flushed, but not with maiden modesty. Line references are to *The Riverside Shakespeare*.

3 Fernie concludes *Shame in Shakespeare* by saying, "The argument of this book as a whole has been that Shakespeare reveals shame as the bridge to the other" (244). Although he is somewhat less concerned than I with spectators, he frequently foregrounds an audience's affective engagement with scenes of shaming.

4 Lemnius (in *The Touchstone of Complexions*) insists that "inwarde vyces, and gracelesse outrages of the mynde … shew oute themselues in the eyes, face, countenance, forehead, eyebrows, and in all the outward shape and habite of the body byside" (fol. 140r).

5 Chief among the early modern writers who were busy unpacking and repackaging the body-book analogy were Michel de Montaigne in France and Francis Bacon in England. Montaigne believed his repeatedly revised essays to be "consubstantial"

with his disease-ridden body. Anatomists from Andreas Vesalius to John Banister read postmortem dissections through the books of Galenic anatomy and, in turn, reinterpreted those volumes on the basis of what they observed in the anatomy theatre. Human passions were codified in such works as Timothy Bright's *A Treatise of Melancholie* (1586), Sir John Davies's *Nosce Tiepsum* (1599), Thomas Wright's *The Passions of the Minde in Generall* (1601), and Robert Burton's *Anatomy of Melancholy* (1621) as an attempt to sort out the various ways that the human spirit inhabited the flesh. The passions were most often represented as female, after the fashion of the four gesturing women (Pleasure, Paine, Hope, and Feare) who appear on the title page of Edward Grimestone's translation of Nicolas de Coeffeteau's *A Table of the Humane Passions* (1621).

6 Darwin, *The Expression of the Emotions*, 325.

7 A notable exception is Krier's excellent study *Gazing on Secret Sights*. Krier meticulously traces classical conceptions of the blush from Virgil and Ovid to the multivalent effects of "abashedness" (157) on such characters as Belphoebe and Britomart in Edmund Spenser's *The Faerie Queene*.

8 Seneca, *Ad Lucilium epistulae morales*, 61. Further references appear parenthetically in the text.

9 In his *Due dialoghi della vergogna* [*Two Dialogues on Shame*], 1592, Annibale Pocaterra expresses the widely held view that women are "weak and dangerous" and that shame is the modest robe that covers "every ugly and stinking indecency" in women. Pocaterra's translator, Werner L. Gundersheimer, skeptical of his author's claim that Nature attempts to defend female modesty by making drowned women float face down (while men float face up), received assurances from the Philadelphia coroner's office that all floaters are to be found face up. See Gundersheimer, "Renaissance Concepts of Shame and Pocaterra's *Dialoghi Della Vergogna*," 53.

10 The most thoughtful of the many treatments of surveillance in the period is Tricomi's in *Reading Tudor-Stuart Texts through Cultural Historicism*, especially his analysis of *The Duchess of Malfi*.

11 Sir Thomas Wyatt locates just such a flush on the face of the male speaker of his sonnet "The longe love, that in my thought doeth harbar," where a personified love "Into my face preseth with bold pretence, / And therein campeth spreding his baner." Meanwhile, "She that me lerneth to love and to suffre / … will that my trust, and lustes negligence / Be rayned by reason, shame, and reverence." See *Collected Poems of Sir Thomas Wyatt*, 3. As Daniel Juan Gil concludes, "For the lady (and apparently for Wyatt) the blush is not understood as the effect of a self-

conscious struggle with forbidden desire" but as a sexually aggressive move that must be controlled by the action of "reason, shame, and reverence," thus creating a new paradigm for courtship. See Gil's "Before Intimacy," 873.

12 As quoted in Cummings, "Animal Passions and Human Sciences," 30. Cummings is mainly concerned in this essay with the difficulties built into sixteenth-century proto-anthropological responses to the apparent lack of shame in New World aborigines.

13 Burton, *The Anatomy of Melancholy*, 1:423.

14 Hawkins, *Partheneia sacra*, 19.

15 See Ornstein, *The Moral Vision of Jacobean Tragedy*, 171–3.

16 Zamir, *Double Vision*, 151–67. Further references appear parenthetically in the text.

17 This response runs directly counter to the wishful image that Brabantio projects of his daughter's sexual self-regulation: "a maiden, never bold; / Of spirit so still and quiet that her motion / Blush'd at herself" (1.3.94–6). The lines recall Seneca's theory of female self-control caused by the ever-present, internalized image of a model father or husband. While Desdemona's "motions" are not, in fact, quashed by any such maiden blush, Shakespeare never presents her desires as licentious.

18 Nussbaum, *Upheavals of Thought*, 301. Further references appear parenthetically in the text.

19 Greenblatt, *Renaissance Self-Fashioning*, 232–54. I find this part of Greenblatt's interpretation very persuasive, though he falls into Zamir's problem of blaming the innocent victim when he says (referring to Iago's multiple slanders) that Desdemona's "erotic intensity … is, I would argue, as much as Iago's slander the cause of Desdemona's death" (250).

20 Levinas, *Totality and Infinity*. Further references appear parenthetically in the text. Levinas's project here and in the other essays I will cite is to undermine Martin Heidegger's argument that the first task of philosophy is understanding the subject of being (ontology), which also involves comprehension of the material world. He also subsequently countered claims made by Jacques Derrida and Michel Foucault for the centrality of the self. Levinas desires to escape the confines of this ontology by arguing for the irreducible singularity of the other (*autrui*), which, by reason of being absolutely apart from the I, has undeniable "ethical standing."

21 Levinas, "Ethics as First Philosophy," 75–8.

22 Levinas, "Philosophy and Infinity," 157. Originally published in *Revue de métaphysique et de morale* 62 (1957), 241–53, quotation from 248.

23 Davis, *After Poststructuralism*, 93.

24 Benhabib, *Situating the Self*, 10. Subsequent references appear parenthetically in the text.

25 The first definition offered by the *Oxford English Dictionary* emphasizes the directorial role of the "supervisor": "one who exercises general direction or control over a business …; one who inspects and directs the work of others."

26 Bullough, "'Psychical Distance' as a Factor in Art," 87–117.

27 Boose, "'Let it be hid': The Pornographic Aesthetic," 22–48.

28 Cartwright, *Shakespearean Tragedy*, 165.

29 Heywood, *An Apology for Actors*, F3^{v}. Further references appear parenthetically in the text.

30 See Barish, *The Antitheatrical Prejudice*. In her essay "Horns of Dilemma," 561–83, Katharine Eisaman Maus refines Barish's findings and, like him, presents especially strong readings of Ben Jonson's plays. Her concept of spectatorship is firmly rooted in the writings of the English Renaissance pro- and anti-theatrical polemicists, and it is insistently presented as a form of male anxiety. Waldron picks up the thread of the argument over the morality of seeing, hearing, and reading plays in "Gaping on Plays," 48–77. Waldron argues vigorously that in *Much Ado* and *Julius Caesar* Shakespeare "put pressure on … two mainstays of the antitheatrical position," namely, privileging solitary reading over play-going and linguistic "purity" over bodily "vulgarity" (58). Surveying a broader selection of early antitheatrical writing, Michael O'Connell had earlier concluded that Ben Jonson's allegiance to humanist "logolatry" (287) confirms his antitheatrical bent, while Shakespeare was far more relaxed about the threats and benefits of theatrical spectacles. See O'Connell, "The Idolatrous Eye," 279–310.

31 Two articles have helped shape my reading of the ethical and linguistic issues raised by this play: Camille Wells Slights, chap. 9 of *Shakespeare's Comic Commonwealths*, and Fleck, "The Ambivalent Blush," 16–23. Fleck sees the ambiguous rhetorical figure of metonymy and its extension into wholesale guilt-by-association to be at the root of Hero's shaming in act 4. Slights establishes the colonial history of the Spanish in Italy as the source of the deference to the overlord's power that corroborates Claudio's false accusation of the innocent but vulnerable Hero. Rhetorical and political slippage combine to shape the narrative of the slandered, colonized bride.

32 Hereafter speeches from this scene will be cited by line numbers only.

33 In a carefully argued article that draws its evidence largely from one of Shakespeare's late plays, Knapp demonstrates that "our ability to make interpretive choice constitutes our ethical responsibility to respond to the otherness of the [stage] image, with

the full understanding that our response may be flawed" (271). See Knapp, "Visual and Ethical Truth in *The Winter's Tale*," 253–78. Making a less-than-certain interpretive choice is not the same thing as jumping to a moral judgment.

34 Taylor, *Pride, Shame, and Guilt*, 57.

35 Ibid., 58. She equivocates on this point, however, arguing that "one may feel shame when quite alone and knowing this to be so," but the solitary response seems to involve the subject's either recalling the presence of an onlooker or shifting her point of view in order to become the onlooker herself.

36 Probyn, *Blush*, 34. Further references appear parenthetically in the text. Probyn extends the pioneering work of the psychologist Silvan S. Tomkins (1911–1991) by arguing for the positive social benefits of the shame-affect. Likewise, Patrick Hart makes the point in his brief essay "The Badge of Shame," that "The blush is the body making itself our good enemy" (7).

37 As Taylor points out (82, n. 13), both Plato in the *Laws* and Aristotle in the *Rhetoric* acknowledge the positive function of shame in an honour-oriented society.

38 See Huebert, "The Female Breast," 205–24.

39 Marion A. Wells attributes Tarquin's fascination with Lucrece specifically to Collatine's iconic representation of her face. While that powerfully lyric evocation of beauty surely energizes Tarquin, so, too, does the challenge of penetrating the walls of his compeer's *domos*. See Wells, "'To find a face where all distress is stall'd,'" 97–126.

40 Augustine, profoundly disturbed by Lucretia's suicide, concludes that "she blushed at the possibility of being believed to be an accomplice of the deed if she were to bear passively the shame that another had actively inflicted upon her" (I.ix) and so sinfully takes her own life. I quote from *The City of God against the Pagans*, 89. Shakespeare lays no such sin at the feet of his Lucrece.

41 All of Lucrece's male kin and friends insist that "her body's stain her mind untainted clears" (1710), but still she is driven by that shameful stain to take her own life for honour's sake.

42 The philosopher Bernard Williams maintains that "The farther that … ethical considerations are involved, the less a watcher needs to be in the actual offing; the idealized other will do." See Williams, *Shame and Necessity*, 221.

43 In his introduction to the 1960 Arden edition of *The Poems*, F.T. Prince claims that "The tragedy of Lucrece is in fact unsuited to direct 'dramatic' presentation" and that "Lucrece loses our sympathy exactly in proportion as she gives tongue" (xxxvi). This sounds suspiciously like trying to silence the victim of rape, a dubious critical

strategy at best. In my reading of the poem, which differs greatly from Prince's, dramatizing, describing, and reenacting are all powerful artistic strategies for capturing Lucrece's tragedy.

44 In her exemplary analysis of the poem's rhetorical strategies, Heather Dubrow makes the point that "Lucrece's contacts with people are marked more by misunderstandings and misapprehensions than by sociability or solace." See Dubrow, *Captive Victors*, 91.

45 The messenger in question is the same groom whom Tarquin threatened to murder along with Lucrece if she refused him, vowing to arrange them in a postmortem embrace as evidence of her unchastity for all Rome to see (515–25, 1632–8).

46 He accomplishes something similar when he has Lucrece's flustered maid apologize for her "sluggard negligence" in not being up before Tarquin's departure, even though she "was stirring ere the break of day" (1277–81). The fault, we know, is Tarquin's, not hers.

47 See Leites (*The Puritan Conscience and Modern Sexuality*, 16–18) on the prudish exercise of such power against women after the seventeenth century.

48 Since the publication of *Visual Pleasure and Narrative Cinema* by the feminist theoretician Laura Mulvey in 1975, extensive work has been done on the male gaze and the ethics of men misreading women's bodies. Prominent early modern instances of flawed male reading appear in the many Renaissance paintings of the suicide of Lucretia. See in particular Hults, "Dürer's *Lucretia*," 205–37.

Mieke Bal adduces persuasive visual/rhetorical evidence that in his 1664 painting of the suicide of Lucretia Rembrandt "writes the spectator into the painting." In this version, Lucretia holds a knife but has not yet stabbed herself; Rembrandt revisited the subject two years later, depicting the moment following the fatal blow. Both scenes perniciously associate rape with self-murder, according to Bal, erasing the true cause of the tragedy (the rapist, who has robbed Lucretia of herself) and causing the spectator to overlook the real horror of rape. Bal goes on to argue: "As the emblematic cultural story of rape, Lucretia's case must be replaced by stories" that describe "both the woman's experience and its meaning for the culture as a whole in which that experience takes place." While Shakespeare's protracted narrative accomplishes this end more completely than do Rembrandt's single images, it still holds the spectator/reader in a troubling bind of male judgment and failed empathy. See Bal's "Calling to Witness: Lucretia" in the collection of her essays entitled *The Art of Viewing*, 93–116, quotations from 103 and 110.

49 Levinas, *Totality and Infinity*, 80.

4
Spectatorship and Repression in Shakespeare's *Twelfth Night*

IAN McADAM

In an article on *Twelfth Night* and the Sonnets that has become required reading for anyone interested in Shakespeare's comedies, or in Shakespeare at all, David Schalkwyk challenges the replacement of "love" by "power" and "desire" in critical discourse on the playwright: "Such a transformation, whereby one argues that 'love is not love' – being instead desire, formations of power, ideological obfuscation of real relations, and so on – runs the risk of simplifying or distorting the concept as it does its work in the complex interactions of Shakespeare's poetry and plays."[1] I respect Schalkwyk's reservation that "we have replaced words that Shakespeare uses frequently with ones he seldom uses and whose theoretical inflections he would have found strange," even though in this discussion I will be very much concerned with "love" as indeed an expression of "desire" underwritten or contained by various mechanisms of social "power." I begin with this critic's observation since my position as well may in part constitute a return to more traditional methodological or ideological assumptions. A consideration of spectatorship in Shakespeare evidently requires some narrowing of focus, and my exploration of the performativity of identity will involve an emphasis on a now neglected truism in critical discourse on Renaissance drama. More than once in my own critical writing I have sought recourse to the succinct formulation of Anne Barton in her discussion of Ben Jonson: "Playing shapes reality, not because it is [always] an agent of deceit and imposture … but because it is a way of uncovering and articulating hidden emotional truths."[2] The key, and obvious, qualification here is that playing certainly does often function as a form of deception – in literature and in life – and when we consider the complex manipulation and layering of spectatorship in Shakespeare we must acknowledge that coercion can exist both from inside and "outside" (as it were) various performances. I propose here to examine such ideological manipulations in *Twelfth Night*, but also to contextualize this examination by including a brief consideration of the somewhat more benign forms of spectatorship that occur in the two antecedent romantic comedies *Much Ado About Nothing* and *As You Like It*. What will remain traditional in my interpretation, nevertheless, will be an insistence on the essential nature of the desires or the "truths" that are being manipulated in the process.

Observing What Ought to Be Hidden

I begin with one of the most famous examples of metadramatic spectatorship in Renaissance drama, act 2, scene 5 of *Twelfth Night*, in which Sir Toby, Sir Andrew, and Fabian observe Malvolio discover and discourse upon a letter purportedly written by Olivia to the steward, encouraging his amorous responses, but in truth fabricated by Maria.

This scene has always struck me as the best textual evidence for a clear awareness, in the early modern mindset, of what we now term the unconscious. Malvolio's notorious exclamation, "By my life, this is my lady's hand. These be her very c's, her u's, and her t's, and thus makes she her great P's" (2.5.83–4),[3] reveals not only the extremely sexual (if unconscious) level of his obsession with Olivia, but – for this moment to constitute an uproarious and ribald joke – the familiarity with such a dynamic on the part of both the onstage and offstage audiences of the play. Through the voyeuristic nature of this scene, Shakespeare attributes to the onstage audience a perspective that cannot be construed as a *moral* superiority – in fact, I will go on to suggest the highly questionable moral position of the observers in this case – but rather simply an ontological superiority, a knowing or understanding that eludes the enraptured Malvolio, and apparently eludes even the slow-witted Sir Andrew until, at least in the BBC production of the play, Fabian whispers in his ear.[4] It is in fact the offstage audience's complicity with, and then increasing reservations concerning,

Fig. 4.1 Stephen Fry as Malvolio, watched by Sir Toby Belch (Colin Hurley), Sir Andrew Aguecheek (Angus Wright), and Fabian (Jethro Skinner) in *Twelfth Night*, directed by Tim Carroll for the Globe Theatre, 2012.

the onstage audience's perspective that leads, in my opinion, to one of the play's most interesting ideological effects. Many readers and viewers will agree that *Twelfth Night* represents Shakespeare's comic sense at its most brilliant and engaging: the episode with the eavesdropping trio hiding, improbably, behind the box-tree (see fig. 4.1), and Malvolio's subsequent appearance, with ludicrous smile and ridiculous cross-gartered yellow stockings, are undoubtedly two of the most hilarious scenes in the canon. And yet the emotional involvement of the offstage audience, ironically, eventually serves to heighten their moral and intellectual discomfort as the tone of the play gradually grows darker and more uncertain.

The gulling of Malvolio in *Twelfth Night* has raised for scholars the political significance of his standing as "a kind of puritan" (2.3.130), and the amount of (natural) condemnation or sympathy such a position would entail for a late-Elizabethan audience. The most obvious level of anti-Puritan satire is, in this case I think, undeniable, and J.L. Simmons has offered a clear description of its general import.

> Maria dupes Malvolio on "his grounds of faith" into interpreting "some obscure Epistles of love" as a "manifestation" of his election. Malvolio's absurd and egotistical reading comically projects what defenders of the Establishment argued to be the inherent danger in Puritanism's essential and foundation[al] principle, its absolute insistence on the unique authority of the Bible in all matters of religion … [Malvolio's] exegesis [of Maria's letter] exemplifies, in the symbolic action, a Puritan's approach to scriptural interpretations in the spirit of self-love, of Bad-Will.[5]

In this sense Shakespeare's satire apparently defends the more conservative, "mainstream" Protestant status quo. But Simmons also argues that "Maria draws the moral of her fable as explicitly as possible in such a profane setting: 'yond gull *Malvolio* is turned Heathen, a verie Renegatho [a Christian converted to Islam]; for there is no christian that meanes to be saved by beleeving rightly [Maria's version of *sola fide*], can ever believe such impossible passages of grossenesse' [3.2.64–7]" (182). Clearly, for Simmons, Maria simply confirms or clarifies the satire on Puritanical excess. Yet her designation of Malvolio as "heathen" signals a crucial complication in the play's satirical strategies and a shifting of sympathies in the direction of pagan or non-Christian sensibilities, which are to become increasingly attractive to Shakespeare over the course of his career. Surely the earthy Maria's insistence on the correct letter of Christian behaviour towards salvation begins to sound almost immediately hypocritical in such a "profane setting." Shakespeare is at least as interested in the dominant culture's rather cynical tendency to use theological strictures to demonize and contain the illicit behaviour of subversive factions, in order to police its own power structures, as he is in simply exposing Puritan ambition or Puritan self-deception.

Moreover, artistically Shakespeare has a keen interest in what Maria terms "grossness." Another earlier commentator on Shakespeare's treatment of Puritanism, Harold Fisch, has described Malvolio as strictly a power-seeker: "He dreams of marriage with Olivia, not because of an invincible desire for her person, but because he will then be in command." For Fisch we need to turn to another "Puritan" in Shakespeare, Angelo in *Measure for Measure*, to see a demonstration of how the "demon of power releases the djin of the libido."[6] But Malvolio's "libido" obviously constitutes a crucial component in his attraction to Olivia, as the reference to her "c's, her u's, and her t's" makes clear. Such a textual moment may be good support for Harold Bloom's suggestion that we are, or should be, engaged in Shakespearean readings of Freud rather than Freudian readings of Shakespeare: "Freud was anxious about Shakespeare because he had learned anxiety from him."[7] Considering "that specifically shameful female signifier – the 'cut,'" Gail Paster argues that the "pun opens out contextually to transform the mediation of the letters into something very like a transgressive encounter." If the joke implicates Malvolio, according to Paster it "works just as vividly to expose Olivia"; its "leveling vision … imagines Olivia and Malvolio together in an act of desire the precise nature of which is left excitingly unclear."[8]

But this levelling, this establishment of a secret affinity or connection between Malvolio and Olivia, has important ramifications for the play's satire on theological attitudes. Many critics, and I think probably most readers, admit to the likelihood of increasing sympathy for Malvolio when, locked in a "dark room," he is treated as a demoniac by Feste as Sir Topaz the curate, this time under the spectatorship of Sir Toby and Maria. In

Trevor Nunn's 1996 cinematic version of the play, Sir Toby has actually furnished himself with a nineteenth-century equivalent of contemporary popcorn and soda pop, as he settles down, comfortably and comically, with biscuit and bottle to watch the show. Nunn's Maria, with perhaps rather more human warmth than is suggested in Shakespeare's text, is obviously uneasy with the proceeding, which somewhat painfully attenuates the comic tone of the scene.[9] Nevertheless, Sir Toby soon experiences his own increasing anxiety over the "control" they are exercising, as Shakespeare's text indicates (4.2.67–71), in spite of the fact that he commends Feste's performance as "exquisite" (62).

Observing Containment

Perhaps the most cogent political reading of the torment of Malvolio has been offered by Donna Hamilton, who suggests a dynamic very similar to the one I have outlined above. Shakespeare, according to Hamilton, focuses ultimately "not on puritanism or on madness or on exorcism, but on the extent to which authority will fabricate [lies and false accusations] in order to protect itself, thus laying bare the strategies of containment, suppression, demonising, and scapegoating that the ecclesiastical officials had been using [in their attacks on Puritans]."[10] We know that Shakespeare was interested enough in writings on exorcism to use Samuel Harsnett's *Declaration of Egregious Popish Impostures* (1603) as a major source for *King Lear* (c. 1604–05). In this work Harsnett exposes the fraudulence of Catholic exorcists in the mid-1580s as a way of indirectly undermining the more recent successes (and popular reception) of Puritan exorcists, specifically John Darrell, near the turn of the century. We might also briefly consider F.W. Brownlow's speculation that while "Shakespeare seems to have found Harsnett's first [satirical attack] on Darrell [*Discovery of the Fraudulent Practises of One John Darrel*, 1599] amusing, he found the *Declaration* disturbing, even horrifying."[11] Hamilton's reading allows us to conjecture that an incipient sympathy for persecuted Dissenters (either or both Catholic and Puritan) may have predated Harsnett's *Declaration*, since it is implicit in *Twelfth Night* (c. 1601–2): "Even as Toby discredits Malvolio by constructing him as possessed and in need of exorcism, so were ecclesiastical officials demonising the puritans, not only by arresting fanatics but by then constructing all puritans as fanatics." Malvolio is poignantly, rather shockingly, tormented not for a "possession" but for an obsession ironically facilitated and encouraged by his very persecutors: "Set up as a mocking parody of an ecclesiastical trial, the [dark room] scene relies … on audience recognition that the entire event is staged, and thus on an awareness that, disagreeable as Malvolio may be, he is innocent of that of which he is being accused." Significantly, "the common criticism of the Darrell trial" – and Hamilton demonstrates that there was an extensive popular reaction in late-Elizabethan society – "was that it was unfair and fixed."[12]

If Shakespeare is indeed playing on recent sympathies aroused by the persecution of Darrell, then the metadramatic spectatorship of *Twelfth Night* could be viewed as subtly working to uncover and defuse the repressive energies built up by the controlling strategies of the politico-religious spectatorship arranged through the discursive practices of the Elizabethan establishment – practices so often imbued with the sense of the theatrical.[13] After Feste's performance as Sir Topaz, Maria remarks, "Thou mightst have done this without thy beard and gown, he sees thee not" (4.2.64–5), even though she herself has directed him to don the disguise at the beginning of the scene. The remark thus constitutes one of those odd Shakespearean moments of apparently gratuitous language and gesture. Was the dark room darker than she anticipated? If so, how could she and Sir Toby have observed the show? Does Shakespeare wish, finally, to emphasize Malvolio's moral blindness, or rather Maria's and Sir Toby's? This disconcerting moment thus strongly encourages the offstage audience to adjust or revise its own moral judgments, through the challenge of attributing motives to Maria's own surprising and seemingly misplaced theatrical concerns.

The possibility of sympathy towards Malvolio is increased through a subtle link – already, as we saw above, implied by Paster – between him and Olivia. Sir Toby calls Olivia "a Cathayan" (2.3.71) which, following Roger Warren and Stanley Wells in the Oxford edition, I take to suggest, in Toby's drunkenly slurred speech, "a Catharan," a proponent of a medieval heresy known for its extreme asceticism and a label applied by

Elizabethans derogatorily to Puritans. I realize this is very much a minority critical position: a rigorously historicized *Shakespeare Quarterly* article treating the "Cathayan" allusion mentions the Warren and Wells reading only to (implicitly) dismiss it, with no effort to refute it other than through a vague insinuation of readers "unsettled by the idea of a Chinese Olivia."[14] But much in the play's ideological context supports the "Catharan" reading. The Catharan label applied by mainstream Protestants, especially defenders of the Elizabethan establishment, to Puritans was, like the accusations of fanaticism or of deliberate deception in exorcism, not infrequently manipulative and reactionary hyperbole.[15] There is some evidence in *Twelfth Night* that Shakespeare is clearly aware of this political motive. The Catharan creed as it emerged in the twelfth century is clearly allied with Manichaeism, characterized by the gnostic assertion that

> The material world and matter were evil, the dominion of the evil spirit. Against him stood the God of the New Testament, whose kingdom was of the spirit, not of this material world. Human souls were spirits imprisoned in the evil, material flesh, and to be freed by the Catharan belief and practices. The Catholic belief in bodily resurrection as well as the whole Church system of sacraments was untrue. Only the unregenerate passed into another material body.[16]

It may be that such "extreme asceticism" could make a connection between Catharan belief and Puritanism plausible, but the attribution to Puritanism of these kinds of gnostic heresies is highly questionable. For the Catharan,

> Life on earth, the devil's domain, was thought of as a dwelling in and with corruption, a penance, a probation. The aim was to have done with such life, such probation, as soon as might be. The unbeliever, though he eventually reached heaven, did not do so immediately after death, but had to continue his penance in another material form. One of the essential ideas of Catharism, then, was the transmigration of souls.[17]

Yet transmigration of souls is exactly the heresy that Malvolio denies during his interrogation by Feste as Sir Topaz the curate: "I think nobly of the soul, and no way approve [Pythagoras's] opinion" (4.2.55–6). In this ideological context, Malvolio could perhaps have just as logically asserted, "I think nobly of the *body*." Clearly Malvolio's "puritanism," unlike Catharism, is *not* beyond the (Protestant) ideological pale,[18] although Feste teasingly, ironically, cruelly responds, "Thou shalt hold th'opinion of Pythagoras ere I will allow of thy wits" (4.2.57–9).

Sir Toby facetiously and drunkenly refers to Olivia as a "Catharan" because of her loss of sensual and sensuous pleasure through excessive grief: "What a plague means my niece to take the death of her brother thus? I am sure care's an enemy to life" (1.3.1–2). The "Catharan" reference significantly establishes a crucial ideological link between the "puritan" Malvolio and Olivia, underlined by Olivia's later admission, "I am as mad as he" (3.4.14). By dramatizing the uncontrollable sexual desires of Malvolio and of the highly sympathetic Olivia, Shakespeare manages a critique of both the self-repression encouraged by (excessive) religious self-idealization, and the political repression arising from the demonization of those struggling to "work through" the reality of their own sexual desires. Obviously Olivia receives the more delicate treatment, both artistically and socially, partly due to advantages of rank. Nevertheless, like her "puritan" alter ego Malvolio, she is driven by barely conscious libidinal desires she hardly understands:

> I do I know not what, and fear to find
> Mine eye too great a flatterer for my mind.
> Fate, show thy force, ourselves we do not owe.
> What is decreed must be; and be this [her passion for Cesario] so.
> (1.5.298–301)

She has indeed "usurp[ed her]self" (1.5.178). Her dilemma is a comic, erotic version of predestination, and surely this is Shakespeare's point: not one's salvation but (the exact nature of) one's sexual desires are beyond one's control. Although the playwright thus rescues the body from gnostic constructions of Satanic corruption, he upholds it as a key determiner of the individual's social and sexual fate.[19]

Observing the Faith in Folly

This apparent appropriation of Reformed doctrine for the purposes of erotic characterization may be consistent with the increasingly "pagan" drift of Shakespeare's artistic interests, which I alluded to earlier, but it is probably a mistake to construe this tendency as specifically or wholly secular, either at this textual moment, or indeed at any point in the playwright's career. Critics have not been blind to the recurring religious significance of the language of *Twelfth Night*. Paul Dean, for example, observes that "the speeches of Feste as Sir Topas, which are usually dismissed as nonsense, have a very precise significance" which finds parallels in Reformation debates concerning the meaning and function of the Eucharist. Such parallels are in fact not confined to Feste's language, for even Antonio's climactic exclamation to Sebastian, "How have you made division of yourself?" (5.1.216), potentially alludes to or recalls, as Dean suggests, controversial claims regarding the inability of Christ's body – at least according to Protestant doctrine – to exist simultaneously in heaven and on earth.[20] Like Dean I don't propose an exhaustive reading of the religious significance of Shakespeare's astonishingly complex mature works, but I wish to emphasize here – as paradigmatic of the playwright's response to theological contexts throughout his career – a speech by Feste which (as far as I am aware) has not been elucidated in scholarship on this play. On the fool's first appearance, as he struggles to regain the favour of Olivia, Feste observes, "bid the dishonest man mend himself: if he mend, he is no longer dishonest; if he cannot, let the botcher mend him. Anything that's mended is but patched: virtue that transgresses is but patched with sin, and sin that amends is but patched with virtue. If that this simple syllogism will serve, so; if it will not, what remedy?" (1.5.40–6). Warren and Wells offer the following explanation: "nothing is absolutely good or bad, but a mixture. Compare *All's Well* 4.3.74–5: 'The web of our life is of a mingled yarn, good and ill together.'"[21] This note may rightly emphasize generally the core of Shakespearean philosophy, but it underestimates here the significance of the theological context, specifically the Protestant emphasis on *sola fide*, and the spiritual and moral insufficiency of the natural man. William Tyndale in *The Obedience of a Christen Man* asserts the familiar Protestant paradox that God must destroy in order to rebuild.

> Whom he loveth him he chasteneth[;] … whom he saveth he damneth first. He bringeth no man to heven excepte he sende him to hell first. If he promise lyfe he sleyth first[;] when he byldeth he casteth all downe first. He is no patcher[;] he can[n]ot bylde on a nother mans foundacion. He will not worke untyll all be past remedy and brought unto such a case that man maye se how that his hande[,] his power[,] his mercy[,] his goodness and trueth hath wrought all togither.[22]

Even if Shakespeare is not responding to this particular passage, the idea was enough of a commonplace within Protestant discourse to render Feste's diction theologically significant in this context. In terms of Christian redemption, one does not put new wine in old bottles.

Nevertheless, my real motive in highlighting this allusion is to contend that Feste's implied (moral) position is really Shakespeare's. The clearest theological response to the fool's question, "what remedy?" would in fact be, "the Atonement" – although a pure theology of grace is quickly qualified, in human experience and indeed in Shakespeare's art, by a consideration of necessary human agency, and human morality. Puritanism itself, as a radically "pure" form of Protestantism that might be expected to uphold the principle of *sola fide*, or faith alone – crucially a faith arising only through the grace of God – soon became notorious for its obsession with Old Testament Law, and with upholding moral codes of behaviour. In early modern studies this contradiction should by now not surprise us: Kristen Poole has helpfully delineated between the antinomian zeal of the radical, "grotesque" Puritan and the strict discipline of the more familiar "killjoy" Puritan in later sixteenth-century cultural conceptions.[23] Malvolio clearly represents a type of the latter, killjoy variety, but as Poole suggests, the former image, most notoriously in the characterization of Falstaff as a reworking of the Lollard martyr Sir John Oldcastle, figures highly significantly in the corpus as well.

I would therefore like to digress briefly in this discussion to consider *Twelfth Night* as a profound culmination, thematically and ideologically, of the triad of plays that includes *Much Ado About Nothing* and *As You Like It*, in a sense that I hope will be more significant than the fact that these texts are often grouped together as the zenith of Shakespeare's achievement in romantic comedy. Several decades ago David Ormerod helpfully identified a crucial dichotomy between "faith" and "fashion" in *Much Ado About Nothing*. In this analysis "fashion" implies superficial conformity to social codes, as opposed to the deeper values and virtues of "faith." Thus the superficial attraction of Claudio for Hero, and her rather pragmatic acquiescence to his romantic interests (the text implies that she may in fact have preferred Don Pedro), contrast with what generations of readers have interpreted as the deeper, more essential passion that emerges between Benedick and Beatrice. But the binary is oversimplified and problematic, since Ormerod assigns "the tutelary deities" Hercules and Blind Cupid to faith and fashion respectively. The former deity suggests "faith" in this reading since "in the Renaissance Hercules' physical power came to symbolize any other kind of heroic strength, whether moral, religious, or intellectual."[24] But to identify a theology of grace with moral strength is in this context historically questionable, and in fact the "mystical" or self-enervating tendencies of Protestantism or Puritanism are indeed, I argue, satirized in this play, specifically through Dogberry and company.

Here I rather surprisingly have to go back almost a century to find an antecedent for my argument: James Westfall Thompson's claim that Dogberry "is manifestly a satire on local Puritan officialdom."[25] On two occasions the comic malapropisms of Dogberry and Verges associate salvation with suffering rather than achievement or reward. In response to Dogberry's initial query to the watch "Are you good men and true?" Verges replies, "Yea, or else it were pity but they should suffer salvation, body and soul" (3.3.1–3). In the later interrogation of Borachio and Conrade, Dogberry exclaims, "O villain! Thou wilt be condemned into everlasting redemption for this" (4.2.53–4). Behind the linguistic ineptitude lies a general association of religious "salvation" – in effect a surrender or loss of self – with masculine inefficacy, a general failure of manliness, certainly a socially undesirable state in Messina (and more generally in the patriarchal contexts of Renaissance drama). Maintaining an aristocratic bias or sympathy characteristic of his earlier work, Shakespeare here still associates such disenfranchisement with the lower classes, as in *A Midsummer Night's Dream* (4.1.202–15), where Bottom's notoriously garbled version of 1 Corinthians 2:9–10 may indirectly attribute spiritual vision to the socially humbled but certainly does nothing to enhance his class status. During the manipulated spectatorship of Benedick, when Don Pedro and Claudio encourage Benedick's passion for Beatrice, Don Pedro ironically commends Benedick as Hector: "in the managing of quarrels you may say he is wise; for either he avoids them with great discretion, or undertakes them with a most Christian-like fear" (2.3.183–6). In spite of the ironic humour, "Christian" behaviour is here tagged as unmanly, and the joke clearly foreshadows Dogberry's advice to the watch that they not "meddle" with or lay hands on thieves or untrue men, since "they that touch pitch will be defiled" (3.3.55–6).

A level of personal assertiveness, and a "dialectical" or possibly even fiercer engagement with others, *Much Ado* implies, benefits not only men. According to Harry Berger, Hero may on some level resent being told by Beatrice that "marriage is virtue's repentance rather than its reward" (in the speech at 2.1.63–9), and Hero both inwardly chafes at and grudgingly admires her cousin's refusal to conform to patriarchal versions of proper womanhood. In preparation for the manipulated spectatorship of Beatrice, Hero instructs Ursula to bid Beatrice

> steal into the pleached bower
> Where honeysuckles, ripen'd by the sun,
> Forbid the sun to enter, like favourites,
> Made proud by princes, that advance their pride
> Against that power that bred it. (3.1.7–11)

But as Berger observes, "the simile does not quite work the way Hero wants it to: the courtly figure strains against the positive quality of its floral subject."[26] When Hero subsequently bitterly muses, "[Beatrice] cannot love, / Nor take no shape nor project of affection / She is so self-endeared" (3.1.54–6), we are reminded of Malvolio, sick of self-love. Nevertheless, Beatrice's assertiveness and self-possession contribute to an eventual romantic fate, an emotionally rich, psychologically mutual marriage with Benedick, infinitely preferable to the one awaiting Hero. Indeed, in the later play the potentially tragic fate awarded the comparably "self-endeared" Malvolio, his social humiliation and alienation, is tempered by a notable reassertion of self-worth. Both Beatrice and Malvolio could be said to justly challenge patriarchal and class strictures. As David Schalkwyk argues, Malvolio's letter of rebuke to Olivia "is shockingly direct." Schalkwyk's exploration of "love and service" leads to his drawing parallels with Shakespeare's Sonnets, but Malvolio's letter, "read out in public, shows no concern for the proscriptions rehearsed in Sonnets 57 and 58, especially regarding the denial of a servant's right to 'accus[e]' the master or mistress 'of injury' (58.8)." Since Malvolio "expresses, in the most forceful, public terms, the duty of care and reciprocity expected of magisterial relationships," it is highly significant "that he should in the end reject all protocols of duty, service, and social distinction" by vowing "I'll be revenged on the whole pack of you" (5.1.368).[27] Malvolio's final response in essence demonstrates what could be termed the Puritan *masculinization* of atonement theology and Pauline self-effacement, a process for which by this point in his career Shakespeare seems to have developed a certain level of sympathy. It is perhaps not surprising that some readers have read Malvolio's final exclamation as Shakespeare's rather uncanny foreshadowing of the Puritan revolution.

Observing Desire

I now return to my initial observation concerning the deeper romantic attraction and (in Malvolio's case) largely unconscious erotic yearning that fuels the final comic, or not so comic, "castastrophe." As implied above, Shakespeare appears to envisage this force, whatever we choose to call it, as beyond the merely social or discursive. My earlier allusion to *A Midsummer Night's Dream* is apropos here, for Bottom's "asinine" metamorphosis emerges clearly as a comic version of the transformation of Actaeon, according to the indispensable reading offered by Leonard Barkan, which establishes that myth as probably the most important classical allusion in Renaissance culture, at least with respect to masculine identity and masculine sexual anxieties.[28] Barkan argues that Actaeon's metamorphosis into a stag merges into or conflates with the image of an ass in Renaissance pictorial depictions, and that this form of horned asininity symbolizes or embodies, through many haunting depictions, the fear of the loss of masculine self-possession, in both sexual and religious senses, in Renaissance art and literature. (Marlowe's *Doctor Faustus* constitutes a major, if still underappreciated, instance.[29]) Dogberry's frustrated and foolish (but also rather poignant) insistence that Conrade's designation of him as "ass" be publicly noted – "[t]he humor derives from the fact that he exacerbates the damage in the very process of trying to repair it"[30] – repeats this motif. Indeed, the Actaeon motif could be said to haunt this entire play through the recurring references to cuckoldry, and the concomitant evocation of masculine fear of feminine power.[31] It is worth noting here that the Actaeon myth, besides evoking male sexual and ultimately religious anxieties, is the myth *par excellence* of the dangers of spectatorship: if Actaeon's original encounter with Diana underlines the dangers of inadvertent spying, the later associations of the myth with cuckoldry underline the social humiliation in being rendered a spectacle, relentlessly exposed and ridiculed as a cuckold.

Yet abject fear and compelling desire seem inextricably joined in *Much Ado About Nothing*, and the Arden editor A.R. Humphreys, building on Shakespeare's oft-observed punning between "nothing" and "noting" (that is, watching, observing), clarifies what could be considered the traditional assertion of essential passion between Beatrice and Benedick: "Not that a sole 'noting/nothing' is the whole reason why Benedick and Beatrice are gulled so readily; the attraction they refuse to admit is already powerfully there, is very clearly 'something.'"[32] Not surprisingly, such readings have been challenged by more recent critics. Stephen Greenblatt argues that the "movement of the play is not so much the unmasking of fraud to reveal the true, virtuous essence within as rather the refashioning, after a dangerous illusion, of the proper image and the appropriate words." Not insensitive to the desire to read a deeply essential love between the two witty lovers, Greenblatt nevertheless insists that "Beatrice and Benedick constantly tantalize us with the possibility of an identity quite different from that of Claudio and Hero, an identity deliberately fashioned to resist the constant pressure of society. But that pressure finally prevails. Marriage is a social conspiracy."[33] This reading, in my opinion, apparently confuses the social construction of a delimiting expression of romantic attraction, a controlling mechanism to contain sexual passion, with the essential reality of that passion.

The ironies that Greenblatt observes in the text do not come close to vitiating the presumed inwardness of the felt passion. *Much Ado* undeniably remains concerned with the tension between "fashion" and "faith." Decades of teaching Shakespeare have sensitized me to the fact that not only are his playtexts carefully structured around thematic binaries or dichotomies, but that it is always dangerous to oversimplify the dynamic relationship between the binaries in any of these texts, or to limit them to the purely political pressures so often emphasized in poststructuralist criticism. Because of my primary emphasis on *Twelfth Night*, I will leave the detailed arguments concerning the tension between artifice and genuine emotion in *Much Ado* to other critics, except to briefly refer here to Philip Collington's fairly persuasive attempt to revive a much older assertion that the play contains key correspondences with Castiglione's *The Book of the Courtier*. Collington acknowledges that both Shakespeare and Castiglione "characterize the world as a stage on which identity is more performance than essence," but then later in his analysis he almost contradicts himself when he observes, "Right from the first scene, Claudio seems attracted to images, whereas Benedick concerns himself with essences."[34] Thus, while Collington does suggest ways that the two eavesdropping scenes work to motivate or compel both Beatrice and Benedick to fulfill already established courtly ideals and social exigencies in order to improve their respective characters, such an analysis does not exclude the reality of their respective desire for each other, and the crucial moral differences they display in contrast to Claudio and Hero.

Moreover, Shakespeare is deeply concerned, at this point in his career, with the tension between the reality, indeed physicality, of sexual attraction and the way it is socially, and personally, *imagined*, since it becomes the central theme of the closely contemporaneous, probably subsequent *As You Like It*. Alan Brissenden succinctly indicates the tight thematic structure of this play, otherwise not remarkable for its rigorous plot construction.

> That Rosalind and Orlando's love, full of comic complexities, lies between the pastoral [and Petrarchan] extravagances of Silvius and the earthy pragmatism of Touchstone is neatly indicated in 2.4 when

> the besotted shepherd goes off crying "O Phoebe, Phoebe, Phoebe!"; Rosalind is reminded of her love, and Touchstone recalls, with a ribald innuendo, his love for the milkmaid Jane Smile.[35]

Certainly "complexities" abound here again. The perfect balance between physical or material desire and romantic idealism eventually achieved in the Rosalind-Orlando relationship may be perceived as a result of the initially rather earthy Rosalind – "some of [this madness] is for my child's father" (1.3.11) – tempering the excessive Petrarchan idealism of the poetry-writing Orlando. But this binary inverts, or the extremes seem to be approached from opposite sides, later in the play, when Orlando disappoints Ganymede because of his careful tending upon Duke Senior – whether or not he has perceived Ganymede's true identity, he apparently gives precedence to the pragmatic, homosocial courting of potentially powerful men – and Rosalind herself seems to have surrendered to the depths of idealized passion: "O coz, coz, coz, my pretty little coz, that thou didst know how many fathom deep I am in love" (4.1.188–9). Such imbalances between artificial codes and genuine passion, and the potentially dangerous lack of reciprocity or mutuality between lovers, might suggest the inextricability of love and fear in *As You Like It* as well as in *Much Ado*. Still, the pastoral *As You Like It*, like the polished courtliness of *Much Ado*, offers a somewhat sunnier world than *Twelfth Night*. Unlike Touchstone's bawdry, Silvius's excessive idealism is finally rewarded with, as Jaques pronounces, "a long and well-deservèd bed" (5.4.185), perhaps because his trials have represented, in the words of Corin's invitation to the spectatorship of Ganymede and Aliena, "a pageant *truly played*" (3.4.47, emphasis added). That is, in spite of the conventional, even possibly hackneyed posturing of pastoral love, there is something undeniably genuine about the depth of Silvius's feelings.

In Malvolio's less happy case, as I have argued, his passion is both conscious and unconscious, and transcends the mere desire for social climbing. That his reflection over Olivia's letter produces an unconscious allusion to "her great P's," or copious urination, might indicate some displaced fear of being overwhelmed by the "leaky vessel" of the female body. Although Gail Paster does indeed construe this comic moment as an allusion to the Actaeon myth – "Malvolio becoming a parody of Actaeon and

Olivia of the naked Diana"[36] – Paster perhaps, in the final analysis, overestimates the extent to which the spectatorship of Malvolio and the false letter implicates the Countess Olivia in a sexual sense. *Twelfth Night* much more obviously alludes to the Actaeon myth in its opening sequence, where Orsino hyperbolically recalls the moment he first laid eyes on Olivia.

> Methought she purged the air of pestilence;
> That instant was I turned into a hart,
> And my desires, like fell and cruel hounds,
> E'er since pursue me. (1.1.19–22)

Here the mythic scenario grants Olivia not a parody, but the dignity, of the goddess Diana. Whether Orsino's desires are genuine – he seems instead to be more enamoured of the Diana-like femininity of the boy Cesario – and whether or not his foppish rhetoric potentially renders him foolish, his social standing, as count or duke, serves to insulate him from the dangerous ridicule that Malvolio suffers.

Observing Antonio

The pattern I have been tracing in *Twelfth Night* of (covert) artistic sympathy for the sexually repressed, and, in Malvolio's case, socially marginalized or subordinated, as well as the ambiguous sexuality evident in Orsino's attraction to Cesario, may cast some light on the role of Antonio, whose homoerotic passion for Sebastian is very difficult to dismiss as simply a standard example of early modern amity. For one thing, Antonio's decision to faithfully "serve" Sebastian, while consistent with Schalkwyk's observation that "[e]very instance of desire in the play is intertwined with service,"[37] is not at all consistent with the tradition of *amicitia*, which insists on an absolute equality between friends. Moreover, a careful consideration of Shakespeare's dramatic versions of amity tends to confirm Robert Stretter's generalization that "the treatment of idealized male friendship in late Tudor and early Stuart drama, on the whole, reflects a move away from an earnestly humanistic didacticism and towards an often scathing mockery of classical friendship."[38] Stretter considers as one example the "disconcerting" offer by Valentine of his fiancée Silvia to his friend Proteus, who has in fact just attempted to rape her, in *The Two Gentlemen of Verona*. The friendship of Antonio and Bassanio is described respectfully by Portia and Lorenzo in act 3, scene 4 of *The Merchant of Venice* as indeed a version of equally reciprocated *amicitia*, although both the desire and the financial assistance are in this relationship in fact quite one-sided, suggesting the tradition of friendship as a convenient mask for Antonio's unrequited, perhaps subconscious homoerotic passion. But surely *Much Ado* constitutes the clearest parody of the sanctity of homosocial bonds as an expression of "spiritual" commitment, with the superficial Claudio quite happy to allow the powerful prince Don Pedro to woo Hero for him, once he has carefully established her desirability from the perspective of his male comrades, and then quite quick to suspect the prince's fidelity in the matter – and, furthermore, quite anxious to *publicly* humiliate her when he mistakenly becomes convinced of her lewdness. And his real motives for marriage were always mercenary rather than romantic; after the supposed death of Hero he is quite prepared to marry, unseen, her "cousin," simply because he therefore stands to inherit the very same estate! Evidently Antonio's self-sacrificing devotion to Sebastian in *Twelfth Night* constitutes something radically removed from Shakespeare's usual take on classical amity.

With the often highly significant scenic juxtaposition of early modern drama in mind, I note that the play's first appearance of Antonio and Sebastian occurs immediately on the heels of the speech by Olivia that I have characterized above as the eroticization of Puritan predestination: "Fate, show thy force, ourselves we do not owe. / What is decreed must be; and be this so." On his first appearance Antonio apparently clings to Sebastian, resisting the latter's proposed separation, which will occur, we (rather surprisingly) find out late in the play, only after they "did … keep company" for "three months before, / No int'rim, not a minute's vacancy, / Both day and night" (5.1.89–91). Sebastian claims the malignancy of *his* fate or predestination in order to justify his desertion of his friend – "My stars shine darkly over me" (2.1.3–4) – and admits that for these three months he has gone under the alias of "Roderigo." Clearly Sebastian has also temporarily "usurped himself," apparently, in this case, highly consciously; like his sister he has a penchant for role-playing, although for me the actual motives for his Roderigo phase remain opaque. On the other hand, Antonio's passion is transparent – "come what may, I do adore thee so / That danger shall seem sport, and I will go" (2.1.42–3) – but not ultimately reciprocal in the way Antonio seems to desire. Nancy Lindheim suggests in Antonio's desire a "contamination of male friendship by the Petrarchan paradigm,"[39] yet the desire here is hardly a discursive *product* of such formulations, and becomes most "Petrarchan" only after Antonio experiences betrayal. (Evidently Antonio experienced some kind of reciprocity, or imagined that he did, during the three months of "Roderigo"?) While it is now critically fashionable to distinguish between the two Antonios of *Merchant* and *Twelfth Night*,[40] I see them in some ways as strikingly similar, struggling with an essential, barely repressed erotic desire desperately displaced through archaic modes of friendship and futile attempts at material (that is, financial) control: the "purse" as a kind of purchase of guarantee. In fact the very emphasis on companionate marriage in Protestant and Puritan discourse of the late sixteenth century serves to highlight the isolation of the two Antonios in these plays, at the same time that, paradoxically, Protestant individualism fuels the intensity of a more radically personal or "inward" desire.

I am therefore suggesting that in Shakespeare homoerotic passion figures as "deeper," less superficially constructed, and in fact less flexible or fluid, than queer theory likes to imply. I don't propose here to engage with the tenets of queer theory or the controversy surrounding them. I will suggest instead, in keeping with my theme of the manipulation of spectatorship, that Shakespeare's interest in Elizabethan demonology, which so decisively informs the gulling of Malvolio, likely extended back to an incident that predates Darrell's turn-of-the-century Puritan exorcisms. In July 1591 a Puritan "prophet," William Hacket, accompanied by his "prophet of mercy," Edmund Coppinger, and his "prophet of vengeance," Henry Arthington, attempted what is sometimes described as a coup against Queen Elizabeth, an event that Shakespeare earlier alludes to in *Titus Andronicus*.[41] One contemporary eyewitness of the insurrection predicted that all three "prophets" would suffer execution, in spite of the conspirators' evident religious madness, which could theoretically or legally exonerate potential criminals in Tudor England by problematizing the existence of a true intent to injure. In fact the witness

> suggested that the "prophet of vengeance," Henry Arthington, would receive a particularly brutal punishment "because he has said the Queen is not to reign any longer, for rejecting the petitions of the faithful, and neglecting the cause of God and his Church, for which she must be punished, though her soul shall be saved." In other words, Arthington's mingling of blasphemy, treason, and Puritan leanings would go hard for him at his trial.[42]

However, as it turned out, only Hacket, the ringleader, subsequently faced prosecution and eventual execution. The man expected to pay the cruellest penalty saved his skin through the state-sponsored composition and publication of *The Seduction of Arthington by Hacket especiallie, with some tokens of his unfained repentance and Submission*.[43] The subtitle crucially adds, *Written by the said Henrie Arthington, the third person, in that wofull Tragedie*, where we see again the theatricalization of the discursive strategies of the Elizabethan establishment. According to historian Owen Williams, *The Seduction of Arthington* presents an astonishing defence for his traitorous blasphemy: "Arthington claims that William Hacket, Satan's minion, had seduced and demonically possessed him during the days leading up to [their seditious] proclamation." As the penitent man relates the story, after being physically embraced by Hacket, Arthington felt himself "verie hot within," which he took as "an extraordinarie motion of the holie-ghost." In Williams's summation, this "curious melding of Galenic humoral theory, demonic possession, and ecstatic religious belief … underscores why Archbishop Whitgift and his supporters feared Puritan … 'prophesyings' so intensely."[44] So why, then, would the Elizabethan establishment actually encourage the publication of Arthington's confession? According to Williams's astute analysis,

> Arthington the demoniac was quick to distance his particular recovery from those of the over two hundred exorcisms reported between 1563 and 1603. In a nod to the bishops and their disapproval of demonic possession and public exorcism, Arthington stressed how he was restored to his "former soundnesse in the knowledge of the truth, without the help of any man mortall"; he claimed that

> God derived more glory from this fact than from contemporary accounts of exorcism at the hands of Catholic priests or through Puritan prayers and fasting.[45]

Thus the discursive representation, the "wofull Tragedie" of *The Seduction of Arthington*, is one more example of a readerly spectatorship devised to confirm the politico-religious power, the godly correctness, of the Elizabethan establishment over the seditious challenges, either Catholic or Puritan, to its authority.

But Shakespeare again, as in the portrayal of Malvolio's false possession and exorcism, counters this portrayal of Satanic corruption via homoerotic possession with the portrayal of an erotic bond whose power is inescapably only just that: an erotic fascination. In place of a homoerotic dynamic that was clearly politicized, factitious, and carefully calculated, Shakespeare offers one completely ingenuous, almost naive. In act 3, scene 4 the exact nature of Antonio's experience is once more, interestingly, left ambiguous. He claims to have "snatched" the youth "one half out of the jaws of death" and to have "Relieved him with such sanctity of love" (3.4.350–2), whereas the description the Captain offers Viola in act 1, scene 2 (1.2.7–16) suggests a virile Sebastian quite capable of saving himself. It is perhaps what Antonio *imagines* that really matters here. At his supposed betrayal by Sebastian, Antonio exclaims in anguish:

> In nature there's no blemish but the mind.
> None can be called deformed but the unkind.
> Virtue is beauty, but the beauteous evil
> Are empty trunks o'er-flourished by the devil. (3.4.358–61)

Here Antonio's demonization of Sebastian is, in one sense, certainly a misplaced reading of the action, insofar as he has mistaken Cesario for Sebastian. Yet, in another sense, what Antonio terms "the blemish in the mind" is from his perspective poignantly accurate, insofar as Sebastian later justifies Olivia's attraction to Cesario with the phrase, "But nature to her bias drew in that" (5.1.254), where the logic of heterosexual normalcy facilitates Sebastian's romantic abandonment of Antonio. It is true that the text does not construct what could be called an overtly homophobic context in response to Antonio's protestations; yet there is a degree of social embarrassment when, in reply to Antonio's assertion, "to his image, which methought did promise / Most venerable worth, did I devotion," the First Officer exclaims, "What's that to us?" (3.4.353–5). This moment constitutes ultimately a refusal of sympathetic spectatorship, a refusal to consider the real grounds of Antonio's outburst. Beyond Petrarchan constructions of idol-worship, and beyond any queer constructions of an endlessly manipulable sexuality, lies the bare fact of Antonio's socially alienated desire. Whatever the exact staging chosen in performance, the text of the play's final scene encourages some recognition of Antonio's isolation; Warren and Wells observe that "directors often make Antonio leave, freed but isolated, in a different direction from the lovers."[46] John Gorrie's BBC production features a lonely Antonio sitting painfully by himself, until driven from the stage by a knowing and taunting glance from Feste. In such productions the play's final tableau thus recalls, or encapsulates, Shakespeare's deliberate juxtaposition of essential, indeed *natural* desire with the kinds of ideological manipulations of sexuality that so often seem created to do service to the state.

That the metadramatic spectatorship of *Twelfth Night* takes on darker political suggestions than the more benevolent versions in *Much Ado* and *As You Like It* might suggest that the later play heralds, or participates in the beginnings of, Shakespeare's tragic period. The development from one play to the next might indicate a greater profundity in the third play of this triad, but it is probably dangerous to underestimate any of the astonishing texts from the playwright's maturity. What is most certain about the conscious highlighting of the mechanisms of spectatorship in Shakespeare is the extent to which he challenges his audiences to accept their *own* responsibility for moral evaluations concerning the relation between the deeper human drives and the consequences of their expression in the social arena – what William Slights in this volume terms "ethically active spectatorship." *Twelfth Night* both encourages a familiar, stereotypical response to the killjoy Puritan, and then a complex and uneasy reassessment of that response. Moreover, religious dissidence is subtly coupled with sexual dissidence in a way that would prove disconcerting and challenging to an Elizabethan audience, and in fact remains challenging, I contend, to our own levels of tolerance and understanding. The actual ontogeny or etiology of desire I think constituted as much of a mystery for Shakespeare as it does for us, but the forms of spectatorship he develops in his romantic comedies emphasize that both desire's inevitability and its variation pose an ongoing challenge of humane accommodation and moral sensitivity for any viewer who becomes ethically involved in the dramatic spectacle.

NOTES

1 Schalkwyk, "Love and Service," 76.
2 Barton, *Ben Jonson: Dramatist*, 226.
3 Quotations are from the Oxford *Twelfth Night* (eds Warren and Wells); from the Oxford *As You Like It* (ed. Brissenden); and from the Arden *Much Ado About Nothing* (ed. Humphreys). References are to act, scene, and line.
4 Gorrie, *Twelfth Night.*
5 Simmons, "A Source for Shakespeare's Malvolio," 181–2.
6 Fisch, "Shakespeare and the Puritan Dynamic," 81–2, 82.
7 Bloom, "Freud: A Shakespearean Reading," 23.
8 Paster, *The Body Embarrassed*, 33.
9 Nunn, *Twelfth Night.*
10 Hamilton, *Shakespeare and the Politics of Protestant England*, 100.
11 Brownlow, *Shakespeare, Harsnett, and the Devils of Denham*, 127.
12 Hamilton, *Shakespeare and the Politics of Protestant England*, 98, 100. In a review of this study, Debora Shuger has criticized Hamilton's association of Sir Toby with Elizabethan ecclesiastical officials as "implausible" (*Shakespeare Quarterly*, 492). In my opinion Hamilton is not forcing "allegorical readings" to the extent that Shuger argues. Malvolio's tormentors collectively suggest the self-serving Elizabethan "status quo" or official ideology quite effectively – rather like dominant high school cliques who isolate and torment "dissidents" for their own amusement and continued control – and in this sense Hamilton's analysis remains highly persuasive.
13 Brownlow's assessment of Greenblatt's reading of Harsnett is relevant here: "Stephen Greenblatt's description of the *Declaration* as 'a massive document of disenchantment' is, besides its hyperbole, too simple and cheery an assessment. Harsnett may have intended to demystify the exorcisms; intentionally or not, he remystified the events by presenting them as performances by a demonic priesthood whose purpose is the subversion of English social order" (*Shakespeare, Harsnett, and the Devils of Denham*, 103–4).
14 Billings, "Caterwauling Cataians," 9.

15 Warren and Wells observe that the word "Catharan" derived "from medieval Latin *Cathari*, 'the pure,' and was applied to puritans, for example by Archbishop Whitgift, 'Puritans or Catharans' (1574), cited by *OED*" (127). William Cowper in *The Bishop of Galloway his Dikaiologie* equates "the Catharan" with the "Novatian" and the "Donatist" (34), all heresies condemned for their excessive emphasis on purity and their rejection of the Church as overly corrupt. Sir Andrew's exclamation, "policy I hate. I had as lief be a Brownist as a politician" (3.2.28–9) appears to participate in this range of references, for the Brownists were frequently labeled "Donatists," as in George Gifford's *A Plaine Declaration that our Brownists be full Donatists*. Andrew implies that a dishonest manipulator is at least as bad as a religious extremist.

16 Previté-Orton, *The Shorter Cambridge Medieval History*, 2:662.

17 Turberville, *Mediaeval Heresy & the Inquisition*, 25.

18 Puritanism is hardly more radical, for example, than mainstream Protestantism in its deconstruction of Catholic sacramental beliefs, even if liturgically more austere.

19 An "essentialist" reading of the body in early modern culture is largely consistent, as the work of Gail Paster generally indicates, with humoral theory. Paster asserts that "Selfhood … in early modern terms … refers to a form of experience intensely physical in kind and expression.… The body and its emotions were understood to be functionally inseparable" ("The Tragic Subject and its Passions," 153). Allison P. Hobgood develops an interesting reading of *Twelfth Night* by insisting that "we must imagine the kinds of bodies who felt [the experience of] shame [which the play evokes], early modern bodies that were distinctly different from our own: bodies that were pre-Cartesian, highly suggestible, emotionally contagious, and driven by their intensely humoral natures" ("*Twelfth Night*'s 'Notorious Abuse' of Malvolio," 3). Through a focus on Malvolio's experience of "shame" – the designation of his emotion may be problematic in this case – Hobgood vacillates between describing deeply unsympathetic and potentially sympathetic responses by early modern playgoers to Malvolio's suffering, but comes down finally in favour of hostility: "If early modern audiences had responded to [Malvolio's] call in *Twelfth Night*'s last moments, reciprocally shaming those who shamed him, they would have had to confront the possibility of something shameful in themselves" (13). As my own concluding remarks will indicate, I believe that Shakespeare in *Twelfth Night* is subtly but significantly working to evoke a greater level of sympathy than such a reading suggests.

20 Dean, "'Nothing that is so is so': *Twelfth Night* and Transubstantiation," 285, 282–3.

21 Warren and Wells, introduction to Shakespeare's *Twelfth Night* (Oxford edition), 105nn43–4.

22 William Tyndale, *The Obedience of a Christen man*, A4r.

23 Poole, "Saints Alive!" 47–75.

24 Ormerod, "Faith and Fashion in 'Much Ado about Nothing,'" 96, n. 3, quoting Richard Knowles, "Myth and Type in *As You Like It*," 14–15.

25 Thompson, "Shakespeare and Puritanism," 229.

26 Berger, "Against the Sink-a-Pace," 14–15.

27 Schalkwyk, "Love and Service in *Twelfth Night* and the Sonnets," 95–6.

28 Barkan, "Diana and Actaeon," 317–59.

29 See McAdam, *Magic and Masculinity in Early Modern English Drama*, 60–6.

30 Lane, "'Foremost in Report,'" 36.

31 Carol Cook observes that "the most persistent theme in the witty discourse of the play's male characters" is "that of cuckoldry," and that the "pervasive masculine anxiety that characterizes … Messina might be read psychoanalytically as castration anxiety; the imagery of horns and wounds in the cuckold jokes points rather insistently in this direction" ("'The Sign and Semblance of Her Honor,'" 187, 186).

32 Humphreys, introduction to the Arden *Much Ado About Nothing*, 4–5.

33 Greenblatt, introduction to *Much Ado About Nothing* in *The Norton Shakespeare*, 1385, 1386.

34 Collington, "'Stuffed with all honourable virtues,'" 287, 291.

35 Brissenden, introduction to the Oxford *As You Like It*, 17.

36 Paster, *The Body Embarrassed*, 33.

37 Schalkwyk, "Love and Service in *Twelfth Night* and the Sonnets," 87.

38 Stretter, "Cicero on Stage," 346.

39 Lindheim, "Rethinking Sexuality and Class in *Twelfth Night*," 691.

40 The first critic to make a clear distinction between the two characters in terms of their sexuality was Pequigney in "The Two Antonios and Same-Sex Love in *Twelfth Night* and *The Merchant of Venice*," 201–21.

41 See "Topicality and Conceptual Blending," where Nicolas R. Moschovakis argues that Shakespeare was familiar enough with the records of this incident to allude to it in *Titus*.

42 Williams, "Exorcising Madness in Late Elizabethan England," 33.

43 Arthington, *The Seduction of Arthington*; STC 799.

44 Williams, "Exorcising Madness," 41, quoting *The Seduction of Arthington*, 15.

45 Williams, "Exorcising Madness," 44–5.

46 Warren and Wells, introduction to Shakespeare's *Twelfth Night* (Oxford edition), 69. Alan Sinfield's suggestion that "a director … might show [Antonio] delighted with his boyfriend's lucky break" as he prepares to move in with Sebastian and Olivia seems to me to be stretching the logic of the social possibilities that Shakespeare presents in the play ("How to Read *The Merchant of Venice* without Being Heterosexist," 66).

5
"Most grateful deceptions of the sight": Optical Technologies in Restoration England

EMILY M. WEST

When London's public theatres reopened after Charles II's restoration to the throne, things looked different: there were only two playhouses, and the old companies' boy actors had, with a Continental flair typical of the cavalier monarch, been replaced by female actresses. In another major break from the pre–Civil War public stage, the new theatres used changeable scenery, along with an increasingly spectacular array of scenic effects, to present both new plays and revivals of Tudor and early Stuart productions. These innovations, drawn from Continental and English court theatre traditions, altered the possibilities of theatre space and dramatic action, and, as Elin Diamond has argued, "introduced a new scopic epistemology" in the public Restoration playhouse.[1] The theatre was hardly the only location of such scopic revolutions. At Gresham College and beyond, optical technologies like the microscope and the telescope radically modified perceptual capacities and imaginative possibilities, and became essential to the wider cultural project of producing empirical knowledge. Following from Joseph Roach's argument that the Restoration stage functioned as "an instrument closely analogous to contemporary optical instruments" in its restructuring of "vision, knowledge, and conquest in their relationships to technology,"[2] this chapter explores the links between Restoration natural philosophy and stagecraft as visual experiences mediated by technological objects. More specifically, I argue that Aphra Behn's 1687 farce *The Emperor of the Moon*, often dismissed as a lightweight entertainment staged largely to exploit the capacities of London's Dorset Garden Theatre, uses the theatre's stage technologies to mount a sophisticated critique of the new science's technologically enabled visual revelations of the natural world.

The Emperor of the Moon is indeed a masterpiece of ephemeral spectacle, one that stretched the considerable resources of Dorset Garden to their capacity. The theatre, originally built for Thomas Betterton and the Duke's Company in 1671, had been conceived of and designed in order to accommodate the most elaborate stage technologies available at the time (see figs. 5.1 and 5.2). The completed structure hosted a series of plays Judith Milhous calls "Dorset Garden spectaculars" – entertainments that brought changeable scenery, flying machines, lighting and sound effects, dance, song, and performance together into a coordinated experience of sensory ostentation.[3] Behn's epic farce in *The Emperor of the Moon* sets the full range of these dazzling effects in motion; *Emperor*, however, was the only one of Behn's nineteen plays to use these kinds of flamboyant scenic effects. As part of the oeuvre of an author who, as many critics have noted, was critically engaged with the capacities of stage representation across her career,[4] *Emperor* emerges as a play particularly concerned with technologies of spectacle: those technologies that modified viewers' perceptual experience in conspicuous ways.[5] As this chapter contends, by recognizing the links between these technologies of spectacle and the optical instruments around which *Emperor*'s plot revolves, we can begin to parse the significance of this play's particular mode of technologically mediated visual extravagance. As I will explore across the following pages, Behn's staging of a technology-obsessed virtuoso's re-education destabilizes nascent hierarchies of perception and knowledge. Binding the virtuoso's scenes of empirical discovery to the "discovery scenes" recently enabled by the introduction of changeable scenery to the English stage, Behn's staging resituates his technologically mediated revelations, embedding them within the kind of spectacular materiality that Royal Society fellows attempted to reject as they sought cultural and intellectual legitimacy. Drawing on the supposed distinction between men's technological ingenuity and women's trifling, ornamental materiality, Behn's sharp critique uses the staged female body and the mechanisms of trivial material display associated with it to disrupt the purportedly transparent function of empiricist perception. Behn's play,

Fig. F.

I contend, ultimately enacts a radical revision of experimental empiricism by privileging experiences of spectacular materiality as sites of knowledge.

The Gimcrack

The Emperor of the Moon (hereafter *Emperor*) tells the story of Doctor Baliardo, a natural philosopher whose particular obsession is the moon, the sovereign of which he believes he can discern through his telescope. Baliardo and his moon-madness stand in the way of two prospective suitors, Don Cinthio and Don Charmante, who have designs on the doctor's daughter and niece, Elaria and Bellemante. In a bid to at once gain Baliardo's consent for their suits and cure him of his misapprehensions, and aided by Scaramouch and Harlequin (the stock *commedia dell'arte* figures who appear as Baliardo and Cinthio's manservants, respectively), Cinthio and Charmante stage an intricate farce for the doctor. In it, they appear as Iredonozar, the titular lunar emperor, and his brother, the Prince of Thunderland, two Rosicrucian spirits who have purportedly bestowed upon Elaria and Bellemante the honour of their affections. The scheme and the play culminate in a series of opulent set pieces representing the supposed moon-royalty's descent to earth and marriage to their sweethearts; after the marriage ceremony, the trick is revealed to Baliardo and he repudiates the "[r]idiculous inventions" that formerly animated his fantasies (3.3.218).

Baliardo is, even before he appears on the stage, associated with an array of optical instruments. As Scaramouch explains the suitors' scheme to Elaria in the first scene, he tells her that he has ready Baliardo's "trinkets here to play upon him" (1.1.114–15). The reference seems vague until, ten lines later, Elaria's governess Mopsophil enters to warn Scaramouch that Baliardo is calling for him: "Run, run, Scaramouch; my master's conjuring for you like mad below: he calls up all his little devils with horrid names,

Fig. 5.1 *Opposite top* Dorset Garden Theatre, exterior.

Fig. 5.2 *Opposite bottom* Johannes Hevelius gazing at the sky through his telescope. From *Selengraphia Gedani* (Gdansk, 1647).

his microscope, his horoscope, his telescope, and all his scopes" (1.1.124–6). As the subject of Scaramouch's jesting reference to the doctor's "trinkets," Baliardo's collection of scopic technologies is marked as so many trivial objects – "small ornament[s] or fancy article[s]" – of little more than decorative value in themselves, and easily turned to the task of duping their operator.[6] The status of Baliardo's instruments as trinketry is emphasized in the next scene, as the doctor makes his first entrance. The stage direction reads, "*Enter Doctor, with all manner of mathematical instruments hanging at his girdle; Scaramouch bearing a telescope twenty (or more) foot long*" (1.2.1). Adorning Baliardo, his instruments first appear onstage not as useful tools but instead as an array of accessories, not all that different from the image of Polish astronomer Johannes Hevelius in an engraving of the time. Divorced from their function as implements to enhance the doctor's perception, they become ornamental objects. Acting primarily as gaudy signs of Baliardo's participation in natural philosophical endeavours, these fancy articles intimate the triviality of this participation and, perhaps, of the endeavours themselves. Attending him, the doctor's immense telescope elaborates this visual joke in a number of ways. Its huge size might at first seem to distance it from the insignificance imputed to Baliardo's other instruments – at twenty feet long, the telescope would have stretched across at least two-thirds of the Dorset Garden stage[7] – but the elaborate trick Scaramouch and Charmante are about to perform using the telescope marks it as the principal "trinket" with which Baliardo will be "play[ed] upon." The most extravagantly scopic of Baliardo's instruments, the telescope is also the most emphatically material: a showy object, it is designed to impress, and meant to be looked *at* as much as looked through. As an article of "personal adornment"[8] and dubious functional value, the telescope is cast as a kind of epic trinket, its exaggerated size only highlighting the mechanism's essential triviality and its owner's perceptual impotence. As an outsized phallic object, it is notably impotent too. A supplement meant to consolidate and conspicuously assert the masculine subject's power within a new model of empirical masculinity that casts this power as optical, Baliardo's telescope instead stages the failure of this technological phallus. Exaggerated to the point of ludicrousness, the instrument diminishes the body it was meant to extend, converting it instead into an object of ridicule.

Behn's critique of optical technologies situates *Emperor* as one of the many Restoration satires that questioned the claims Royal Society members made for their value. Such instruments, as Steven Shapin and Simon Schaffer have influentially shown, were key to the production of empirical matters of fact, verifying the objectivity of natural knowledge by artificially mediating "the perceptual competences of a human being and natural reality itself."[9] One of the most ruthless of the satires of the Society's modest witness, his array of instruments, and the supposed purity of his artificially augmented perception was Thomas Shadwell's *The Virtuoso* (1676), an important context for Behn's representation of Baliardo and his trinkets.[10] In it, Shadwell lampoons the titular character, Sir Nicholas Gimcrack, whose philosophical pastimes include learning to swim "*upon a table*," with the guidance of a frog and a swimming master (asked whether he plans to practise in water, Gimcrack explains that he is content to explore "the speculative part of swimming").[11] One of the main targets of Shadwell's satire on the new science in *The Virtuoso* is the use of optical technologies. The inappropriateness of Gimcrack's investment in optical instruments is a running joke in the play, as when Gimcrack's niece Clarinda describes her uncle as a "sot that has spent two thousand pounds in microscopes to find out the nature of eels in vinegar, mites in cheese, and the blue of plums which he has subtly found out to be living creatures" (1.2.7–10). Gimcrack's outlay is farcical not only because of its extravagance, but also because this extravagance is wildly out of proportion with the subjects of his instrumental inquiry, which are both materially and intellectually minute. Gimcrack's philosophical project is one of material trivialities, as the Lady Gimcrack confirms when she characterizes her husband's laboratory as "a spacious room where all his instruments and fine knacks are" (2.1.289–90). Knackery, trinketry, toys: Gimcrack's inquiry, focalized through one such trivial object, amounts to a collection of so many others. The knowledge that is his "ultimate end" is destined to join this array of useless curios. As he proudly asserts, "I seldom bring anything to use; 'tis not my way" (2.2.84–6).

Gimcrack was a lasting figure in critiques of the new science pursued across the Restoration and early eighteenth century; Joseph Addison even revived him in a series of essays in the *Tatler* in 1710. For Addison, Gimcrack exemplified natural philosophers' inclination to attend only to "mean and disproportioned Objects," and the related tendency of "Observations of this Kind" to "alienate us too much from the Knowledge of the World, and to make us serious upon Trifles." Addison identifies this error as one of perception, since "whatever appears trivial or obscene in the common Notions of the World, looks grave and philosophical in the Eye of a Virtuoso." Gimcrack's eyes – augmented by his array of expensive optical instruments – are organs that transmute "Refuse" into "Treasure." Thus misapprehending objects that should act only as "diversions, relaxations, and amusements," the virtuoso inappropriately makes them the "Care, Business, and Concern of Life."[12] Addison's essay, in its reprisal of Shadwell's critique, shows how Gimcrack came to represent a mode of perception profoundly distorted through its affiliation with trifling objects. Apprehending the world through a trinketry lens, and rendering his empirically adduced knowledge of it a series of mere knacks, Gimcrack's folly is perhaps best encapsulated by his name, a word Johnson describes as connoting "[a] slight or trivial mechanism." "Supposed, by *Skinner,*" Johnson writes, "to be ludicrously formed from *gin*, derived from *engine*," a gimcrack is an inane diminutive, a technology of triviality.[13] In critiques of the new science such as those launched by Shadwell, Behn, and Addison, the designation "gimcrack" attaches to the natural philosopher's optical instrument in the sense of a "mechanical contrivance" or a "scientific apparatus," but also in the sense of "a showy, unsubstantial thing … a useless ornament, a trumpery article, a knick-knack."[14] As these critiques make clear, however, the term "gimcrack" comes to signal the broader technology of perception enabled by such trivial mechanical contrivances. The gimcrack, linked with the body as artificial organ (or gaudy accessory), transmits its triviality to that body and to the subjectivity informed by the primary impressions it produces,[15] just as any articles refracted through the gimcrack's lens come to share its qualities.

The idea of the gimcrack is a useful interpretive tool to bring to bear on Behn's representation of optical technologies in *Emperor*. Baliardo himself is clearly a version of Shadwell's Gimcrack, and by identifying Baliardo's array of instruments not simply as trinkets in the way they are explicitly designated, but, more specifically, as the gimcracks their material qualities and epistemological effects demonstrate them to be, we can recognize how they participate in a debate about optical technology's mediatory functions that had wide-ranging implications for the status of knowledge, the body, and the subject. Recognizing the gimcrack also allows us to see how the play is concerned not only with the politics of spectacle, as Al Coppola has argued,[16] but with the complex ways that optical technologies operated upon subjects to produce particular *kinds* of visual experience and spectacular effects. Finally, as I will briefly outline before moving on to examine more closely the way Baliardo's instruments function in the play, the gimcrack has particular kinds of gendered significations that inform both Baliardo's character and the effects of Behn's satire more generally.

Francis Grose's *A Classical Dictionary of the Vulgar Tongue* includes an entry for "gimcrack" with two definitions, both of which attach themselves to particular bodies. One of these, "a person who has a turn for mechanical contrivances," is predictable, but the other, "a spruce wench," seems at first incongruous.[17] Yet, when we consider the gimcrack's suggestions of materiality, triviality, and unrestrained consumption, the word's association here with a woman's body – one that is "spruce," or "smart in appearance" and "apparel"[18] – comes as no surprise. And, right around the time that Behn's *Emperor* premiered, female bodies were increasingly being "spruced" with optical instruments, as "glass-grinders found a new public among women for whom they manufactured exquisite microscopes which many ladies wore dangling from their bracelets."[19] It was during the 1680s that the microscope began what was perceived as a "decline" from "a sizeable and relatively inaccessible tool of male-dominated science" to "the portable commodity popular with middle- and upper-class women that it had become by the early eighteenth century," as Deborah Needleman Armintor has traced.[20] These "pocket microscopes," available in "brass, silver, and ivory models" and "sold in elegant snuffbox-sized containers," functioned as decorative accessories. Yet the instruments' optical functions were not merely incidental: in fact, these small microscopes were able to transmit images to the eye "much more clearly at greater magnification" than the larger models used by Robert Hooke and the Royal Society.[21] Regardless of their capacities, the miniature instruments were widely seen to literalize the qualities imputed to optical technologies by critics like Shadwell as they became ornamental toys in the hands (or on the wrists) of ladies. As the example of the pocket microscope demonstrates, whether it spruced a female body, decorated a natural philosopher's laboratory, or dangled from a virtuoso's girdle, the gimcrack was a mechanism intimately linked with early modern constructions of gender. The aggressively material triviality the gimcrack both represented and produced was linked with the ornamented female body and the feminized realm of fashionable consumer objects. And, as gimcracks, Baliardo's philosophical trinkets are technologies that ultimately enact the virtuoso's emasculation, even, and indeed especially, that enormous, exaggeratedly phallic telescope.

The Discovery Scene

My analysis thus far has concentrated on the ways Baliardo's instruments signify as they accompany the doctor into the playing space. Before long these instruments are put to use, and so initiate the metatheatrical farce that is continually elaborated through the remainder of the play. Soon after Baliardo and his telescope take the stage, Charmante joins them, pretending to be a Rosicrucian cabalist sent to induct Baliardo into that society. If Baliardo can demonstrate his purity, he can join the cabal, and he can demonstrate his purity by being able to see Rosicrucian spirits through his telescope. As the stage direction describes:

> *[Doctor Baliardo] looks in the telescope. While he is looking, Charmante goes to the door to Scaramouch, who waited on purpose without, and takes a glass with a picture of a nymph on it, and a light behind it, that as he brings it, it shows to the audience. Charmante goes to the end of the telescope.*

Charmante asks Baliardo, "Can you discern, sir?" to which Baliardo responds, "Methinks I see a kind of glorious cloud drawn up – and now – 'tis gone again." Charmante suggests that, since the doctor as yet sees no figure, he should make "a short prayer to Alikin … shake off all earthly thoughts, and look again." While the doctor is distracted by his prayer, "*Charmante puts the glass into the mouth of the telescope,*" and when Baliardo looks again, "Astonished, ravished with delight," he sees "a beauty young and angel-like, leaning upon a cloud" (1.2.78–86). Charmante continues the deception, egging the doctor on.

> CHARMANTE: Seems she on a bed? Then she's reposing, and you must not gaze.
> DOCTOR: Now a cloud veils her from me.
> CHARMANTE: She saw you peeping then, and drew the curtain of the air between. (1.2.87–91)

Charmante's trick here is, most obviously, an entertaining set piece through which the audience is invited into the trickster-hero's omniscient, satirical perspective of Baliardo's telescopic misapprehensions.[22] At the same time, the scene offers a sophisticated comment on the ways that stage and scientific technologies act upon the spectator's sight, ultimately suggesting that these processes are analogous.

Charmante's optical gambit here is one that involves particular actions and effects: namely, the sudden appearance of a new vista and the equally sudden "drawing" of this vision from view. These actions and effects replicate those of another optical manoeuvre, one enabled by the new scenic technologies of the Restoration's public stages: the discovery scene. Discovery scenes were a representational strategy that used mobile scenery to generate striking visual revelations of concealed stage spaces, and were among the most recognizable and commonly used effects associated with the new changeable scenery. This scenery was constructed from painted flats and set in a series of staggered grooves running the length of the stage.[23] What we might call a single set (but Restoration authors and audiences referred to as a "scene") was normally composed of two of these flats, each extending from the wings to meet in the middle of the stage and thus, together, forming a complete visual representation of one space. At cues indicated by the stage directions, these lightweight flats could be drawn apart to "discover" a further playing space behind them, which was itself usually backed by another set of scenic flats set in grooves farther upstage.[24] As a number of critics have shown us, scene changes on the Restoration stage were treated quite differently than our present-day understanding of stage conventions would suggest. Richard Southern begins his book on changeable scenery by emphasizing that "the changing of scenes was intended to be visible; it was part of the show; it came into existence purely to be watched."[25] As a "*playing* thing" this "dynamic scenery" functioned not as a backdrop but as an "operative factor" in the drama, with scene changes happening in full view of the audience, and often with characters still onstage.[26] The popularity of the discovery scene in Restoration drama was a function both of this spectacular scenic mobility and of the pleasure audiences took in viewing its rapid transformations of the stage space, transformations that allowed them to be "'transported' from one place to another without leaving their seats."[27] It is precisely this mode of visual revelation – "[t]he movement of painted flats, the discoveries of previously unseen interiors" – that Elin Diamond credits with introducing a "new scopic epistemology" for its Restoration spectators.[28] While the visual experience of scenic discovery was indeed new to the public stages of Restoration London, the scenic technologies that enabled these discoveries had been regularly used in the English court theatre since the early seventeenth century – a significant detail, and one I will discuss further below.

That Charmante's optical trick stages a discovery scene for Baliardo is evident not only from the kind of visual effect it produces – the "Astonish[ing]" revelation of a previously unseen space (1.2.85) – but also from the language both trickster and dupe use to describe the manoeuvre. Conjugations of the verb "to draw" are used twice in this short vignette (once by Baliardo, once by Charmante) to explain what the doctor sees through his telescope, characterizing his visual experience with a term universally used in the context of the Restoration stage to describe the action of scenic movement, and repeated in countless stage directions indicating where "the scene draws." The content of the tableau revealed to Baliardo links this telescopic spectacle even more strongly with the tradition of stage discoveries. The play of concealment and exposure inherent to the discovery scene often had an erotic dimension, and the disclosure of a sexualized female body in a private space was a common stage discovery. This kind of disclosure drew simultaneously on the visual appeal of the mobile scenery and of the actresses who were a similarly novel presence on the public stage. Baliardo's nymph, found "reposing" on a bed of clouds, plays on this convention, one that is particularly significant within the context of Behn's dramatic oeuvre.

Behn's creative and innovative use of stage space and scenic effects in her plays has been noted by critics like Derek Hughes.[29] Hughes argues that Behn used these scenic resources not just to make her dramatic work visually engaging, but, more particularly, to "examine the different ways in which men and women control space."[30] Behn's use of discovery scenes exemplifies her critical engagement with Restoration stage technologies and the scenic effects they produced. In his work on performance and theatrical representation in the Restoration, Peter Holland describes Behn's deployment of discovery scenes as "positively obsessive" and "an exception to the rule" of contemporaneous works "so pronounced as to necessitate consideration." Holland notes that in her ten comedies alone (not including the farces, such as *Emperor*) "there are no fewer than thirty-one discoveries, many of them needing much of the scene to be acted upstage."[31] Holland suggests that these disclosures cater to a scopophilic gaze, centring as they repeatedly do on women caught in "scenes of undressing, dressing or bedrooms,"[32] while Hughes argues that Behn's discoveries "emphasize a juxtaposition between different kinds of space" within a gendered spatial field.[33] Susan Green agrees that the effects of discovery in Behn's work have to do with gender; linking the discovery's effect to the disruptive presence of the Restoration actress onstage, she contends that the scenic manoeuvre "occurs over and over again because the female body, signified by the female actresses themselves, is always, and perhaps awkwardly, present to her audience."[34] As these scholars make clear, for Behn scenic effects in general, and the discovery scene in particular, were a key part of her works' interrogations of interlinked structures of gender, space, spectatorship, desire, and power, and this field of concerns is a context within which Baliardo's telescopic discovery must be read.

Through this telescopic discovery, the staged female body enters the scene of empirical philosophical investigation as a disruptive presence, calling attention to the limits of the knowledge produced by the virtuoso and his instrument, and its damning affiliation with fantasy, illusion, and spectacle. With the trick, Behn thus mounts a kind of dual discovery, one in which Baliardo's delectation of the nymph exposes his artificial vision's failure to distinguish artifice from empirical truth. The discovery reveals that the new territories visible through Baliardo's instruments are as easily interchangeable with sham fantasies as the doctor's intellectual engagement is with sexual excitement. In this way, the trick does more than lampoon the virtuoso's pretensions to chaste rationality and his "prurient curiosity veiled as disinterest."[35] By proposing that the boundary between philosophical observation and spectacular illusion is muddy at best, Baliardo's telescopic revelation ultimately suggests an inherent equivalency between stage and scientific discoveries.

Behn was not the only one who noticed a resemblance between these two kinds of technologically mediated revelations. Prominent members of the Royal Society had been expressing concerns about the likeness of their experiments to popular entertainments for years. A letter written from Christopher Wren to William Brouncker in 1664 and subsequently published in the Society's proceedings is illustrative. The letter was written amidst the Society's preparations for a visit from the king (a visit considered particularly important because, at that time, the Society still hoped to gain an endowment from the Crown).[36] Wren, attempting to decide on an appropriate demonstration of the Society's methods for the monarch, writes:

> The solemnity of the occasion, and my solicitude for the honour of the society, make me think nothing proper, nothing remarkable enough ... if you have any notable experiment, that may appear to open new light into the principles of philosophy, nothing would better beseem the pretensions of the society; though possibly such would be too jejune for the purpose, in which there ought to be something of pomp. On the other side, to produce knacks only, and things to raise wonder, such as KIRCHER, SCHOTTUS, and even jugglers abound with, will scarce become the gravity of the occasion. It must therefore be something between both, luciferous in philosophy, and yet whose use and advantage is obvious without a lecture; and besides, that may surprise with some unexpected effect, and be [commendable] for the ingenuity of the contrivance. Half a dozen of experiments thus qualified will be abundantly enough for an hour's entertainment and I cannot believe the society can want them, if they look back into their own store.[37]

In order to honour the Society and impress the king, Wren recognizes that the presentation of experiments must be spectacular – or, as Coppola puts it, he "knows that the Royal Society needs a little scientific razzle-dazzle."[38]

At the same time, too close an affiliation with spectacle easily renders an experiment a mere knack (or gimcrack), unserious and intellectually vacant, and ultimately fit only to raise wonder. Wren's criticism of Athanasius Kircher and his follower, Kaspar Schott, is particularly interesting in this regard, as Kircher had a fascination with mechanical inventions and optical instruments that in many ways mirrored that of the Royal Society fellows.[39] Kircher was particularly known for his writings on the magic lantern, a proto-cinematic technology that projected "various images, and spectres on a wall, or other white surface, so odd and surprising, that those who are not in the secret, think them the effect of magic."[40] Developed at the same time as other optical technologies like the microscope and telescope and utilizing the same principles, the magic lantern was not nearly far enough removed from these more philosophically inclined instruments for the Society's comfort. Wren, who clearly has the magic lantern in mind as he writes his letter, struggles with the challenge of mounting an experimental program that will "open new light into the principles of philosophy" for its observers without turning the Society's works into an empty series of sensational entertainments (or, more dangerously, suggesting that that is what they already are). The compromise Wren lands on, a demonstration that is "luciferous in philosophy" but that, designed for an effect "obvious without a lecture," appeals only to the eyes, does not seem as different from knacks and jugglers as he might hope. In fact, this imagined philosophical spectacle, planned to "surprise with some unexpected effect, and be [commendable] for the ingenuity of the contrivance," precisely replicates the optical and epistemological functions of the public stage's new scenic technologies. In his work on the microscope (written in the same year as Wren's letter), Henry Power argues that scientific technologies, in their mediatory function, *remove* natural philosophy from the threat of becoming merely an elaborately staged fantasy. "[W]ithout some such Mechanical assistance," Power contends, "our best Philosophers will but prove empty Conjecturalists, and their profoundest Speculations herein, but gloss'd outside Fallacies; like our Stage-scenes, or Perspectives, that show things inwards, when they are but superficial paintings."[41] In Wren's formulation, however, the scene of technologically mediated philosophical discovery is the unmistakable double of the staged discovery scene, no matter how vigorously he, or other Society fellows, might deny a resemblance between the two.[42]

The telescope trick Behn mounts in *Emperor* lampoons this consonance, as the scene of philosophical discovery reveals its modest witness to be a participant in an illusory kind of spectacular entertainment. That this exposure is accomplished through the disruptive appearance of a staged female body alerts us to how these questions of discovery, knowledge, embodiment, and material display are implicated in a larger shift between different modes of subjectivity. Will Pritchard, drawing on Cynthia Lowenthal's work, notes that critical accounts of the Restoration self depict it as "exterior and outward," but with "a sense of anxiety attendant upon that externalized self, a lingering unease with the knowledge that human surfaces are 'provisional, liable to manipulation, and subject to self-conscious and self-generated transformation.'"[43] This anxiety was one increasingly "displaced and projected onto women," in an effort to "cast women as 'the only counterfeits' and to position men as the possessors of stable selves capable of penetrating women's disguises," a penetration to be accomplished through the same kind of empirical optical strategies used by the Royal Society.[44] Caught by a trick in which he is seduced by a painted, literally superficial female body – associated through its discovery with the painted body of the actress and which, despite its actual transparency, he cannot see through – Baliardo is utterly taken in by the kind of feminized spectacle his technologically mediated vision is meant to penetrate. Moreover, the trick emphasizes the way these optical technologies, as gimcracks, reflect only illusory trivialities back to those who rely on them to repair their vision, producing a subject informed by fantasy rather than sober empirical witnessing. Behn, displaying her own mastery of spectacle through the complex staging of the telescope trick, lampoons the virtuoso who utterly fails to master the scene of discovery, or to perceive that he is the one it exposes. Behn's demonstrative entertainment engages with material spectacle in a complex way: the doctor is not laughable here simply because he over-invests in trinketry, but because his gimcrack optics claim a rational transparency that the instruments' material qualities and effects belie. By immersing the kind of masculinist, technological empiricism Baliardo represents in a scene of spectacular stagecraft, Behn reveals how they already mirror each other, while affirming the power of the feminized, material spectacle the virtuosos purported to reject.

The Finale

After a series of escalating tricks, *Emperor*'s final scene brings about their culmination with the performance of an extravagant show for Baliardo (and the Dorset Garden audience), one that stretches the theatre's scenic capabilities to their full extent. This show is a farce called "*The World in the Moon*," through which Baliardo "shall be so imposed upon, as shall bring matters magnificently about" (1.1.107–9). Scaramouch, Harlequin, and the two lovelorn Dons have converted an abandoned gallery on Baliardo's estate into a makeshift theatre and, hustling the doctor there, promise him that now, "with the help of your telescope, you may discover all" (3.2.397–8). The play opens into an ostentatious, exoticized scenic fantasy as Baliardo and the Dorset Garden audience are treated to a series of scenic discoveries that reveal vistas of Parnassus adorned with living statues, Kepler and Galileo descending from the sky in chariots, a massive zodiac machine from which twelve actors representing the signs disembark, and an equally large moon-machine that waxes and wanes, then opens to reveal the lunar royalty inside, to name just some of the final scene's effects.

The lavish staging of this scene makes *Emperor* one of the most sensational of a series of similarly elaborate plays it joined on the Dorset Garden stage. Through their deployment of technologies of spectacle, *Emperor* and its fellow Dorset Garden spectaculars worked more explicitly than other Restoration dramas in the tradition of Stuart court masques. These masques had organized dance, song, verse, and stunning scenic effects around and through the bodies of powerful court figures, including the monarchs themselves. While masque texts were written by prominent playwrights like Ben Jonson, the text was far from the most important part of the proceedings. More germane to the political theatre of the Stuart court were the evanescent, occasional aspects of the entertainment, such as the courtiers chosen to perform in the masque, the symbolic formations they created through their choreographed and spontaneous movements, and the exquisite scenery and scenic machines that were customarily torn apart as an extension of the performance in a calculated display of conspicuous destruction.[45] As a political event, the masque thus functioned within a code of courtly display through which "virtue was defined as the creation of its appearance"[46] and power worked "primarily by making itself visible";[47] in this paradigm, the "artful trifle" was imbued with consequence, "the surface was, in a sense, precisely what mattered," and "the trivial assumed a startling importance."[48] While Jonson would attempt to enshrine his poetry as the masque's "spirit" enlivening the proceedings' material, ephemeral "carcass" in the published text of Queen Anna's 1605 *Masque of Blackness*, it was this "bodily part" that produced the entertainment's meaning, and its political and social force.[49]

It was the masques' "bodily part" that lived on in Restoration stagecraft: As Southern demonstrates, all of the new scenic technologies and effects introduced onto the commercial stage after the Restoration – changeable scenery and the discovery scenes it enabled chief among them – had their roots in Stuart court theatre.[50] And, though these new scenic technologies were undoubtedly popular with Restoration audiences, there was considerable and sustained anxiety about the effects of these technologies on the dramatic works they accompanied, and on playgoers. Mary Pix, for example, in the prologue to *The Deceiver Deceived*, describes effects-heavy plays as "nonsense" dressed up with "powder[ed]-pimp of Dance, Machine, and Song," which "put together make it hard to say / If Poet, Painter, or Fidler made the Play," while James Wright valorized the antebellum plays that "cou'd support themselves, merely from their own merit; the weight of the Matter, and goodness of the Action, without Scenes and Machines," unlike the contemporary drama.[51] In 1664, Richard Flecknoe, moved like so many others to consider "the difference betwixt our Theaters and those of former times," reflects that pre–Civil War productions

> were but plain and simple, with no other Scenes, nor Decorations of the stage, but onely old Tapestry, and the stage strew'd with Rushes (with their Habits accordingly) whereas ours now for cost and ornament are arriv'd to the heighth of Magnificence; but that which makes our stage the better, makes our Playes the worse perhaps, they striving now to make them more for sight, than hearing; whence that solid joy of the interior is lost, and that benefit which

men formerly received from Playes, from which they seldom or never went away, but far better and wiser then they came.[52]

Flecknoe nostalgically imagines an era in which plays' intellectual substance instilled a corresponding wisdom in their audiences, and contrasts this golden age with the present day, in which drama, having dispensed with depth altogether, is characterized primarily by a surface "ornament" and "Magnificence." Yet when he turns to consider the scenic apparatus more closely, Flecknoe is clearly enthralled by this very splendour: "Scenes and machines," he writes, "are excellent helps of imagination, most grateful deceptions of the sight, and graceful and becoming ornaments of the stage, transporting you easily without lassitude from one place to another; or rather by a kind of delightful Magick, whilst you sit still, does bring the place to you." In this description, the ornamental, tricking qualities of scenic technologies – their "gloss'd outside Fallacies" – are shown to be central to the unique pleasures of modern drama, as the striking discoveries the scenes and machines enable produce novel experiences of the playhouse space, and of space and time more generally. More intriguingly, Flecknoe's characterization of scenes and machines as "excellent helps of the imagination" suggests that these technologies have some kind of relationship with their spectators' subjectivity, which, if it does not resemble the "solid joy of the interior" supposedly produced by the drama of former times, is no less potent. This suggestion is extended when we consider the epistle dedicatory for *Love's Kingdom*, the playtext to which Flecknoe's reflections on drama are attached.[53] Flecknoe writes that he hopes the published version of the play will find more approbation than the produced one, which was not "rightly represented."[54] While Flecknoe believes that printing the play will "shew its Innocence" of the failings ascribed to it by the bad production, he notes that in its printed version it "wants much of the Ornament of the Stage"; this, however, "by a lively imagination may easily be supplied." Flecknoe's dedication reveals that the scenes and machines seen to "ornament" dramatic works are in fact crucial to the plays, such that they must be provided in their absence to approximate the dramatic experience. Further, Flecknoe's assurance that his readers will easily be able to supply these effects shows that, barely three years after their debut on the public stage, scenes and machines had become "helps of the imagination" not only to the spectator witnessing their action in the playhouse but to the same subject well after she or he had left the performance space. This dedication reveals that, counter to Flecknoe's later assertion, the new scenic plays do, in fact, produce joys of the interior. Describing the imagination as a moving toyshop through which the playhouse's pleasurable visual and epistemological discoveries may be continually restaged (and new ones created), Flecknoe demonstrates how scenic technologies quickly found their double in a mental machinery.

These reflections from Flecknoe, Wright, and Pix express a number of the ways that scenic technologies signified differently once they were displaced from the Jacobean and Caroline court, where their conventions had been developed, to the public, commercial Restoration playhouse. While in the Stuart court the masque's splendour had functioned visually and politically as part of a system in which status depended "for its very existence upon material display," where power was "either visible or non-existent,"[55] and in which this play of surfaces functioned symbolically as a scientific revelation of truth, in the context of the public stage, and of a public that came increasingly to value a subjectivity imaginatively comprised of interior depth, the same scenic manoeuvres came to appear to some suspiciously superficial, trifling, and deceptive. As a trivial, aggressively material mechanism believed to transmit its triviality both to the drama it structured and to that drama's spectators, the scenic apparatus is deprecated in these critiques as a kind of gimcrack. Like the gimcrack lampooned by critics of technologically mediated experimentalism, scenic technology is made suspicious through its association with ostentatious, increasingly feminized materialism and frivolous display; like the gimcrack, it was believed to make those whose perception it mediated "serious upon trifles"; like the gimcrack, it produced an empirical experience, and thus a subjectivity, inappropriately informed by spectacular fantasy. In different but importantly linked ways, the scientific and scenic gimcrack are both optical technologies that signal the Restoration subject's unstable, rapidly shifting experiences of material culture, empirical knowledge, and gendered embodiment.

The links between scientific instruments and scenic technologies ultimately structure the climax of Behn's *Emperor*. The stage tricks I have analyzed above demonstrate how Behn uses the perceived equivalencies between scientific and stage technologies to mount a sophisticated critique of Royal Society virtuosi and their optical apparatuses. Through her use of dazzling, masque-like staging techniques in the play's closing scene – including multiple scenic discoveries; stylized, ornamental, and emblematic bodies; and complex machine effects – Behn draws on the history of scenes and machines and on the Restoration debate about their mediatory function to extend and nuance this critique. We can see this in the language used in the closing moments of the play, as Baliardo comes to understand that what he is watching is a farce rather than a lunar visitation. "My heart misgives me ... Oh, I am undone and cheated in every way!" Baliardo cries as Scaramouch deliberately shatters the illusion (3.3.191–2). The false Kepler exhorts Baliardo to "Be patient, sir, and call up all your virtue; / You're only cured, sir, of a disease / That long reigned over your nobler faculties," explaining that "It was not in the power of herbs or minerals, / Of reason, common sense, and right religion, / To draw you from an error that unmanned you" (3.3.193–9). Cintho soon joins "Kepler," explaining to Baliardo that he is not the Prince of Thunderland and that there is "no such person, sir. / These stories are the phantoms of mad brains, / To puzzle fools withal; the wise laugh at 'em"; Charmante concurs that the supposed moon-world is merely a collection of "Ridiculous inventions" (3.3.213-18). Baliardo is convinced, and with a Faustian injunction to "Burn all my books, and let my study blaze," he renounces his folly, thanking Charmante and Cinthio for the "glorious miracle" they have effected.

The doctor's description of the elaborate show performed for him as a "cheat" recalls contemporary characterizations of stage effects as tricking "deceptions of the sight," but the scene quickly complicates this identification. The designation "cheat" attaches with more force to the "phantoms" Baliardo has taken for reality because he has read about them and, more importantly, seen them through his telescope. As the play has repeatedly shown and this scene emphasizes, Baliardo's optical instruments have failed to extend his perception, and act instead to confuse and obfuscate his faculties with ludicrous fantasies. And, while the scenic apparatus might at first appear to function in a similar, straightforwardly deceptive way, we should notice that the elaborate show has succeeded in re-educating Baliardo where "reason, common sense, and right religion" have failed. The show accomplishes this through the revelation of its effects' mechanisms, of their status as a simultaneously spectacular and trivial optical technology. In the finale's series of escalating scenic discoveries, the third and most important exposure is of the technology of discovery itself. The final scene works to restage the discovery scenes Baliardo has totally misapprehended in the first and second acts, this time foregrounding the scenic apparatus as apparatus so that the doctor is able to recognize painted representations and tricking bodies for what they are. This final revelation does not suggest that scenic gimcracks are a collection of useless, bombastic nonsense: instead, they find their most fruitful use when they are recognized *as* gimcracks. It is, after all, the scenic spectacle – in all its superficial magnificence and powder-pimped knackery – that finally produces the most valuable empirical knowledge of the world for Baliardo: "I see there's nothing in philosophy," he finally declares, his language foregrounding the notably optical nature of his "glorious" lesson (3.3.230–1).

This outcome is particularly significant given the links the play draws between scenic and scientific technologies. Advocates of optical instruments, such as the Royal Society fellows, believed that the value of these devices inhered in their ability to accurately transmit objective facts about the world; the utter transparency of the instruments' artificial operation was believed to repair and extend the limited perceptual faculties of the human body. This transparency of function was critical to the production of empirical truths: as Crary notes, "it was crucial that the distorting power of a medium, whether a lens, air, or liquid, be neutralized, and this could be done if the properties of that medium were mastered intellectually and thus made effectively transparent through the exercise of reason."[56] While Baliardo claimed this rational transparency for the operations of his optical instruments, Behn has repeatedly foregrounded the ways that the instruments' material qualities interrupt and confuse their supposedly transcendent function. In the last scene, as Baliardo's telescope fails to help him recognize its gimcrack double in the play's scenic apparatus, the scenic technology takes over the scientific instrument's role of revealing empirical information. Behn calls on the links between scientific discovery and scenic spectacle that the Royal Society fellows so vigorously attempted to deny, centring the scenic apparatus's flamboyantly ornamental materiality as a mechanism of rational knowledge and denouncing transparency as a cheat.[57] The play's finale accomplishes what Behn promised *Emperor's* dedicatee, the Marquis of Worcester: that a spectator of "refined sense" watching the play would, "through all the humble actions and trivialness of business, find nature there" (274). Behn's dedication, which directs the spectator not to look past the play's trivial trappings but to look *through* them, positions its trifling apparatus as a technology of empirical revelation, one that substitutes material mechanism for rational transparency.

Behn's *Emperor* stands as a document of the shifting relationships that were forged between optical technologies and the human body in Restoration England, and of Behn's own interrogation of the ways their mechanisms mediated perceptual experience. Her critique of the optical instruments believed by some to correct the failings of human sense satirizes the mechanisms' gimcrack qualities: their immersion in a feminized realm of consumer display in which they circulate as showy knacks and useless ornaments. Behn's stance is familiar from attacks on the virtuoso from Shadwell to Addison, but her treatment of the relationship between technologies of the new science and of the new Restoration playhouse is not. Behn's recuperation of the gimcrack through *Emperor's* extravagant culminating entertainment is a manoeuvre informed by her critical interest in material spectacle, an interest itself influenced by her feminism and Toryism. *Emperor* extends Behn's career-long project of using scenic design to explore the intersections of power, gender, space, and spectatorship on the Restoration stage, and links it with a complicated nostalgia for the traditions of court theatre. In the epistle dedicatory, Behn indicates the ways in which the play looks backward to the reign of the recently deceased Charles II (writing that the play was originally "calculated for his late majesty of sacred memory, that great patron of noble poetry, and the stage, for whom the muses must for ever mourn") and further still to the political theatre of the antebellum Stuart court. "'[T]is a great pity," she writes, "to see that best and most useful diversion of mankind, whose magnificence of old was the most certain sign of a flourishing state, now quite undone by the misapprehension of the ignorant, and misrepresentings of the envious" (274). Behn has in mind the dramas of the past more generally (later mentioning the "admirable plays" of

Shakespeare, Fletcher, and Jonson), but the way she links staged magnificence and state power evokes most vividly the court masque's organization of spectacular trivialities to generate political authority. It is this "useful diversion" that Behn restages with *Emperor*'s final act, arranging the masque's scenic technologies into a new formation that produces empirical knowledge, and does so through the revelation of its own trifling mechanisms. With this final, extravagant show, Behn constructs a perceptual technology out of the materials cast off by the modest witness: the bodily part whose "gloss'd outside Fallacies" [58] his new scientific optics both renounced and promised to penetrate. The mode of personal and political power of which the masque was rapidly becoming a relic is thus revived, and its ornamental spectacle – now, increasingly, debased and feminized – occludes the philosopher's instrumentalized vision in order to correct it. Behn's play, as it lampoons Baliardo's gimcrack misapprehensions, exposes and reframes the gendered binaries produced by the empirical subject's technology of perception.

NOTES

1 Diamond, "Gestus and Signature," 521.

2 Roach, "The Artificial Eye," 143, 134.

3 Milhous, "The Multimedia Spectacular on the Restoration Stage," 41–66.

4 See, for example, Hughes, *The Theatre of Aphra Behn*, and Lewcock, "More for Seeing than Hearing," 66–83. Citations from the play (by act, scene, and line) refer to *The Rover and Other Plays*, ed. Spencer.

5 In a reading that recognizes and differently explores the play's engagement with spectacle, Al Coppola connects *Emperor*'s scenic magnificence to the political spectacles mounted in the midst of the Exclusion Crisis in London. Coppola traces Behn's diagnosis of "what appears in the play as a linked network of social abuses that all derive from improper peeping, what we might call a 'culture of spectacle,'" and her critique of "the irrational credulity stoked by Whig politics during the Exclusion Crisis, which the Court faction had inadvisably embraced in James's reign" (67). See Coppola, *The Theater of Experiment*.

6 Emphasizing this turn, "trinket," in a verb form used through the seventeenth and eighteenth centuries, itself connoted trickery and deceit: see Zuroski Jenkins, "Defoe's Trinkets: Fiction's Spectral Traffic," in *A Taste for China*, especially 114–15.

7 For the probable dimensions of the stage, see Muller, "Flying Dragons and Dancing Chairs at Dorset Garden."

8 *Oxford English Dictionary Online,* s.v. "trinket, n.1," last modified March 2013, http://www.oed.com/view/Entry/206184.

9 Shapin and Schaffer, *Leviathan and the Air-Pump,* 77.

10 The title of Shadwell's play offers us another, less flattering label for the Restoration man of science. While the term virtuoso "originally had positive associations, referring to a man of learning," in the 1660s it came to denote "a person engaged in 'futile and indiscriminate study'" (Chico, "Gimcrack's Legacy," 30).

11 Shadwell, *The Virtuoso,* 2.2.1–84. Further references appear parenthetically in the text. References are to act, scene, and line.

12 Addison, "No. 216," in *The Tatler,* 486.

13 Johnson, *A dictionary of the English language,* "gimcrack."

14 *Oxford English Dictionary Online,* s.v. "gimcrack, n. and adj.," last modified March 2014, http://www.oed.com/view/Entry/78334.

15 The *Oxford English Dictionary* definition of "gimcrack" lists alternate meanings of the word as an "affected showy person" or a "fanciful notion."

16 Coppola explores how Behn "lampoons an excessively credulous virtuoso only to direct the audience's own untrustworthy gaze toward the threat posed by enthusiasm to domestic and civil harmony" (67) in the context of the Exclusion Crisis, but does not address the gendered materiality of Behn's spectacle. See Coppola, *The Theater of Experiment.*

17 Grose, *A Classical Dictionary of the Vulgar Tongue,* 98–9.

18 *Oxford English Dictionary Online,* s.v. "spruce, adj. and adv.," last modified September 2014, http://www.oed.com/view/Entry/187868.

19 Hope Nicolson, introduction to Shadwell's *The Virtuoso,* xx.

20 Needleman Armintor, "The Sexual Politics of Microscopy in Brobdingnag," 620. Needleman Armintor draws on Fournier's *The Fabric of Life* and Wilson's *The Invisible World* for her argument about gender and microscopy.

21 Ibid., 623.

22 The trick continues with a second glass plate depicting the lovelorn emperor, setting Baliardo up to believe in the lunar monarch's supposed interest in Elaria.

23 Frans and Julie Muller, "Completing the Picture," 677.

24 For information on the construction and use of Restoration scenery, Richard Southern's 1951 monograph *Changeable Scenery* remains an invaluable source. I have

also drawn on the more recent work of Frans and Julie Muller, Jocelyn Powell's *Restoration Theatre Production*, and Peter Holland's *The Ornament of Action.*

25 Southern, *Changeable Scenery*, 17

26 Ibid., 142, 139.

27 Frans and Julie Muller, "Completing the Picture," 677.

28 Diamond, "Gestus and Signature," 521.

29 See Hughes, "Aphra Behn and the Restoration Theatre," e-book.

30 Ibid.

31 Holland, *Ornament of Action,* 41.

32 Ibid.

33 Hughes, "Aphra Behn and the Restoration Theatre."

34 Green, "Semiotic Modalities of the Female Body," 138.

35 Benedict, *Curiosity*, 62.

36 See Hunter, *The Royal Society*, 15–16, for more information on the financial situation of the Society during its first years.

37 Birch, *The history of the Royal Society*, 1:288.

38 Coppola, *The Theater of Experiment*, 8.

39 See Fletcher, *A Study of the Life and Works of Athanasius Kircher.*

40 Chambers, *Cyclopædia*, 2:8. See also Warner, *Phantasmagoria*, 137–43, for a critical account of Kircher's magic lantern.

41 Power, *Experimental philosophy*, 18. Power's link between misguided scientific work and staged spectacle draws on the *New Organon*, in which, as Coppola notes, Bacon "decried all the false philosophical systems that had been erected, both ancient and modern, as 'Idols of the Theater,' those 'illusions which have made their homes in men's minds from the various dogmas of different philosophies.'" See Coppola, *The Theater of Experiment*, 1.

42 An apocryphal detail too intriguing not to reference here is that Wren himself is popularly believed to have been the architect of Dorset Garden Theatre. Diana De Marly, revisiting the evidence, has suggested a more likely candidate: Robert Hooke. See De Marly, "The Architect of Dorset Garden Theatre," 119–24.

43 Pritchard, *Outward Appearances*, 27.

44 Ibid.

45 McManus, *Women on the Renaissance Stage,* 5, 9–10.

46 Ibid., 8.

47 Bevington and Holbrook, introduction to *The Politics of the Stuart Court Masque*, 3.

48 Ibid.

49 Jonson, "The Queen's Masques," 47, 50.

50 Southern, 32–5, 138.

51 Pix, *The Deceiver Deceived,* 3; and Wright, *Historia Histrionica*, 6.

52 Flecknoe, *Love's Kingdom.*

53 The dedicatee is Flecknoe's patron, the Duke of Newcastle.

54 Paul Hammond suggests that Flecknoe's dismissal of the new scenic effects in his "Short Discourse" is an attack on Davenant specifically, as a kind of revenge for the failure of *Love's Kingdom* when the Duke's Company performed it. Flecknoe's immortalization as a hack in Dryden's *Mac Flecknoe* suggests that the failure may have stemmed from the text rather than the production. See *Oxford Dictionary of National Biography*, s.v. "Richard Flecknoe (*b. c.*1605, *d.* in or after 1677)," by Paul Hammond, last modified 2004, doi: 10.1093/ref:odnb/9682.

55 Bevington and Holbrook, introduction to *The Politics of the Stuart Court Masque*, 3–4.

56 Crary, *Techniques of the Observer,* 64.

57 The genre of Behn's play contributes to this political critique, as farce was itself associated with trivial excess – for example, John Dryden wrote, in the preface to 1671's *An Evening's Love*, that farce "consists of forc'd humours, and unnatural events" and entertains with "what is monstrous and chimerical," and Nahum Tate contrasted farce, whose "Business … is to exceed Nature and Probability," with other genres, like tragedy and comedy, that "subsist upon Nature." These assessments are quoted in Peter Holland's "Farce," 121–2.

58 Power, *Experimental Philosophy*, 18.

6

Dying in Earnest: Public Executions and Their Audiences

RONALD HUEBERT AND DAVID McNEIL

Public executions as practised in early modern England drew large numbers of spectators, and we are therefore interested in asking: is it fair to describe them as theatrical events? We are of course indebted to Foucault for drawing attention to the cultural meanings embedded in these spectacles.[1] But our purpose here is to see the execution not so much from the point of view of those exercising power as from the position of those who are there (for whatever reason) to watch. There is no shortage of evidence of a wide variety of audience participation in "theatre of the gallows," according to Peter Lake and Michael Questier.[2] We are in full agreement with this judgment, even though the specific evidence we will be citing is often quite different from the cases they write about. Indeed, we would go so far as to claim that the spectator's response is an often neglected aspect in accounts of this rather ghoulish kind of theatre. It is just this neglect that we hope to remedy.

To an extent, all public executions in early modern England followed a script, especially those arising from high-profile political cases, some of which we will be describing. However, just as in live theatre, there was always the unanticipated and the possibility that something might miscarry, so here the real excitement had to do with what was not predictable: the behaviour of the condemned and of the crowd. An execution for high treason in particular might be compared to a five-act interactive improvisation: act 1, the trial and sentencing; act 2, the procession from prison to scaffold; act 3, the execution itself, including the last words and the displaying of the severed head (sometimes the heart) for all to see; act 4, the dismembering or disembowelling; and act 5, the displaying of certain body parts in various places.[3] The last two steps could be strictly judicial, but in cases where the criminal's body became an object of anatomical study, they could be scientific as well.[4] While the outcome from sentencing to execution was set, there were many details that had to be experienced "in the moment," so to speak. Afterwards, pamphlets and broadsides (and later newspaper articles) conveyed in print what only a small percentage of the population had seen live. This material could be said to provide a kind of second-hand spectatorship, or vicarious access to the event. Our purpose here is to focus specifically on how the presence of the spectators inflected the event both politically and theatrically.

On the subject of eliciting sympathy for the condemned, there is a prominent vein in the textual material we will be considering that finds a parallel in the fictional literature of the early modern period. For instance, critics like Ramesh Mallipeddi have analyzed instances of spectacular suffering that featured female victims or the enslaved.[5] This includes the she-tragedies of the late-seventeenth and early-eighteenth centuries along with their precursors and successors. While acting metaphors dominate the writing about historical figures, plays like *The Beggar's Opera* and *The London Merchant* (with the additional lines) stage execution scenes, usually without depicting the ultimate act. Nevertheless, the ultimate act could very well be described by a character and hence resemble the literary representation in texts like Aphra Behn's *Oroonoko*. What is deemed suitable to be spoken or read is not suitable to be seen.

English courtiers were fond of using theatrical metaphors to describe their own lives, including the ending they imagined for themselves and one another. "What is our life?" asks Sir Walter Ralegh; "a play of passion." And the rest of the short poem from which we have taken these phrases is an extended metaphor in which "Our mothers wombs the tyring houses be / Where we are drest for this short Comedy." The last six lines underscore the notion of spectatorship and link it to the final performance available to us.

Heaven the Judicious sharp spectator is,
That sits and markes still who doth act amisse,
Our graves that hide us from the searching Sun,
Are like drawne curtaynes when the play is done,
Thus march we playing to our latest rest,
Onely we dye in earnest, that's no Jest.[6]

Stephen Greenblatt has written at length about the ways in which this metaphor inhabited Ralegh's various real-life performances, including his last and most spectacular scene, on the scaffold.[7] Literary examples of spectatorship are of utmost importance for anyone who wishes to understand the culture of the past. They help us to imagine the range of expectations that early modern spectators might have brought with them when they attended events, like public executions, no longer available to most of us.

In the rest of this chapter we will be using textual and visual resources in the effort to provide the reader with the closest approximation to a spectator's position at several such events. We begin with the beheadings of Sir Thomas More (1535) and Lord Lovat (1747), events that can be taken as chronological bookends to our discussion as a whole. We then offer a brief segment on the execution of women, taking as our key examples three early modern women who were burned at the stake. The executions of Charles I (1648/9) and the Duke of Monmouth (1685) both illustrate, but in strikingly different ways, the unexpected results that can arise on such occasions. In a concluding discussion we will comment on the special qualities that must indeed have brought a theatrical thrill to spectators on these occasions, a thrill made only more potent by the dangers to which they were exposed.

"A parte of his owne"

On 6 July 1535 Sir Thomas More was escorted out of the Tower by the Lieutenant and led to the scaffold erected on Tower Hill. The sequence of events that led to this outcome is too familiar to require rehearsal; suffice it to say that More had repeatedly shown himself unwilling to endorse the desire of Henry VIII to secure a divorce from Katherine of Aragon so as to enable him to marry Anne Boleyn, and that the record of non-compliance had made him a marked man, guilty of treason. At his execution Sir Thomas acknowledged the spectators who had assembled by asking for their prayers and for them "to beare witness" that he was about "to suffer death in *and* for the faith of the holy catholike chyurche."[8] The scene is described in *The Lyfe of Sir Thomas Moore, Knight*, composed by More's son-in-law William Roper some twenty years after More's death, widely circulated in manuscript, and first published in 1626. Roper's view of More, as a courageous hero beset but not defeated by historical circumstances, is on the whole endorsed by many subsequent authors, even if they correct or supplement Roper's account.

Roper animates his account of the execution with anecdotes designed to make More appear admirable. He notes that More's final journey from Westminster Hall, where he was sentenced, to the Tower, where he was imprisoned, provoked an unscheduled interruption by his favourite daughter, Meg (coincidentally Roper's wife), who pushed her way through the crowd, including "the garde that with halberds *and* bills wente round aboute him," then "imbraced him, toke him about the neck, and kissed him" (Roper, 97). Sir Thomas himself was deeply moved, and sent Meg a letter from the Tower telling her "I never liked your manner [towards me] better then when you kissed me last" (Roper, 99), a sentiment that can be confirmed by consulting More's extant correspondence.[9]

Roper had a profound influence on subsequent interpretations of More's execution, but not a monopoly. The book widely known as Hall's *Chronicle* offered a portrait of More that included some reservations. More's celebrated wit was acknowledged, but with the qualification that "it was so myngled with taunting and mocking, that it seemed to them that best knew him, that he thought nothing to be wel spoken except he had ministered some mocke in the communication."[10] The desire for a witty riposte seems to have motivated More even when, as he was led to execution, "a poore woman called unto him" asking him to return to her important documents she had submitted to him when he was Lord Chancellor. "He answered, good woman have pacience a litle while, for the kyng is so good unto me that even within this halfe houre he will discharge me of all busynesse, and help thee himselfe" (Hall, 3P4^{v}). Indeed More was no longer in a position to answer the request, but he might have resisted belittling the "poore woman" who made it.

Spectators matter very little in Roper's account, possibly because he himself was not an eyewitness. The only member of More's family to attend the execution was his adopted daughter, Margaret Giggs, who was among the informants consulted by Thomas Stapleton before he composed his account of More's life, in Latin, while in exile in the Low Countries for thirty-five years (1563–98). Stapleton has an appreciation for the spectacle of the execution, and he uses the best evidence available to him to reconstruct it. Margaret Giggs, Stapleton recalls, "once showed me a lifelike image, made with great skill, of More going out to the place of execution, and in accordance with that image I have described here his appearance and demeanour."[11] The details in Stapleton's account link More's execution to that of his (and Stapleton's) great master, Jesus Christ: "His beard was long and disordered, his face was pale and thin from the rigour of confinement. He held in his hand a red cross and raised his eyes to heaven. His robe was of the very poorest and coarsest … by it he was made like to Christ, who willed to be poor" (Stapleton, 187–8).

Nicholas Harpsfield's account of More's death, written during Mary Tudor's reign but not published until 1932, incorporates virtually all of the incidents and words already cited, but also adds new material, including an observation about a kind of spectatorship that must have been almost commonplace for early modern city dwellers. More lost his head, to be sure, "And the saide head sett upon London bridge, in the saide Citie where he was borne and brought up, upon an high pole, among the heades of traitours: A rufull and a pitifull spectacle for all good Citizens and other good christians."[12] Here we are reminded that the essence of the public execution, especially that of political traitors, was that it played a role in the life of the body politic: the cutting off of a particular member was an ocular spectacle designed for deterrence.

We close this vignette on Sir Thomas More with an anecdote that occurs in every version of the execution that we have been able to consult.[13] In preparation for his date with destiny, More "changed himself into his best apparel" (Roper, 102). The Lieutenant of the Tower, noting that his fine garments would be appropriated by the executioner, advised

More to change his mind. Eventually, More "altered his apparel" (Roper, 102) so that the executioner got only what he deserved, namely, the forgiveness of his victim and an angel (that is, a gold coin worth eight shillings and sixpence). The books and manuscripts cited earlier offer divergent interpretations of this event. It would be possible to argue that the Lieutenant of the Tower hoped to defraud More of a considerable legacy, or that More's mood changed from exultation to humility, or that God was directing More to reject worldly vanity in favour of submissive plainness. The particulars of the case could be (and were) cited in support of whichever argument was being advanced.

None of the early accounts of More's execution, however, attribute to him what seems most obvious: the desire to be the star of the last spectacle in which he would play a part. Richard Marius, his fine modern biographer, does make this point: "He was, as always, ready to be at his best before an audience."[14] That's why he put on his most splendid costume, and that is no doubt also why, on reconsideration, he changed into the garment of suffering. More would certainly have agreed with Ralegh that "Heaven" is the "Judicious sharpe spectator," but he was accustomed to playing for a worldly audience, too. The most frequently cited anecdote about More's boyhood makes exactly this point. When he served as a page in Cardinal Morton's household, young More would enhance the festive entertainments by "stepp[ing] in among the players, *and* never studyeng for the matter, make a parte of his owne there presently among them, which made the lookers on more sporte then all the plaiers beside" (Roper, 5). The spontaneous wit on display led More's patron to predict great things for the lad. He was right, of course, though he could not have predicted that More's most memorable scene would be performed on a scaffold at Tower Hill.

Setting the Stage and Accommodating the Spectators

As a number of scholars have already claimed (see 164n3), the theatricality of a public execution could be said to include the scripted "show trials" (common in the case of those accused of high treason) and all the staging involved in the processions of the accused to and from the prison to the courtroom and ultimately to the site where the sentence was carried out.

The usual site for important high treason trials was Westminster Hall, where carpenters were employed in constructing a set that was appropriate for what was to be acted out. And because voyeurism confers a sense of power on the part of the voyeur over the object of his or her gaze, the trial staging could include the construction of secret viewing rooms. This feature apparently marked the set of the trial of the Gunpowder Plot conspirators in 1605/06; a few compartments were built to conceal James I and others, who could then watch the fate of those who had tried to blow up Parliament without themselves being scrutinized.[15]

This accommodation of private viewers seems also to have been part of the trial of Lord Lovat in March of 1747. A detailed plan (a two-page foldout) of the construction that was done inside Westminster Hall appeared in *The Gentleman's Magazine* the following month.[16] For instance, under "s," which referred to Lord Orford's gallery, which ran down the left side of the hall, one finds the note that a private compartment was set up there so that Princess Amelia, the second daughter of George II, could watch "incog. with a spying glass." To observe without being observed seems to have been a privilege reserved for members of the royal family. In any case, the plan did provide *Gentleman's Magazine* readers with rather precise knowledge of who saw what, after the fact. Their sense of spectatorship was a step removed, nevertheless the reader must have felt as though even this mediated access to the proceedings was important as news.

Lovat's execution on 9 April 1747 was the last beheading on Tower Hill for high treason. In almost every respect it was handled according to the long-established convention for such events. Since he was held at the Tower, Lovat's trial at Westminster Hall necessitated processions back and forth through the city. For viewers, Tower Hill had tradition and predictable comforts, especially for those invited to watch from one of the houses lining the site on the west and north sides. Commoners were routinely executed at Tyburn, but the authorities who were charged with the executions did select other sites that had either had an appropriate association or promised something new for spectators. One principle that does seem to have been followed in this case was choosing a site of execution that was also that of the original crime, or at least near to it. If Cromwell and his party were laying to rest the principle of monarchy along with Charles I, then their selection of the Banqueting House as the place for the execution – the preferred space for English royalty – was most fitting. Likewise, as Paula Backsheider recognizes, Charing Cross, that great crossroads of London situated within view of the Banqueting House, was appropriate for the execution of the regicides that followed after the Restoration. (The bodies of Oliver Cromwell, John Bradshaw, and Henry Ireton, who had died prior to this time, were disinterred and desecrated at Tyburn.[17]) This principle also seemed to dictate some of the sites chosen for the execution of those convicted in the 1780 Gordon Riots over a century later.[18]

When multiple trials were being conducted, as they were in the summer of 1746 for the Jacobite rebels, different locations seem to have been selected to maximize the impact on spectators. The common rebels were tried near St Margaret's Hill in Southwark, and the condemned nine, including Francis Townley and George Fletcher, were drawn to the place of execution, Kennington Common, on 30 July. On the same day the Jacobite Lords Kilmarnock, Balmerino, and Cromartie were paraded through the city from the Tower to their trial at Westminster Hall. Lord Lovat, who had been arrested on an island in Loch Morar in the Scottish Highlands the month before, arrived in London on 15 August and joined them in the Tower. Though Cromartie would be granted a reprieve, Kilmarnock and Balmerino were beheaded on Tower Hill three days later.

Not only were multiple sites used for groups but the times could be staggered. The Gunpowder Plot conspirators were executed in two groups of four at the end of January 1605/06: the first at the western end of St Paul's Churchyard on 30 January and the second (the last of whom was Guy Fawkes) the next day in the Old Palace Yard at Westminster. The strategy was to maximize the spectacular fate and punishment of those who sought to overthrow authority by making the stage as expansive as possible, both spatially and temporally, without losing the intensity of the event. Common criminals, of course, were taken from Newgate, down Holborn and then St Giles, then Tyburn (now Oxford), before finally arriving at the gallows. Stops were often made at the Old Bailey and the Bowl Inn in St Giles, the latter for a toast.

The mode of transportation to the place of execution was chosen with the purpose of humiliating the condemned. The "sledge" or litter (sometimes referred to as a "hurdle"; see *OED* sub. 4) was a simple wooden structure designed so that prisoners could be dragged behind a horse without banging their heads and losing consciousness. The Jacobite commoners were brought three to a hurdle to Kennington Common to be hanged and quartered. A "tumbrel," or two-wheeled cart, was also a popular mode of transportation. Hogarth depicts the condemned apprentice being taken to the Tyburn gallows in a tumbrel in Plate 11 of his *Industry and Idleness* series, which was released just a few months after Lovat's execution.[19] By the time of the French Revolution, the tumbrel would be the standard mode of transport for prisoners going to the guillotine; traditionally in Europe it is associated with moving and dumping manure. The Gunpowder Plot conspirators were taken by barge from the Tower to Westminster. Water transport may have been preferred for security reasons, as London streets were narrow and congested in 1606. In any case, the mode of transport was part of the penal show designed to humiliate the prisoner and impress those watching.

While there is a tendency to think of the spectators at public executions as bloodthirsty, and no doubt many were, there were also those who were emotionally connected to the accused and who had to suffer the agony of seeing a loved one tortured. There were two such individuals among the spectators on Kennington Common on that Wednesday in July 1746 when the Jacobite commoners were hanged and then dismembered. One was Charles Deacon, a rebel who had been granted a reprieve because of his youth; his older brother Thomas was not. A guard of soldiers carried Charles in a coach and made sure that he saw Thomas hanged and dismembered.[20] Another was the fiancée of James Dawson, who, ignoring the pleas of her "kindred," attended his execution. When it came time for the dismembered corpse to be burned, the young woman got close enough in a hackney coach to see the fire. The last body part to be tossed in was the heart of the man she had expected to marry the day before. When the executioner then shouted "God save King George," Dawson's fiancée is said to have died on the spot, while "the multitude of spectators gave a great shout."[21]

Since Lord Lovat was not clearly in arms with the rebels when apprehended, it was decided to proceed with impeachment, and these hearings began in December 1746. His actual trial for high treason was delayed until March 1747. The record of these events and related documents collected by T.B. Howell in 1816 amounts to over three hundred pages of text (much of it word-for-word transcription of the proceedings). It includes frequent complaints by Lovat, who was about eighty years old, about his poor mobility and fatigue.[22] Lovat accused those who testified against him of lying, and suggested that they were given incentives to do so. He also complained that those he wished to call as defence witnesses were intimated or obstructed.[23] Nothing could be more integral to the English judicial system than the reliability and availability of witnesses. Even though testimony is "heard" and goes into the record as text, the use of the term "witness" is not just a matter of semantics but a reflection of how spectation (or seeing) is closely associated with knowledge. Having lost his argument regarding his unfair treatment with regard to witnesses, Lovat is depicted as displaying a stalwart decorum and dignity, even a kind of bizarre gaiety.[24]

As a man with a reputation for brutality and deviousness, Lovat had already been the subject of much popular curiosity. That would not change. Charles Petrie says simply: "Legend has been busy with his last days."[25] On one trip through the city to his trial, a woman is said to have shouted at him through the carriage window, "You'll get that nasty head of yours chopped off, you ugly old Scottish dog!" to which he replied, "I believe I shall, you ugly old English bitch."[26] The account that became part of John Villette's 1776 collection *The Annals of Newgate; or, malefactors register* emphasized Lovat's mimic theatricality:

> he desired one of the Warders to lay a pillow upon the floor, at the feet of the bed, that he might try, if he could properly perform his part in the tragedy in which he was next Thursday to be the chief actor; and after having kneeled down, and placed his head upon the foot of the bed, he rose up, and said, "by this practice, I believe, I shall be able to act my part well enough."[27]

The day before his execution Lovat is said to have "cracked his jokes merrily with the Warders that attended him, the barber that shaved him, and almost every one that came near him."[28] The legend of the last man to be beheaded on Tower Hill for treason resembles the last figure in a dance of death.

What the contemporary public saw in terms of records was not a collection like Howell's but a steady stream of individual items: first there were the broadsides and pamphlets that came either before, during, or immediately after the trial and sentencing; then came the same for the execution (copies of dying speeches, sometimes peddled before the event occurred). Within a week of the trial/sentencing and then the execution(s), there were newspaper accounts, many of which were reprinted in the monthly magazines. Finally, many of these documents ended up in collections like Howell's years later, or in popular publications like *The Annals of Newgate*.

Coverage in *The Gentleman's Magazine* was limited to summaries and brief notices of a few sentences. One such story ran in the April 1747 issue, and it quickly delineates the disaster that happened on Tower Hill the day Lovat was executed.

> Just before he came from the *Tower*, a scaffolding [which we understand to be a viewing-stand] by the ship alehouse near *Barking Alley*, built from that house in many stories, with near 1000 persons on it, fell down all at once, by which 8 or 10 persons were killed on the spot, and many had their arms and legs broke. Among the kill'd were Mr *Hindman*, of the inspector's office; M. *Goldney*, woolen-draper in *Black-Fryers*; a servant to the king's locksmith; Mr *James Johnson*, just come from the *W. Indies*, and three other men; 10 persons died the next day of their bruises, in the *London* infirmary and St *Thomas*'s hospital, as did the master carpenter of the scaffold, and his wife, who was selling beer underneath when it fell.[29]

This description offers the most specific detail regarding the individuals who lost their lives in the disaster and it is tempting to note the ironies. The couple who would have profited monetarily from the spectators – namely the carpenter and his wife – are killed. A brief victim portrait and the story of one miraculous survivor are offered in a letter by Horace Walpole: "A scaffold fell down, and killed several persons; one, a man who had rid post from Salisbury the day before to see the ceremony; and a woman was taken up with a live child in her arms."[30] It is unfortunate to lose one's life after travelling across the country to get a view of a beheading, and there is nothing like the miraculous rescue of a child from the wreckage of a disaster to draw Walpole's comment and the eyes of posterity. Contemporary pamphlets on Lovat or the rebellion tend not to mention the disaster. However, one exception comes from James Ray, who finishes his 408-page history of the rebellion with the incident and the sentence, "[S]o that as he [Lovat] had caused much Destruction in his Life, the like Fate attended him on the Day of his Death."[31] To reiterate, subsequent publications like this one constitute a second-hand spectatorship.

There are about a half dozen popular prints of the Tower Hill beheadings of the Jacobite lords, which, like the pamphlets, can be understood as extensions of the public execution itself. Perhaps the most famous of these is the one that carries the inscription "A True Representation of Tower Hill, as it Appeared from a rais'd point of View on the north side, Aug. 18th 1746 …" and the subheading "Published by act of parliament." The view is towards the southwest, with three spectator-stands on the left in front of the Tower moat, two immediately facing the scaffold, and another farther east. While it is difficult to make out much detail with the houses on the far side, there is a Dutch print ("*De Onthoofding vande Rebellige Lords op Groot Tower Hill*") that clearly shows more spectator-stands built up against the houses here (see fig. 6.1). It is reasonable to assume that the general layout would have been the same for Lovat the following April. In any case, the description of the collapsed spectator-stand in *The Gentleman's Magazine* puts the structure near Barking Alley, which is marked with two red dots just to the left of the letter *T* on the 1720 Strype map as reproduced by The Grub Street Project (see fig. 6.2), which matches up with the visual detail of the Dutch print. Both prints feature an orderly sea of faces and figures, with the only difference being that in the Dutch one there is an outer rim to the crowd in the foreground that features some of the more carnivalesque features that are also part of the scene by Hogarth and the engraver of the Anne Askew print (see fig. 6.3 below).

Looking closely at the housing reveals that every available space is occupied by spectators, many of whom seem to be sitting on what one assumes would be makeshift benches. It is probable that it is one of these houses on the right to which James Johnstone was invited to watch the execution of the Scottish peers. Johnstone was a Jacobite officer who had avoided capture at Culloden and who had slowly made his way from the Highlands down to Edinburgh and then London, where he was in hiding in the summer of 1746. Having no idea that his tenant was a Jacobite

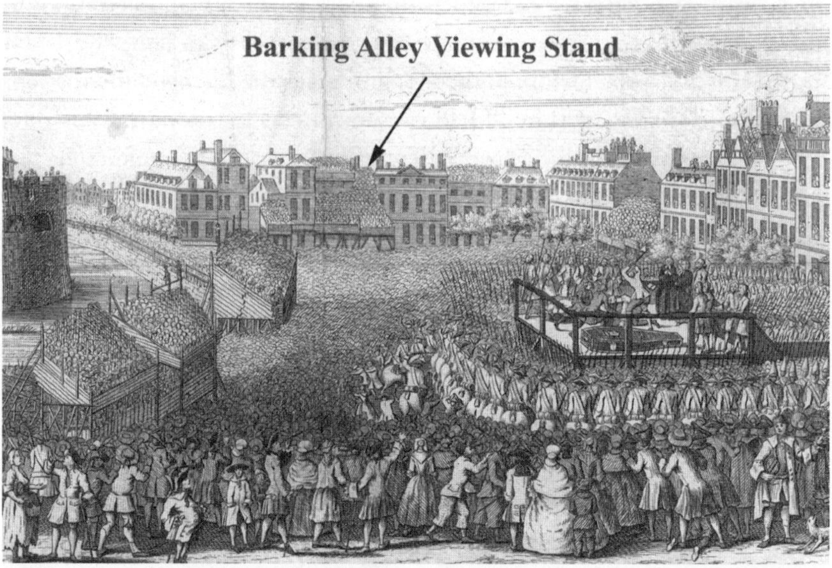

Fig. 6.1 *Top* Detail from the Dutch print indicating the location of the Barking Alley viewing stand at the beheading of Balmerino and Kilmarnock, 21 August 1746.

Fig. 6.2 *Bottom* Detail from The Grub Street Project reproduction of the 1720 Strype map showing Barking Alley.

himself, the landlord invited Johnstone to a friend's house that had a view of Tower Hill and from where they would be able to watch the executions. Understandably, Johnstone made his excuses, claiming that "he had a heart too sensible to take pleasure in that sort of spectacle."[32]

A close examination of "A True Representation of Tower Hill" discussed above reveals that although the overall impression is of crowd control, there are some "carnivalesque" elements similar to those identified by Thomas Laqueur in his classic study of public executions.[33] In the right-hand corner of the foreground is a band of spectators, including a woman selling broadsides (here one assumes the dying speeches of the condemned), and finally a dog or two scampering about. These are drawn with some accuracy, as are the principal figures on the scaffold and the soldiers who surround it (two or three lines deep and holding pikes). The dominant impression is one of authority; every space at ground level not already accounted for is filled with lines meant to convey a shoulder-to-shoulder crowd pressing in. The sense of overall authority, as far as the crowd is concerned, is subtly undermined by mundane detail (some vendors, etc.). In this respect the image bears a similarity to the popular woodcut representing the execution of Anne Askew.

One of the most infamous of carnivalesque moments was recorded by Giacomo Casanova. When Robert Damiens was tortured over the course of some hours in Paris in 1757, Casanova was with a party of revellers who rented a room overlooking the Place de Grève; he describes how he nonchalantly enjoyed the food and drink, and then noticed a couple fornicating among the group watching from a window. (Only later did Casanova discover that the sexual interaction was actually an assault.) Needless to say there is something sickening about such nonchalance in the face of what can only be called barbarous authority, and representations of the carnivalesque generally work to accentuate this barbarity and elicit disgust from the reader/viewer.[34]

Neil R. Storey points out that since one had to pay a fee for a place on one of these temporary viewing-stands, an execution that did not happen, as in the case of a last-minute reprieve, could result in violent disputes between the viewers wanting refunds and those who were taking in the money.[35] It seems that all manner of private property could be let for such purposes; in January 1664, Samuel Pepys records how he joined a crowd to see the hanging of a convicted robber named Turner: "there I got for a shilling to stand upon the wheel of a Cart, in great pain, above an hour before the execution was done – he [the condemned] delaying the time by long discourses and prayers one after another in hopes of a reprieve."[36] Impatience with such dying discourses seems to be common with Pepys, who learned the details about what Turner was saying in a coffeehouse afterwards. This hanging was an example of locating the execution near the site of the crime (Leadenhall and Lyme Streets), and Pepys claims that the crowd was "at least 12 or 14000 people."[37]

So being present at an execution did not necessarily mean that one had a good view of the proceedings or even heard the dying words of the condemned. Pepys's experience of Sir Henry Vane's execution in June 1662 is a case in point. Vane details the reasons for his actions (much too fully for Pepys's liking), and when the blow is finally struck, Pepys cannot view it because, in his words, "the Scaffold was so crowded that we could not see it done."[38] Later Pepys gets a much more detailed account of what Vane said from Boreman, a man who was on the scaffold. With his wonderful curiosity with respect to human detail, Pepys also relates how Vane apparently "had a blister or Issue upon his neck, which he desired them not to hurt" and how the trumpeters were brought near the scaffold to drown out the condemned man's speech.[39]

That spectatorship was the point of public executions is obvious, and critics have repeatedly noticed how a great many factors (political, social, theatrical) were involved in how the central participants and the audience behaved. First, the participant category, or the dramatis personae, included the condemned, the executioners, the clergy, and other officials. The purpose of the having clergymen on the scaffold was ocular – i.e., to exact a public confession and repentance. Obviously this was what the authority wished to see, but other than a sheriff and the executioners, government officials were generally not present, and judging from the first-hand accounts of Pepys or Evelyn, what was actually witnessed or heard was largely unknown, varied, and unpredictable.

The interaction between the condemned and the executioner was central. Beheading accounts commonly contain details about the condemned checking the sharpness of the blade, tipping the executioner, and requesting a "sign" for the final blow.[40] On his part, the executioner could ask that an item of clothing in the neck area be removed. Beheadings, reserved for peers and the nobility, required a solid and accurate stroke of some force, a good blade, and often a display of the head. However, things could miscarry. There are countless popular stories related to botched jobs – most notably those concerning Mary Queen of Scots, Lord Russell, and the Duke of Monmouth.[41] There were often two executioners on hand: one swung the axe, and the other caught the head and held it up for all to see. This was the climax of the event. However, this practice had fallen off by the time of Lovat's execution, and he is said to have tried to confirm that his head would not be thus displayed. It was also conventional for those guilty of treason to have their hearts extracted and held up to view: "behold the heart of a traitor." Further dismemberment was accorded treasonous commoners. Spencer has commented on how the exposing of the entrails had something to do with the association of evil with innards.[42]

Commoners guilty of high treason were hanged, but "not until death"; a short drop was done to incapacitate the prisoner but leave him conscious before the disembowelling and dismemberment began. One of the most famous examples of defiance was displayed by the regicide Thomas Harrison, who had his genitals cut off and was being disembowelled with a hot poker when he managed to actually land a punch on the executioner![43] The best that condemned traitors could hope for was to conceal their fear, perhaps reiterate their rebellious principles, and turn the scene into one that confirmed the cause. Either that or take control of the event itself, which is essentially what Guy Fawkes did in 1606. His hanging was conducted in the Old Palace Yard, so temporary gibbets were set up with ladders rather than scaffolds. The executioner was supposed to let the condemned man up only a rung or two for a short drop, but Fawkes was able to quickly mount high enough so that when he hurled himself off the ladder his neck snapped and that was the end as far as he was concerned.

How the crowd reacted was another unpredictable aspect. Often a majority of those present was predisposed to be sympathetic, or not, towards the condemned, and this predisposition certainly factored in how they reacted to the performances of the participants. If the condemned was unpopular, as the regicides were following the Restoration of Charles II, then maximum pain and suffering could garner a positive response. If popular, then silence might mark the occasion, or a demonstration of defiance or equanimity on the part of the condemned might garner respect from the crowd.[44] If the executioners did their jobs well in either extracting pain or not, then the crowd was apt to respond positively. Conversely, the crowd could express its displeasure if an execution was botched.

Towneley's and Fletcher's heads were displayed on Temple Bar Gate (the traditional western entrance to the city), which during the eighteenth century seemed to be the place reserved for Jacobite rebels, although the real reason is that there was no more room on London Bridge. In any case, the heads were mounted on tall poles and joined that of a previously executed Jacobite, Colonel Henry Oxburgh. Oxburgh's head had been on display since 1716 when his was added to those of Sir William Perkins and Sir John Friend, who had plotted the assassination of William III in 1696. The mounting on poles was done so that rats or birds of prey couldn't make a quick feast of the display. According to Neil Storey, the last of the heads fell off the Gate in 1772.[45] With ghoulish curiosity, Geoffrey Abbott has outlined exactly what happened to Townley's head from the time it fell off Temple Bar to when it was interred in St Peter's Parish Church, Burnley, in August 1947.[46] Like choosing the sites and routes between prison cell, trial court, and execution place, decisions about where to display the severed body parts were calculated and designed to maximize spectating. One might miss the execution and dismembering, but if you moved about London at all, it was impossible to miss the evidence. So it was for John Evelyn who records how, on 17 October 1660, he was too late to see the execution of the regicides Thomas Scott, Adrian Scrope, John Cook, and John Jones at Charing Cross "but met their quarters mangld [sic] and cut & reaking as they were brought from the Gallows in baskets on the hurdle."[47] The entire event, from trial to sentence to final destination, was an exercise in penal spectation, and with historians like Storey and Abbott its ghoulish aspect is kept alive.

Burning Women

The distribution of punishments at the end of the Elizabethan play *The Tragedy of Master Arden of Faversham* includes, at least for readers and spectators today, a small surprise. Mosby, the lover of Alice Arden, who has conspired with her in the murder of Master Arden, and Mosby's sister

Susan, also an accomplice, are sent to London, "Where they in Smithfield must be executed."[48] Two servants who knew about the murder but didn't cry foul, Michael and Bradshaw, will remain in Faversham, where they too "must suffer death" (18.32). Alice herself will be sent to Canterbury, "where her sentence is she must be burnt" (18.31). The sentencing, announced in the play by the Mayor of Faversham, agrees in detail with the source material in Holinshed's *Chronicles*.[49] But nobody explains the odd discrepancy between Alice Arden's punishment and that of her accomplices.

The difference rests on English legal history, beginning with the Treason Statute of 1351, which specifies in detail the distinction between high treason and petty treason.[50] Briefly, high treason is an act of defiance against the king (direct military defiance, for example, or violation of his consort, and a limited number of parallel offences, including the production of counterfeit coins). Petty treason, by contrast, is an act of defiance against one's social superior in the established hierarchy: against one's lord, if one is a knight; against one's prelate, if one is a clergyman; against one's husband, if one is a wife. So a woman who finds the authority of her husband intolerable and contrives to kill him as a result will eventually be found guilty not of murder, but of petty treason.

Significantly, punishments for high treason and petty treason are inflected by social position and gender. An untitled gentleman found guilty of high treason would suffer drawing, hanging, and quartering, whereas a nobleman would suffer simple beheading. (Hence the implicit compliment paid Sir Thomas More by Henry VIII's merciful revision of his sentence.) Women found guilty of treason might also qualify for decapitation in special circumstances, as did Anne Boleyn. But for most women it was far more likely that both high treason (such as counterfeiting) or petty treason (such as husband killing) would end in fire. As the authoritative summary of ancient English law succinctly observed, "And if a woman be attainted of any treason, let her be burnt."[51]

To complicate matters and to prevent confusion, we need to acknowledge that burning had been for centuries the signature punishment for heresy. The Church of course maintained the legal fiction that it burned no one: that it merely handed heretics over to the secular arm for appropriate punishment. The net result however was that people of both sexes who held dissenting views were burned at the stake. This paradigm will be confirmed in the story of Anne Askew's burning, soon to follow. But just before we reopen her case, it would be worthwhile to pause and reflect on the truth that, in early modern England, women had three possible avenues that might lead them to death by burning: heresy, high treason, and petty treason. While these are quite separate categories to the legalistically minded, we should perhaps be alert, in the discussion that follows, to some of the ways in which they overlap.

The story leading up to the burning of Anne Askew for heresy on 16 July 1546 has been frequently told and widely disseminated, both in the sixteenth century and in our own time. Within months of the burning, John Bale published two autobiographical accounts by Askew of her interrogations by Henry VIII's heresy hunters;[52] these accounts, though divested of Bale's commentary, were taken up by John Foxe as primary source material for his account of Askew in the so-called "Book of Martyrs."[53] If the Protestant Reformation gave Askew her first opportunity for celebrity, the recovery of women's writing begun in the twentieth century gave her a second chance. Readers today may choose from retellings that border on the sensational (Lindsey), that strive for nuance (Luckyj), that advertise theory (Coles), or that claim to transcend all of these in the name of history (Loewenstein).[54] Any of these versions may be usefully supplemented by consulting Diane Watt's careful and impeccably documented account in the *Oxford Dictionary of National Biography.*[55]

The earliest printed narrations of Askew's burning were prepared by authors who were not eyewitnesses to the event. Bale tacitly admits this when he writes: "Credyblye am I infourmed by diverse duche merchauntes which were there present, that in the tyme of their sufferynges, the skye abhorrynge so wicked an acte, sodenlye altered coloure, and the cloudes from above gave a thonder clappe, not all unlike to that is written, Psal. 76. The elementes both declared therein the high dyspleasure of God for so tyrannouse a murther of innocents."[56] Foxe reprints the autobiographical materials by Askew, though not Bale's commentary, in his fairly protracted account of her martyrdom. And he adds what appear to be circumstantial details: Askew's dialogue with Nicholas Shaxton, for example, the man chosen to preach just before the burning, because he had earlier recanted the heresy which Askew and her three male companions stood accused of.

Fig. 6.3 Woodcut from John Foxe, *Acts and Monuments* (1583).

Foxe comments briefly on the spectators: "The multitude and concourse of the people was exceeding, the place where they stoode beying rayled about to keepe out the prease."[57]

What might appear to be visual confirmation of this judgment can be observed in the woodcut that accompanies Foxe's narrative (see fig. 6.3). But we should be careful not to expect a precise correspondence between the image and the events of 16 July 1646. The woodcut first appeared not in Foxe's book, but in Robert Crowley's *The Confutation of XIII Articles, Whereunto Nicolas Shaxton, late byshop of Salisburye subscribed and caused be set forthe in print in the yere of our Lorde MCxlvi whe[n] he recanted in Smithfielde at London at the burning of mestres Anne Askue, which is lively set forth in the figure followynge.*[58] Precisely what Crowley meant by the words "*lively set forth*" (presuming them to be his) is open to interpretation, but he cannot have supposed them to mean "accurately and realistically recorded" as they might have been interpreted later by readers and writers familiar with photography. Sara Lanier Smythe, the scholar who has produced an exhaustive study of the woodcuts in English books of exactly this period, has argued persuasively that the image was not created by someone who had seen the burning first-hand. She points out that "the clothing of the soldiers and spectators" is not sixteenth-century dress; rather, the designer is alluding to "Early Christian martyrdoms … by depicting the soldiers as Roman centurions and the spectators as Roman citizens."[59] She also points out that, in the background, "we seem to have a lateral view of a church" rather than the west front view of St Bartholomew's that would have been visible from Smithfield.[60] On stylistic grounds, Smythe believes the designer to have been Continental rather than English, and she notes that the woodcut's first printer (John Day) often employed Flemish artisans. As to the close correspondences between the woodcut and Foxe's account, she points out that "Foxe relied on the accounts of others for many of his descriptions, and here he may have used the woodcut, which illustrated his text, as one of his sources."[61] Two mundane details require notice. One is that in the bottom-left corner there appears to be a mishap as a table has fallen over, sending some spectators crashing to the ground; this offsets the spectators in the bottom-right corner who perch on a wagon to get a better view. The second is that about halfway up the left side is a dog chasing what seem to be some smaller creatures (see fig. 6.4). The effect is reminiscent of Bruegel's peasant calmly walking on as Icarus falls into the ocean. It would be fair to say that all of the textual and visual evidence other than these mundane details is directed towards the goal of creating a martyr. Perhaps none of this work was done by eyewitnesses, but that doesn't matter. Spectators are cited nonetheless to authenticate the narrative: think of Bale's "duche merchauntes" or the "multitude" held back by a railing in Foxe and the woodcut. It would be tempting to say that martyrdom requires a witness, so the spectator will be fabricated if need be.

But then we may ask: Will the real spectator please stand up? And he does. He turns out to be John Louthe, who, after reading the story of Askew's burning in *Acts and Monuments*, wrote to Foxe in 1579 with additional information that he claims to remember: "the day afore her exequetione, and the same day also, she hadd an angel's countenance, and a

Fig 6.4 Detail from a woodcut in John Foxe, *Acts and Monuments* (1583).

smylyng face," writes Louthe.[62] "And afore God, at the fyrst puttyng-to of the fyar theyre felle a lytle dewe, or a few pleasante droppes apon us that stode by, and a pleasant crackynge from heaven."[63] Louthe isn't confident about how he should interpret these events, but they do inspire him with courage: "I could not, for feare of damnatione, stand by and say nothing agaynste theyre cruelte; therefor I with a lowed voyce, lookyng to the cownsell, sayd, 'I axe advenganse of yow all that thus dothe burne Chrystes member.' I hardly escaped a cartar's blow at that same worde, and forthwith departed."[64] Louthe may indeed be an eyewitness, but there's a gap of thirty-three years between his experience and the retelling, and that is certainly a filter by means of which Askew may have become even more angelic than she was, and the spectator bolder in support of her.

In 1546 and for many years after that there could have been no such thing as a disinterested spectator. The burning of heretics inevitably polarized spectators into opposing camps. So far we have drawn evidence only from witnesses who believed Askew to be a martyr. But this was not the view of Myles Huggarde, who may have been a first-hand witness too, and who had doubtless already developed the "abhorrence of religious nonconformity"[65] that would motivate him to seek out and testify against persons suspected of heresy. He declared that Anne Askew "was of suche charitie, that when pardon was offered, she defied them all, revyling the offereres thereof, with suche opprobrious names, that are not worthy rehersal."[66] Her own words, Huggarde implies, are enough to condemn her. Here too it is easy to see that the spectator does not occupy a neutral position. Protestant supporters of Askew, when they described her refusal of the pardon offered, invariably noted that it was offered only on condition of her recantation. To refuse pardon on these terms is yet another act of Christian courage. With as much zeal as other witnesses demonstrate when they strive to construct a martyr, Huggarde observes the same events but with the explicit aim of identifying and annihilating a heretic.

Our second female victim has been chosen, not for her celebrity, but for her obscurity. She was a woman who killed her husband in 1652, and who was convicted of petty treason and burned at the stake. All of this might have disappeared from the historical record with little more than a trace were it not for John Evelyn, who wrote these cryptic lines in his diary for 10 April 1652: "I went again to Lond: & next day, passing by Smithfield, there was a miserable creature burning who had murder'd her husband."[67] As Evelyn's twentieth-century editor surmises, this "creature" may well have been Prudence Lee, whose story is told as a kind of afterthought in a pamphlet that targets far more important figures. Still, in the final paragraphs of this text, we are told that Prudence was married to Philip Lee, a Bailiffe, that "being jealous of her husband" and finding him "in company with another woman … she drew her knife and stab'd him."[68] The crime scene, however, is not what interests the pamphleteer. Prudence Lee's performance at her own burning is enough to put her, for one fleeting moment, at the centre of attention. She arrives at Smithfield accompanied by two sheriff's officers "attired in a Red Wastecoat" (7). After confessing her errors and warning other women to "do nothing rashly, especially against their husbands" (8), she submits to the inevitable: "Then the Executioner setting her in a pitch barrel, bound her to the stake, and placed the straw and Faggots about her; whereupon she lifting up her eys towards Heaven, desired all that were present to pray for her; and the Executioner putting fire to the straw, she cried out: Lord Jesus have mercy on my soul; and after the fire was kindled she was heard to shrike out terribly some five or six several times" (8). If this is in fact what Evelyn saw and heard, then it's remarkable that he can shrug it off so easily. Prudence Lee reminds us, if reminders are needed, that people may burn to death and leave only a very small mark on the historical archive. In a sense, we are lucky to have so much as heard of her.

Unlike Lee's story, that of Catherine Hayes (the last women to be burned alive in England, in 1726) is well known. While it has been suggested that executioners strangled their female subjects before lighting the fire as a gesture of compassion, such kindness was not accorded Hayes. She, along with two male accomplices, was reputed to have brutally killed her husband, dismembered the corpse, and tossed the parts into the Thames. When the head was retrieved and identified, Hayes and her accomplices were tried and found guilty. These details were generally known at the time of the trial and sentencing. The popular historian Fred McLynn has suggested that an angry crowd protested when the executioner looked as if he was going to perform the usual compassionate gesture – more possible evidence that the spectators had some control over what exactly happened.[69] However, the account in the *Annals of Newgate* implies that the flames were simply too much for the executioner to work around as he tried to strangle the subject.[70] Women's bodies continued to be burned, but not while the women were still alive.

Of all the public executions in early modern England, perhaps there is none so heart-wrenching as that of Elizabeth Gaunt, who was burned at the stake for the crime of helping James Burton (who had been involved in the Rye House Plot) escape to Amsterdam. What made her case sympathetic was that Burton himself, after hiding out in London following the failed Monmouth Rebellion, came forward as a witness against her, after having heard that James II had pronounced the hiding of traitors a worse crime than treason itself. Gaunt had not lifted a hand against anyone, but found herself the victim of James II's brutal vindictiveness. One wonders just how aware of these details the spectators were as they watched, and if they felt the heat of the fire as it engulfed Elizabeth Gaunt. MacAulay tells the story in a manner to elicit maximum respect and sympathy for the condemned.

> To the last she preserved a tranquil courage, which reminded the spectators of the most heroic deaths of which they had read in Fox.

> William Penn, for whom exhibitions which humane men generally avoid seem to have had a strong attraction, hastened from Cheapside, where he had seen Cornish hanged, to Tyburn, in order to see Elizabeth Gaunt burned. He afterwards related that, when she calmly disposed the straw about her in such a manner as to shorten her sufferings, all the bystanders burst into tears.[71]

MacAulay may be guilty of reading his own knowledge of Foxe into his understanding of the crowd's reaction to Gaunt's execution. Exactly how Gaunt could have "disposed the straw" while tied to the stake is anybody's guess, but it makes for a moving image. Ultimately, MacAulay's statement implies commonly held beliefs – that texts can serve as a window through which posterity views history, and that this vicarious experience helps shape reactions in the present. There is no way to verify if William Penn and the other bystanders had a thought for Anne Askew while watching Elizabeth Gaunt burn, but MacAulay makes sure that his reader does.

"The royal actor"

James VI of Scotland, soon to become James I of England, could perhaps have shown greater concern for the possible ironies of spectatorship when he applied this metaphor to his own situation (and by extension to his son's): "A King is as one set on a skaffold, whose smallest actions & gestures, al the people gazingly do behold."[72] Unlike his father, Charles did not enjoy making a spectacle of himself; by the time it was his turn to embody the metaphor, the option of heroic leadership was no longer available, or at least the prospect of such action was receding with each of Charles's political errors. For him, the royal actor's part was a tragic role, and this may indeed be what James Shirley was recalling when he observed, years after the royal execution, that "Death lays his icy hand on Kings," as sure as on the rest of us.

> Scepter and crown
> Must tumble down,
> And in the dust be equal made,
> With the poor crooked sithe and spade.[73]

Fig. 6.5 A German engraving showing the execution of King Charles I.

Charles's execution in January 1648/49 was of course a political event with a long history of causes and an even longer history of consequences. But it was a theatrical event as well, to judge by evidence of several kinds, both visual and verbal. A German representation of this event (see fig. 6.5) shows it taking place in front of the Banqueting House in Whitehall, on a platform stage elevated to a height of perhaps six or seven feet, and surrounded by hundreds (perhaps thousands) of spectators, many of whom can see blood gushing from the newly decapitated corpse. Images of this kind were suppressed in England, but Continental artists could not be controlled.

Some of the most celebrated textual responses to the execution of Charles I represent it in explicitly theatrical terms. Andrew Marvell's famous "Horatian Ode upon Cromwell's Return from Ireland" (written just months after the execution) enumerates among Cromwell's heroic achievements the capture of King Charles at Carisbrooke Castle, and then pauses in its relentless pursuit of Cromwell to offer this cameo appearance to Charles.

> That thence the royal actor borne
> The tragic scaffold might adorn:
>   While round the armed bands
>   Did clap their bloody hands.
> *He* nothing common did or mean
> Upon that memorable scene:
>   But with his keener eye
>   The axe's edge did try:
> Nor called the gods with vulgar spite
> To vindicate his helpless right,
>   But bowed his comely head
>   Down as upon a bed.

There is admiration for Cromwell in this poem (the kind of admiration that's mixed with fear), but the lines we've quoted don't match up with Cromwell's recorded positions. A far closer match would be Thomas Fairfax, who could not bring himself to sign the petition demanding the king's execution (his unruly wife evidently called out her view that regicides would be committing treason from the gallery in Westminster Hall on the day the matter was being debated), who would shortly resign his position as commander in chief of the New Model Army, and would then offer Marvell employment as tutor to his young daughter Mary. It is perhaps unfair to isolate the lines we've quoted from the rest of the poem, but they do seem to us unalterably sympathetic to Charles.

There is now no way of determining whether Marvell was in the crowd of spectators who saw the "royal actor" perform on the "tragic scaffold"; he may have been an eyewitness, or he may have depended on the words of others. One report by a spectator who was certainly there is recorded in the *Memoirs of the Last Two Years of the Reign of King Charles I*, written by Sir Thomas Herbert, who identifies himself as groom of the chambers to his Majesty. After serving in the Civil War on the side of Parliament, Herbert had been appointed in 1647 to serve as a personal "attendant to the captive Charles I." This was a tricky position to occupy, but "Herbert successfully walked the tightrope of keeping both the Parliament and the army on the one hand and Charles I on the other satisfied with how he did his job."[74] It was he, therefore, who slept on a pallet beside the king's bed on the last night of Charles's life, and it was he who accompanied the king, just how far it would be difficult to ascertain, on the final journey described by Herbert as follows:

> Colonel *Hacker* attending still at the Chamber-Door, the King took notice of it, and said, *Open the Door,* and bade *Hacker* go, he would follow. A Guard was made all along the Galleries and the Banqueting House; but behind the Soldiers abundance of Men and Women crowded in, though with some Peril to their Persons, to behold the saddest sight *England* ever saw. And as his Majesty pass'd by, with a chearful Look, heard them pray for him, the Soldiers not rebuking any of them; by their silence and dejected Faces seeming afflicted rather than insulting. There was a Passage broken through the Wall by which the King pass'd unto the Scaffold; where, after his Majesty had spoken a little, the fatal Stroke was given by a disguised Person.[75]

If the tension in Marvell's poem registers as literary ambiguity, the still more palpable tension in Herbert's prose grows out of the divided loyalty that he must certainly feel, and which he attributes, with some considerable skill, to the other spectators: the soldiers first, but members of the audience, too, all of whom are living through a difficult and demanding event.

The metaphor of Charles as an actor, playing his last and most memorable scene in the bitter cold of January 1649, becomes a virtual commonplace in many other accounts of his execution, though at times it is a commonplace quite beautifully expressed.[76] The verbal restraint in the two passages just cited only intensifies their theatrical power. Conversely, the rhetorical over-indulgence in Laurence Echard's account may cause resistance in readers not committed to the royalist agenda. Echard ends his narration of the event by declaring, "Thus fell the ROYAL MARTYR King *Charles* the First, in the 49th Year and Strength of his Age, both after a happy and comfortless Reign of twenty three years, ten Months and three Days."[77] And if such an estimate by itself strains credulity, then it will be difficult to absorb this description of the theatrical ripple effect: "The venerable Archbishop *Usher*, from a Window, swooned at the Sight of the fatal Blow, as at a Prodigy too great for Heaven to permit, or the Earth to behold: And as the Rumour of his Death spread throughout the Kingdom, Women miscarry'd, many of both Sexes fell into Palpitations, Swoonings and Melancholy, and some, with sudden Consternation, expired" (2: 646). The one spectator named here can indeed be identified as James Ussher, archbishop of Armagh, who "watched and wept from the roof of the countess of Peterborough's house in London."[78] But the subsequent palpitations of many kinds can't be confirmed, because they are only imagined. They still belong to the history of spectatorship, however, at least as elements of the royalist imaginary.

It would appear from the images and texts cited so far that, in his most vulnerable moment, Charles I was a figure with whom many of his subjects sympathized, perhaps even to the point of veneration.[79] Were there representations from an overtly critical standpoint? Indeed there were, as would hardly be surprising in a culture so radically divided as this one was in 1649. What is more surprising, perhaps, is that the ideological opponents of Charles I, like his allies, use the trope of the royal actor to refer to this pivotal event. John Goodwin, an Independent minister who had supported first Parliament and then the New Model Army against the king, wrote in support of the royal execution as follows: "I think there are few men amongst us, but will grant, that the King was not onely the Supreme person, but the Supreme Actour also in the tragedie of bloud, which hath been lately acted upon the stage of this Nation; yea and had more of the guilt of the bloud shed in it, upon his conscience, than all his fellow-Actours besides, put together."[80] When his opponents call Charles "the Supreme Actour," however, what they are alluding to is not his courage in defeat but his skill at dissimulation.[81]

The question raised here requires a look at one further text, the king's book, *Eikon Basilike*, purportedly written by Charles himself as his last gift to the English people. Modern scholars are inclined to assign the authorship of this work to the king's chaplain, John Gauden, but royalists in the seventeenth century believed that Charles had written it himself.

The iconography of the frontispiece, engraved by William Marshall (see fig. 6.6), makes an obvious appeal for us to think of Charles as a Christ figure. "The Explanation of the EMBLEME" is printed on the bottom half of the page, in Latin and in English. We quote a few of the most pertinent English lines:

> That Splendid, but yet toilsome Crown
> Regardlessly I trample down.
> With joie I take this Crown of thorn,
> Though sharp, yet easie to be born.
> That heavenlie Crown, already mine,
> I view with eiess of Faith divine.

And so began the cult of King Charles, a cult that had to go underground in the mid-seventeenth century, because its very rhetoric was offensive to iconoclasts like John Milton, but a cult that flourished nonetheless and that seeks to keep the figure of Charles the martyr alive even today. In *Eikonoklastes*, Milton ridiculed the "besotted and degenerate baseness" with which his contemporaries "are ready to fall flat and give adoration to the image and memory of this man who hath offered at more cunning fetches to undermine our liberties, and put tyranny into an art, than any British king before him."[82] But Milton's view did not carry the day. Having first become available on the day of the royal execution, the king's book appeared in thirty-five editions by the end of 1649; within a decade it had been translated into five European languages, rewritten as verse, and set to music. We cite these particulars as reported in Elizabeth Skerpan Wheeler's essay, which begins with the claim that, if presented with *Eikon Basilike*, "A modern brand manager would call it 'the King Charles experience.'"[83] The king who had seemed so distant from his subjects throughout his reign was now readily accessible; once so secretive, he was now sincere. The Charles who speaks in these pages, whether his words are the king's own or Gauden's, is able to give candid and plausible accounts of his own motives in every situation, even when the political consequences of his actions (which he doesn't try to explain) are disastrous. This reader-friendly Charles is nonetheless an actor still, though now to call him the

Fig. 6.6 Engraved frontispiece by William Marshall for *Eikon Basilike* (1648/9).

royal actor might seem a stretch. In chapter 26 Charles gives an account of his capture at Holmby Castle, and then looks forward with uncertainty: "What part God will have Mee now to act or suffer in this new and strange scene of affairs, I am not so much solicitous; som little practice will serv that man, who onely seek's to represent a part of honestie and honor."[84] This approach to the actor's role, of course, is one that every reader of the king's book could appropriate for her- or himself.

If the execution of Charles I was (in every meaningful sense of the term) a theatrical performance, it was a performance that could be said to bring into positivity the category that Jacques Rancière has called the emancipated spectator.[85] The new political order unfolding in England was a bold and brave experiment indeed. But if its leaders believed that executing King Charles would help to secure the republic, or even that they could control the consequences of their performance, they were sadly mistaken. The event itself, including the distribution of the king's book, would now belong to the spectators and would therefore be subject to their collaborative reinterpretation.

"Honest and Innocent in the sight of God"

If Charles I performed well at his execution (defiant but not wildly so), then the opposite might be said for the Duke of Monmouth and his executioner when the latter beheaded the former on Tower Hill in the summer of 1685. Just as his ill-fated rebellion fell well short, so did Monmouth's behaviour on the scaffold leave much to be desired, both for those who may have harboured sympathy for him and for those who supported authority in the person of James II. Monmouth did not own his treason; neither did he embrace it. Rather he laid blame on his co-conspirator, Fergusson, and this kind of finger-pointing, even if accurate, does not tend to earn respect.

Two aspects of the accounts of Monmouth's execution involve spectatorship. First, Monmouth himself invoked the idea of an observing deity, in much the same manner as Walter Ralegh, when he tried to justify his relationship with his mistress, Lady Henrietta Wentworth. Second, John Evelyn would record how the crowd attempted to get at the executioner, John Ketch, after the latter botched the job ("the wretch made five Chopps before he had his head off, which so incens'd the people, that had he not ben guarded and got away they would have torne him in pieces").[86] Evelyn was working from the first-hand knowledge of Dr Tenison, Rector of St Martin's, who was sent by James II to serve as one of Monmouth's attendants. MacAulay may have sensationalized Monmouth's lack of defiance, just as Aphra Behn may have over-emphasized his romantic infatuation with his mistress.[87] Nevertheless, the main and indisputable elements of the story do not lend themselves to an interpretation that would see his performance as admirable from any point of view.

The contemporary pamphlets reproduce an extended fictionalization of what was said on the scaffold, and it is suggested that Monmouth's only rehearsed speech had to do with the virtue of Lady Henrietta.

> Then he began as if he was about to make a premeditated Speech in this manner. M. *I have had a Scandal raised upon me about a Woman, a Lady of Vertue and Honour. I will name her; the* Lady Henrietta Wentworth. *I declare, that she is a very Vertuous and Godly Woman. I have committed no Sin with her; and that which hath passed betwixt Us, was very honest and Innocent in the sight of God.*[88]

Clearly, defiance was part of the duke's performance, but it was not of the kind that garnered respect for the condemned. Right up until the execution itself, the bishops attempted to get Monmouth to admit his blame in the armed rebellion, and right up until the last he managed to not quite satisfy them with his answers. He did not display absolute bravado or contrition. After a considerable dialogue, one of the bishops drew Monmouth's attention to the public nature of the moment: "Here are great numbers of Spectators, here are the *Sheriffs*, they represent the *Great City*, and in speaking to them you speak to the whole City; make some satisfaction by owning your *Crime* before them."[89] At this point, the stage direction reads "*(He was silent here.)*" Aphra Behn in her version of the story did not let Monmouth off, at least as far as the submissive letters to James II were concerned, but she also implied that his affection for his mistress was an honourable position.

He is said to have done the standard things – including a bid to the executioner to do his job well: "Do not hack me as you did my Lord Russell."

Monmouth apparently gave the man six guineas and promised him some gold from his servant if he did the job well. In all probability, no further payments were made. The first blow only slightly injured Monmouth. As Evelyn remarks, five strokes had to be taken. At one point Ketch apparently dropped the axe and couldn't go through with the job. He was strongly urged to continue and had to use a knife to sever the head. The crowd apparently pressed forward wishing to get hold of Ketch and register their disgust.[90] This interpretation of the event may itself be owing to Monmouth's popularity as somebody who would have protected the status of Protestants in England. The botched execution reflects an unjust execution. However, there is one point on which the executions of Charles I and the Duke on Monmouth were similar – in the aftermath, those who sympathized with the condemned pressed forward with handkerchiefs to dip into the blood of the martyr.

Steven Wilf documents how in 1783 early modern England moved away from the spectacular public execution, "the large-scale public processions" (at Tyburn and elsewhere), to carefully restricted and controlled events: "England discovered the importance of imagination in criminal punishment."[91] However, we have demonstrated that even the depiction and reception of the public event relied very much on convention (much of it theatrical) and on the imagination. The need for spectators who would bear witness to the execution seems to remain constant through the long historical stretch from which our examples have been taken. What changes is the kind of investment the spectators make in the events they are observing. In our earliest examples, drawn from the reign of Henry VIII, spectators on both sides of the Catholic/Protestant divide are described as behaving in ways that underscore their belief in an absolute power (whether Henry's or God's or both) and their conviction that what they are witnessing matters in the grand scheme of things. By the late seventeenth century, interpretation of a beheading (as in Monmouth's case) had become far more subjective. And by the time of Lord Lovat, many of the old securities had been shattered. Attending an execution was no longer an act of faith, but a recreational occasion (for some) or a business opportunity (for others). The collapse of the viewing-stand is an adventitious metaphor that might stand for ideological insecurity as well. Over time, the spectator at a public execution had become a skeptic of sorts, no longer able to justify the absolute severity of the punishment, no longer convinced of the absolute depravity of the condemned, no longer confident in even the technical skill of the executioner. If the spectator as skeptic has emerged from this inquiry, we should hardly be surprised; the story we have been telling here begins in Martin Luther's time and ends in the age of Voltaire and David Hume.

NOTES

1 Foucault, *Discipline and Punish.*

2 Lake, *The Antichrist's Lewd Hat,* 270.

3 Few subjects in the study of early modern culture in Europe have drawn more attention than that of public executions, and furthermore, given the *public* nature of the subject, it is not surprising that much has already been said about the spectators at such events. This work may itself be seen as a kind of natural curiosity insofar as public executions have largely disappeared in the West; they may also be said to constitute an imagined spectatorship – scholars view these executions through the window of their various representations in texts and images, and we view them through the lens of the analytical commentary that accompanies them. What follows here is not an exhaustive list of this work, but, in our estimation, one that provides the best examples and documentation for the presence of spectators and the pattern we describe. See Fagan, *The Lure of the Arena,* 51–74; Mitchell, *Shakespeare and Public Execution,* 16–19; Linebaugh, *The London Hanged,* 19; Spencer, *Killers of the King,* 149–52; Wilf, "Imagining Justice: Aesthetics and Public Executions in Late Eighteenth-Century England," 51–78; and Sawday, *The Body Emblazoned,* 54–78.

4 See Huebert, "Performing Anatomy," 9–26.

5 Mallipeddi, *Spectacular Suffering.*

6 Ralegh, *The Poems of Sir Walter Ralegh,* 48.

7 See Greenblatt, *Ralegh: The Renaissance Man,* 14–25.

8 Roper, *The Lyfe of Sir Thomas Moore, Knight,* 103. Roper's *Lyfe* is the most important source for Robert Bolt's twentieth-century interpretation of More, *A Man for All Seasons* (1960), though it is not the inspiration for the dyspeptic, ascetic, and narcissistic representation of More that haunts the pages of Hilary Mantel's *Wolf Hall* (2009).

9 See More, Letter 218, "To Margaret Roper," in *The Correspondence of Sir Thomas More*, 564.

10 Hall, *The Union of the Two Noble and Illustre Famelies of Lancastre and Yorke*, 3P4^{v}. Hall died in 1546, and Grafton claims to have brought to completion the later segments of this work. It is impossible to tell, therefore, whether this view of More is Hall's or Grafton's.

11 Stapleton, *The Life and Illustrious Martyrdom of Sir Thomas More*, 188.

12 Harpsfield, *The Life and Death of Sr Thomas Moore*, 217.

13 This includes all of the works already cited, and also Ro. Ba., *The Life of Syr Thomas More,* 258.

14 Marius, *Thomas More: A Biography*, 513.

15 For details about this aspect of the constructed set in Westminster Hall, see Fraser, *Faith and Treason*, 219.

16 *The Gentleman's Magazine and Historical Chronicle*, April 1747.

17 Paula Backscheider refers to this series of events (i.e., the regicides executed in October 1660 and the exhumed bodies of Cromwell, Bradshaw, and Ireton desecrated the following January) as "hideous but magnificent theatre"; see *Spectacular Politics*, 7.

18 For a detailed description of the planning and organization of the executions that followed the Gordon Riots in 1780 (including the suggestions by Edmund Burke), see White, "Public Executions and the Gordon Riots," 204–25.

19 Hogarth's print has been the subject of several commentaries, perhaps the most famous being Laqueur, "Crowds, Carnival and the State in English Executions, 1604–1868," 305–55.

20 "A Brief Description of several of their friends," in Howell, *A Complete Collection of State Trials*, 18: 376–8.

21 "An Extract of a Letter dated at London, July 31, 1746" and "A Brief Description of several of their friends," in Howell, *A Complete Collection of State Trials,* 18:375–8. The latter document also adds the hyperbole, "there was present the greatest number of spectators ever seen together in the memory of man, some thousands of whom had waited in the rain several hours, to see the execution of these unhappy men. But was observed, that the mob offered no insults to any of the prisoners this day, though they behaved very rudely to them in passing to and from their trials."

22 See Howell, *A Complete Collection of State Trials and Proceedings*, 18:530–858.

Ronald Paulson notes that Hogarth did his famous sketch of Lovat when the latter was held for three days at St Albans on his way to the Tower. Dr Webster apparently examined him at the White Hart Inn and thought "his patient's illness was more feigned than real"; Paulson makes no mention of how Lovat had been transported; see Paulson, *Hogarth: His Life, Art and Times,* 2:58.

23 Howell, *A Complete Collection of State Trials and Proceedings*, 18:816–24.

24 His final address to the court before sentencing is recorded as "My lords, I am very sorry I gave your lordships so much trouble in my trial; and I give you a million of thanks for your being so good in your patience and attendance, whilst it lasted." See Howell, *A Complete Collection of State Trials and Proceedings*, 18:827.

25 Petrie, *The Jacobite Movement*, 124.

26 Ibid.

27 Villette, *The Annals of Newgate; or, malefactors register*, 280.

28 Ibid.

29 *The Gentleman's Magazine and Historical Chronicle,* April 1747, 6 [197]. To distinguish this structure from the "scaffold" proper, which refers to the platform on which the execution took place, we will use the term "viewing-stand." Contemporary documents consistently refer to both structures (execution platform and viewing-stand) as "scaffolds."

30 Walpole, *Horace Walpole's Correspondence with Sir Horace Mann,* 3:386.

31 Ray, *A compleat history of the rebellion*, 408. Ray claims the viewing-stand was "next the Bars" and that there were "about 400 People" on it when it collapsed, or 600 fewer than reported in *The Gentleman's Magazine.*

32 Johnstone, *Memoirs of the Chevalier de Johnstone*, 2:128. Johnstone also passed on the opportunity to view the execution of the Jacobite commoners (including Townley and Fletcher) at Kennington Common on 30 July. While one assumes that he had reason to fear his own exposure (i.e., he should have been among the Manchester regiment prisoners), the reason he gives in his memoirs is that he was too much in love to give his comrades any thought; see *Memoirs*, 2:136.

33 Laqueur, "Crowds, Carnival and the State in English Executions, 1604–1868," 305–55.

34 Casanova, *The Memoirs*, Episode 11, "Paris and Holland," chap. 1. Location 19194–19225.

35 Storey, *London: Crime*, 128.

36 Pepys, *Diary of Samuel Pepys*, 5:23.

37 Ibid.

38 Ibid., 3:108–9.

39 Ibid.

40 For a history of executioners, see Abbott, *Lords of the Scaffold.*

41 For the execution of Mary Queen of Scots, see Scott, *The Tragedy of Fotheringay*, 255: "she lying very still on the block, one of the executioners holding of her slightly with one of his hands, she endured two strokes of the other executioner's axe … and so the executioners cut off her head saving one little gristle, which being cut asunder he lifted up her head to the view of all the assembly … Her lips stirred up and down almost a quarter of an hour after her head was cut off." These details are repeated on the *English History* website by Marilee Hanson, posted 9 February 2015, accessed 13 October 2016. http://englishhistory.net/tudor/execution-mary-queen-of-scots/.

According to John Evelyn, it took "Jack Ketch" five blows to sever the head of Lord Russell, executed for treason on 21 July 1683. See Evelyn, *The Diary of John Evelyn*, 4:456. Again the details are repeated at "1683: Lord Russell, Whig Martyr," ExecutedToday.com, posted 21 July 2014, accessed October 13, 2016. http://www.executedtoday.com/2014/07/21/1683-lord-russell-whig-martyr/.

Finally, MacAulay is critical of Monmouth's behaviour and the performance of "Jack Ketch" (so named to protect the man's real identity). See MacAulay, *The History of England*, 476. His description is reproduced at the website "The Execution of Monmouth," *A Theory of Civilisation*, accessed 13 October 2016. "1685 [15 July]: James Scott, Duke of Monmouth," ExecutedToday.com, accessed 14 November 2018. http://www.executedtoday.com/2008/07/15/1685-james-scott-duke-of-monmouth/.

42 Spencer, *Killers of the King*, 151.

43 Ibid., 155.

44 Behn's Oroonoko, who casually smokes while being dismembered, is a sensational example from the novel.

45 Storey, *London: Crime, Death and Debauchery*, 125. Storey's book is full of sensational grotesquerie.

46 Abbott, *Lords of the Scaffold*, 53. Abbott tracks the history of several body parts post-execution, including that of Lord Lovat; see 48–59.

47 Evelyn, *Diary of John Evelyn*, 3:259.

48 *The Tragedy of Master Arden of Faversham*, ed. Wine, *The Revels Plays*, 18.29. Subsequent references, in parentheses, are to scene and line.

49 See Appendix 2, in *The Tragedy of Master Arden of Faversham*, ed. Wine, 158.

50 See *The Statutes of the Realm*, 25 Edw. 3, Stat. 5, c. 2.

51 *Britton*, 41.

52 *The First Examinacyon of Anne Askew* (1546) and *The Lattre Examinacyon of Anne Askew* (1547), both of which are printed, along with Bale's voluminous commentary in Askew, *The Examinations of Anne Askew*.

53 Foxe, *The Seconde Volume of the Ecclesiastical Historie, Conteining the Acts and Monuments of Martyrs*, 1234–40. Subsequent references are to *Acts and Monuments*.

54 See, respectively, Lindsey, *Divorced, Beheaded, Survived*, 190–7; Luckyj, *'A Moving Rhetorike*,' 123–7; Coles, *Religion, Reform, and Women's Writing*, 17–44; and Loewenstein, *Treacherous Faith*, 69–101.

55 Watt, "Askew [married name Kyme], Anne (c. 1521–1546), writer and protestant martyr" (2004).

56 Askew, *The Examinations of Anne Askew*, 154.

57 Foxe, *Acts and Monuments*, 1240.

58 Crowley, *The Confutation of XIII Articles*.

59 Smythe, "Woodcuts in English Books," 76.

60 Ibid., 77.

61 Ibid., 75.

62 Louthe, "Reminiscences," 41.

63 Ibid., 44.

64 Ibid., 45.

65 Bradshaw, "Miles Huggarde."

66 Huggarde, *The Displaying of the Protestantes*, E8^{v}.

67 Evelyn, *Diary of John Evelyn*, 3:64.

68 *The Witch of Wapping*, 7–8. Though Prudence Lee's story seldom appears in the vast scholarly archive we are citing in this chapter, it is referred to (briefly but appropriately) by Bannerjee in *Burning Women*, 166.

69 McLynn, *Crime and Punishment in Eighteenth-Century England*, 122.

70 Villette, *Annals of Newgate*, 1:426.

71 MacAulay, *History of England*, 1:519.

72 James I, *Basilikon*, R1.

73 Shirley, *Honoria and Mammon*, K1.

74 Fritze, "Herbert, Sir Thomas."

75 Herbert, *Memoirs*, 193–4.

76 See, for example, the accounts by Echard, Kennett, Clarendon, and Hume, among others, as discussed by Siebert in "The Aesthetic Execution of Charles I," 7–27.

77 Echard, *The History of England*, 2:645.

78 Ford, "Ussher, James."

79 For intelligent commentary on the principal divisions, and careful presentation of relevant documents, see Kesselring, *The Trial of Charles I.*

80 Goodwin, *Hybristodikai*, 63.

81 See Loewenstein, "The King Among the Radicals," 104–6.

82 Milton, *Complete Poems*, 784.

83 Wheeler, "*Eikon Basilike* and the Rhetoric of Self-Representation," 122.

84 *Eikon Basilike: The Pourtraicture of his Sacred Majestie,* 3.

85 See Rancière, *The Emancipated Spectator*, 13–15.

86 Evelyn, *Diary of John Evelyn,* 4:456.

87 For Aphra Behn's version of the Monmouth Rebellion, see the last part of *Love-Letters Between a Nobleman and his Sister (1684–7)* in *The Works of Aphra Behn*, 2:397–439.

88 "An Account of what passed at the Execution of the Late Duke of Monmouth," 1–2.

89 Ibid., 3.

90 All details in this paragraph are taken from MacAulay, *The History of England*, 1:487–8. John Dryden was obviously not thinking of Monmouth's fate when, in making an analogy between the fineness of raillery and the art of execution, he cited Jack Ketch's wife on her husband's skill: "Yet there is a vast difference betwixt the slovenly Butchering of a Man and the fineness of a stroak that separates the Head from the Body, and leaves it standing in its place. A man may be capable, as *Jack Ketch's* wife said his servant, of a plain piece of Work, a bare Hanging; but to make a Malefactor die sweetly, was only belonging to her husband." *Works of John Dryden*, 4:71.

91 Wilf, "Imagining Justice," 51.

7
Looking at John Donne Looking at God

RONALD HUEBERT

The question I will be raising is this: when he left written evidence of being profoundly moved by the presence of God, was it a Protestant or a Catholic deity that John Donne had in mind? Nowadays this question could be brushed aside as trivial, both by ecumenical believers and by skeptics of almost any stripe. But in the culture that Donne inhabited four hundred years ago, it was urgently real. Negotiating the Reformation was strikingly difficult for someone born into an English Catholic family – the great-grandson of Sir Thomas More's sister Elizabeth, to be precise – who would spend the last sixteen years of his life as a priest in the Church of England.

Situating Donne's religious orientation in this way puts him into the middle of a contentious debate about the propriety and/or efficacy of images of the divine in Christian worship. Medieval Catholicism had left a rich and beautiful heritage of religious icons in churches throughout Europe, including England, in manuscripts, on tombs, in monastic houses, and in private places of worship as well. Reformation thinkers tended to be hostile to such imagery, and could easily find evidence in scripture to support their viewpoint; the second commandment, "Thou shalt not make unto thee any graven image" (Exod. 20:4), was a convenient point of departure. This is not the place to retell the story of Reformation iconoclasm, but a few brief allusions to events in England may be useful. Early on in the reign of Edward VI, Archbishop Cranmer promoted a policy of removing images from places of worship;[1] the King subsequently wrote to Nicholas Ridley, recently appointed bishop of London, "to give substantial order throughout all your diocese, that with all diligence all the altars in every church or chapel, as well in places exempted as not exempted, within your said diocese, be taken down; and in the lieu of them a table set up in some convenient part of the chancel, within every such church or chapel, to serve for the ministration of the blessed communion." Ridley did his best to comply, "and in the church of Paul brake down the wall standing then by the high altar's side."[2] To Cranmer, Ridley, and many others, these were steps necessary to secure a reformed English church. In our own time these events have been narrated from the diametrically opposite point of view; Eamon Duffy retells the story in which "churchwardens cooperated in the removal and destruction of images," but he resituates what was happening here by adding that "all over the country horrified traditionalists watched as the lead given by Cranmer and the royal visitors unleashed a wave of destruction."[3]

When allowance has been made for polemical embellishment on both sides, the narrative still stands. Catholics were accustomed to approach the divine partly with the help of images; Protestants were forbidden to do so, on the grounds that the Word of God, as printed in the vernacular and spoken in the acts of worship, is the only reliable guide. Even when you acknowledge that, in Donne's lifetime especially, the Church of England was the scene of vigorous contestation between those who thought the Reformation hadn't gone far enough and those who thought it had gone too far, the opposition between seeing the image of God and hearing his Word still stands. And for Donne, this rift seems to have been in many ways a treacherous one.

"Seek true religion"

There is copious evidence in the Donne archive that the change I have just alluded to was difficult for him. In "An Advertisement to the Reader" prefixed to the polemical tract *Pseudo-Martyr*, Donne claims to be "derived from such a stocke and race, as, I believe, no family, (which is not of farre larger extent, and greater branches,) hath endured and suffered more in their persons and fortunes, for obeying the Teachers of Romane Doctrine, then it hath done."[4] And the toll was indeed a heavy one. It included the protracted exile to Italy of one of his uncles, Ellis Heywood, S.J., the imprisonment, torture, and deportation (1584) of another uncle, Jasper Heywood, S.J., and the arrest of his younger brother Henry for the crime of harbouring a Catholic priest, followed by imprisonment in Newgate, where Henry would die of the plague (1593). Eventually Donne would take the view that God does not require excessive self-sacrifice of the kind his relatives made. But the revision of his doctrinal position could not eradicate the memories of his boyhood and youth. As Donne says quite casually and with, I think, complete sincerity in a letter to Sir Henry Goodyer, people are better off spiritually if they can stay with the church they grew up in: "You shall seldom see a coin, upon which the stamp were removed, though to imprint it better, but it looks awry and squint. And so, for the most part, do minds which have received divers impressions."[5] The metaphor here would suggest that changing one's religion is not an entirely voluntary project, or at least not one that can be completed by an act of will alone.

By the time Donne wrote this letter to Goodyer (c. 1610), he seems wiser and more pessimistic than he was in "Satire 3," a youthful exercise in which the speaker advises his auditor to "Seek true religion," and then invents a series of fictional characters who, for shallow reasons, conduct their searches according to the models available in Rome, Geneva, and England, or who, for equally shallow reasons, reject all the alternatives or accept them all. None of these searchers has the integrity the speaker requires, because the search is going to be a demanding one.

> On a huge hill,
> Cragged, and steep, Truth stands, and he that will
> Reach her, about must, and about must go. (30–1)

Donne here seems eager to declare his own intention of climbing this hill. But whether he was able to arrive at the top is a question that, for now, must remain open.

If the Reformation was a troubling phenomenon for Donne, his attitude towards it has been a troublesome question for his biographers and interpreters. John Carey took a strong position when he argued, in *John Donne: Life, Mind and Art* (1981), that after having been raised a Catholic Donne in effect remained a Catholic for the rest of his life. Not a contented Catholic, mind you, because in his own eyes he was an apostate, a status he earned because ambition led him to conform to what he thought the patronage network would require. Subsequent biographical readings have all been responses to, modifications of, or attempted refutations of Carey's point of view. Dennis Flynn, in *John Donne and the Ancient Catholic Nobility* (1995), made a case for a softer interpretation of Donne's relationship to his Catholic past, one in which Donne regrets having blemished the honour of his family. More recently John Stubbs, in *Donne: The Reformed Soul* (2006), has argued that Donne was able to accept and adapt to Reformation values in ways that Carey had not been willing to admit.[6] Lucid and persuasive articles by Gregory Kneidel (on Donne's so-called conversion), Paul Stevens (on the pressure of nationhood on Donne's religion), and Lukas Erne (on the location of "Show me dear Christ thy spouse so bright and clear" in the Donne canon) have not settled the debate so much as shown why and how it matters.[7]

The personal history of Donne's religious life challenges us, at every turn, to measure the gap that may separate public confession and private conscience. Jeanne Shami has indeed addressed this question,[8] and has pointed out some of the errors of anachronism we are likely to promote if we carry out this task without historical awareness.[9] Relying on her compendious knowledge of the religious commitments Donne was willing to make in his sermons, Shami points out that the public ground he claimed for "our Church" was a moderate middle between opposite extremes: idolatry on the one hand, separatism on the other.[10] Still, there may be a further trap that even deeply learned scholars could fall into, namely, the view that a private relationship with God is no more than the sum of its public parts. My assumption in the argument that follows will be the opposite of this one; for me, Donne is a writer whose private thoughts, including his private thoughts about God, were profoundly hidden except in those rare instances when, and under those specific circumstances where, he chose to reveal them.[11]

"That Spectackle of too much waight for mee"

The poem to which I now turn has been known to most readers of Donne since the publication of the first edition of his *Poems* (1633) as "Goodfriday, 1613. Riding Westward." Donald R. Dickson has recently studied the twenty-three manuscripts in which this poem circulated, and he has come to the conclusion that the most authoritative copy is that in the Dolaucothi manuscript held in the National Library of Wales.[12] Although the title varies considerably from one manuscript to another, the circumstances leading to the composition of this poem are to a surprising degree recoverable. In the spring of 1613 Donne had been spending time with Sir Henry Goodyer at Polesworth, Warwickshire. Good Friday fell on 2 April that year, so we have grounds for presuming that Donne set out on that date to visit Sir Edward Herbert at Montgomery Castle in Wales. We can't be certain about the details of his journey, except that Donne had reached Montgomery Castle by 7 April; and we can draw some confident inferences about the act of writing itself because, as John Stubbs points out, "Donne liked to compose on horseback."[13]

The first printed text and the manuscript copy agree that the direction of Donne's journey was "Westward," a point that can be confirmed by locating Polesworth and Montgomery on any reliable map and observing the horizontal distance of about seventy miles that separates them. The circumstances are important because they help to situate, among other things, the significance Donne wants to embed in the metaphors of vision in this text. While the speaker is, as he puts it, "caryed towards the West," his "Soules forme bends towards the East" (lines 9–10), because that would take him to the site of the Crucifixion, the precipitating event of the Easter narrative. But the speaker cannot look directly at this scene, for reasons that virtually come pouring out as soon as the reader asks. First, there's the direction of the speaker's travel, which ensures that he's facing westward, and not towards the eastern location of Calvary. Next, there's the Old Testament prohibition spoken by God when Moses asks to see his glory: "Thou canst not see my face: for there shall no man see me, and live" (Exod. 33:20). This prohibition is virtually quoted – "Who sees Gods face, that is selfe life must die" (line 17) – and it is supported too by a long philosophical tradition, beginning as far back as Heraclitus and explicated in copious detail by Pierre Hadot in *The Veil of Isis*, which holds that certain spiritual mysteries are too secret to be revealed to human minds. Beyond this, the speaker is surely aware of the resistance to images of divinity within Reformation Christianity. These are powerful reasons to lead the speaker to believe that he won't be permitted to see "That Spectakle of too much waight for mee" (line 16).

But he's not easily discouraged. Indeed, he turns to wondering whether he might be allowed to see not the Saviour himself, but his "Miserable Mother,"

> Who was Gods Partner here and furnished thus
> Halfe of that Sacrifice which ransomed us. (lines 31–2)

This is an amazing sidebar that deserves more commentary than it is ever given.[14] Yes, there are ways in which Mary the Mother of God can be shown as sharing in the story of the Crucifixion. But *half* of the sacrifice? Well, a learned theologian might say that, in order to create our Saviour's dual nature, the spiritual essence was provided by God the Father, and the corporal matrix was the Virgin Mary's contribution. Even on that analysis, *half* seems a very generous designation of the Virgin Mother's share.

Having described the things that he cannot / dare not / must not see, the speaker now draws a distinction between "mine Eie" (line 33), which sees nothing more unusual than the Warwickshire countryside, and "my Memorie" (line 34), which brings back the Crucifixion scene: "O Saviour as thou hangst vppon the tree" (line 35). Perhaps the contrast here is between Donne's adult perceptions in 1613 and his memories of the Catholic iconography available to him as a boy. But the memories could be more recent than this. Just a year earlier Donne had taken one of his more extended trips to France, Germany, and the Low Countries, as secretary to Sir Robert Drury. Between December 1611 and April 1612 Donne was in Drury's entourage in the cathedral city of Amiens, in Picardy, and in Paris.[15] These months away from home doubtless offered Donne many opportunities for looking at images of God, the first of which would have been immediately available in the stone carving that represents Christ treading on a lion and a basilisk (c. 1220) on the exterior of Amiens Cathedral (fig. 7.1). The image here is often referred to as the beautiful God (the

Fig. 7.1. *Right*
Stone carving of Christ as the "Beau Dieu" (c. 1220).

Fig. 7.2 *Opposite*
Stone carving of *La Vierge Dorée* (1240–45) at Amiens Cathedral.

"Beau Dieu"), and in this phrase itself is embedded a Catholic satisfaction that Reformers may have found difficult to endorse. A parallel problem would have arisen with the carving of the Virgin Mary (1240–45) decorating the same cathedral and known as "La Vierge dorée" (fig. 7.2). This image is certainly not the "Miserable Mother" of Donne's poem; indeed, the Virgin Mother seems to be engaged in blissful communion with her divine Son, an attitude that may have been enhanced by the gilding that covered her image until the eighteenth century and which supplied the pretext for her soubriquet.

When Drury and his party left Amiens for Paris in March 1611/12, the images of Christ and his Mother available to Donne would have been multiplied many times over. I have chosen to reproduce one specimen of the Crucifixion, an oil-on-wood panel created for the Grande Chambre of the Parlement of Paris, circa 1452 (fig. 7.3), and attributed to a painter from Flanders or the north of France, perhaps the enigmatic figure known only as the Master of Dreux Budé. Whatever the questions of interpretation

that might arise from this picture, it is clear that Christ's "Miserable Mother," standing at the foot of the cross, dressed in her traditional blue, and wiping a tear from her eye with a corner of her napkin, is indeed the *mater dolorosa* of Donne's memory.

But the poem does not end with the Virgin Mary, or under the auspices of memory. The speaker chooses to interrupt nostalgia, so as to reinterpret his literal position: "I turne my back to thee but to receave / Corrections" (lines 37–8). Suddenly he is in the presence of the stern Reformation deity who loves and chastises with schoolmasterish care: "For whom the Lord loveth he chasteneth, and scourgeth every son whom he receiveth" (Heb. 12:6). By the end of the poem, Donne will gladly accept such punishments in preparation for the happy day when he will be able to see God, face to face.

Fig. 7.3 *Crucifixion*, Grande Chambre, Parlement of Paris.

"Going out of sight"

Less than two years after the ride of "Goodfriday, 1613," Donne was ordained a priest in the Church of England (23 January 1614/15) and Chaplain-in-Ordinary to the King (March 1614/15); soon he would be installed as Divinity Reader at Lincoln's Inn (24 October 1616).[16] While he was still getting accustomed to his new role as a clergyman, in the spring of 1618/19, Donne was invited to serve as Chaplain to the Earl of Doncaster (formerly Lord Hay) on a diplomatic mission that would take him abroad once again, certainly to Bohemia, and probably to other locations in the decentralized territory then known as Germany. Donne anticipated this trip with trepidation. The principal sources in support of this claim are Donne's poem "A Hymn to Christ, at the Author's last going into Germany," his letters to Sir Henry Goodyer (9 March 1618/19) and Sir Robert Ker (April 1619), and his farewell sermon preached at Lincoln's Inn (18 April 1619). The circumstantial reasons for his fear, partly because there are so many of them, don't seem to add up to a full explanation, even after the intelligent account by Jeffrey Johnson.[17] Yes, Donne knew that the diplomatic mission upon which his patron had embarked was beset with difficulties: a mediation between the Vienna-based house of Habsburg and the newly elected King Frederick of Bohemia was bound to trigger alarm bells, even though Donne could not have known (as we with the easy help of hindsight do) that he was being invited to oversee the early phases of the Thirty Years' War.[18] Yes, the recent death of Donne's wife, Ann More, had left him emotionally vulnerable at a time when all of his positive energies were required. And yes, his anxiety about physical infirmities may have been more urgent than what we might think appropriate nowadays for a forty-seven-year-old man. But all of these contingencies are, I believe, either less or more than what we need to explain Donne's mood at this time.

The unacknowledged cause of Donne's fear is, I believe, memory, a theme he does explore in the farewell sermon, and one that he anticipates with great beauty in the "Goodfriday, 1613" poem already discussed. In what follows I will be suggesting that Donne's memory of his Roman Catholic boyhood created an acute feeling of exposure on this occasion, when the delegation to which he was assigned hoped to mediate between Catholic and Protestant partisans. I will begin with his valedictory sermon, because the theme of memory is overtly present in the entire discourse. I will proceed then to the letters and the poem, where memory, though present by implication only, is nonetheless a decisive carrier of Donne's emotional meaning.

For his text on the occasion of saying farewell to his regular congregation of Lincoln's Inn benchers, Donne chose Ecclesiastes 12:1, "Remember now thy Creator in the days of thy youth." The prose of the sermon is animated by many of the rhetorical techniques and stylistic virtues that made Donne a famous preacher in his own day. As he divides his topic into subheadings in his opening paragraph, Donne plays an oral riff on the words "remember" and "memory." "Here then the holy-Ghost takes the nearest way to bring a man to God," Donne announces, "by awakening his memory."[19] Eventually the memory will be remade into a beautiful metaphor:

> we may be bold to call it the Gallery of the soul, hang'd with so many, and so lively pictures of the goodness and mercies of God to thee, as that every one of them shall be a catechism to thee, to instruct thee in all thy duties to him for these mercies. And as a well made, and well plac'd picture, looks alwayes upon him that looks upon it; so shall thy God look upon thee, whose memory is thus contemplating him, and shine upon thine understanding, and rectifie thy will too. (2:237).

As so often in Donne's poetry, the metaphor points in two directions at once. The Christian enjoys the pictures in his gallery, because they remind him of God's blessings. But God looks back at the Christian, using his eternal vigilance to evaluate and, if necessary, "rectifie" his follower's behaviour.

The theological interpretation of memory embedded in this metaphor is perfectly at home in the discursive world of the sermon.[20] But the visual appeal of the gallery metaphor is especially striking when compared to Donne's later representations of memory as an aural phenomenon. In the Whitehall sermons of 4 March 1624/25 and 1 April 1627, as Catherine Evans has recently and persuasively shown, Donne relies on the figure of the echo to suggest how memory works within us.[21] In the first of these two sermons Donne builds his extended metaphor with patience and wit: "The Scriptures are Gods Voyce; The Church is his Eccho; a redoubling, a repeating of some particular syllables, and accents of the same voice."[22] Donne doesn't stop here, of course, but continues troubling his metaphor until he arrives at the sacrament of holy communion which, as his auditors know, Christ asked them to perform "in remembrance of me" (Luke 22:19). In the second Whitehall sermon Donne gives a virtual explication of his metaphor, adapting it with delicate precision to the practices of the Reformed church: "when men have a Christian liberty afforded them to read the Scriptures at home, and then are remembred of those things at Church,"[23] then the voice of God will be heard in its proper echo.

In the Lincoln's Inn sermon, Donne gives his auditors (many of whom he knows as friends) a much more personal reading of memory as well. This pattern is especially visible in his final paragraph, where he proposes "to make up a circle, by returning to our first word, remember" (2:248). And return he does, again and again: "In my long absence, and far distance from hence, remember me, as I shall you" (2:248). He entertains the possibility that he will "never meet" his parishioners again, until "we have all passed the gate of death"; even so, he enjoins his auditors, "Remember me thus, you that stay in this Kingdome of peace, where no sword is drawn, but the sword of Justice, as I shall remember you in those Kingdomes, where ambition on one side, and a necessary defence from unjust persecution on the other side hath drawn many swords" (2:248–9). Clearly Donne wants the faculty of memory to do a great deal of work for him: bringing to mind the mercies God has favoured him with; reminding him, where necessary, of lapses in his faith that need to be rectified; and binding him in Christian fellowship to those he must leave behind. These are, if you like, the positive achievements of memory. In his more personal utterances he will allow himself to exhibit greater vulnerability.

Donne's letter to Sir Henry Goodyer (9 March 1618/19) is frequently and appropriately cited to illustrate his misapprehensions about the German voyage to which he is now committed. "I leave a scattered flock of wretched children, and I carry an infirm and valetudinary body, and I go into the mouths of such adversaries as I cannot blame for hating me, the Jesuits, and yet I go."[24] Donne's wife Ann had died on 15 August 1617, of which more later; hence the "scattered flock" about which Donne is concerned. He is aware also of his physical weakness (a "valetudinary body") and a past record of having offended his Jesuit opponents. All of this the letter to Goodyer does indeed offer us. But it also places a special pressure on the idea of memory that is, so far as I can tell, never mentioned in the commentary this letter has called forth. "For your commandment in memory of Mr. Martin," Donne writes, "I should not have sat so many processes, if I could incline my thoughts that way. It is not laziness, it is not gravity, nor coldness towards his memory or your service; for I have thought of it oftener and longer than I was wont to do in such things, and nothing is done" (2:122). Goodyer's nominee for Donne's memorial tribute is Richard Martin (1570–1618), a barrister who did admirable work on many fronts, served in the House of Commons, and rose at length to be Recorder of the City of London.[25] Why was Donne unable or unwilling to *remember* Martin in ways that Goodyer wanted him to? There is no easy answer to this question, but there is the suspicion that memory, for Donne, was not immediately at the service of will.

And with this thought in mind I turn to the letter to Sir Robert Ker (April 1619) in which Donne, now on the eve of his trip to Germany, asks for the safekeeping of an enclosed manuscript of his poems, and the custody of "another book" (283) which we know to be his early justification of suicide, *Biathanatos*. "It was written by me many years since," says Donne, "and because it is upon a misinterpretable subject, I have always gone so near suppressing it, as that it is only not burnt … Keep it, I pray … let any that your discretion admits to the sight of it know the date of it, and that it is a book written by Jack Donne, and not by Dr Donne" (283). Here if ever is an admission of the ambiguity of memory. Jack Donne is the persona invented to distance this youthful treatise from the mature (and now theologically responsible) Dr Donne. But with the best will in the world, Dr Donne can't simply let go of Jack Donne. Don't publish it, Donne says to Robert Ker, but don't burn it either: "I only forbid it to the press and the fire … between these two, do what you will with it" (283). What Donne remembers from his impetuous younger days may no longer have his full approval, but he is not willing to cancel, to assign to oblivion, the person he once was.

The great poem Donne wrote to anticipate his departure to Germany does not use the word "memory," but I think it will soon be clear that the idea is everywhere present in this text. I am referring to "A Hymn to Christ, at the Author's last going into Germany," a poem of four brief stanzas in which the speaker prepares for the eventuality that he will not return. "In what torn ship soever I embark," he begins, "That ship shall be my emblem of thy ark" (lines 1–2). Then he imagines disasters: that the sea may swallow him, or that Christ may look upon him with "clouds of anger" (line 5). Whatever else may be going on here, this is clearly a poem about escaping detection, about going out of sight. In the opening stanza the speaker seems nervous about attracting a stare of disapproval from his divine master, but he reassures himself that, no matter what he might fear, the loving eyes of Christ will shine upon him: "yet through that mask I know those eyes, / Which, though they turn away sometimes, / They never will despise" (lines 6–8). But the reassurance he appears to have won in this opening stanza is repeatedly questioned in the rest of the poem. In the second stanza the speaker disappears into a kind of spiritual hibernation: just as the sap descends to the tree's root in winter time, so "in my winter now I go" (line 14) to regions underground, where communication between the soul and Christ will not be subject to interference. And in the final stanza this pattern is underscored by announcing a "divorce" (line 25) that now separates the speaker from the "false mistresses" (line 28) of the past: namely, his ambition, his intellectual brilliance, his desire for advancement. Instead of showing himself in the conspicuous places where these desires might be fulfilled, the speaker now wants to withdraw: "Churches are best for prayer that have least light" (lines 29–30). Significantly, Donne has here moved the devotional practice of his soul into an environment that he might well have remembered from his early days as a Catholic. He does not imagine prayer in the sunlit and whitewashed houses of worship that Dissenters are inclined to promote. For Donne's speaker, meditation is an activity that strives to be inconspicuous, except to the eye of Christ.

If I am right about this poem, and its relationship to the texts that surround it, then Donne felt vulnerable to the prospect of exposure on the eve of his trip to Germany in 1619. And there were sufficient reasons to provoke this feeling. He knew that he would be required to preach to "the Winter Queen," the much admired daughter of James I, the iconic princess of Protestantism, the wife of Count Frederick, newly elected King of Bohemia. He may not have been aware of the political minefield into which this obligation was inviting him, but he must certainly have been aware that his heritage as a Catholic would not recommend him to these patrons. Donne was, in my view, a person of endless creativity, and I find it difficult to imagine him so hemmed in by constraints and prohibitions as this poem and the documents surrounding it would suggest. But I am also willing to imagine that the summer of 1619 was not, for Donne, a time when his normal moods would have prevailed. If he was someone who, in other circumstances, loved to be the centre of attention, just here and now he didn't want to be observed. What he really wanted was the chance to disappear, just once, into darkness.

"For whom the bell tolls"

Donne's distinguished service as a priest led before long to his election and installation as dean of St Paul's Cathedral (1621). Two years after that he fell seriously ill with so-called relapsing fever, and while he believed himself in danger of dying, he wrote twenty-three *Devotions Upon Emergent Occasions* in the form of a day-by-day record of his struggle with the disease and the spiritual inferences he was able to draw from these events. This work was rushed into print in 1624, only weeks after his recovery. As the title page declares, each devotion is divided into three parts: a meditation, an expostulation (these are further described as "*Debatements with God*"), and a prayer.[26]

The book I have written under the title *Privacy in the Age of Shakespeare* contains a chapter called "Private Devotions." The research I did for this chapter led me to read widely across the spectrum of devotional manuals available to English Christians in the sixteenth and seventeenth centuries. And while I was reading these texts I asked myself, inter alia, whether there were any real differences, after each one had entered his or her prayer closet, between the devotions of an English Protestant and an English Catholic. I came to the provisional conclusion that, yes, there were polemical, semiological, and iconographical differences. Polemical differences: Protestant piety differs from Catholic in the first instance because Protestants never tire of saying that they're not Catholics and are happy not to be. Semiologically, Protestants insist on filling the margins of their meditative texts with biblical citations, including chapter and verse, while Catholics don't feel the need to do so. Iconographically, there has been a spectacular and inescapable demotion of the Virgin Mary in Protestant piety. This is not the place to fill in my outline with examples that would verify it. But perhaps one illustration can be cited, in part because it could be read in support of all three of the categories just proposed. Edward Wetenhall, a young and well-placed clergyman in the Church of England, opens his devotional manual, *Enter into Thy Closet* (1666), with a series of quite literal instructions for the creation of a prayer closet. Ideally, it should be a cheerful room, with plenty of natural light, in the top storey of one's house. The furniture should be sparse but appropriate: a table, a stool, and a couch on which to recline. Required study materials are a Bible, a copy of *The Book of Common Prayer*, two blank manuscript books, plus pen and ink. The crowning touch is his plan for the wall above the "*Praying desk*" (B4^{v}) as he now calls the table: it should be decorated with a monochrome hanging (Wetenhall prefers green) so as to provide the eye with no distractions. Plenty of opportunity for biblical citation here, but no image of the Virgin Mary, indeed no traditional iconography of any kind.

Where then would Donne's *Devotions* stand if measured by these criteria? The hundreds of references to holy scripture in the margins would place him with the Protestants. The biblical references are not uniformly distributed; overwhelmingly they appear in the margins of the Expostulations, very occasionally with the Prayers, and never with the "Meditations upon our Humane Condition" (to cite the title page) which begin all twenty-three devotions. Perhaps Donne is closer to the spirit of the Reformation in his "*Debatements with God*" than when he's just thinking or praying. Yes, if you really want to argue with God, you'll want to have the biblical evidence to do so. Also counting in favour of a Protestant reading of the *Devotions* is the complete absence of the Virgin Mary: a spectacular absence, one might observe, in view of the role assigned to her in "Good-friday, 1613. Riding Westward."

But of the polemical markings of Donne's prose text as Protestant, there is not a trace. Instead, he announces his intention to seek the word of God "not from *corners*, nor *Conventicles*, nor *schismatical singularities*, but from the association, & communion of thy *Catholique Church*, and those persons, whom thou hast always furnished that *Church* withal" (39). Donne's readers will of course know that by "*Catholique*" he means "universal"; or will they? Will they perhaps be aware of his unwillingness to distance himself from the religion of his childhood, just at the point where you might expect him to?

I will suspend this question without a direct answer in order to add the further thought that many sensitive readers of Donne's *Devotions* have found in this text a spiritual quality in tune with Roman Catholic teaching, and influenced (either positively or negatively or both) by the *Spiritual Exercises of Ignatius of Loyola*. Some years ago, Anthony Raspa measured this relationship by observing, in the excellent introduction to his edition of the *Devotions*, that Donne's creative choices resulted in "a literary form that had an aesthetic effect on the reader akin to the ascetic experience of Ignatius" (xxxix).

The tension between overt Protestantism and residual Catholicism is observable even in the most famous passage of this text, which I am about to quote. This of course is the description of the passing bell, rung out as a signal that someone in the parish was in danger of imminent death.

> The *Bell* doth toll for him that *thinkes* it doth; and though it *intermit* againe, yet from that *minute*, that that occasion wrought upon him, hee is united to *God*. Who casts not up his *Eie* to the *Sunne* when it rises? but who takes off his *Eie* from a *Comet*, when that breakes out? who bends not his *eare* to any *bell*, which upon any occasion rings? but who can remove it from that *bell*, which is passing a *peece of himselfe* out of this *world*? No Man is an *Iland*, intire of it selfe; every man is a peece of the *Continent*, a part of the *maine*; if a *Clod* bee washed away by the *Sea*, *Europe* is the lesse, as well as if a *Promontorie* were, as well as if a *Mannor* of thy *friends*, or of *thine owne* were; Any Mans *death* diminishes *me*, because I am involved in *Mankinde*; And therefore never send to know for whom the *bell* tolls; It tolls for *thee*. (86–7)

There can be no doubt about the brilliance of this, or about the sincerity that allows Donne, whatever his personal fears, to draw us into kinship with all humankind. He prefaces this passage by observing, yet again, that "The *Church* is *Catholique, universall*, so are all her *Actions; All* that she does, belongs to *all*" (86). Again, this is Donne at his most generous, most open-hearted. His *Catholique* church may well be the one he describes, but the Roman Catholic Church would have employed a different set of rules. In Catholic Europe, a bell was indeed rung at the death of a parishioner. Friends and family would then send to know for whom it was done. Only after they had ascertained that, yes, their loved one had died – only then could they begin the long and expensive investment in praying for the soul of the departed one. This practice is not mentioned by Donne in the three devotions in which he deals with the tolling of bells, but I think it is present, perhaps not to Donne's eye (or, in this instance, his ear), but nevertheless to his memory.

"She whom I loved"

Donne's holy sonnets might be expected to yield opportunities to observe him profoundly moved by the presence of God. But even here we should be careful: some of the sonnets are holier than others.

The one I am about to turn to, "Holy Sonnet 17," may not be the holiest of them, but it is one of the most intimate, both by virtue of its subject matter and as marked by its limited circulation. This poem did not appear in the first edition of Donne's *Poems* (1633), nor in any other early edition; it was not included in the manuscript sources in which his divine poems circulated, except for one: the Westmoreland MS, copied in the hand of Donne's friend Rowland Woodward and held in the Berg Collection of the New York Public Library. This manuscript was purchased by Sir Edmund Gosse in 1892, who then printed the poem in his *Life and Letters of John Donne* (1899).[27] The poem cannot have been written earlier than 15 August 1617, the date on which Ann More died, age thirty-three, after more than fifteen years of marriage to Donne, having borne twelve children including a stillborn daughter delivered shortly before her death.

Holy Sonnet 17

Since she whom I loved hath paid her last debt
To nature, and to hers, and my good is dead,
And her soul early into heaven ravished,
Wholly in heavenly things my mind is set.
Here the admiring her my mind did whet
To seek thee God; so streams do show the head,
But though I have found thee, and thou my thirst hast fed,
A holy thirsty dropsy melts me yet.
But why should I beg more love, when as thou
Dost woo my soul, for hers offering all thine:
And dost not only fear lest I allow
My love to saints and angels, things divine,
But in thy tender jealousy dost doubt
Lest the world, flesh, yea Devil put thee out. (270)

The attributes of God in this poem are quite remarkable. He experiences fear, jealousy, and doubt. In part these are attributes that could be supported by biblical citation: "for I the Lord thy God am a jealous God" (Exod. 20:5). And in part they may be the inevitable result of an anthropomorphic approach to deity. When man makes God in his own image, God is bound to exhibit some of man's idiosyncratic vulnerabilities.

But I think something more interesting is going on in the poem. The speaker wants to reassure God. Since "she" has died, "Wholly in heavenly things my mind is set." I find it difficult to believe this claim, and I suspect that God did too. After all, what sense are we to make of the line, "A holy thirsty dropsy melts me yet"? We could begin by reading John Carey's gloss on "dropsy": "an immoderate desire for more." At this point the desire to capitalize the word "more" becomes almost irresistible, especially when the word is insisted upon in the very next line.

What I am trying to show, of course, is that this poem, like so many sonnets before it, sets up a love triangle. God appears to have won Ann More's soul from the outset; she's been "ravished" away from Donne and "into heaven." But a negotiation of some sort appears to be underway. God is wooing Donne's soul, apparently offering all of his love as a replacement "for hers." This is a God who seems eager to claim Donne, and to ensure that he is not supplanted by his traditional enemies: the world, the flesh, and the Devil.

Still, what does all this have to do with the tension between Protestant and Catholic allegiances? Rather more than might be apparent at first blush. God in this poem doesn't seem to align perfectly with the image of deity that Donne offers from the pulpit to his congregation at St Paul's, and certainly not with the stern paternal eminence of much Protestant rhetoric. He seems much more tolerantly interested in human weakness than the God of the Protestants, and hence more open to negotiation as well. He seems to enjoy working with a woman, especially if she can act as an intermediary, so as to ensure the eventual allegiance of an insecure follower. And the follower in this case implies that he may have given "love to saints and angels, things divine"; to me this phrase sounds like a memory of Donne's Catholic past. Not that the Church of England renounces saints and angels, but I think the opportunity to "love" them as "things divine" would have been more openly available in the religious culture of Donne's Catholic boyhood.

So we have a pattern that emerges from the texts under close and particular scrutiny. Overt allegiance to Protestant conventions and expectations, in all cases, comes into conflict with a memory (explicit or implicit) of a religious culture that Donne learned first as the faith of his family. This is not an inflexible template but a pattern that allows for some variation from one text to another. Indeed, I would say that it allows for dissonance: for what Donne himself described as the coin "that looks awry and squint" when the original impression is corrected. Perhaps it would be fair to say that, even in his religious utterances, Donne exhibits what Samuel Johnson found to be characteristic of metaphysical wit: "a combination of dissimilar images, or discovery of occult resemblances in things apparently unlike." Or again, "The most heterogeneous ideas are yoked by violence together."[28] What has long seemed characteristic of Donne's verbal style may well have been true of his spiritual life as well.

Conclusion

The question of spectatorship in Donne's poetry has been foregrounded by previous readers, but always in relation to his erotic verse. William Shullenberger pointed out a generation ago that many of Donne's most famous love poems, including those that claim to celebrate intimacy between the lovers, depend for much of their rhetorical effect on an imagined third person: the intruder in "The Canonization," the sexton in "The Relic," the jilted lover himself in "The Apparition," the personified figure of the Sun in "The Sun Rising," and even the apparently neutral observer in "The Ecstasy." This is not the place to outline the ingenuity of Shullenberger's arguments concerning spectatorship as a means for suggesting privacy, as a strategy for confuting paternalism, and as a rhetorical device for bringing the reader into the poem.[29] The point is rather that, in thinking about spectatorship in Donne's religious writing, I have had Shullenberger's treatment of the erotic verse in mind as a precedent. Looking at John Donne looking at God has not been the same as looking at Jack Donne looking at a woman he loves, but there are similarities nonetheless.

In both instances, I would argue, memory is required to take on a powerful role in valorizing the images that we see. And the authority given to what we see, in both erotic and religious writing, is a mark of the degree to which Donne is indelibly linked to his heritage.

The tension between official Reformation doctrine and residual Catholic yearning need not have been, in all cases, as occult as I have made it out to be. If the texts I've selected here for the access they give us to Donne's inner life are compared with some of his public pronouncements, the differences will be far more striking than subtle. Take for example this excerpt from a sermon Donne preached at Paul's Cross, 24 March 1616/17: "I know the Fathers are frequent in comparing and paralleling *Eve*, the Mother of Man, and *Mary* the Mother of God … But … The Virgin *Mary* had not the same interest in our salvation, as *Eve* had in our destruction; nothing that she did entred into that treasure, that ransom that redeemed us."[30] One way of situating what Donne is up to here would be to cite the material circumstances in which he was obliged to work. Here we are given real assistance by John Gipkyn (fl. 1594–1629), whose rendering of Old St Paul's (fig. 7.4) helps us to imagine what a Paul's Cross sermon would have felt like in 1617. The open-air pulpit stands near the front left-hand corner; from it, the preacher would be addressing members of the public stationed in the yard, but also civic dignitaries, nobility, and perhaps royalty seated in the galleries above the standing-room spectators.[31] It's clear that, under the circumstances depicted here, no preacher is offering simply his own opinion on a theological text, question, or controversy. As to the part played in our redemption by the Virgin Mary, has Donne changed his mind so radically since Good Friday 1613, just four years earlier? Or has he recognized that, as a priest in the Church of England, preaching in a conspicuous public location, he must be careful to stay on message?

Still, I would like to give the last word not to the Dr Donne who knows he must conform to the doctrine of his Church and the wishes of his King, but to John Donne the devoted son of a mother who remained a lifelong Catholic, through three marriages and years of living abroad. On the occasion of the death of his sister Anne, perhaps in 1616, Donne sent his mother a letter of condolence. The tribulations of her life, Donne tells her, are God's way of ensuring that she will have no leisure to stray while

Fig. 7.4 Old St Paul's, by John Gipkyn (fl. 1594–1629).

he guides her to her destination, "which is his glorious Kingdom." His mother's status as a lifelong Catholic has no bearing on Donne's assessment of where she's going, nor for that matter on how she ought to get there: "As long as the Spirit of God distills and dews his cheerfulnesse upon your heart, as long as he instructs your understanding, to interpret his mercies and his judgments aright; so long your comfort must needs be as much greater than others, as your afflictions are greater than theirs."[32] In the same letter Donne offers his mother material reassurance, by telling her that there will always be room in his household for her, should she require it. And indeed, she lived the last years of her life, after the death of her third husband, with Donne at the deanery. Faced with a choice between a narrow, sectarian commitment to the Church of England and the more liberal conviction that salvation is available through many Christian churches, Donne chose the latter. It was not an easy choice, and we can admire him for having the courage to make it when and how he did.

NOTES

1 See Hoak, "Edward VI (1537–1553)," *Oxford Dictionary of National Biography*, online.

2 Foxe, *Acts and Monuments*, 6:5, 7.

3 Duffy, *The Stripping of the Altars*, 462.

4 Donne, *Pseudo-Martyr*, ed. Anthony Raspa, 8.

5 Donne, *Donne: The Major Works*, 197. Unless otherwise noted, Donne citations are from this volume, and will be identified by page numbers in parentheses only or, in the case of longer poems, line numbers within parentheses.

6 See, respectively, Carey, *John Donne*; Flynn, *John Donne*; and Stubbs, *Donne: The Reformed Soul.*

7 See, respectively, Kneidel, "Donne's 'Via Pauli,'" 224–46; Stevens, "Donne's Catholicism," 53–70; and Erne, "Donne and Christ's Spouse," 208–29.

8 See Shami, "'Trying to Walk on Logs in Water,'" 92.

9 See Shami, "Labels, Controversy, and the Language of Inclusion," 135–57.

10 See Shami, *John Donne and Conformity*, 19–24.

11 See Huebert, "'Study our Manuscripts': John Donne's Problems with Privacy," 1–22.

12 Dickson, "The Text of Donne's Good Friday Meditation," 87–106. The full text appears on pages 104–5, under the title "Good Fryday / Made as I was riding Westward that daie," and it is the source for the quoted excerpts that follow. Subsequent references will include line numbers in parentheses.

13 Stubbs, *Donne: The Reformed Soul*, 286.

14 Though John Baxter does come close when he writes, "The description of Mary as 'God's partner,' who furnishes 'half' of the sacrifice, gives to Mary the sort of prominence that she holds among Catholics, a reminder that Donne was himself born into a Catholic household." See "Perilous Stuff," 99.

15 See Bald, *Donne and the Drurys*, 85–103.

16 See Bald, *John Donne: A Life*, 302–19.

17 Johnson, "Gold in the Washes," 199–207.

18 For a succinct and informative account of the diplomatic issues facing the English delegation, and of the events that led up to them, see "The Torn Ship," chap. 17 of Stubbs, *Donne: The Reformed Soul*, 332–51.

19 Donne, "A Sermon of Valediction at my going into Germany, at Lincolns-Inne, April 18. 1619," in *The Sermons of John Donne*, 2:235. Subsequent references are to this edition.

20 A fairly rich archive of scholarship has grown up around the question of Donne's theological position here, especially as it responds to St Augustine's figuration of memory as a third part of the rational soul, and thus parallel to the Holy Ghost, the third member of the Holy Trinity. See, for example, Friedman, "Memory and the Art of Salvation," 418–42; Guibbory, "John Donne and Memory as 'the Art of Salvation,'" 261–74; and Andrew Hiscock's chapter on Donne, "'Tell me where all past yeares are': John Donne and the obligations of memory," in *Reading Memory*, 165–91. None of these studies draws any connection between memory and Donne's early Roman Catholicism.

21 Evans, "'The church is his Eccho,'" 3.

22 Donne, *Sermons*, 6:223.

23 Ibid., 7:401.

24 Gosse, *The Life and Letters of John Donne*, 2:121.

25 See Zaller, "Martin, Richard (1570–1618)," *Oxford Dictionary of National Biography*, online.

26 The original title page is reproduced in Donne, *Devotions Upon Emergent Occasions*, 1. All subsequent references to the *Devotions* are from this edition.

27 Gosse, *Life and Letters of John Donne*, 2:370–1.

28 See the "Life of Cowley" in Johnson's *Lives of the English Poets*, 1:20.

29 See Shullenberger, "Love as a Spectator Sport," 46–62.

30 Donne, *Sermons*, 1:200.

31 See Cook, *Old St. Paul's Cathedral*, 70.

32 Donne, *Selected Prose*, 149.

8

Sidney Visualized: Thomas Lant's *Sequitur celebritas* (1588) and the Funeral Construction of an English National Hero

RICK BOWERS

This essay concerns the remarkable graphic publication that accompanied the funeral of Sir Philip Sidney and, through its complicated effects of spectatorship, continues to construct the consciousness of Sidney as national hero. The book published by Thomas Lant and Theodor De Bry titled *Sequitur celebritas et pompa funeris* (1588) contains thirty separate plates easily broken up and joined sequentially to illustrate the entire funeral procession. Indeed, a hundred years after Sidney's death, John Aubrey would still remember – as a boy of nine in 1635 – seeing Lant's book in precisely this state on the walls of an alderman's house in Gloucester, and describe it with some wonderment as follows: "engraved and printed on papers pasted together, which at length was, I beleeve, the length of the room at least; but he had contrived it to be turned upon two Pinnes, that turning one of them made the figures march all in order. It did make such a strong impression on my tender Phantasy that I remember it as if it were yesterday."[1]

Today, we have the technology to reproduce these wondrous effects in digital form. A multimedia electronic edition of Lant's plates, titled "The Funerary Procession of Sir Philip Sidney: An Early Modern Multimedia Site and Pedagogical Venture," is readily accessible at www.michaelharrison.ws/sidney/. This file features a continuously looping five-and-a-half-minute flash presentation of Lant's plates scrolling right-to-left across the screen with the accompanying music of William Byrd, written for the occasion of the procession.[2] This updated audiovisual format still depends on the original pages of Lant's printed book, and yet this twenty-first-century multimedia presentation might also be said to actualize what an early modern display (as witnessed by Aubrey in 1635) sought to literalize: the strong impression of an unprecedented visual and metaphorical funeral display, expressing – even as it constructs – a new form of public national heroism.

That unnamed alderman whose display so impressed a young John Aubrey in 1635 effectively created and enacted an imagined spectatorship in the boy that created meanings along the lines of history, patriotism, and esteem. Aubrey in turn transported that "strong impression" through time to his reporting of the experience sometime in the final decade of the seventeenth century, a report at last collected and first published at the end of the nineteenth. Such a widely extended awareness enacts a form of "extended mind," a visualized cognitive ecology described recently within Shakespeare studies as "the multidimensional contexts in which we remember, feel, think, sense, communicate, imagine, and act, often collaboratively, on the fly, and in rich ongoing interaction with our environments."[3] In effect, we share spectator consciousness across time with Aubrey and that alderman, as well as with everyone else at the actual funeral – those identified and also the greater, overwhelming, unrepresented number of those who cannot be identified – in addition to all those who have since viewed Lant's document after its publication within an imagined community of spectators impossible finally to enumerate.

A Hero's Funeral

Recent work on Sidney, even Richard Hillyer's *Sir Philip Sidney, Cultural Icon*, focuses strictly on literary-historical evidence and makes only minor reference to Lant's book.[4] Alan Stewart's critical biography *Philip Sidney: A Double Life* begins suggestively with Lant's text but relates the funeral simply in retrospective terms as "the last master-stroke of a major propaganda exercise."[5] In 1980, editors Godshalk and Colaianne produced a facsimile edition of Lant's work in the Scholars' Facsimile Reprint series with the following standard memorial observation: "The grandeur of the ceremony and the number of participants depicted are important indicators of England's sense of loss."[6] A more recent annotated edition by Elizabeth Goldring in 2014 handsomely reproduces each plate of British Library copy C.20.f.12 to localize the funeral with political immediacy: "The public mourning for Sidney almost certainly was manipulated and inflated for political ends by both his uncle, the Earl of Leicester, and his father-in-law, Sir Francis Walsingham."[7] No doubt. But the mourning for Sidney, already months after the fact of his passing, was generating more complicated social effects on the people of England. I argue that something more powerful, something beyond immediate political strategy, unprecedented and ongoing, manifests itself in Sidney's funeral through considerations of what might be termed cognitive spectatorship across time.

The evolution of this material "thing" – this illustrated text depicting Sidney's funeral –from printed text in 1588, to moving pictures in 1635, to digital forms in 2015, while it does not include the live viewing of actual spectators, involves three layers of spectatorship: the book format, including Lant's contemporary document as well as the modern editions mentioned above and their readership; that unnamed alderman's installation, including the young John Aubrey and other contemporary viewers; the digital website multimedia and other digital forms, including images at Early English Books Online – all of which include possible digital counting through page-hits and recorded website visits. Collectively such formats register an imperfect record of viewership, but the impression reiterated throughout and across time suggests enormous numbers of spectators. Indeed such evolution of materials – from printed paper, to reassembly of pages, to virtual pages and even digital sound – also effectively parallels the expanded nature of spectatorship itself at the actual funeral, and the sharing of meanings through time by altruistically patriotic English men and women.

I analyze Lant's document in terms of spectator consciousness across time and go beyond standard memorial observations of loss to describe Sidney's funeral in relation to its sense of extended cognitive *gain*. Doing so will involve consideration of the following questions: What visual signals concerning military significance, mourning, celebration, heraldry, fame, and meaning were being realized here? Why were they so long-lasting? How do they relate to the construction of Sidney's image as Protestant hero? I read the signals of Lant's little-considered publication to argue for the creation of a new military and political and decidedly *public* English national heroism – one that emits unifying meanings in excess of local understanding and immediate perceptions. Such signals go beyond mourning. They engage within even as they exceed the speculative descriptions of "literary mourning" contained in Gavin Alexander's *Writing After Sidney*: "Whether it was an orchestrated effort or a spontaneous show of grief, the scale of the literary mourning of Sidney is staggering."[8] Preceding all such retrospection, however, the immediate signals within Lant's graphic document – readily accessible to all – actively create a complex and unprecedented visualization within early modern English culture.

Such visualization cannot easily be summarized. Historian David Cressy rightly argues that elaborate contemporary funeral rituals in England "survived the Reformation, not because they found justification in Protestant theology but because they served deep-rooted social and familial needs."[9] I fully agree, but in the case of Sidney's funeral I am arguing for a cognitive relation to shared spectatorship across time, one that involves a future-oriented national need exceeding its own significance in the very moment of its realization. In "The Mourning for Sidney," John Buxton provides the standard literary-historical judgment: "He seemed to his contemporaries to exhibit to perfection those qualities which went to make up the ideal courtier of Castiglione's description, which they wished to emulate."[10] Yes, he formed a pattern for elite courtiers. But he also appealed to a much wider public within and beyond the collective visualization of Lant's text – public, unlettered, English – relating to "forms of nationhood" and "imagined community," as argued by later critics such as Richard Helgerson and Benedict Anderson. In my reading, the funeral of Sir Philip Sidney – calculated to live on long after the actual event – marked the birth of his public availability as English national hero and ratified an equally public availability of English national consciousness. Reflective spectatorship on a massive scale endows Sidney's death with profound public meaning. Moreover, this form of meaning manifests itself as a deeply implicit mutual regard of consciousness through time, effectively forming a national consciousness that operates both as consolation and as identification.[11]

Sidney's Imagined Communities

In his important study of nationalism titled *Imagined Communities*, Benedict Anderson issues the following reminder:

> In an age when it is so common for progressive, cosmopolitan intellectuals (particularly in Europe?) to insist on the near-pathological character of nationalism, its roots in fear and hatred of the Other, it is useful to remind ourselves that nations inspire love, and often profoundly self-sacrificing love. The cultural products of nationalism – poetry, prose fiction, music, plastic arts – show this love very clearly in thousands of different forms and styles.[12]

It is therefore worth remembering that Fulke Greville, Sidney's well-known first biographer, asserts at the very beginning of his memorial that he "loved him." Greville famously recounts Sidney's decision to "cast off his cuisses; and so, by the secret influence of destinie, to disarm that part, where God – it seems – had resolved to strike him."[13] As well, he originates the oft-reported battlefield episode of Sidney, fatefully wounded, suppressing his own thirst and passing his water bottle to an equally wounded private soldier with the immortal words, "Thy necessity is yet greater than mine."[14] Easily dismissed for its obvious and overstated sentimentality, this famous story also creates a deeply altruistic image – one of self-sacrificing love in relation to an unknown, unnamed, invisible but profoundly affiliated other.

Less emphasis is placed on another key point of Greville's document: misplaced but active publicity in relation to a lovable public image somewhat out of public control. On day sixteen of Sidney's improving recovery, Greville reports, "The joy of their hearts over-flowed their dis-creation, and made them spread the intelligence of it to the Queen and all his noble friends here in England, where it was received, not as private, but as publique good news."[15] Unfortunately, the news of his recovery was greatly exaggerated. After confirmation of Sidney's death, Greville reports that the States of Zealand made application to the Queen and her Privy Council to bury Sidney at their own public expense. But no. Sidney would be interred in London at the centre of English national life. His funeral procession would be outdoors and on the street, and everyone would be allowed to attend. It would be a huge public event, regulated only by the route of the official procession (see fig. 8.1) and by the selective reporting of Lant's description. Moreover, this massive funeral would effectively bankrupt Sidney's father-in-law, thereby broadcasting its valuable public significance even as it bankrolled a priceless future of imagined national consciousness.

In *Crowds and Popular Politics in Early Modern England* (2006), John Walter declares: "Crowd actions can best be understood as claims to exercise political agency in the context of a popular political culture that was drawn from a dialogue with the discourses of state, Church and commonwealth."[16] Sidney's funeral certainly exercised political agency within state, Church, and Commonwealth, as well as within a new national sense of mourning and pride. Walter's analysis of crowds, however, focuses on protest as his main topical category, so that the early modern crowd is considered almost exclusively in terms of class warfare and resistance in the historical process of urbanizing and developing itself as the "mob" of oppositional social, political, and economic force. Likewise, in an article focused on Sidney's funeral, Ronald Strickland settles for literalized observation of the reinforcement and production of "modes of subjectivity appropriate to the feudal and proto-capitalist social orders of Renaissance England."[17] But I am arguing at once for a wider purview – involving connection with an imagined community outside of local titled lords and wealthy families and systems of trade and exchange – as well as for a focused sense of the unnumbered spectators at the funeral of a specific English noble, in order to reach for connection with a new national consciousness ratified by the sacrifice of a distinct national hero. This imagined community admits of diversity in church, class, and national consciousness in 1588, in Aubrey's time a half century later, and within subsequent generations of readers in an extended consciousness through time. Those crowds on the street at the funeral for Sidney become sharers, spectators at once admittedly compliant but also self-regulating and participatory, through their perceived togetherness as mourners mobilizing a new national and future-oriented English imagined consciousness.

In discussing such a crucially public and progressively national consciousness, Anderson characteristically italicizes the adjective *imagined* because, as he points out, "the members of even the smallest nations will never know most of their fellow-members, meet them, or even hear of them, yet in the minds of each lives the image of their communion."[18] For excommunicated England, adrift on an island of Protestant, Elizabethan political and national reform, Thomas Lant's series of representations of Sidney's funeral provides the first visual guide to just such a communion. Herein Sidney appeals to a national English imagination as a hero around whom the truths of a national consciousness cohere, a hero who moves through and within a public and mutually realized sociological landscape of distributed cognition that stretches over centuries.

This late-Elizabethan communion expresses itself as opposed to previously public cultural systems related to religious commonalty and dynastic certainty. What is publicly crucial here involves interpretation, a perceived mutuality of meanings related to shared and proliferating texts. Such texts are heraldic, civic, institutional, social, and military. They exist in numerous copies. Consequently, passé Latin text manifests itself less as powerfully authoritative and more as merely indicative. Within Lant's book, every instance of Latin is immediately translated into English. Hence the phrase "*Sequitur celebritas et pompa funeris*" forms merely the opening clause of a lengthy description beginning "Here followeth the manner of the whole proceeding of his funeral."[19] Power here – "the whole proceeding" – involves new alliances and new perspectives regarding English, European, and Dutch Protestantism combined with the objective truth-language of architecture involving the destination of St Paul's Cathedral along an undefined London streetscape. Curiously, but also purposefully, that London streetscape of Lant's text is sanitized, even whited out, on an unpopulated low horizon. It presents and identifies each sequential aspect of the funeral parade – representative "poor men," officers, troops, mourners, and others of the official cortège, as well as freemen from a number of London guilds – scrupulously eliding any crowds or external onlookers or even recognizable features of London along the parade route from the armoured Minories outside Aldgate in east London all the way to St Paul's Cathedral. Such features, common to more usual celebratory texts, would only be a distraction here. (See fig. 8.1 for the route of the procession.)

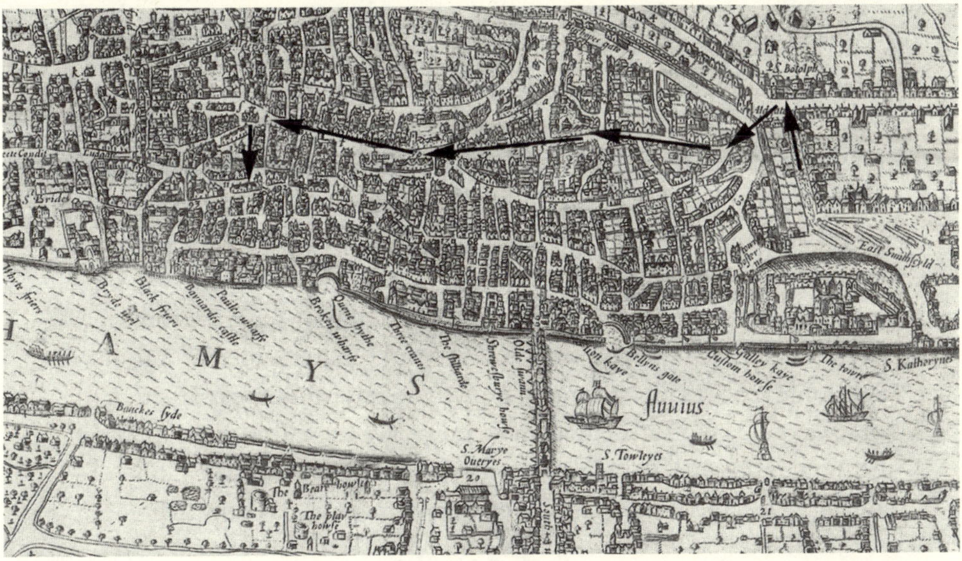

Fig. 8.1 John Norden, *Map of London* (1593), showing Sidney's funeral procession route.

This graphic sparseness exists as a form of "perspective," a way of relating subjects and objects and calculating the nature of their mutual engagement along the lines argued by Erwin Panofsky in his classic study of Renaissance optics *Perspective as Symbolic Form*. Through realist perspective, Panofsky observes, "the claim of the object (to use a modern term) confronts the ambition of the subject."[20] The objective visualization of Sidney's funeral – always already in multiple copies and now virtually unlimited in access through digital form – provides an unlimited horizon in space and time for subsequent readers and observers. The actual spectators of the funeral parade of 1587 merge into the reported communion of Lant's text and on into the transcendent allegiance of shared patriotic Englishness. With each step of this distributed cognitive parade through time, spectators and participants become more abstract, more removed, but also paradoxically more numerous and more powerful within the unrepresentable diversity of this imagined community.

Then, as now – perhaps even more so now through digital presentation – the reader-as-spectator experiences what Anderson calls a "unisonance." Opposed to "dissonance," such unity creates a specific effect, a powerful self-replicating connection through time. Some years ago Elizabeth Eisenstein shrewdly observed a characteristic of all printed materials, that they "address an invisible public from afar."[21] Such is the figurative effect of literary texts. But by reproducing the visual actuality, the "thing-ness" of Sidney's funeral, Lant's graphic text addresses an invisible public in terms of a literalized *felt* experience. We unify in the *now* as observers of Sidney's funeral rites and representations, extending beyond the moment of their actual realization on 16 February 1587. We who perceive Lant's text in the *now* feel a participation with those actual perceivers from *then*. Those thousands of people on the street at the actual funeral – variously emotional, chaotically bounded only by space, and unrestrained, even somewhat dangerously democratic – no longer exist. It is *we* who exist in the moment of our ambitiously collective, simultaneous perception of – and unprecedented but equally novel involvement in – a national heroism.

A New National Protocol

The very first page of Lant's document depicts the notorious *Black Pinnace* – the "ship of death" that carried Sidney's body over the North Sea from Flushing, in the Netherlands, to London. The "view" of Lant's readers already exceeds that of those thousands of mourners attending Sidney's actual funeral, and includes biographical details of his wounding, subsequent death, and mournful transportation back to England. Plate 2 begins with the funeral's end, picturing the realistic interior of St Paul's Cathedral with a ceremonial bier centrally placed to receive Sidney's coffin. From here the document depicts the parade as it passes right-to-left, east-to west into the image, across the next twenty-eight pages of plates. Significantly, the parade begins with two conductors of the poor and thirty-two poor men, each representing a year of Sidney's thirty-two years of life. This important semiology relates to humility and limitation, but also to generosity of human representation. What follows is overwhelming in terms of sheer numbers, heraldic colour and symbolism, military trappings, musical participation; it includes aristocratic mourners mounted, afoot, and carrying the coffin – itself at the centre of the document draped with heraldic significance – all the official heralds of England, a delegation from Holland, the Lord Mayor of London, aldermen and sheriffs of the City, the Company of Grocers, "of which he was free," and the London civic guard fully armed marching three by three to the number of some three hundred men "who so soone as hee was interred honored the obsequy with a double volley."[22]

Clearly, this is not the funeral of a mere knight, or even a pure and successful one in shining armour. Previous commentators, such as Sander Bos et al. in "Sidney's Funeral Portrayed," take pains to count up and identify the seven primary mourners, which would have been customary for a baron's funeral, as opposed to the usual five for a knight.[23] More recently, in "Sir Philip Sidney and the Politics of Elizabethan Festival," Elizabeth Goldring declares with confidence that Sidney's funeral "was essentially a royal one in all but name."[24] But beyond the baronial technicality of Bos et al. and the overstated estimation of Goldring, Sidney's funeral surpassed even royalty in its complexity and cost. Its value is impossible to quantify. It represented a massive breach of protocol – but it clearly did so for the purposes of a new *national* protocol.

Public protocol is usually reassuring and conservative, accenting Goldring's insightfully factual observation that "deviations from established protocol for the funeral of a knight must ultimately have been approved by the College of Arms," and further that "the heralds of the College would not have dared to give their assent unless the queen herself had agreed to the ceremony."[25] In this regard, Queen Elizabeth I had clearly agreed – but agreed to a heightened ceremony already out of her control. Through a sense of shared public mourning, Sidney's funeral was not aimed at enforcing the hierarchical dissymmetries of power, control, and protocols of public order central to Elizabethan royal processions, as argued most recently by William Leahy.[26] Instead, Sidney's funeral display appealed to a sense of felt unity in the spectators themselves – not from the top down but from the side of the street, which represents the dominant perspective of Lant's illustrated text. Such perspective momentarily captures a new, loosely connected, and heightened public consciousness in the process of its own making. Graspable in the moment, Sidney's funeral communicates even as it enacts a paradoxical "life of its own" – in the moment of its own realization on the streets in 1587 and within consciousness through time.

In fact, the only previous examples of a publicized funeral-pictorial work such as Lant's include those for the funeral ceremonies of King

Ferdinand of Aragon at Brussels in 1519, the funeral of Charles V, again at Brussels, in 1558, and the funeral of Prince William of Orange at Delft in 1584. These are all royal and Continental and materially commemorative funerals. Sidney's stands alone as English and non-regal and constructed beyond the mere necessities of commemoration. Indeed it stands without an actual tomb ever having been constructed. The funeral itself and its published depiction in Lant's document stand in as Sidney's only material monument. As Nigel Llewellyn observes, "Such was its success and so powerful were the images produced by [Lant and] De Bry that a permanent monumental body in the form of a sculpted tomb was never erected."[27] There are times when powerful images of spirit cannot be contained materially. Sidney's funeral *was* his monument, ratified through an unusual recorded experience of mass spectatorship.

The final plate of Lant's document provides numbers and commentary already experienced in graphic form throughout the previous twenty-nine plates.

> He was carried from the Minories (which is without Aldgate) along the cheefe streets of the Cytye unto the Cathedrall church of St Paules the which streets all along were so thronged with people that the mourners had scarcely rome to pass. The houses likewise were as full as they might be of which great multitude there were few or none that shed not some tears as the corps passed by them. Of the mourners every Gentleman had a man, every knight 2, some Noblemen 12, some more, some less as also sundry English Captaynes of the low Countrie with divers other Gentlemen that came voluntary and are not in this woorke expressed, so that the whole number were about 700 persons.[28]

It is important to remember that these numbers relate only to the official procession, and that they emphasize excess in every case. Indeed, the document suggests excessiveness throughout in terms of its collective felt effect of stretched experience of feeling, of importance, of grandeur, of people (regulated and unregulated), and of generally incalculable and all-encompassing totality.

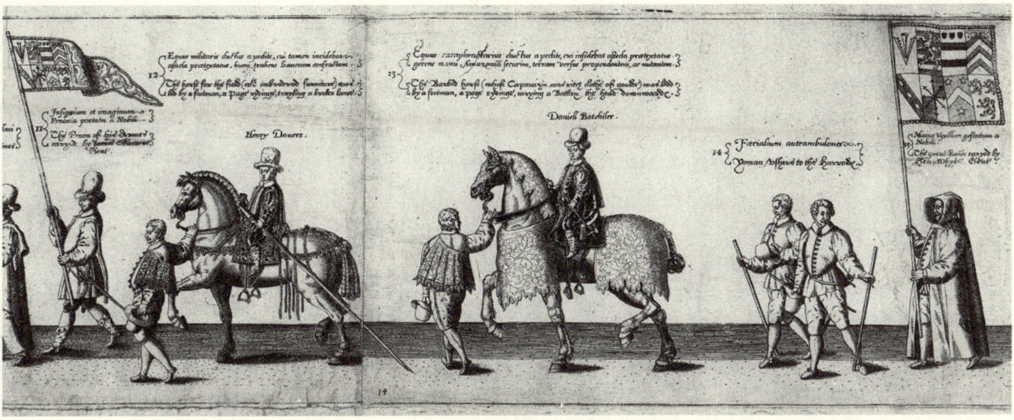

Fig. 8.2 "Earles and Barons of his kindred and frendes," from Thomas Lant, *Sequitur celebritas et pompa funeris* (1588), Plate 18.

A Lasting Spectacle

Could all of this have been an attempt to distract the English public from the execution of Mary Queen of Scots a few days earlier, or to intensify (or better yet, suppress) the anti-Catholic fervour that resulted? Either way, the reign of Elizabeth I (and by extension all Elizabethans) benefits most materially from this heraldic funeral display so richly invested with meanings beyond itself. As Llewellyn also observes, "For some years after Sidney's death his horse was presented to her [Elizabeth] at the start of the annual Accession Day tilt, in an act of official mourning and an extension of the death ritual."[29] Further, the Earl of Essex not only married Sidney's widow but also attended the 1590 Accession Day tilt dressed entirely in black in memory of his dead friend. Such gestures clarify and powerfully reinforce Sidney in experiential terms as the dead but ever-loving friend.

Significantly, Sidney's friendship also contains a demonstrably physical power and responsibility to protect. That horse of Sidney's just mentioned features in the document (fig. 8.2) as follows: "The Horse for the field … led by a footman, a page ryding, trailing a broken lance." Sidney – he who was now broken himself physically forever – was of course a star performer at the tilts and had broken many a lance. But the next image in the sequence features another horse, "The Barbed horse (whose Caparison was with Cloth of Gold) was led by a footman, a page ryding carrying a

Battle axe, the head downward."[30] The mock battles and the real battles are over. We, the beneficiaries, find ourselves at the very centre of the funeral at this point, and Sidney's two powerful war horses precede "The Great Banner," the presence of which was normally reserved for the funeral of a baron and all ranks upward. However, as is clear throughout both on the page and within public consciousness, Sidney's funeral is *not* a normal funeral.

As if to ratify the stratospheric social mobility of this funeral, *all* of the chief heralds of England follow, "carrying the Hatchment and Dignitye of his Knighthoode."[31] Visually central and meaningful to these proceedings, the six heralds are hooded, gravely dignified in procession, and carry aloft the significant equipment of Sidney's complex knighthood. They include:

> William Seagar, alias Porticullis, who carries his spurs.
> Humphrey Hales, alias Blewmantle, with the armoured gauntlets.
> Nicholas Paddy, alias Rouge Dragon, carrying the helmet.
> Richard Lea, alias Richmond, carrying his sword and shield.
> Robert Glover, Somerset, who holds Sidney's (literal) coat of arms.
> And finally Robert Cooke, Clarencieux King of Armes, marshal of the entire event.

These material objects of Sidney's armour feature ceremonially. As signifiers of rank and dignity, they are intended to adorn the funeral monument, which, in Sidney's case, will never be built. But they also feature as stylized body parts, disassembled by the heralds within their esoteric rites, and reassembled in the collective imagination of all who find themselves allied with Sidney and his English causes. Make no mistake, this funeral represents a significant national assembly – both sequentially and imaginatively – as a new national communion.

And the accompanying music? Plate 4 depicts and identifies "ffyffs and drommes playing softely." Neither celebratory nor mourning, these instruments are subdued, "softely" pitched at keeping time while drawing attention to the spectacle and drumming significant realizations within the consciousness of a receptive public. One of the drummers catches our eye and makes a momentary connection, as do one or two of Sidney's "kindred and frendes" marching across Plates 9, 10, and 11. Fifes and drums appear again at the end of the procession to reinforce and maintain funereal tempo to the end. Somewhat surprisingly, Plate 5 includes four trumpeters carrying their instruments upside down. With bells up and mouthpieces pointed to the ground, no brassy clarion call will stir the emotions here. Insisting on class significance, Goldring observes that trumpets were more usually restricted to royal funerals.[32] Their presence here however, ceremonial and without fanfare, again signals significance and restraint. Beyond the usual protocols for a knight, they suggest new protocols for a nation. This funeral does not signal emotional assertions of grief elevating themselves into sectarian ideals. There is no cry for recompense, no rationalization for loss. *Pace* Goldring and others: bellicose national Protestantism and the fight against popery in general hardly assert themselves here. Rather, a new consciousness is gained: a deeper positive national consciousness, rising above sectarian strife in a mutual understanding of community and purpose – a purpose "softely" drumming the presence of a powerful absence into the consciousness of those in attendance and those of us beholding the document after the fact, a national English consciousness felt and claimed almost by default in relation to ourselves and to each other.

Sidney's coffin forms the powerfully visual centrepiece of the funeral even as it forms the centre of Lant's document at Plate 16 (fig. 8.3). It is draped in layers of velvet armorial splendor. The smudged ink of this plate testifies materially to over four hundred years of human fingers actually touching the document at this point, literally connecting to it and pointedly defining its significance. This connection, noticeable on the photographed British Library copy for Early English Books Online (EEBO), is routinely cleaned up for textual reproduction. Such editorial intervention effectively erases the powerfully physical immediacy of the documentary artifact. But even four hundred years of fingers pointing out Sidney's coffin fails to define the heroism that itself cannot be contained within a coffin. The image of Sidney documented here already exceeds its own reporting to thrive within the totality of the event: the colours, trappings, and sense of occasion of official participants – titled and untitled – within

Fig. 8.3 Funeral cortège, from Thomas Lant, *Sequitur celebritas et pompa funeris* (1588), Plate 16.

the funeral procession, and everyone else, including spectators, readers, and English men and women of all classes and conditions, everyone over time who self-identifies as English.

In "Death be very proud: Sidney, Subversion, and Elizabethan Heraldic Funerals," J.F.R. Day argues the complex and at times contradictory presence of heraldic symbolism and enumeration to explain Sidney's funeral in traditional terms of mourning and respect. The massive military presence at Sidney's funeral certainly gives pause, but Day readily explains it, even as he admits to perplexity in the very next breath: "These officers might well be expected to attend the funeral of a comrade. But this does not explain why after the corpse come 300 citizens of London armed with a variety of muskets, 'small shot,' pikes, halberds, and the like, accompanied by fife and drum."[33] I would argue that these unofficial citizens, powerfully moved and self-determined, even somewhat subversively involved, perform a new form of conscious mobilization, witnessed by thousands of other fellow citizens on the street that day who are unrecorded in Lant's document but who live on after the event within an imagined community of connected readers and viewers. Like other commentators, Day overlooks the crucial absent-presence of the people, their diversity then and now, and their relation to subsequent generations. He de-emphasizes "subversive" readings of Sidney's funeral, but his crediting of a new and unprecedented, even post-medieval "pride" in the proceedings speaks to Sidney's funeral in all of its meaningful excessiveness and new sense of collective realization.

Having died for his country, in another country, asserting a unified Protestant cause in such a public way, Sidney achieved something at once specific but infinitely replicable: a new national consciousness connecting the truths, hopes, and ideals of a nation. He achieved, not the sacrifice of a private soldier or even of a retrograde medieval martyr, but rather the moral grandeur of a national hero, one who is always available, always generously reproducible, within the consciousness of any member of the imagined English community. Conflicted regal heroes such as Henry V or King Arthur or even Henry VIII evolve as the products of poetry, history, and mythology. Sidney as national hero seems to thrive from the day of his funeral as an unassailable product of collective imagination. That he would now live on forever was not a pious consolation. Rather, he could now be collectively understood and asserted with all the power of a new sense of national mission and of national consciousness. Such a collective consciousness in relation to Sidney precedes and outlives the more readily explicable "explosion" of literary mourning observed by documentary historians and interpreters.

England had never had a unifying cultural and military hero like this, but it needed one in 1587–88 with which to face a deadly ideological opposition from continental Europe – specifically, the Spanish threat, very much alive until the Armada's destruction in August 1588. Sidney had died in the Netherlands in a Protestant cause, but his funereal meanings rise above domestic religious factions in favour of national assertion and creativity. As itemized by music historian John Harley, the well-known English Catholic composer William Byrd wrote funeral songs for Sidney, including the famous "Come to me, Grief, forever" and "O that most rare breast, crystalline sincere."[34] Sidney's father-in-law, Sir Francis Walsingham, so easily reduced as anti-Catholic spymaster, may very well have commissioned the songs. That multimedia flash file mentioned at the outset of this essay features the sound of continuous choric voices singing "Come to me, Grief, forever." As a unifying, consoling, distinctly sincere but also rare and self-replicating image of national generosity and strength, Sidney continues to thrive. An emergent English "unisonance" finds place, guided and iconographically represented within Lant's text, to assert itself as well beyond the simplicities of reactionary sectarianism.

Sidney's remarkable funeral *was* forever – but not the grief. England was not saying goodbye. Rather it was saying hello to a singular but infinitely reproducible hero. In this regard, Sidney dazzled others within the relatively short span of his life, and over four hundred years later Lant's graphic account of his funeral procession continues to connect cognitively within a sense of our own mutually affiliated, diverse consciousness as spectators. It did so for John Aubrey in 1635. And it does so for viewers of Lant's text today. Sidney was not mourned as a king – in the standard formula: the King is dead; long live the King – but recognized then as now emphatically as a national hero. To kings (and queens) the state constantly says goodbye. To the true hero, always publicly available, the state and everyone living says hello, *forever*.

NOTES

1 Aubrey, *Brief Lives*, 280. That the STC2 records six copies of Lant's book in existence – none of them complete – suggests that dismantled display was its usual state in its own time. For my oral presentation of this essay at the conference of the Canadian Society for Renaissance Studies, University of Victoria, June 2013, I printed the British Library copy of Lant's text from Early English Books Online, connecting all pages together (8 1/2" x 11") and taping them across the classroom blackboard of Cornett B108. At twenty-seven feet long, my display was yet some ten feet short of the total of the actual printed pages of the text, most of which measured 7 5/8" x 15". See Hind, *Engraving in England*, 132.

The actual document bears the date 1587 on page 2, but 1588 on the final page, suggestive of the immediacy of the event of Sidney's funeral on 16 February 1587, but also that the actual publication occurred later. STC2 includes both dates for the book and numbers it 15224.

2 Harrison, Lord, and Quilligan, "The Funerary Procession of Sir Philip Sidney: An Early Modern Multimedia Site and Pedagogical Venture" [Flash Presentation].

3 Sutton and Tribble, "Cognitive Ecology as a Framework," 94.

4 See Hillyer, *Sir Philip Sidney, Cultural Icon.*

5 Stewart, *Philip Sidney: A Double Life*, 3.

6 Colaianne and Godshalk, eds., *Elegies for Sir Philip*, viii.

7 Goldring, ed., "The Death [1586] and Funeral Procession [1587] of Sir Philip Sidney," 284.

8 Alexander, *Writing After Sidney*, 57.

9 Cressy, "Death and the Social Order," 99.

10 Buxton, "The Mourning for Sidney," 47.

11 For thoughtful twentieth-century considerations in this regard, see Wittman's suggestive study titled *The Tomb of the Unknown Soldier.*

12 Anderson, *Imagined Communities*, 141.

13 Greville, *Works*, 4:129.

14 Ibid., 4:130.

15 Ibid., 4:132.

16 Walter, *Crowds and Popular Politics*, 11.

17 Strickland, "Pageantry and Poetry as Discourse," 19.

18 Anderson, *Imagined Communities*, 6.

19 Lant, *Sequitur celebritas et pompa funeris*, 2.

20 Panofsky, *Perspective as Symbolic Form*, 68.

21 Eisenstein, "Some Conjectures about the Impact of Printing," 42.

22 Lant, *Sequitur celebritas*, 2. In her edition, Goldring notes the attendance of freemen from at least three other livery companies, unmentioned in Lant's document but recorded within their own company books: Merchant Taylors, Skinners, and Drapers. See Goldring, "The Death and Funeral Procession of Sir Philip Sidney," 338.

23 See Bos, "Sidney's Funeral Portrayed," 51.

24 Goldring, "Sir Philip Sidney and the Politics of Elizabethan Festival," 199.

25 Ibid., 209.

26 See Leahy, *Elizabethan Triumphal Processions.*

27 Llewellyn, *The Art of Death*, 68.

28 Lant, *Sequitur celebritas et pompa funeris*, 30.

29 Llewellyn, *The Art of Death*, 67.

30 Lant, *Sequitur celebritas et pompa funeris*, 14.

31 Ibid., 15.

32 Goldring, "Sir Philip Sidney and the Politics of Elizabethan Festival," 206. See also

Goldring's informative note in her edition, "The Death and Funeral Procession of Sir Philip Sidney," 324.

33 Day, "Death be very proud," 197.

34 Harley, *William Byrd*, 280.

9

"Watching the Watchers": The Spectatorship Game in Ned Ward's *The London Spy*

DAVID McNEIL

Contextual Background

One of the most common entertainments is watching people get drawn in to what is known as the "shell game." Some equivalent to this kind of swindle – a "confidence trick" – is depicted in Ned Ward's *The London Spy* when the narrator (usually referred to as "the Spy") and his companion enter a "most Crowded" betting shop at Bartholomew Fair: "[L]ike Poor Spectators, with willing Hearts and low Pockets, [they] stood in the Rear, peeping as Boretto Pensioners at the Groom-Porters, over the Shoulders of those that Raffled."[1] What the Spy and his guide observe exactly is "this Ridiculous Vanity, that whatsoever the Gentlemen won, they presented to the Fair Lady that stood next" (265). That the "Fair Lady" and the operator (and possibly one of the "Gentlemen") are working together is pointed out by the guide, and thus Ward presents one of the basic patterns he uses to describe hazard and economic opportunity in late-seventeenth-century London. In the following essay, I will trace what I call this "swindle model" in episodes dealing with financial venture in *The London Spy*, and pay particular attention to how the flow of capital from the fools to the knaves becomes, for Ward, a pronounced subject of spectatorship.

Ward's work is as much about Londoners gawking at the sights of the town as it is about the sights themselves. *The London Spy* initially appeared in the form of eighteen monthly instalments, from November 1698 to

May 1700, and can be generically linked to a few literary traditions. First, one is tempted to see it as a kind of tourist guidebook in the manner of John Stow's *A Survey of London* (1603), and yet its capricious structure, popular (as in common) prose style, and emphasis on London's low-life amusements render it quite a different animal. Given these latter features, one should not be surprised that Ward's work is ignored in the critical commentary on tourist literature, for proper tourism is a genteel pastime.[2] Second, its visitor-guide format is a classical trope, which might be traced back to Aeneas's trip to the underworld (*The Aeneid*, book 6), and which in the eighteenth century would become a standard narrative technique in satires like Delarivière Manley's *The New Atalantis* (1709) and Eliza Haywood's *Memoirs of a Certain Island* (1724). Lastly, the idea of walking the streets of the metropolis would become a poetic commonplace in works like John Gay's *Trivia; or the Art of Walking*, Richard Savage's *The Wanderer* (Canto III), and Samuel Johnson's *London*. While Ward's primary purpose is to give readers a view of London, he also points their gaze to the American colonies by marking London's plantation offices as the entry to indentured service there. As he locates economic themes and subjects along a path of ambulation, Ward's narrator anticipates some steps of John Thelwall in *The Peripatetic* (1793), although it must be admitted that the former is more satiric than the latter and *almost* devoid of sensibility.[3]

Notwithstanding these connections, *The London Spy* is ultimately a unique satiric work that draws on the basic seventeenth-century subgenres of character writing and the literary sketch. While critics have recognized the important influence the work has had on English satire (Jonathan Swift's, for instance) and on subsequent periodicals like Joseph Addison and Richard Steele's *The Spectator*, the full extent of these and other intertextual connections is still being mapped out (see below on Centlivre).[4] Because the style and content of Ward's writing are decidedly popular, Ward can be said to be working in a tradition directly opposed to that of learned wit. That said, Ward, in the manner of Rabelais, appeals to the stomach as well as offering the lure of the spectacular; readers can almost smell the food and feel the drink go down. Still, it is not surprising that Ward was one of the main targets of Alexander Pope when the latter wrote *The Dunciad*.[5] Rather than classical allusions, in Ward we find what Peter Briggs calls "earthy metaphors."[6] Everything is compared to something outrageously lewd or familiar. We also get a commoner's view of the urban morass that is London in the 1690s: the streets, the taverns, the people. While it is generally accepted that Addison and Steele were writing for the emerging middle class – or serving the middle-class discussions of high art (e.g., aesthetics, *Paradise Lost*, poetry, and drama), Ward was appealing to a lower audience, and we can easily recognize this purpose when we consider his topics: popular entertainments, food and drink establishments, observations on historical sites. Briggs refers to this perspective as "the reporter's eye" (76). Ben Neudorf and Allison Muri have done substantial work identifying not just the ostensible "vice and villainy" that catch Ward's eye, but the precise nature of the corruption behind what presents itself as civic nobility, like the financing of the Monument commemorating the Great Fire of 1666.[7]

The still popular travel guide is the essential form of literary spectatorship here, a text to serve the curious. In fact, Hunter Davies published *The New London Spy* in 1966, with the intriguing subtitle *A Discreet Guide to the City's Pleasures*.[8] One Amazon reviewer describes it as a fascinating step back in time to the city during the 1960s: "pubs and clubs to galleries, gambling, and gals … and a good deal more."[9] If we consider such texts as part of the literary activity known as psychogeography – that is, the writing about place that highlights the author's emotions and his/her sense of drift – then our subject takes on a layering of time that gives it a more general appeal. Catharina Löffler examines both Thelwall's *Peripatetic* and Ward's *The London Spy* in *Walking in the City*, her recent study of the literary psychogeography of the eighteenth century, and what she argues about the latter text supports many of the points made here.[10] It could be said that Löffler charts a new direction in the field insofar as writers on psychogeography have tended to focus elsewhere. For example, Merlin Coverley's primer on psychogeography and its presence in English literature includes Daniel Defoe rather than Ward, probably because in a work such as *A Journal of the Plague Year* not only is the sense of London locales pronounced, but the narrator is caught up in a kind of psychological nightmare that isn't far off the gothicism that Coverley sees as part of psychogeography.[11] As mentioned, the mood of *The London Spy* is decidedly satiric rather than gothic, and as such the work might be part of another vein of literature that has not received the notice from the genre's critics, like Coverley, who associate the psychogeographic with traditional figures like the French *flâneur* of the nineteenth century. As much as psychogeographic elements persist throughout Ward's work, I am concerned with tracking one specific kind of spectatorship, or drift, if you will, and that has to do with what might be called the "swindle model," in a broad economic and cultural sense.

To appreciate fully the swindle model in *The London Spy* it is helpful to imagine what it was like to live in London at the end of the seventeenth century, in the years leading up to England's great reach for what would come to be known as the British Empire. When the Dutch Prince of Orange became William III of England, he brought with him the administrative expertise that was responsible for the rise in Holland's overseas trade and commerce, and the "embarrassment of riches" that followed. The Bank of England was established in 1695, and Lloyd's Coffee House (founded by Edward Lloyd in 1688 in Tower Street) expanded and moved to Lombard Street in 1691. Needless to say, banking and insurance go hand in hand. With the break with the House of Stuart would come a new political ideology that was committed to the money interest – that is, the interest of the new-start investors and speculators who would fuel England's surge to empire over the next century. And, as with many new movements, there would be a counter-movement, a conservative backlash. Obviously Ward was not the first English writer to satirize the human desire to gawk at the world or to feed one's stomach, or even to perpetrate a swindle, yet the specifics of his vision of how economic need and curiosity are connected does occur in a unique historical context.

But what was Ned Ward's position in the face of this economic activity? He had made a trip to Jamaica to seek his fortune, and apparently it was not a success. Back in London, trying to earn a living, Ward gave other would-be adventurers and indentured servants an idea of the experience by publishing his travelogue, *A Trip to Jamaica* (1698), and its popularity encouraged him to write more – to open the eyes of his readers to the city of London. In this essay, I trace what Ward offers us about spectatorship in late-seventeenth-century London, and in particular how it relates to economic activity having to do with overseas trade and commerce. Ned Ward's life clearly demonstrates that the man wrote to sustain himself, and that he might just as well have run a small business as earn a living through his pen. In fact, this is exactly what Ward would eventually do. As a writer he was especially prolific, from his first successful publication, *A Trip to Jamaica* in 1698, until 1712, when he opened an alehouse between St John Street and Clerkenwell Green. After establishing himself in business, he continued to publish works over a period that extended another seventeen years (1712–29).

Following the Money

Ward's narrator in *The London Spy* begins in the east end of the city, proceeds west as far as St James's Park, and then returns to the east end (this includes a diversion to Mob's Hole, Essex). Among the most spectacular passages are the visits to Bedlam, Smithfield Market, Bridewell, Westminster, Covent Garden, Bartholomew Fair, and the Tower. The most extended and perhaps best description of a London event is that of Bartholomew Fair, which happened the last week of August and first of September; another notable event comes right at the end of the work, and that is John Dryden's funeral procession on 13 May 1700.[12] In any case, the cyclical structure (east-west-east) seems appropriate given the pervasive satirical mode of the work itself; human corruption being ubiquitous, one's experience tends to lack any sense of progress. The east end of London was also its financial centre, as it would continue to be for the next three centuries. (Some of the banks, like Barclays, have now relocated to Canary Wharf.)

So the Spy and his guide begin their journey in the east end, where there is a concentration of activity associated with overseas trade and fortune: ships, goods, naval factors and supplies. Only, for the low-life Spy (or Ward himself), what is on display is, more accurately, the illusion of money, and here one finds the first instance of the swindle model. The narrator and his companion reach the Office of Plantations in Pudding Lane, just east of the Monument. (It was in Pudding Lane, at Thomas Farriner's bakery, to be exact, that the Great Fire of 1666 is said to have started.) The companion describes the work of the plantation office agents as seducing indentured servants. The Spy refers to peeping in at a "Gateway, where [h]e saw three or four Blades well drest, with Hawkes Countenances, attended with half a Dozen Ragamuffinly Fellows, showing Poverty in their Rags, and Despair in their Faces, mixt with a parcel of young Wild

Striplings like Run-away Prentices" (52). A detail from a map of Billingsgate and Bridge Wards (see fig. 9.1) shows a number of possibilities where one could imagine a gateway, but the Plantation House is not identified. The fact that it moved locations a number of times subsequently only complicates matters when working with other early-London reference works.

The Spy's companion or guide then observes that it is the agent, the person who sells the indenture, who makes the money.

> Those fine Fellows who look like Foot-men upon a Holy-day, crept into cast Suits of their Masters, that want Gentility in their Deportments answerable to their Apparel, are Kidnappers, who walk the Change, and other parts of the Town, in order to seduce People, who want Services, and Young Fools crost in Love, and under an uneasiness of mind, to go beyond Seas, getting so much a head of Masters of Ships, and Merchants who go over, for every Wretch they trapan into this Misery. Those Young Rakes and Tatterdemallions you see so Lovingly hearded, are drawn by their Fair Promises to Sell themselves into Slavery, and the Kidnappers are the Rogues that run away with the Money. (53)

Ned Ward seems to be speaking from experience as an adventurer or indentured servant. At the beginning of that work, the narrator comments, "I now began to peep into the *Business* of the World, and chang'd the Company of those who had nothing to do but *Spend Money*, for the conversation of such whose practice was to *Get it*."[13] And the opening statement reads, "*The Condition of an Author is much like that of a* Strumpet" (*TJ*, np). One is paid for a service rendered. The narrator is the victim of the promotional tract that was designed to make the unsuspecting regard America as a land of opportunity. A conservative skeptic, Ward is having none of it.

The passengers all have "one Design, to patch up their *Decay'd Fortunes*" (*TJ*, 9). One, an Irishman, has been bribed with drink, and the narrator believes him to be "*Kidnap'd*" (*TJ*, 11). The portrait we get of Jamaica itself is a demonized version of colonial life as something for criminals, where the fools meet the knaves. There is a huge body of literature, fiction and non-fiction, primary and secondary, on the subject of the indigent being trepanned – that is, fooled, bamboozled – into venturing on a colonial

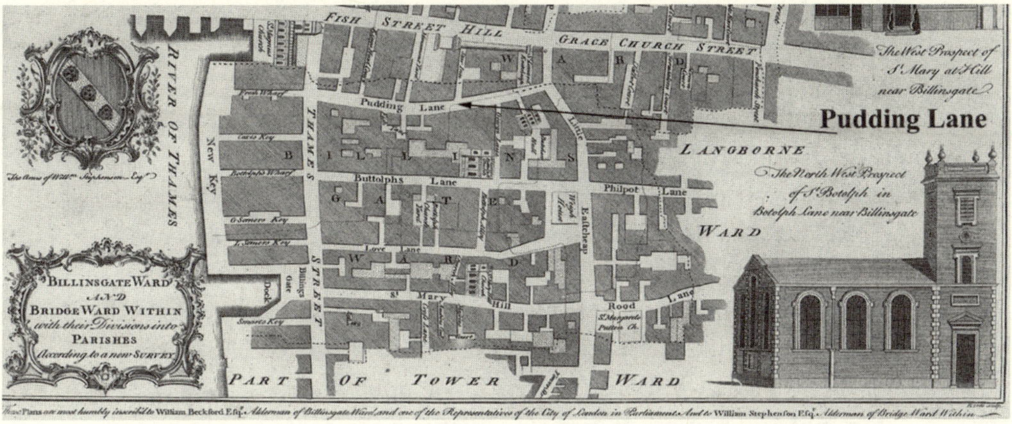

Fig. 9.1. Detail from Billingsgate Ward and Bridge Ward, showing Pudding Lane: cartographer Richard Blome, surveyor John Stow (1720).

project having to do with the Americas.[14] It is easy to characterize the subject of physical entrapment as reflective of one's economic condition: nothing to do but sell yourself into indenture. Ward's satire falls into this category, and can be associated with what would eventually be labelled a Tory world view. New money is suspect.

The counter-narrative may be found in the fiction of Defoe, whose narrators, like Moll Flanders and Colonel Jack, make fortunes with plantation operations in the American colonies. Ward also published *A Trip to New-England* the next year, but critics from Howard Troyer forward have found that the derivative nature of the detail here suggests that the account is bogus, that Ward was simply repeating clichés from other works.[15]

We must now pull back from Jamaica and rejoin our pair in *The London Spy*, who, after stops at the Monument, Gresham College, and Bedlam, take a tour of the Royal Exchange (also in the heart of the financial district). Here the Spy follows the "big" money as opposed to the paltry sums earned by the indenture-agents. Perhaps "respectable" is a better adjective, at least as far as "new" money is concerned, since "new" and sudden wealth tends to be suspect. The Royal Exchange was reserved for trade in commodities. Stockjobbers, or what we know as stockbrokers, were banned from the premises in 1698, just prior to Ward's writing. One of the most well-known and positive Whig narratives of money and commerce can be found a little over a decade later in Addison's *The Spectator* no. 69, published 19 May 1711. Addison's idealized view of world trade approaches ecstasy as the economic is depicted as a reflection of the political, and the business transaction is shown as the equivalent of worldly political diplomacy.

> It gives me a secret Satisfaction, and, in some measure, gratifies my Vanity, as I am an *Englishman,* to see so rich an Assembly of Country-men and Foreigners consulting together upon the private Business of Mankind, and making the Metropolis a kind of *Emporium* for the whole Earth. I must confess I look upon High-Change [editors' note: "The time of greatest activity on the 'Change"] to be a great Council, in which all considerable Nations have their Representatives. Factors in the Trading World are what Ambassadors are in the Politick World; they negotiate Affairs, conclude Treaties, and maintain a good Correspondence between those wealthy Societies of Men that are divided from one another by Seas and Oceans, or live on the different Extremities of a Continent.[16]

It is certainly noteworthy that the work from which Addison borrows his spectating metaphor, namely Ward's *The London Spy*, castigates the "Hawks of Mankind" or merchants at the "'Change," and rather than some sense of international harmony we are treated to a series of ethnic epithets and clichés. The description of the French merchants who "talk more with their Heads and Hands than with their Tongues" seems harmless enough, but then there are the "*Bumfirking Italians,*" the garlic-reeking Spaniards, the "vagabond" Jews, the "reddish hair and freckly faces … of Scotch and Irish" (66–9). Xenophobia run amok.

In the last few sections of *The London Spy* we are back in the east end, and the Spy serves up a description of Jonathan's Coffee-House at the end of Part 16 and then a character sketch of a "banker" at the beginning of Part 17. What first attracts the attention of the Spy is the look of concern he sees on the faces of a group of people, "as if they had received News of the French Landing, or that an Army of Irish Papists had taken possession of the Stocks Market, in order to Massacre the Protestants, and Plunder the City" (390). Jonathan's was one of two coffee houses in Exchange Alley, where stock trading was concentrated; the other was Garraway's, a little farther east. Both are located on The Grub Street Project representation of the 1720 Strype map (see the high-resolution, marked-up version online).[17] Ward's portrait is what we would come to see as the Tory reactionary position against these new financial endeavours, which emphasizes crowd behaviour and ultimately employs the classical and simplistic binary of "knaves" and "fools" (391–2). According to this model, all money flows from the fools to the knaves as in the D'Urfey song, "The Hubble Bubbles," made popular during the sharp rise and crash of 1720, in which the narrator observes two tables, one happy and the other despondent, reflecting the direction in the flow of money.

Part 16 concludes with the character of a "stockjobber" (391–2). At times the "fool," at times the "knave," the stockjobber both makes and loses money as he is either victimizing others or himself victimized, according to how he manages the margins between what he has to pay for a stock and what he can sell it for. There is no sense of being compensated for risk, which is the argument in favour of the market. Debt management is not a service in Ward's cynical but naive thinking. The narrator compares the jobber's love of uncertainty to the Royal Oak Lottery and games of hazard. The Royal Oak Lottery was named after the holiday, celebrated on 29 May, to commemorate the Restoration; it alludes to Charles II having successfully escaped being captured by the Roundheads by hiding in an oak tree. Recognizing the popularity of lotteries during the 1690s, Anne Murphy has argued that, contrary to Dickson's classic position that saw lotteries as a phenomenon contrary to the new world of finance, the lotteries should be seen as instruments whereby potential capital was mobilized.[18] Ned Ward makes no less than seven references to the Royal Oak Lottery in the course of *The London Spy* and they are all negative with respect to surrendering oneself to fickle fortune. The last two of these references come in Part 16. The first is simply a statement on the unpredictable fate of a vessel captain, "the Sea a meer Royal-Oak-Lottery" (372). In the next character, a stockjobber is said to be a lover of "Uncertainty, as some Fools are of the Royal-Oak-Lottery" (391–2). While there often is an element of chance in stock fluctuation, the profession truly prides itself on the opposite – managing risk, being able to read future trends and strategize on the basis of anticipated developments. The reality might be seen as a combination of mental acumen and hazard; we can observe this in many card games that involve a chance distribution and the skill of effectively exercising short-term memory. For Ward, the stockjobber indulges in "Faith" and "Hope" but not "Charity" (392).

A good portion of Part 14 is taken up with lotteries. The Spy comments on how the desire to discuss lottery details pushes "Modesty and Plain dealing" aside, how the newspapers are ignored, how the state of trade with France or the Scottish settlement in Darien are ignored: "it was as much as London cou'd do to Conjure together such Numbers of Knaves as might Cheat 'em fast enough of their Money" (339). Here it is the guide who eschews the idea of "Fairness" to posit the standard argument against games of chance as tying up resources (human and capital) that could be invested in practical production. The pair then witness a lottery at Mercer's Chappel, and they remark on how the individuals in the crowd might have their number drawn only to discover the paltry nature of the prize. Part 14 concludes with a poem on lotteries that invokes the same dance between the knaves and fools ("where the Gain in Justice is too large, The very Profit is alone a Cheat") and concludes with a mention of the "late Act" (343), a reference to the 1698 statute against lotteries, a law that lasted only a decade (10 & 11 William c.17).[19]

Ward's picture of Jonathan's Coffee-House is disappointing and offers nothing like the dramatic detail of Susanna Centlivre's scene in *A Bold Stroke for a Wife* (4.1), where the viewer can enjoy the art of news manipulation and observe how it affects stock prices. The character of the stockjobber operates in a fairly mechanical replication of the binary structure of knavery and folly; no allowance is made for the economics of debt management. The few graphic images we have of Jonathan's are from the eighteenth century and do not satisfy our ocular curiosity.

For a more entertaining drama of financial manipulation along the lines of Centlivre's 1718 play we can turn to another Ned Ward work, *The Weekly Comedy* or *The Humours of a Coffee-House*, which features an engaging list of characters including the projector, Whim, who cheats an unsuspecting city beau named Prim.[20] Troyer notes that this comedy is essentially a reorganization of passages that first appeared in Ward's journal *The Weekly Comedy*, which appeared in 1699 just as Ward was producing *The London Spy*.[21] In any case, *The Weekly Comedy* is a fictionalization of coffee-house culture complete with stock characters, a format that Addison and Steele would copy a decade later with *The Tatler* and *The Spectator*. Following the money here is again a simple version of watching it flow from the fools to the knaves. One thinks of Swift, who was writing pretty much the same thing at the same time in *A Tale of a Tub*. What we encounter here is a version of the seventeenth-century "character sketch."

Section 17 of *The London Spy* begins with a general discussion of money and banking, and once again Ward reveals his fear and suspicion of the new financial tools – of investment in particular. A story is told of a "Person of Quality" who observes a banker interacting with a merchant; the merchant turns down the banker's proposal and then offers to discuss his move with the "Person of Quality" at the latter's convenience. The latter tells his coach to wait for him at Lloyd's Coffee House and seeks out the merchant. The merchant relates the extortion-like practices of the banker and the "Person of Quality" steps in to finance the merchant directly, to their mutual benefit. What follows are some simple verses on the mysterious nature of the banking profession:

> His dealings are so dark a mystery,
> No man can truly tell, though ne'er so much so wise.
> Whether he thrives or that he honest be,
> Until the black-palmed miser breaks or dies. (400)

This general portrait does remind one of Mr Merdle in Charles Dickens's *Little Dorrit*, but *there is* something fundamentally mysterious about the function of a banker. Using capital to make more capital is a skill that depends on covert measures; it also inspires in characters like Merdle a desire to detect the source of the money flow. Rather than getting any recognition for risk management, the banker is demonized as somebody engaged in "Jewish and unlawful practices" (399–400). This view, of course, is part of a long history in Western civilization of both usury and anti-Semitism. (See also chapter 12, 314–17.)

I concur with Briggs that *The London Spy*, like the later *Spectator* papers, has "a … built-in visual bias … Their methods of reporting are journalistic … In short, they become people watchers and readers of visible circumstances and social behaviours."[22] However, although the caricatures can be entertaining, Ward's view is interesting only as it documents the backlash against the emerging financial institutions. That said, we are at least pointed to the east-end London locales where we might observe the spectacle of capital flows. The "money flow" has its high-commodity channel at the Royal Exchange and its low-service channel at the Plantation Office. In between (literally on the map) is trading in stocks, which will, over the course of the next three centuries, be subject to demonization as risk management becomes entangled with market and news manipulation.

Gawking and Enticement

Given what the Spy sees as the underlying flow of money from the fools to the knaves, the human propensity for gawking in *The London Spy* is often part of the prelude to a financial transaction. The curiosity business is best represented by the trip to the Tower and to the major fairs. As far as the Tower is concerned, the Spy reveals that his rural origins make him susceptible to the novelties of London: "I had oftentimes in the Country heard wonderful Tales and Tidings from Higlers, Hawkers, Carriers, Drovers, and such like" about the "amazing Objects, together with many other Inticing Rarities, to be visited at a small Expence" (298). Despite the fact that these stories were "received from the Magnifying Mouths of some Boobily Bumpkins, who had stolen so much time from their Waggons and Hay-Carts, as to be Spectators of these surprizing Curiosities" (298), the Tower episode presents human spectatorship in a rather straightforward manner. Escaping from the guild mobs attending the Lord Mayor's procession, the pair make their way east and come across Tower Hill, the famous site of political executions (see chapter 6); the Spy simply remarks on how the place makes him feel a safety in the middle-station of life where one cannot be viewed as any kind of threat to the prevailing power. It may be a commonplace observation (but one that merits notice) that when a place is associated with history-making events, it becomes endowed with a meaning that will inspire reflection among those who, in the future, happen upon it.

Then the pair encounters a classic case of competition between two street engagers: a prophet and a piper. They make no comment on the fact that the piper wins the crowd, and the prophet denounces it. Popular

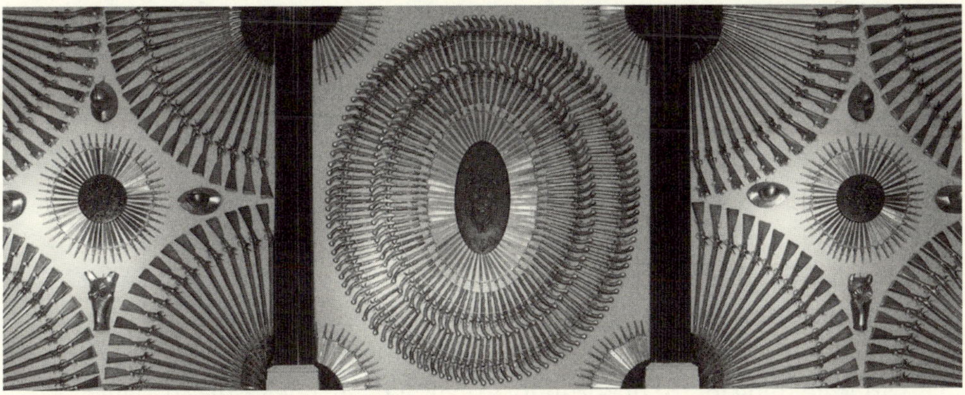

Fig. 9.2 King's Guard Room, Hampton Court Palace.

legend is part of the curiosity appeal of the zoo animals at the Tower – the woman who gets too friendly with the lions and has her arm ripped off, the caretaker who gets caught in a pen with a lion who ends up licking his face. And, of course, for an extra penny one can see more big cats, eagles, and owls. Several more curiosities are described, and then the pair encounters the armoury (as it still is in the Tower, at Hampton Court, and at Edinburgh Castle) displayed in elaborate symmetrical detail and pattern on the wall (see fig. 9.2).[23] The Spy notes "A Wilderness of Arms, whose Locks and Barrels were kept in that Admirable Order" and concludes: "such Mischievous Implements disguis'd under the Form and Figure of a Musical Instrument, which Breaths forth nothing but Peace, Innocence, and Delight, and Harmony, is putting the Devil into a Canonical Robe, or, as I said before, a Wolf into Sheeps-Cloathing" (310). Still, the mood is not satirical. The Spy and his guide appear satisfied that they are getting their money's worth of spectating.

Hence, *The London Spy* contains episodes pertaining to spectatorship that range from the panegyrical to the satiric. We have noted several of the latter. For an example of the former, there is the Spy's reaction to seeing Isaac Fuller's murals at the Crown Tavern at the end of Duck Lane:

> at first Entrance, I discern'd the Masterly Strokes of the fam'd *Fuller*'s Pencil, the whole Room being Painted with that commanding Hand, that his Dead Figures appear'd with such Lively Majesty, that they begot Reverence in us, the Spectators, towards the Awful Shadows;

> our Eyes were so Delighted with this Noble Entertainment, that every Glance gave new Life to our weary Senses. (122)

Isaac Fuller (1606?–1672) painted murals in a number of London taverns (e.g., the Sun, near the Royal Exchange, and the Mitre in Fenchurch Street).[24] For the Spy, ocular curiosity is as natural an appetite as that for food and drink, and there is nothing that undermines the enthusiasm expressed for Fuller's "Dead Figures." Of course, the pair has not had to barter anything for the opportunity to look at them; nor are they designed to lure the Spy and his guide into some other activity. Not only can pecuniary factors shape how curiosity is depicted, curiosity itself is largely determined by one's previous experience. And so when the pair arrive at St James's Palace they note how a "Fingalian conjurer" stops to inform a group of "Country Hobbies" of the story behind "the whale rib" displayed in the first court (169). Similar to the knave/fool binary that characterizes much of the cash flow, so the spectacle of curiosity features the sophisticated and street-wise urbanite against the country bumpkin.

However, there are several instances of spectatorship that do not fall into these binaries. For example, at the end of their second day, the Spy and his guide are placed in the "Poultry Compter" for apparently having contravened some general curfew. Here they witness a scatological christening of sorts as one of the prisoners is treated to a face-wash from the contents of the chamber pot, an act that puts the "Spectators … into an excessive laughter" (81) – another passage in the spirit of Rabelais. Later, the pair find themselves browsing the stalls in St Paul's churchyard, where some "smutty prints" attract the attention of a crowd of "spectators" that easily outnumbers those reading sermons (96–7). But Ward generally does not titillate with sexual voyeurism, at least not in the manner of amatory fiction, and this tendency is seen in the episode at Bridewell, the correctional institution, which stands out for containing definite strains of sensibility in an otherwise satiric narrative. First, the Spy marks a "Ghastly Skeleton weeping" and remarks that the "sad appearance … call'd for Mercy and Compassion" (132). After serving up a catalogue of brutal cases, he returns to his usual deception motif to account for how this punishment spectacle arises: "I thought the Offenders had been Popish Penitents, who by the Delusion of their Priests, were drawn thither to buy Lashes by Auction" (135). The reader is then given information identifying a specific individual, something that rarely occurs with Ward. One "Ed-th T-ll" is sentenced to a public flogging, and this means that she "was forc'd to show her tender Back, and tempting Bubbies to the Grave Sages of the Grave Assembly" (135). The ironic repetition of "Grave" along with the Spy's decision to forgo the entertainment, designed as he says to satisfy "the Curiosity" of "the Spectators," clearly sets the pair apart (135–6).

Just as *The London Spy* as a whole seems to serve as a diversion for the non-Londoner who may not be especially aware of what the city has to offer in the way of ocular amusement, so the "Excursion" to "Mob's Hole" in Essex reflects the endlessly deferred nature of human diversion in general, since it represents a flight from the urban (so recently embraced). We now follow the pair as they join the traffic, or the "herd" of people and vehicles, leaving the city for a hunter's feast in Essex northeast of the city (see fig. 9.3). Their first stop is at the Globe in Mile End (a public house, it seems) to fortify themselves with "a precious sirloin of roast beef … and … a flask of rare claret" before they continue the to a calf-roast at a house in "Mob's Hole." Here the Spy and his companion no sooner join the bustle in the house than they make their escape up into one of its garrets. The Spy then produces his watch for a maid who wishes to know the time, before entering the kitchen where the roasting calf is located. However, the meat is so well done as to resemble "the side of a blackamoor" and so they escape the bustle on their return via a coach from Stratford.

The London Spy *as a "Time-Fixed" Narrative*

Since people-watching is best done at large public gatherings, it should not be surprising that *The London Spy* also features time-fixed occurrences such as annual celebrations and special events. Hence, the description of "May Fair" comes in Part 7, which originally appeared in May 1698; this fortnight of pleasure, a relatively new addition to the calendar, operated for almost a century, from 1686 to 1764, between Piccadilly Road and Curzon Street (or what subsequently would be called "Shepherd's Market"). Here the pair take a coach through the throng in hopes of taking

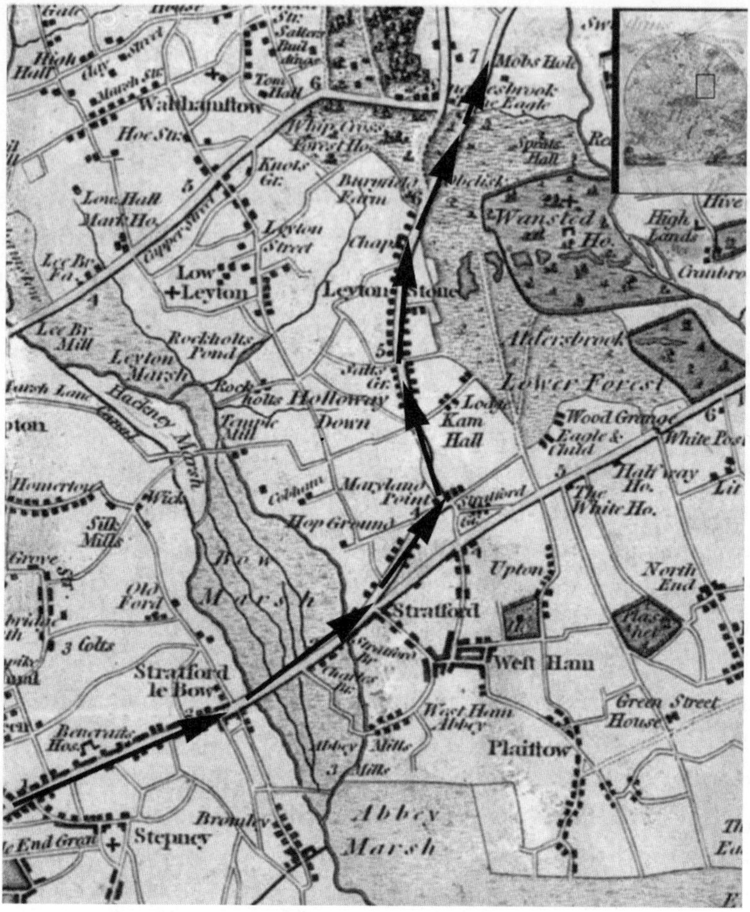

Fig. 9.3 Spy's Route to Mob's Hole, Essex. Detail from Fairburns Map.

in the "gazing multitude"; what they find is the competition among the various performers to draw a crowd. As for the people, the Spy provides the following rather scathing description.

> We now began to look about us, and take a view of the Spectators; but could not, amongst the many Thousands, find one Man that appear'd above the degree of a Gentlemans Valet, nor one Whore that could have the Impudence to ask above Six-pence wet and Six-pence dry, for an Hour of her Cursed Company. In all the Multitudes that ever I beheld, I never, in my life, saw such a Number of Lazy,

> Lousie-look'd Rascals, and so hateful a Throng of Beggarly, Sluttish Strumpets, who were a Scandal to the Creation, meer Antidotes against Leachery, and Enemies to Cleanliness. (166)

The class-conscious and misogynist elements are clear in this passage, but so are Ward's rhetorical flourishes that smack of Rabelaisian energy and undercut the moralistic satire.

Similarly, the description of Bartholomew Fair first appeared in the August and September instalments for 1698 (Parts 10 and 11 in the *Compleat* version) since the fair took place in late summer. This longstanding event was held at Smithfield from 1133 to 1855; by 1641 the fair had stretched to two full weeks, but by the time of Ward's writing it had been scaled back to four days.[25] Ward choreographs how human curiosity is set in motion, and dances through the steps towards its satisfaction. What first greet our pair when they arrive by coach are the loud and various sounds and – after they seek "a convenient House to Smoke a Pipe, and over-look the Follies of the Innumerable Throng" (229) – the smells rather than the sights. Then the reader is given descriptions of what lures operate to draw the gaze, beginning with the "Merry Andrew" (231), a performer whose task it is to draw a crowd and induce it to enter the booth, to commit financially. The pair leave the spectating comfort of their window seat and re-enter a coach, which allows them to penetrate another part of the fair crowd. Eventually, the coach is again abandoned, and the pair go on foot to brush more closely with humanity at play. A woman is seen walking on her hands, and her upside-down performance leads the Spy to remark on its fittingness based on the degradation of the female mouth versus her lower parts, a misogynistic observation with which the guide agrees: "Truly … I [th]ink you are much in the right on't; for a Woman is a mere Receptacle, and to see her standing on her Legs is an Unnatural … Posture" (233). Throughout *The London Spy*, a rough pattern emerges as the narrator's position and movement often involves a fixed window seat, then a mobile coach, and finally this on-foot watching and close interacting.

The final shift here is to give oneself up to one of the "Merry Andrews," to take the lure and actually pay a fee to enter one of the many tents and satisfy one's curiosity about what is displayed within. The guide is the one who encourages this move: "let us fling away Six-pence a piece, and see what's to be done within-side; methinks, says he, there is something in this sort of Activity, that is both Diverting and Amusing" (233). It is not enough to watch; one must eventually join in. The ultimate entertainment value of the experience is balanced: after a long series of various performers, the Spy expresses his satisfaction with the tumbling and disappointment with the dancing.

As with all the most engaging writing, Ward's text contains an impression of authenticity that comes from precise and detailed observation. As the Spy and his guide take in Bartholomew Fair from their window seats, they are waited on by a servant who strikes them as a little too anxious to sell the wares of the house and ultimately intrudes on their spectating pleasure: "[He] Plagu'd us as constantly with his Impertinent Do you call Sirs, every two Minutes, as surely as the Clock strikes every Hour, till at last he had to affront us with his over Diligence, that we were forc'd to tell him we would Kick him down Stairs if he came any more till we call'd him" (230). The pair overindulge with the roasted pork and start to feel nauseated. The Spy becomes physically engaged with a woman in the crowd, only to discover later that she has done so in order to pick his pocket. Hoping to find the ultimate entertainment, the pair eventually enter a tent and are struck by the degree of snack-nibbling and spectator-to-spectator flirting going on in the expectant audience, which breaks "out into Bear-Gardens Acclamation of Show, Show, Show, Show; till at last, in answer to their loud-Mouth'd Importunities, the Curtain was drawn up" (248). It might be said that there are points of strong commonality between 2018 and Ward's London when it comes to human spectation and specific behaviours.

Another annual event was the Lord Mayor's Parade, usually held on 29 October (that being a Sunday in 1699 it took place the following day), and as we would expect it comes up in Part 12, corresponding to that month. While a sense of the calendar (spring, summer, fall) characterizes certain episodes like this one, the fictional time of the narrative as a whole unfolds as a day-to-day experience in eighteen parts (each covering a day or so), adding up to approximately one month.[26] Here we witness the essential middle-of-the-road conservativism of the Spy as he comments on the reassurance that the new Lord Mayor, Richard Levett, is a member of the "Established Church" (220).[27] Levett had risen from humble begin-

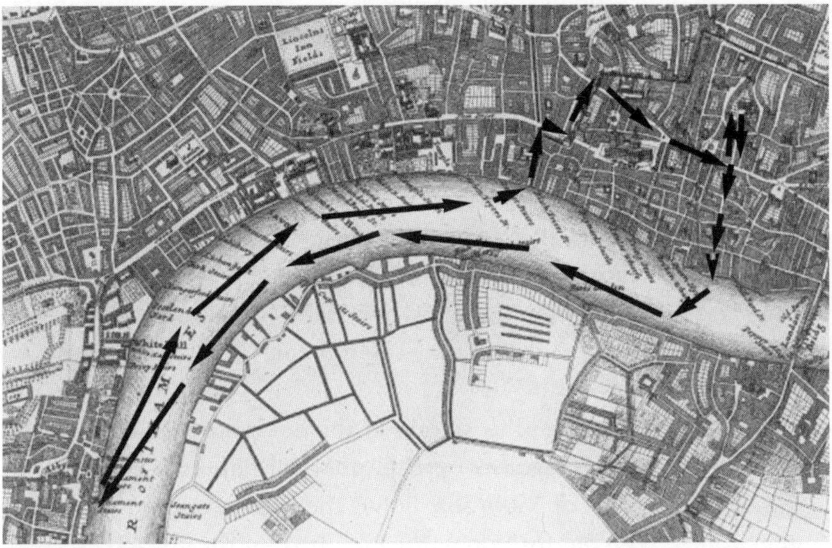

Fig. 9.4 Lord Mayor's Parade Route, 1699: Guildhall to Westminster and back.

nings as a haberdasher and trader in tobacco and linen and in 1698 found himself appointed a director of the Bank of England;[28] the following year he was elected, as per protocol, to the position of lord mayor of the City of London by Common Hall, a body comprised of the senior members of the livery companies. Our pair find a place at the end of Blow Bladder Street (just a little northeast of St Paul's and essentially the extension of Cheapside) where they become part of the "Innumerable Multitude of the Gaping Spectators" (292). One might speculate that they were catching the parade making its way back from the "Amphibious Journey to Westminster-Hall" (292), as that reference precedes Ward's detailed description. The event, according to the *Triumphs of London* (1699), would have begun with a general assembly at Levett's house at 7:00 a.m., with the parade proper beginning "from *Guildhall* … through *Cheap-side* to Three Cranes Wharf," then by barge to Westminster and back only as far as "*Dorset* Stairs … and thus with the whole Cavalcade, moves forward toward *Cheap-side*."[29] (See fig. 9.4.)

The first object of the Spy's attention is the bank of ladies crammed into the windows, peering out to observe the festivities. A sentence easily captures Ward's penchant for simile and distinctive – often Latinate – diction: "[t]he Windows of each House, from the Top to the Bottom, being stuffed with Heads, Piled one upon another, like Skulls in a Charnel-house, all gazing at the Lobcocks in their Coney-skin Pontificalibusses with as much Intention, as if an Indian Prophetess had been Riding thro' the City upon the Back of a Tyger" (293). The nominal object of the crowd's gaze is the parade of colourful pageants (*OED*, n3 "floats"), many representing specific guilds and surrounded by marching apprentices, but the Spy and his companion soon find themselves caught in the swarm of bodies that begins to press physically upon them:

> my Friend and I were thus staring at the Spectators, much more than the Show, the Pageants were advanc'd within our view, upon which such a Tide of Mob over-flow'd the Place we stood in that the Women cry'd out for Room, the Children for Breath, and every man … strove very hard for his Freedom. For my own part, I thought my Intrails would have come out of my Mouth … (293–4)

The Spy improvises a kind of counter-list of the celebrated virtues, represented by specific figures, beginning with "the four Principal Vices of the City, viz. Fraud, Usury, Seeming Sanctity, and Hipocrisie" and "those three Vanities … Falsehood, Pride and Incontinency" (295). In between five pageant items, described in some detail, Londoners amuse themselves by passing around a leather-apron stuffed with some odious substance, then a kennel soaked cloth, and after that "a Bullocks-Horn … fill'd with Kennel-water," which is "pour'd … down Peoples Necks" (296). The pattern here is for spontaneous, earthy celebrations to fill out and essentially usurp the carefully planned ones; there also seems to be a considerable lag time between the pageant floats, which seems right if this was the day-long parade coming to its end.

Another calendar event is the Christmas carnival in December, which is alluded to at the beginning of Part 14 (December 1699) but not really addressed in any detail. Here the pair, having just left the Tower, find themselves in the poor district marked by the seafaring culture around the quays. And the last "event" episode is not an annual celebration but a one-

Fig. 9.5 Dryden's Funeral Procession: Physicians' Hall to Westminster. Detail from Strype's *New Plan* (1720).

time only occurrence: John Dryden's funeral procession. The mood is solemn; any ironic implication about the spectacle is at first completely absent. Among Dryden's biographers, Walter Scott and Charles Ward seem to have the most to say about the funeral procession, and both allude to its description in *The London Spy*,[30] which reminds the reader that despite Ward's rhetorical flourishes, his purpose is also to simply give readers news of the month.

Dryden, whose leg was inflamed with gout, had apparently refused to have it amputated, and he died of gangrene on 1 May 1700. His body was embalmed by William Russell and left at Physicians' Hall until four o'-clock on 13 May, when it was taken by procession to Westminster and laid between Chaucer and Cowley. The route presumably would have been from the Hall either straight down Warwick Lane (or up around Newgate and down the Old Bailey) to Fleet Street, along the Strand, Charing Cross Road, White Hall, and finally Westminster (see fig. 9.5). Whereas Sir Philip Sidney's funeral procession was very much an east London event, beginning from the Minories outside Aldgate and ending at St Paul's

Cathedral (see chap. 8, fig. 8.1), Dryden's was a west end affair. Ward's account proceeds chronologically from the ceremonies performed at Physicians' Hall to those at Westminster; it then includes an elegy to the poet, which, while not of the stateliness of Dryden's own works in this genre, is fitting and serious.

However, while the subject would seem to then be exhausted, Ward goes back to focus on one particular detail that touches on the satiric and has to do with a typical urban problem – traffic. Dryden's funeral is an opportunity not just to see off the great poet and dramatist, but for the well-to-do themselves to be seen. Unfortunately, the "quality coaches" block Chancery Lane and prevent the "Hackney whore drivers" from getting past the King's Head Tavern (this is at the intersection of Chancery Lane and Fleet Street). What follows is a fierce verbal battle between the coachmen of these two groups, and just as the blockage seems to get worked out, Ward's eye is attracted to another procession, this one honouring a prizefighter from Dorset Garden (located just a little to the east and down by the river). So, high art is in Ward's text swallowed by the low. The fighter it seems has "like a true cock … won the day after he had lost an eye in the battle" (324). Once a grand venue to stage elaborate technical spectacles like Aphra Behn's *The Emperor in the Moon* (see chapter 5), Dorset Garden had subsequently become the site for more popular entertainments, like prizefighting. The Spy is led to understand that the fighters "mauled one another stoutly, to the great satisfaction of the spectators," and so the elegy to Dryden is quickly followed by a lyric on the prizefighter.

As a once-spectacular theatre become less so, Dorset Garden and its history have already been commented on by the Spy after the return from Mob's Hole. A rough coach ride makes the pair seek wherry transport and they disembark at Dorset Garden, on the Thames (see chap. 5, fig. 5.1). Here the guide informs the Spy of the fate of the building as a house of high entertainment and of the demise of the theatrical culture of the city.

> For this, says he, is one of the Theatres, but now wholly abandoned by the Players; and, 'tis thought, will in a little time be pulled down, if it is not Bought by some of our Dissenting Brethren, and Converted to a more Pious Use, that may in part Atone for the sundry

> Transgressions occasion'd by the Levity which the Stage of late has been so greatly subject to. (148)

The idea of the exchange as swindle also marks this observation, as the guide suggests that the only inhabitants now are "Rats and Mice" and perhaps a caretaker to insure that no "decay'd Lover of the Drama should get in and steal away the Poets Pictures, and sell 'em to some Upholsterer for Roman Emperors" (148). The spatial and temporal intersect in the Spy's encounter with the culture of Dorset Garden, and so it is generally with psychogeography, for the city locales and institutions are experienced at a specific time in history. (For the record, Dorset Garden Theatre was demolished in 1709.)

Conclusion: Westminster in Time and Space

This intersection of the spatial and temporal is especially notable when the Spy first sets eyes on Westminster Abbey, that "Awful Pile," and is struck with "Rev'rence and Amazement" (178). Entering the cathedral to the sound of chiming bells and "Divine Heavenly Musick," the pair seems overwhelmed with a sense of spirituality (178). After taking in the Trained Bands drilling in the Palace Yard, which is satirically depicted, and hearing some of the proceedings in Westminster Hall (the oldest part of the palace) which afford some amusement, the pair comes across the ruins to the old clock tower, and the guide registers a general regret about the destruction of historical objects: "There's nothing … concerns me more, than to see any piece of Antiquity Demolish'd. It always puts me in mind of the Ignoble Actions of the Sanctified Rebels in the late Domestick Troubles, who made it their Business to deface Old Images" (186–7). The reflection makes clear how the exclusivity of Ward's text belongs more to its precise time – the eighteenth months from November 1698 to May 1700 – than its exact place, London, even if both are only vicariously experienced by the reader. While Ward's language and rhetoric in *The London Spy* belong very much to late-seventeenth-century popular English literature, there are landmarks that remain familiar. These latter retain a sense of the tangible that stands in contrast to temporal events like Dryden's funeral procession or Bartholomew Fair.

Another tangible object that endures is the equestrian statue of Charles I in Charing Cross.[31] Like all statues, it is not an ocular swindle but a physical monument designed to elicit reflection on the historical. And so the Spy inserts a poem on the monarch that concludes with the following lines: "Thus the Mad Crowd who could no Ills foresee, / Of Just Restraint endeavouring to be free, / Took off thy Head, because themselves would Headless be" (203). Ward leaves posterity a seminal text in literary spectatorship that ranges from basic human curiosity to more profound instances of psychogeography. It might be said that reading *The London Spy* with all the resources offered by The Grub Street Project is a kind of textual and cartographic time-travelling. While the major key is satirical conservativism, there are also moments when the satiric modulates to the panegyric, when the minor key can be heard, a straightforward expression of awe. It is not "ills [we] foresee" – it is a past at which we laugh and wonder when Ward's fiction prompts us to imagine London's sounds, her smells, her fabric, and, of course, her sights.

NOTES

1 Ward, *The London Spy Compleat*, 265. Subsequent parenthetical references are to this edition. The Grub Street Project reproduces not only Ward's text, but a number of others, and includes several maps and other source materials. My own research on Ward is heavily indebted to The Grub Street Project, and several of the places referred to in this essay are identified on a high-resolution digital reproduction of Strype's 1720 map. It is worth mentioning that there is a John Strype website that provides much more cartographic information on early modern London; see Merritt, *Strype, Survey of London [online]*.

2 For example, neither Esther Moir not Carole Fabricant makes any mention of Ward in their respective works, *The Discovery of Britain*, 254–75, and "The Literature of Domestic Tourism," 310–11.

3 Judith Thompson, "Introduction," 24–32. The passage in which the Spy denounces the flogging of a woman in Bridewell (discussed later in this essay) is an example of how sensibility can intermix with satire in *The London Spy*.

4 See "The Curious Eye" section of Benedict, *Curiosity*, 92–117, for comments on *The London Spy* and its spectator-context. For a Habermasian analysis of *The London Spy* with respect to *The Tatler* and *The Spectator*, see Pollock, *Gender and the Fictions*, 10, 34–54. Pollock summarizes what he sees as Addison's use of *The*

London Spy as follows: "Addison appropriates and transforms three key elements from the *London Spy*: Ward's deployment of the anonymous observer as a new kind of public intellectual, his idea of the essay periodical as a vehicle for wide-ranging cultural critique, and his association of the critical observer with specific urban spaces and forms of sociability" (35).

5 See Troyer, *Ned Ward of Grubstreet*, 196–202.

6 Briggs, "Satiric Strategy in Ned Ward's London Writings," 76.

7 Neudorf, "The Satirical Topography of Ned Ward's *The London Spy*."

8 Davies, *The New London Spy*.

9 See Walsh, Amazon review of *The New London Spy*.

10 Löffler, *Walking in the City*, 214–40.

11 Coverley, *Psychogeography*.

Other writers associated with psychogeography do make passing reference to Ward; see Ackroyd, *London: The Biography*, 136–8, 445, 547, and 652. The first reference (136–8) is to Bartholomew Fair, and Ward's description of this annual event is noted by many historians; for instance, see Morely, *Memoirs of Bartholomew Fair*, 264–72.

12 The Bedlam visit will remind readers of the description provided by Swift's narrator in Section IX of *A Tale of a Tub*.

13 [Ward], *A Trip to Jamaica*, 6. All subsequent parenthetical references are made to this edition and abbreviated *TJ*.

14 For an introduction to the subject, see Coldham, *Emigrants in Chains*.

15 For a summary of the evidence and suggestions about Ward's source material, see Troyer, *Ned Ward of Grubstreet*, 21–3.

16 Addison, *The Spectator*, 69, 1:292.

17 The Grub Street Project: 1720 London (Strype). See http://grubstreetproject.net/london/#map=3/categories=6/@47403,48781,95772.

18 See Murphy, "Lotteries in the 1690s," 227–46, and Dickson, *The Financial Revolution in England*, 54.

19 See Ashton, *A History of English Lotteries*, 50–1.

20 *The Humours of a Coffee-House, A Comedy* appears in *A Collection of the Writings of Mr. Edward Ward* (1717); the play does not seem to have been produced. Ward's characters include Snap (sharper), Scribble (newswriter), Prim (a beau), and Whim (a projector). They resemble Centlivre's Prim (a Quaker), Tradelove (a merchant), and Fainwell (the hero). It seems probable that Centlivre (like Addison, Steele, and Swift) was influenced by Ward.

21 Troyer, *Ned Ward*, 244, 273–4.

22 Briggs, "Satiric Strategy," 80.

23 One can easily get an impression of what the Spy is talking about by consulting some online photography; see Reeve, "Tower of London: Royal Armoury"; Gareth, "Armoury Images Hampton Court," Flickr. Similar arrangements can be seen in the Great Hall at Edinburgh Castle. Despite the Spy's comments on the aesthetical impression made by such elaborate symmetry, it is worth noting that these arms still played a role in the military power of England.

24 For information on Isaac Fuller and his works, see Croft-Murray, *Decorative Painting in England*, 1:43–4, 220–1.

25 It was scaled back to four days in 1691.

26 Day one consists of Parts 1 and 2, but thereafter it is impossible to ascertain exactly when a day ends. There is a gap between Parts 5 and 6. The end of Part 6 is the excursion to Mob's Hole. Part 7 sees the pair take a wherry to Dorset Garden, and Part 8 a coach to St James's Palace and Park, thence to the Mall, Westminster (the Abbey then the Hall), and a survey of the burnt-out ruins of Whitehall, the last and greatest fire having occurred in January 1698. Part 9 covers the area around the Naval Office, Charing Cross, the Strand, the New Exchange, and Covent Garden. Another day? Most of Parts 10 and 11 describe Bartholomew Fair. Part 12 begins at a coffee house in Aldergate St and then moves to Blow Bladder St, where the Lord Mayor's parade is observed (29 October). Part 13 covers a trip to see the rarities at the Tower. Part 14 (December 1699) covers the Christmas Carnival. Part 15 opens with a statement to the effect that the author will henceforth offer "characters," the first being a victualler. Part 16 begins with the guide leaving the Spy after "about a month since" (281), and given all the detail and places covered thus far, a month seems a plausible estimate of the fictional time. Much of the rest of Part 16 concerns the Spy meeting with a seafarer. The Spy and guide reunite in Part 17, which describes bankers and a christening. Part 18 covers Dryden's funeral procession (13 May 1700), a prizefighter from Dorset Garden, and a Guildhall trial.

27 The 1697 elected Lord Mayor, Humphrey Edwin (barber-surgeon), was a Non-Conformist and his parade lacked pageantry. He was followed by Levett's predecessor, Francis Child (goldsmith), who restored the grand spectacle of the parade. In fact, his parade had been choreographed by none other than Elkannah Settle and was commemorated with a folio publication with plates: Settle, *Glory's Resurrection: Being the Triumph of London Revived.* With a total of six pages including four leaves of plates representing only the four pageants and sculptures (and no people), the

publication is a considerably smaller version of Lant's volume on Sir Philip Sidney's funeral; see chap. 8. For details about Levett's parade, see *The Triumphs of London.* (For Hogarth's use of the Lord Mayor's Parade in the *Industry and Idleness* series, see in this volume chap. 12, 302–3.)

Paula Backscheider comments on similar works, like *London's Triumph Presented* (1662), that commemorated the early years of Charles II's reign; see *Spectacular Politics,* 36–9, 49–56.

28 Frances, *A History of the Bank of England,* 2:262.

29 *The Triumphs of London* (1699), 2–3.

30 See Scott, *The Life of Dryden,* 370–2; and Ward, *The Life of John Dryden,* 317–18. Scott cites Ward (i.e., *The London Spy*) on Dryden's refusal to have his leg amputated as if it were authoritative.

31 First created by Hubert le Sueur in 1633, the statue disappeared during the interregnum until it was restored in 1675. It replaced the original Eleanor cross on that site.

10

Prospect Views: Landscapes, Knowledge, and Political Spectatorship in the Eighteenth Century

FRANS DE BRUYN

In August 1789, Edmund Burke recorded his first reaction to the French Revolution in a letter to the Irish statesman Lord Charlemont, in which he described recent events in France revealingly as a "Spectacle."

> As to us here our thoughts of every thing at home are suspended, by our astonishment at the wonderful Spectacle which is exhibited in a Neighbouring and rival Country – what Spectators, and what actors! England gazing with astonishment at a French struggle for Liberty and not knowing whether to blame or to applaud![1]

Like a theatregoer after the opening scene of an extravagant production, Burke professes astonishment at what he is seeing but is noncommittal about his eventual judgment of the performance. His comment makes an apposite *terminus ad quem* for a collection of essays on early modern spectatorship in Britain down to the turn of the eighteenth century. From the outset of the Revolution, Burke viewed events in France as spectacle, but how are we to understand this? What does it mean to be a spectator of political events unfolding at a distance internationally, and what, exactly, does such an act of spectatorship entail? And in the context of this collection, what is distinctive about the ways in which the eighteenth century understood political spectacle and spectatorship?

At one level the answer to these questions is straightforward: conceiving of political events as a theatrical spectacle draws on an ancient topos in Western thought, famously summed up in Shakespeare's adage, "All the world's a stage." This conception of *theatrum mundi* or "theatre of the world," which evokes a cosmic order in which all are divinely ordained to play their allotted roles, certainly informs Burke's repeated characterizations of revolutionary events in the 1790s as alternately tragedy or farce. Indeed, this dimension of his analysis of the Revolution, especially in *Reflections on the Revolution in France* (1790), has attracted considerable commentary.[2] In this essay, however, I should like to explore a quite different kind of spectatorship, also invoked by Burke in his writings on France, one that derives from contemporary conventions of landscape representation. As will appear, these conventions pose problematic questions about the role of the spectator and the epistemological status of spectatorship in the eighteenth century.

The event that provoked Burke to write *Reflections on the Revolution in France* was a sermon preached by the Reverend Richard Price, a Dissenting clergyman, at a meeting of the London Revolution Society on 4 November 1789 celebrating the 101st anniversary of the Glorious Revolution. In the peroration of his sermon, Price rejoices that he has "lived to see … an arbitrary monarch surrendering himself to his subjects."[3] Price describes himself as a "witness" to the French Revolution, but Burke dismisses the preacher's account of what he has "lived to see" as the product of a depraved taste, like that of a theatre audience hungering after lurid sensation: "A cheap, bloodless reformation, a guiltless liberty, appear flat and vapid to their taste. There must be a great change of scene; there must be a magnificent stage effect; there must be a grand spectacle to rouze the imagination." In the sentences immediately following, however, Burke presents Price as a very different kind of spectator, one who, "viewing, from the Pisgah of his pulpit, the free, moral, happy, flourishing, and glorious state of France, as in a bird's-eye landscape of a promised land," sees the country not as a theatrical spectacle but as a landscape beheld from a commanding prospect.[4] Like Moses, who was shown the Promised Land from the summit ("Pisgah") of Mount Nebo but never entered it, Price imagines that he has been vouchsafed a glimpse of Europe's future as a continent of liberty.

This marked alteration in spectatorial perspectives mirrors the larger movement of Burke's text, in which an account of events in Paris during the summer and fall of 1789, presented to the reader as a tragic narrative, gives way to a lengthy, sober political and economic analysis of the Revolution's impact on contemporary France. Metaphorically, this analysis is rendered as a prospect view. The reader is invited, in words that echo Burke's description of what Price sees from "the Pisgah of his pulpit," to share in an ocular survey of the French landscape:

> [W]hen I consider the face of the kingdom of France; the multitude and opulence of her cities; the useful magnificence of her spacious high roads and bridges; the opportunity of her artificial canals and navigations opening the conveniences of maritime communication through a solid continent of so immense an extent; when I turn my eyes to the stupendous works of her ports and harbors, and to her whole naval apparatus, whether for war or trade; when I bring before my view the number of her fortifications, constructed with so bold and masterly a skill and made and maintained at so prodigious a charge, presenting an armed front and impenetrable barrier to her enemies upon every side; when I recollect how very small a part of that extensive region is without cultivation ... I behold in all this something ... which demands, that we should very seriously examine, what and how great are the latent vices that could authorize us at once to level so spacious a fabric with the ground.[5]

Burke here sums up the argument of his treatise in a bravura periodic sentence of almost three hundred words, in which verb phrases of seeing and mental reflection – "consider," "turn my eyes," "bring before my view," "recollect," "behold" – mark him as a Lockean spectator for whom sense perception (especially sight), together with the mind's deliberations on the deliverances of the senses, is the basis of what we know. Burke's text shifts perspective from a conception of spectatorship as little more than sensation (and sensationalism) to spectatorship conceived as an avenue to knowledge.

I propose in this essay to trace how a literary convention that began by insisting on the actual ocular experience of looking at a landscape from a specific vantage point (in John Denham's *Coopers Hill*, James Thomson's *The Seasons*, and John Dyer's *Grongar Hill*, for instance) evolved over the eighteenth century in ways that transformed actual sight into imagined sight and eventually abandoned sight altogether.[6] The reasons for such a transformation are numerous and complex, involving a growing gap between the literary convention and what it was meant to represent. In some instances, the landscape surveyed was too vast to be visible to the naked eye; or the view might be conceived temporally rather than spatially, extending into past and future. A prospect view could be a (re)construction or a composite, created by an act of imagination, rather than a view available to the naked eye. The very act of perception (what do we actually see when we are seeing, or how do we see what we are seeing?) or the epistemological basis of the prospect view was itself increasingly called into question. Prospects appeared also in a variety of genres: not just landscape poetry, but prose genres of topographical and political description, such as tours, chorographies, states, surveys, and statistical tables.[7] By the end of the eighteenth century, the poetic convention was giving way to new ways of "seeing," as the nascent science of statistics supplanted the ocular reach of the poetic prospect. In all of this the role of the spectator and the status of spectatorship were perpetually in flux.

Prospects and Understanding

A landscape prospect is not normally referred to as a spectacle, nor is an admirer of such a view customarily thought of as a spectator, so a word of justification is in order at the outset for considering topographical representations from the perspective of spectatorship. In his *Dictionary of the English Language*, Samuel Johnson defines *spectacle* as "A shew; a gazing stock; anything exhibited to the view as eminently remarkable," but also more generally as "Anything perceived by the sight." A *spectator*, meanwhile, is "A looker-on; a beholder." What marks an object as a spectacle, in Johnson's definition, is that it is exhibited to the public gaze, which it attracts by virtue of some "remarkable" attribute that excites curiosity or admiration. Eighteenth-century garden landscapes, particularly those commissioned by wealthy landowners, were consciously designed by landscape gardeners to be spectacles in this sense, as the poet William Cowper scornfully notes in *The Task*: "Estates are landscapes, gazed upon awhile, / Then advertised, and auctioneer'd away."[8]

Stephen Daniels cites these lines in arguing that eighteenth-century landscape prospects functioned like stage scenery, consciously designed as backdrops for the theatrical self-presentation of the gentry: "In the various sites of their power, from assize courts to ox roasts, the style of the gentry had always been theatrical, and landscape parks were perhaps the most theatrical sites of all."[9] He contends that polite culture in the eighteenth century was itself "a highly, and self-consciously, theatrical environment." Even landscapes not sculpted for the purpose by a garden designer were "framed" rhetorically as "scenic attractions with guidebooks, marked paths and viewpoints."[10] This sort of "staging" of landscape is precisely what eighteenth-century poets themselves sometimes undertook in their descriptions of prospect scenes, such as Thomson's view of the Thames Valley west of London, seen from the vicinity of Richmond Park:

> Here let us sweep
> The boundless Landskip; now the raptured Eye,
> Exulting swift, to huge Augusta send,
> Now to the *Sister-Hills* that skirt her Plain,
> To lofty *Harrow* now, and now to where
> Majestic *Windsor* lifts his Princely Brow.
> …
> Heavens! what a goodly Prospect spreads around,
> Of Hills, and Dales, and Woods, and Lawns, and Spires,
> And glittering Towns, and gilded Streams, till all
> The stretching Landskip into Smoke decays!
> Happy Britannia![11]

Like other eighteenth-century theatrical spectacles, this rhetorically staged landscape is designed to evoke a moral, prompted in this instance by the mind's reflection on the visible prosperity of the scene. Landscape features are selected and highlighted for political purposes, as well as on account of their geographical prominence. The term "prospect" suggests also a projection into the past and future: prospects can be temporal as well as spatial. With the mind's eye, visible prospects furnish mental perspectives along with physical ones – what Samuel Johnson refers to in his *Life of Denham* as "historical retrospection, or incidental meditation."[12]

Despite the obvious constructedness of these landscape descriptions (to say nothing of the landscapes themselves), the prospect view succeeded rhetorically as a literary (and painterly) convention because it in fact modelled the manner in which the mind was thought to work and how we come to an understanding of the world around us. Despite their artifice, Tim Fulford argues, representations of landscape in eighteenth-century poetry "asked to be read and seen as 'just representations of general nature' ... to be judged disinterestedly as reflections of the scene rather than approved as rhetorically persuasive social or political argument."[13] Prospect views conveyed an air of detached objectivity because everyone assented to the underlying premises of spectatorship – the processes of sight and insight, sensation and reflection – that prospect poems in effect embodied and performed. Ralph Cohen describes how these premises gave rise to what he calls an "Augustan mode" of poetry: "Augustan poetry converts inherited poetic features or conventions by relating them to scientific spatial assumptions, to philosophical assumptions regarding the acquisition of knowledge by experience, experiment, and observation, and to religious assumptions that connect local observation with God's presence in infinity."[14]

Richard Jago, for example, attests to this epistemological consensus by his adoption, as an epigraph to his poem *Edge-Hill, or, the Rural Prospect Delineated and Moralized*, Joseph Addison's opening statement on the pleasures of the imagination in *The Spectator* no. 411: "Our Sight is the most perfect, and most delightful of all our Senses. It fills the Mind with the largest Variety of Ideas, converses with its Objects at the greatest Distance, and continues the longest in Action, without being tired or satiated with its proper Enjoyments."[15] In *Elements of General Knowledge* (1802), Henry Kett, a tutor at Trinity College, Oxford, invokes the prospect view as a self-evident metaphor for the process of acquiring knowledge. He clearly takes for granted that his readership will share the structure of beliefs that informs his analogy. To educate is to open up for the student "the interesting prospects of a charming country."

> I shall conduct him, who commits himself to my directions, from a low and narrow valley, where his views have been closely confined, to the summit of a lofty mountain: when he has reached the proper point of view, he will feel his faculties expand, he will breathe a purer air, enjoy a wider horizon, and observe woods, lakes, mountains, plains and rivers, spreading beneath his feet in delightful prospect. From this commanding eminence, I shall point out such places as are most deserving his researches.[16]

Nothing, seemingly, could be more natural, Kett suggests, than to conceive of learning in this way as an inventory of "Prospects, distinctly and deliberately surveyed." To undertake such a survey is to assist the mind in its natural operations: "By studies thus diversified, the mind … is enabled, by the combination of many particular ideas, to form those general principles, which it is ever eager to embrace, and which are of eminent use in the conduct of life."[17]

Yet, as Ralph Cohen, John Barrell, and other scholars have noted, this apparently universal mental operation was in fact circumscribed in a particular way, making it available only to a privileged and defined class of individuals.[18] A mind habitually focused on "any one pursuit" or trained to a specific profession, craft, or occupation cannot escape a partial perspective on things, partial both in the sense of embracing only parts or constituents rather than a totality and in the sense of an undue predisposition towards a biased outlook. In order to grasp in its entirety what a prospect view lays out before the spectator, it is necessary to bring to it a mind detached and free of self-interest, with the leisure to train itself to a liberal perspective on things, for (in Kett's words) "comprehensive views of learning and science are calculated to produce the best effects upon the mind."[19] In eighteenth-century Britain such impartiality was thought to reside with the landowning class, for they, by virtue of the privilege, education, and independence that landownership afforded, were deemed, in Edmund Burke's words, "To stand upon such elevated ground as to be enabled to take a large view of the wide-spread and infinitely diversified combinations of men and affairs in a large society."[20]

From a twenty-first-century perspective it is easy to detect the ideological bias of this rationale for the convention of the prospect view. Much is omitted or invisible when the landscape is viewed thus, from a perspective ostensibly comprehensive, but seen actually from above and at a distance. The urban landscape of London, for instance, is reduced in *Coopers Hill* to a smoky smudge on the horizon.

> Under his [St Paul's] proud survey the City lies
> And like a mist beneath a hill doth rise;
> Whose state and wealth the business and the crowd,
> Seems at this distance but a darker cloud:
> And is to him who rightly things esteems,
> No other in effect than what it seems.[21]

Barrell argues that this effacement of the urban scene is necessary, given that the "town, buried in smoke and divided by interest, inhibits a clear and disinterested vision of the world."[22] The farmer and the rural labourer similarly dwindle to invisibility in such a bird's-eye perspective: the landscape that is the fruit of their labours seems magically laid out in all its productivity before the viewer.

Despite this, the distanced, extended prospect was frequently accorded a kind of epistemological privilege. Fulford points to the philosopher George Berkeley, who observes that

> he who stands close to a palace, can hardly make a right judgment of the architecture and symmetry of its several parts, the nearer ever appearing disproportionately great. And if we have a mind to take a fair prospect of the order and general well-being, which the inflexible laws of nature and morality derive on the world, we must, if I may so say, go out of it, and imagine our selves to be distant spectators of all that is transacted and contained in it; otherwise we are sure to be deceived by the too near view of the little present interests of ourselves, our friends, or our country.[23]

Berkeley's observation appears in *A Discourse on Passive Obedience*, a polemical pamphlet defending a controversial political and religious doctrine. Writing in a more philosophical context, he would doubtless have acknowledged the case to be more complex than he states it here. As he writes in the introduction to *A Treatise Concerning the Principles of Human Knowledge*, "the largest Views are not always the Clearest, and … he who is Short-sighted will be obliged to draw the Object nearer, and may, perhaps, by a close and narrow Survey discern that which had escaped far better Eyes."[24]

If anything, the tendency of eighteenth-century philosophical inquiry was to call into question the basis and extent of epistemological certainty. In book 4 of *An Essay Concerning Human Understanding*, John Locke addresses what he regards as inevitable limits to the scope of human knowledge, especially when, as is very often the case, only probable certainty is possible rather than demonstrative proof. He writes of the need in such circumstances to exercise judgment, which requires laborious and careful attention.

> The mind sometimes exercises this *Judgment* out of necessity, where demonstrative Proofs and certain Knowledge are not to be had; and sometimes out of Laziness, Unskilfulness, or Haste … Men often stay not warily to examine the Agreement or Disagreement of two *Ideas*, which they are desirous or concerned to know; but, either incapable of such Attention, as is requisite in a long Train of Gradations, or impatient of delay, lightly cast their Eyes on, or wholly pass by the Proofs; and so, without making out the Demonstration, determine of the Agreement or Disagreement of two *Ideas*, as it were by a view of them as they are at a distance, and take it to be the one or the other, as seems most likely to them upon such a loose survey.[25]

Locke characterizes undisciplined reflection here in spatial terms as viewing from a distance, which results in a "loose survey" rather than a rigorous comparison of ideas. He understands distance here not as affording a synthesized overview, as Berkeley suggests, but as impeding precision of understanding. Seeing from a distance makes it difficult to discern the parts that make up a whole (or the constituents of an idea) and to understand their relations.

In *A Treatise of Human Nature*, David Hume considers the problematic epistemological status of observation that extends through space or time. Things contiguous to us strike our imaginations "with a peculiar force and vivacity," but that power is weakened by spatial and temporal distance.

> When we reflect, therefore, on any object distant from ourselves, we are oblig'd not only to reach it at first by passing thro' all the intermediate space betwixt ourselves and the object, but also to renew our progress every moment; being every moment recall'd to the consideration of ourselves and our present situation … The *fewer* steps we make to arrive at the object, and the *smoother* the road is, this diminution of vivacity is less sensibly felt, but still may be observ'd more or less in proportion to the degrees of distance and difficulty.[26]

This weakening influence of objects on the imagination is even more noticeable over a span of time, for spatial distance can be surmounted by the spectator, but temporally we have direct experience only of the present moment, so as events recede into the past, our conception of them fades correspondingly. Interestingly, for Hume, our psychological tendency to anticipate future events, and the natural progression inherent in thinking forward rather than backward, render such events more vivid to the imagination than past occurrences, with the consequence that our conception of future time is stronger than the past.

In short, if a distant prospect, an overview, offers no more than a "loose survey" of objects, in Locke's phrase, how can a landscape prospect be defended as an adequate procedure (or metaphor) for arriving at a reliable, comprehensive understanding of things? Can such a prospect, such a landscape, be viewed as anything more than a theatrical spectacle or an object of aesthetic pleasure? As will appear, Burke (among others) argues that it can, though his sardonic dismissal of Price's bird's-eye prospect of France as an intoxicated "rapture," provoked by his breathing too deeply "the fumes of his oracular tripod," signals his determination to impart a philosophical rigour to what would otherwise invite rejection as an empty rhetorical gesture.

Prospect Views, Survey Lines, and Maps

Writers who employed prospects in their works addressed these knotty questions in various ways and with varying degrees of self-awareness. Their responses point in sometimes contradictory directions. Topographical poets – at least those who employed a determinate point of view in their prospect surveys – tended to emphasize the physical, reportorial accuracy of their descriptions. (Denham's *Coopers Hill*, for example, has an identifiable physical vantage point, whereas Alexander Pope's *Windsor-Forest* does not.) John Wilson Foster argues that the distinctive features of the prospect view evolved to accentuate scientific, documentary accuracy. He emphasizes "how in topographical poetry the eye became a physical instrument instead of being confused with the muse and fancy, how point of view became fixed and limited instead of omniscient, how perspective became physically credible instead of ideal and unrealistic, and how the poet became an observer instead of an omnipresent witness."[27] Others, such as writers of political "states" and "surveys," insisted less on circumstantial accuracy in their landscape overviews, using them, rather, as representative preliminary statements intended to anchor or contextualize the detailed, methodically organized information that follows in their texts.

A number of such prose "states," focusing on England or Great Britain, appeared at the beginning of the eighteenth century. What distinguishes the bird's-eye views in these texts from poetic prospects later in the century is that they offer composite overviews, tending towards the emblematic, of the country as a whole rather than a perspective from a specified viewpoint. Robert Morden's *The New Description and State of England* (1701) is a case in point, opening with the declaration that "*MAGNA BRITANNIA*, or *Great Britain* is, and hath always been reckoned since its first Discovery, most Noble, most Fruitful, most Excellent, and most Blessed Island of the World, not only in regard of its Soil, Situation, Climat, and other natural Conveniencies, but also in respect of its brave, valiant, beautiful, skilful, and industrious Inhabitants." To this encomium he adds, "And of this Island … 'tis not disputable nor questionable but that *England* is the chief, the most fruitful, the wealthiest, and the most convenient for the Habitation of Mankind."[28] These overviews appear with such regularity that they must be considered one of the defining features of the genre of the state. Guy Miège's *The New State of England* is another case in point: "Of all the *States* of Europe, there's none more happy than *England*, whether we consider the Advantages of its *Situation*, the Temperateness of its *Air*, the Richness of its *Soil*, the happy temper of its *Inhabitants*, or the Blessed Constitution of its Government."[29] The catalogue of topics proper to such a descriptive overview (like a poetic blazon, or record of virtues and excellences, applied to landscape) eventually evolved into the statistical categories that political statisticians came to use in their states, surveys, and gazetteers.

The generic, emblematic character of these introductory overviews is even more obvious in an earlier example, Edward Chamberlayne's *Angliae Notitia* (1669), which describes England in terms identical to those used by Virgil to celebrate his native land in the second book of the *Georgics*.[30] Virgil's Italy is temperate, fertile, favourably situated, free of noxious plants and animals, blessed with prosperous towns and cities, and populated by a hardy, self-reliant race. Chamberlayne's England mirrors these glories in well-nigh every particular.

> It is blessed with a very fertile wholesome *Soyle*, watered abundantly with *Springs* and *Streams*, and in divers parts with great *Navigable Rivers*; few barren *Mountains* or craggy *Rocks*, but generally gentle pleasant *Hills*, and fruitful *Valleys*, apt for *Grain*, *Grass*, or *Wood* … [H]er *Valleys* are like *Eden*, her *Hills* like *Lebanon*, her *Springs* as *Pisgah*, and her *Rivers* as *Jordan* … O happy and blessed *Britain*, above all other Countries in the World, *Nature* hath enricht thee with all the blessings of *Heaven* and *Earth*: Nothing in thee is hurtful to Mankind, nothing wanting in thee that is desirable, in so much that thou seemest another World placed besides, or without the great World, meerly for the delight and pleasure of Mankind.[31]

Virgil's panegyric on Italy is clearly designed to recall the classical myth of a bygone Golden Age, just as Chamberlayne's encomium on England recalls, in biblical cadences, the Garden of Eden and the Promised Land. Such an idealized landscape is not designed as a faithful representation of an actual scene, to be viewed and reflected upon by a spectator; instead, it offers itself as a kind of hypothesis, to be confirmed factually by the wealth of information subsequently provided. As I have argued elsewhere, these overviews "provide a unifying framework by means of which the discrete particulars and facts collected by the authors can be placed, compared, and interpreted."[32] They offer a way to overcome the perennial gap between part and whole in the acquisition and interpretation of knowledge.

The term "state" often appeared interchangeably with the term "survey" in the titles of these descriptive accounts. A case in point is Thomas Cox's six-volume *Magna Britannia antiqua & nova: or, a New, Exact, and Comprehensive Survey of the Ancient and Present State of Great-Britain* (1738). To "survey" a landscape, as opposed to summing up the "state" of a place or thing at a particular time (the word "state" connoting a relatively static tableau or "snapshot"), is to engage in an active, methodical process that unfolds spatially and temporally. This is precisely the kind of movement that prospect poetry strives for, and the word "survey," as Foster points out, appears regularly in the lexicon of topographical poets. Denham writes, for instance, in *Coopers Hill* of how his eye "descending from the Hill, surveys / Where *Thames* amongst the wanton vallies strays"; Thomson, after laying out the prospect of the Thames Valley in *Summer*, prays for "Public Zeal" to eye the land with "equal, wide survey"; Samuel Johnson declares, in the opening lines of *The Vanity of Human Wishes* (a poem of moral topography), "Let Observation with extensive View / Survey Mankind, from *China* to *Peru*"; and Jago announces in *Edge-Hill* his purpose to "scan" the landscape attentively, "with accurate survey."[33]

An important link between the discursive structure of the prose "state" or "survey" and the poetic spectacle of the prospect is made explicit in Jago's preface to *Edge-Hill*. The title of his poem, he writes, refers to a place notable "for its extensive, and agreeable Prospect" and also for its historical significance as the site of the first pitched battle of the English

Civil War (the Battle of Edgehill in 1642). Jago explains the procedure he undertook to render poetically these two "Circumstances of natural Beauty, and historical Importance."

> His Business ... was, first to select a Stock of Materials fit for his Purpose, and then to arrange them in the best Order he could. Both these Points he endeavoured to effect, not only by consulting his Eye, but also by considering the Character, Natural History, and other Circumstances of such Places as were most likely to afford Matter for Ornament, or Instruction of this Kind; forming from the Whole, by an imaginary Line, a Number of distinct Scenes, placed in the most advantageous Light.[34]

An appropriate "Stock of Materials" and their methodical arrangement – these are the key features that link the states of Chamberlayne, Miège, and Morden, in their organization and content, to Jago's prospect poem. But the basis of Jago's arrangement, as Foster argues, is not just the analytical categories of the political economist but, equally important, the eye of the observer, who in this instance adopts the methods of scientific observation.

The "imaginary Line" that Jago refers to in his preface is in fact a survey line, as Foster explains:

> His procedure is as methodical as any surveyor's. From his first station on the summit of Edge-Hill, he scans, as far away as Ragley Hall, the northwest to southwest sector, in an orderly and sweeping motion. His second station at the castle on Ratley Hill affords him a view of the countryside farther north, as far as Coventry in his first session and Birmingham in his second. His third station, after an "evening walk along the hill to the N.E. point," gives him the countryside northeast of Edge-Hill as far away as Northampton. In this schematic way, Jago surveys about 180 degrees of the circular prospect theoretically available to him. If we plot Jago's many bearings with the aid of a map, the result resembles triangulation.[35]

Jago strives for an air of scientific authority by adopting the professional techniques of land surveying, a science that achieved its modern-day accuracy in the eighteenth century with the introduction of the theodolite and the extension of triangulation networks across entire countries, notably France and Britain. Some readers, among them Andrew Chalmers, thought the outcome at best a mixed success. *Edge-Hill*, he concludes, "has some passages not destitute of animation, but it is so topographically exact, that to enjoy it the reader must have a map constantly before him."[36]

Chalmers's assessment points up an ironic circumstance: the desire to make a poetically rendered topographical representation more comprehensive, more accurate, succeeds only by displacing one form of representation with another. Careful land surveying in the late eighteenth century went hand in hand with advances in cartography (the period of the French Revolution saw the establishment of the Ordnance Survey), and maps in the period incorporated triangulation diagrams to verify their scientific basis. As a consequence of this Enlightenment mapping process, maps have acquired, in Matthew Edney's phrase, "a privileged status as objective bearers of truth," a status "epistemologically distinct from that accorded to other representational strategies, such as writing and landscape imagery, which are widely recognized as flexible and problematic."[37] Chalmers's remark suggests that Jago's strategy of adopting the eye of the surveyor as his structural point of view in *Edge-Hill*, designed to give his poem an air of scientific objectivity, ends with the creation of a poem that requires what the surveyor's labours are calculated to produce – a map – in order to be enjoyed and understood. Rather than resolving the ongoing question of representational fidelity and comprehensiveness, Jago's poem simply defers it by his adoption of a poetic structure based on a mathematical representation of space.

Yet, Jago's experimental marriage of poetic and mathematical surveying manifested itself elsewhere as well, notably in two poems by William Wordsworth describing Black Combe Mountain, which lies in the south-west corner of the Lake District near the Irish Sea. Wordsworth declares the view from the top of Black Combe the greatest prospect in all Britain: "This Height a ministering Angel might select: / For from the summit of

BLACK COMB ... / the amplest range / Of unobstructed prospect may be seen / That British ground commands."[38] The view itself is a 360-degree vista, described by the poet in terms that recall the surveyor's art:

> low dusky tracts,
> Where Trent is nursed, far southward! Cambrian hills
> To the south-west, a multitudinous show;
> And, in a line of eye-sight linked with these,
> The hoary peaks of Scotland ...
> Right at the imperial station's western base,
> Main ocean, breaking audibly, and stretched
> Far into silent regions blue and pale; –
> And visibly engirding Mona's Isle [Isle of Man]
> That, as we left the plain, before our sight
> Stood like a lofty mount, uplifting slowly
> (Above the convex of the watery globe)
> Into clear view the cultured fields that streak
> Her habitable shores, but now appears
> A dwindled object, and submits to lie
> At the spectator's feet. – Yon azure ridge,
> Is it a perishable cloud? Or there
> Do we behold the line of Erin's coast?[39]

Wordsworth gives compass headings for the directions in which his gaze is successively carried, from south (Trent) to southwest (Wales), thence by a surveyor's "line of eye-sight" to the northeast (Scotland), and finally west (towards the Isle of Man and the Irish coast). The prospect encompasses the political entities that make up Great Britain, though Ireland, as James Garrett notes, is only "doubtfully perceived," its unclear outline mirroring its problematic inclusion in the United Kingdom.[40] But the contiguous lands of England, Scotland, and Wales present a harmonious spectacle: "Look homeward now! / In depth, in height, in circuit, how serene / The spectacle, how pure!"[41]

"View from the Top of Black Comb," as Wordsworth titled this poem, is generally read in tandem with a companion piece, "Written with a Slate

Pencil on a Stone, on the Side of the Mountain of Black Comb." The latter poem connects the convention of the prospect view with the science of surveying and the project of map-making that this science subserves. "Written with a Slate Pencil" takes as its theme the national "trigonometrical surveys," under the direction of William Mudge, then underway to accurately map Great Britain. The poem tells of a "geographic Labourer" on the summit of Black Combe, who there

> pitched his tent,
> With books supplied and instruments of art,
> To measure height and distance; lonely task,
> Week after week pursued!—To him was given
> Full many a glimpse (but sparingly bestowed
> On timid man) of Nature's processes
> Upon the exalted hills. He made report
> That once, while there he plied his studious work
> Within that canvass Dwelling, colours, lines,
> And the whole surface of the out-spread map,
> Became invisible: for all around
> Had darkness fallen—unthreatened, unproclaimed—
> As if the golden day itself had been
> Extinguished in a moment; total gloom,
> In which he sate alone, with unclosed eyes,
> Upon the blinded mountain's silent top![42]

A number of critics have observed how "Written with a Slate Pencil" questions the limits of the nationalistic, military-sponsored drive to survey and map the nation by the surveyor's lines of sight. Garrett points, for instance, to Wordsworth's uncertainty at the time he wrote these two poems about the value of an "imperial prospect view with its 'grand terraqueous vision'" in view of the dangers such a project might pose to local autonomy and distinctiveness.[43]

The darkness that descends upon the geographical labourer suggests that describing the land by means of mathematical measurement, rather than attending (with the aid of imagination or the mind's eye) to "Nature's processes," is to surrender to what Wordsworth in *The Prelude* terms the "tyranny" of sight, the "most despotic of our senses." He there describes a time when his eye, the eighteenth-century emblem of empiricism, wrested a "wider empire for the sight" and laid his "inner faculties asleep."

> The state to which I now allude was one
> In which the eye was master of the heart,
> When that which is in every stage of life
> The most despotic of our senses gained
> Such strength in me as often held my mind
> In absolute dominion.[44]

The limits of spectatorship are vividly dramatized in the "darkness visible" that prevents the geographer's eye from prosecuting its task. In the context of our present discussion, this same darkness can be read as Wordsworth's contribution to the questioning of comprehensiveness and epistemological adequacy that the use of the prospect view repeatedly prompted.

Future Prospects: States, Surveys, and Early Statistics

In the concluding pages of this essay, I return to the prose states and surveys of the eighteenth century and their use of the convention of the prospect view. Wordsworth himself bridges the poetic and prose traditions of the landscape prospect in *A Guide through the District of the Lakes in the North of England*, first published in 1810. In a well-known passage that opens the first section of the *Guide*, he describes having seen in Lucerne, Switzerland, a model of part of the Swiss Alps: "The Spectator ascends a little platform, and sees mountains, lakes, glaciers, rivers, woods, waterfalls, and vallies … lying at his feet." The delight he feels in viewing this spectacle, a Lilliputian, scale-model representation of a vast landscape, is supplemented with a "more substantial pleasure": for by means of the bird's-eye view the model affords, "the sublime and beautiful region, with all its hidden treasures, and their bearings and relations to each other, is … comprehended and understood at once."[45] Once again, the distant view promises unified understanding, though in this instance that knowledge comes from viewing a representation of a greater landscape than the human eye is capable of seeing from a terrestrial vantage point.

Wordsworth has no equivalent model of the Lake District to proffer his reader, so he solicits the imagination instead to supply the deficiency by placing the reader at the summit of "Great Gavel, or Scawfell" – or, rather, on "a cloud hanging midway between those two mountains." From here, the view is of eight valleys "diverging from the point, on which we are supposed to stand, like spokes from the nave of a wheel."[46] This circular view with its radiating spokes bears an obvious affinity with the survey lines measured by the surveyor, and it has been observed that Wordsworth may well have taken his cue from James Clarke's diagram in *A Survey of the Lakes of Cumberland, Westmorland, and Lancashire* (1789) of sight lines looking south from Penrith Beacon, a diagram that tellingly places a human eye at the nodal point (see fig. 10.1).[47]

Clarke's description of the prospect from Penrith Beacon begins, "If the day be clear, you see Cumberland spread out like an immense map under you," and it proceeds, like Wordsworth's wheel, to catalogue the visible sights in all directions. As for his accompanying diagram, Clarke assures the reader that when properly aligned, "the Plan will … explain the country round, much better than the generality of guides will be able to do," even better, presumably, than his own verbal description.[48]

Alan Liu observes that Wordsworth's *Guide*, like other guides, tours, gazetteers, states, and surveys of the time, supplements its prospects and topographical views with "details of local administration." He accounts for this circumstance in a Foucauldian manner, arguing that this mixture of materials reflects the "politics of the picturesque" in Wordsworth's time, which strove to "police" the rural landscape and its inhabitants: "The picturesque … was the late-eighteenth- and early-nineteenth-century idea of bureaucracy as 'natural.' … [O]nly so can we account for the fact that the strength of Wordsworth's own *Guide* lies precisely in its supervision of landscape and population together (Sections I and II of the 1835 edition)."[49] Liu illustrates his argument by juxtaposing the panoramic wheel of Wordsworth's landscape prospect with another panorama, this one contained in an unpublished manuscript of materials apparently intended for inclusion in a revised version of the *Guide*. The latter lays out the view of Lancaster Castle from its principal tower, a prospect that includes the unhappy spectacle of the prisoners confined there pursuant to

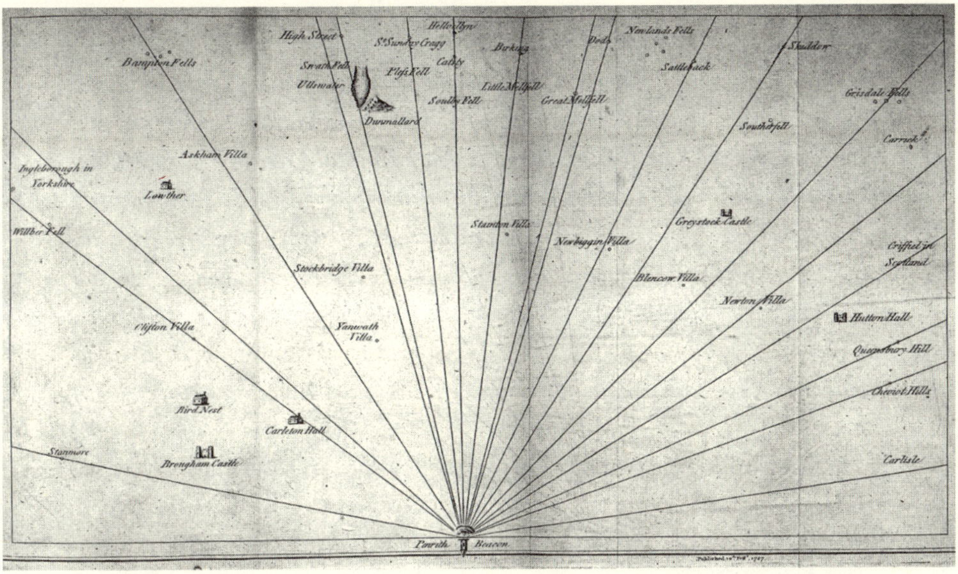

Fig. 10.1 James Clarke's diagram in *A Survey of the Lakes of Cumberland, Westmorland, and Lancashire* (1789) of sight lines looking south from Penrith Beacon.

"those coercive duties of civil polity which the infirmities of Men have rendered necessary."[50]

What Liu identifies in Wordsworth's *Guide* and similar texts at the beginning of the nineteenth century – their mixture of physical description and politico-social information – had in fact been a feature of such texts for over a century, as we have seen in the states of Chamberlayne, Miège, and Morden. This circumstance suggests a less minatory explanation for the generic combination in these texts of what Liu calls a "supervision of landscape and population together." On its own, an ocular view of the landscape makes a problematic claim to comprehensiveness, so, like the prospect poet's adoption of the scientific perspective of the land-surveyor, the prose observer in states and surveys supplies a wealth of factual information to substantiate the unified overview with which the work customarily begins. This information, much of it descriptive but becoming progressively more numerical towards the end of the eighteenth century, was organized according to standardized categories which were presented in the form of tables and, sometimes, pioneering charts and graphs. The title of one such text, Thomas B. Clarke's 1791 survey of European states, enumerates the standard categories and illustrates the fact-gathering, taxonomic methodology of the enterprise: *A Statistical View of Europe, in Respect to the Forms of Government, Administration of Justice, Religion and Manners, of Each Nation, with Considerations on the Clergy and Literary Bodies, Agriculture and Productions of the Soil, Navigation, Money, and Political Interests; and a Distinct View of the Dominions, Extent, Population, Number of Inhabitants to a Square Mile, Chief Towns, with Their Size and Population, Revenues, Expences, Debts, and Military and Naval Strength of Each State.*

By the 1790s, the compilers of such collections of information had acquired a designation and an academic discipline, as Clarke's title reveals: they were statists or statisticians, and they practised what was coming to be known, in German universities especially, as a science of statistics that made use of "statistical tables" (though this was not as yet the mathematics-based applied science familiar to us today).[51] Henry Kett, who, as we have seen, deemed the prospect view a paradigmatic metaphor for the young gentleman's acquisition of knowledge, embraced this new discipline in *Elements of General Knowledge*.

> With respect indeed to foreign nations, the objects of his most useful attention are the actual power, the nature of their present governments, the state of civilization, sciences, and arts, their natural and artificial advantages, their population, produce, commerce, and relative importance in the scale of political greatness. This constitutes a branch of study, which has been of late years much cultivated by the Germans, and is distinguished by the name of *Statistics*. Travellers and statesmen must not claim this study as their own exclusive province, since it will be found extremely useful to every English gentleman.[52]

The growing reliance on numbers and tabular presentations in the descriptive accounts produced by pioneering statisticians suggests a parallel with the adoption by landscape poets of techniques of surveying in their prospect views. The turn to numerical data promised, as Mary Poovey argues, an objective form of representation apparently transparent and free from theory and value. Numbers seemed to be "simple descriptors of phenomenal particulars."[53] And they could represent (or describe) spaces and aggregates too great to be encompassed by the human eye. But numbers as a mode of representation tend towards abstraction and away from visual spectacle, a trend that the invention of graphs and charts was designed to counteract. Just as survey lines facilitated the perfection of the map as a mode of representing the landscape, so too numerical data spawned the creation of new visual tools. Instead of inferring national wealth from the prosperous appearance of the countryside, for example, one could visualize it in diagram form as a line or bar graph plotted over time.

It remains to consider the impact of these modes of visualization on the prospect view temporally conceived, rather than spatially perceived. This, in turn, brings us back to Burke's rejection of Richard Price's prophetic prospect of France's future (in the *Reflections*) in favour of his own statistically supported survey of the kingdom. The link between physical and temporal prospects is encapsulated in the Renaissance commonplace that "Geography and chronology are the eyes of history." New technologies of visualization (maps and chronological charts), perfected through the sciences of surveying and statistical description, strengthened the connection, as Kett affirms: "[Geography] assists the memory by the various associations of ideas, with which it furnishes the mind; and the prospect of a country presented by a map, or a globe, recalls the memorable transactions, which have been performed in it, and revives the recollection of its illustrious men."[54] But a temporal prospect, as Hume had observed, can point forward as well as backward. Prospects in this sense are expectations: the word once meant, as the *OED* reminds us, "Forethought; consideration or knowledge of something in the future." These senses have a biblical warrant as well. In the view God grants Moses of the Promised Land from the summit of Mount Nebo (Deut. 34) and in Satan's temptation of Jesus on the top of "an exceeding high mountain," from which he is offered "all the kingdoms of the world, and the glory of them" (Matt. 4), visible prospects are associated with prophecy.

The link is made explicit in John Milton's *Paradise Lost*, which concludes with the prospect of the future that the archangel Michael unveils to Adam from the highest point in Paradise, the amplitude of the visible scene giving way to a view of cosmic and human history down to the end of time.

So both ascend
In the Visions of God: It was a Hill
Of Paradise the highest, from whose top
The Hemisphere of Earth, in clearest Ken
Stretcht out to the amplest reach of prospect lay.
Not higher that Hill nor wider looking round,
Whereon for different cause, the Tempter set
Our second *Adam* in the Wilderness,
To show him all Earth's Kingdoms, and their Glory.[55]

Wordsworth recalls this moment in the opening line of "View from the Top of Black Comb," where he declares the mountain's summit a "Height a ministering Angel might select" for the "unobstructed prospect" it affords. The same Miltonic conceit inspired Burke in his 1775 *Speech on Conciliation with America*. Striving to make his audience understand the immense importance of America to Britain and to grasp what the future might hold, Burke imagines a ministering angel in 1704 showing a youthful Lord Bathurst (who in 1775 was ninety-one years old) the future prospect of America: "Suppose, Sir, that the angel of this auspicious youth … should have drawn up the curtain, and … whilst he was gazing with admiration on the then commercial grandeur of England … should point out to him a little speck … and should tell him – 'Young man, There is America – which at this day serves for little more than to amuse you with stories of savage men, and uncouth manners; yet shall, before you taste of death, shew itself equal to the whole of that commerce which now attracts the envy of the world.'"[56]

Burke asks his auditors in the House of Commons to pause for a moment and, as it were, admire the view: "Mr. Speaker, I cannot prevail on myself to hurry over this great consideration. It is good for us to be here. We stand where we have an immense view of what is, and what is past. Clouds, indeed, and darkness, rest upon the future. Let us however, before we descend from this noble eminence, reflect that this growth of national prosperity has happened in the short period of the life of man."[57] The future, he acknowledges, is uncertain, but in offering his listeners a prospect view of America, he hopes to prognosticate with some degree of probability the future course of events. He does so after furnishing an impressive survey or state of the Thirteen Colonies, buttressed by a wealth of statistical information. As with his prospect view of France in the *Reflections*, Burke ventures to predict what the future holds, not on the basis of Price's prophetic inspiration, but by means of a comprehensiveness built on a minute and thorough attention to detail.

Edward Chamberlayne held forth this emancipatory potential in his introductory remarks to *Angliae Notitia*. "Although the main aim is to inform all men of the *Present State* of this Kingdom," he tells the reader,

> yet divers *Reflections* are made upon the *past State* thereof, that so by comparing that with the present, some men may thereby not only be moved to endeavour the *Restauration* of what was heretofore better … but also in some measure may *fore-see* without consulting our *Astrologers* and *Apocalytick* men, what will be the *future* state of this Nation: according to that Excellent Saying, *Qui respicit praeterita & inspicit praesentia, prospicit etiam & futura. A good Historian by running back to Ages past, and by standing still and viewing the present times, and comparing the one with the other, may then run forward, and give a Verdict of the State almost Prophetick.*[58]

In the *Reflections*, Price's oracular enthusiasm for the visionary prospect he sees from his pulpit is a latter-day avatar of Chamberlayne's visionary "Astrologers and Apocalytick men." By contrast, Burke's prediction of what the future holds for France, as with his earlier prospect of America in the 1770s, illustrates how a literary convention grounded in procedures of mindful seeing and spectatorship underwent a transformation in the course of the eighteenth century as new technologies such as surveying, map-making, and statistical analysis sought to surmount the limitations of the naked eye.

NOTES

1 Burke, "To Lord Charlemont – 9 August 1789," in *The Correspondence of Edmund Burke*, 6:10.

2 See, for example, Melvin, "Burke on Theatricality and Revolution," 447–68; and De Bruyn, *The Political Genres of Edmund Burke*, chaps 4 and 5.

3 Price, *A Discourse on the Love of Our Country*, 49.

4 Burke, *Reflections*, 8:115.
5 Ibid., 179–80.
6 A full bibliography of some three hundred such poems is given in Aubin, *Topographical Poetry*, 298–314 ("Hill-Poems"). Two illuminating studies of the prospect poem are Cohen's "Augustan Mode," 3–32; and Foster, "The Measure of Paradise," 232–56.
7 In the late eighteenth century "states" designated publications that presented in tabular form descriptive, taxonomic, comparative information about political jurisdictions. See Frans De Bruyn, "From Georgic Poetry to Statistics and Graphs."
8 Cowper, *The Task*, Book 3, "The Garden," in *The Poems of William Cowper*, 2:182, lines 755–6.
9 Daniels and Seymour, "Landscape Design and the Idea of Improvement 1730–1900," 500. See also Daniels and Cosgrove, "Spectacle and Text," 57–77; and Daniels, *Fields of Vision*.
10 Daniels, *Fields of Vision*, 47.
11 Thomson, "Summer," lines 1408–13 and 1438–42, in *The Seasons*, 124–5.
12 Johnson, *Life of Denham*, in *The Lives of the Most Eminent English Poets*, 1:238.
13 Fulford, *Landscape, Liberty, and Authority*, 4.
14 Cohen, "Augustan Mode," 9.
15 *The Spectator*, 411 (21 June 1712).
16 Kett, *Elements*, 1:xxxix.
17 Ibid., 1:xxv–xxvi.
18 See Cohen, *Unfolding*, 63–4, 100–1, and *passim*; Barrell, *English Literature in History*; and Fulford, *Landscape, Liberty, and Authority*, 3–6.
19 Kett, *Elements*, 1:xxiv.
20 Burke, *An Appeal from the New to the Old Whigs*, in *Writings and Speeches*, 9:448.
21 Denham, *Coopers Hill*, lines 25–30, in *Expans'd Hieroglyphicks*, 140.
22 Barrell, *English Literature*, 60–1.
23 Berkeley, *Passive Obedience*, 37.
24 Berkeley, *The Works of George Berkeley*, 6:32–3.
25 Locke, *An Essay Concerning Human Understanding*, 653.
26 Hume, "Of Contiguity," in *A Treatise of Human Nature*, 428.
27 Foster, "The Measure of Paradise," 233.
28 Morden, *The New Description and State of England*, 1.

29 Miège, *The New State of England*, 7–9. Chandler discusses the development of the genre of the "state" in England in *1819: The Politics of Literary Culture and the Case of Romantic Historicism*, 120–7.

30 See *Georgics*, book 2, lines 136–76.

31 Chamberlayne, *Angliae Notitia*, 5–6. Another instance that closely echoes Virgil is Camden's, *Britain*, 3.

32 See De Bruyn, "From Georgic Poetry to Statistics and Graphs," 117.

33 Jago, *Edge-Hill*, 2.49–50.

34 Jago, preface to *Edge-Hill*, vi.

35 Foster, "Measure of Paradise," 252–3. Foster illustrates diagramatically the sequence of "bearings" taken by Jago in book 1 of his poems (see Foster, 254).

36 Chalmers, "The Life of Jago," in *Works of the English Poets*, 17:283.

37 Edney, "Reconsidering Enlightenment Geography," 165. For an overview of the emergence of the Ordnance Survey, see Delano-Smith and Kain, "Mapping the nation," in *English Maps*, 216–24.

38 Wordsworth, "View from the Top of Black Comb," lines 1–5, in *The Poetical Works*, 2:289–90.

39 Ibid., lines 5–9, 13–25.

40 Garrett, "Surveying and Writing the Nation," 81.

41 Wordsworth, "View," lines 28–30.

42 Wordsworth, "Written with a Slate Pencil," lines 14–29, in *Poetical Works*, 4:199.

43 Garrett, "Surveying," 90. The phrase Garrett cites, from "Written with a Slate Pencil," actually reads, "the grand terraqueous spectacle, / From centre to circumference, unveiled" (lines 10–11). See also Wiley, *Romantic Geography*, 150–69; and Liu, *Wordsworth: The Sense of History*, 91–103.

44 Wordsworth, *The Prelude*, in *Poetical Works*, 2:430, 432 (lines 171–95).

45 Wordsworth, *A Guide*, in *The Prose Works*, 2:170. The *Guide* was published in five successive editions between 1810 and 1835.

46 Ibid., 2:171.

47 See Kelley, "The Economics of the Heart," 24, and n30. See also Wiley, *Romantic Geography*, 153–60, esp. 158.

48 Clarke, *A Survey of the Lakes*, 22.

49 Liu, *Wordsworth: The Sense of History*, 100.

50 Wordsworth, "[An Unpublished Tour]," in *Prose Works*, 2:290–1.

51 For an account of the emergence of a science of statistics at the end of the eighteenth century, see De Bruyn, "From Georgic Poetry to Statistics and Graphs," 110–15.

52 Kett, *Elements*, 1:241.

53 Poovey, *A History of the Modern Fact*, 4.

54 Kett, *Elements*, 1:246.

55 Milton, *Paradise Lost*, in *Complete Poems*, 11.376–84.

56 Burke, *Speech on Conciliation with America*, in *Writings and Speeches*, 3:115.

57 Ibid., 3:114.

58 Chamberlayne, *Angliae Notitia*, "To the Reader," A4v–A5.

11

A Case Study on Spectatorship and the Visual Arts: Democritus and Heraclitus

JOHN LEPAGE

Robert Burton takes up spectatorship at the outset of *The Anatomy of Melancholy* in a monologue portraying Democritus Junior as an "Anticke" and "Personate" actor intruding on "this common Theatre."[1] The top-middle panel of the title-page illustration features Democritus of Abdera in dramatic pose, sitting on a prospect above his garden with pen in hand, distracted yet facing and engaging the viewer (fig. 11.1).

Such is his presence that we might think the quirky philosopher the subject of the work. We would not be far wrong. His scion, Democritus Junior, is the virtual image of ourselves – the living proof of our melancholy – and Democritus Senior is the ancient mirror in which we see ourselves – the actor playing our part in history and laughing at the ridiculous part *we* play. Burton got the idea for Democritus Junior from Erasmus's *The Praise of Folly*, also a dramatic monologue, a work that implicates its auditors as stand-ins for Folly onstage in the theatre of the world.

On some level, to say that Burton and like-minded humanists were preoccupied with spectatorship depends on nothing more than recognizing the pervasiveness of the *theatrum mundi* topos and acknowledging its extensive role in literature and other arts.[2] My object is to make clear how self-conscious this preoccupation was for the early modern period. To do so, I will explore the relationship between the theatre metaphor and the visual arts and examine the relationships among history painting, portraiture, and still life. I will argue that the visual arts make explicit what is in

Fig. 11.1 Detail from the title page of Burton's *Anatomy of Melancholy* (1638).

literature an implicit concern with spectatorship. Burton's Democritus Junior was the most elaborate expression of what was widely perceived to be an important literary trope.

Like his ancient forebear, Democritus Junior has little in common with the readership of *The Anatomy of Melancholy*: he is a pagan philosopher and a learned polymath whose intellectual abstraction is so extreme that it borders on self-parody. Even so, he embodies the melancholy experienced by all human beings. He speaks, in short, not just for himself but for his auditors. Such is his gift for reaching out to humanity that he all but banishes the pretensions of art, let alone philosophy. In the hierarchy of early modern painting, for example, he dislodges the most important visual arts genre of the fifteenth and sixteenth centuries: the history, or "famous men," painting. He reveals that mundane aspects of life can be more compelling than heroic narratives drawn from the distant past.

The image of Democritus relied on a thematic relationship with his pre-Socratic antagonist, Heraclitus.[3] Together they evoked the comic and tragic masks of the ancient theatre, for, in keeping with their satirical responses to folly through laughter and tears, as well as aspects of their philosophies (Democritus's concept of cheerfulness and Heraclitus's notion of flux), they had long been celebrated as the Laughing and Weeping Philosophers. This rigid symbolism aside, they stood for the spectrum of human emotions and their public expression. They were at once distinctive characters and stereotypes of common humanity. Because they represented wide-ranging emotions, however, they pointed to theatre roles people might play that resisted stereotyping.

My study begins by examining a historical context in which Democritus and Heraclitus were linked to artistic representation of the human character. Ancient Roman theatres were notorious for the caprices of their audiences, which made them microcosms of the world at large. On the Roman stage, heightened realism pandered to the masses while reflecting social moods and perspectives; it underscored the dynamic interchange between freedom and authority and the gap between artistic representation and reality.[4] In the same way, to set a long-dead philosopher with a distinctive personality in a contemporary audience, as Horace did with Democritus in the act of satirizing theatre realism, was both a striking literary device and an instance of hyperrealism. Inasmuch as portrait painters in the early modern period took up the device, it had more in common with still-life art than with history painting, for its focus was on the present – and on the art of representing the present. Democritus and Heraclitus were subjects for domestic art – representations of the common stage of humanity through which spectators might see, not the image of famous men, but themselves.

Early modern portraits of the philosophers built on tensions already evident in group portraits on historical subjects, in which different actors in a scene vied for public attention. Democritus and Heraclitus indicated forces undermining history and flattening the social, political, and artistic landscapes, heralding the values of middle-class culture and the rise of individualism. Portraits of Democritus and Heraclitus were hypostatized, "still-life" realizations of human life set on the visual-arts stage for the free interpretation of society.

"The shifting and empty delights of the eye"

Burton was inspired to create Democritus Junior by Erasmus, but his source was a verse epistle by Horace on the public function of poetry. Horace begins *Epistle* 2.1, addressed to Augustus, by registering Rome's debt to Greek antiquity, which had once stultified its artistic production. But the tide has turned, Horace says, for the arts have been democratized and it is now fashionable for everyone to write poetry. He likens the change to the Roman theatre, which was then subject to the whims of public taste. The comparison is awkward, since it glosses over differences between poetry as a spoken art and theatre as a spoken and visual art, and for a time we think Horace intends to change subjects. He lays out the initial anxiety felt by the Romans in imitating Sophocles, Thespis, and Aeschylus, saying that they felt they could capture the spirit of tragedy but not live up to the Greeks in other ways. Comedy was easier, he says, but less indulged by audiences. What at first appears to be a discussion of theatre genres soon documents artists' lack of resolve in the face of public reception and reveals how tormented they are by the stature of the ancients, and yet distracted by their own desire for praise and fame. The climax of his example comes when theatre writers find no other course than to yield to their audiences.

> And often, if a poet *is* brave, he is disconcerted and put to flight by the fact that the majority (deficient, however, in rank and virtue), stupid, illiterate, ready to fight it out with any of their betters who differ from them, call for bears or boxers in the middle of the play. That's what the plebs enjoy. In fact, even the knights have now transferred all their pleasure from the ear to the shifting and empty delights of the eye. The curtain is up for four hours or more while squadrons of horses and hordes of foot pour over the stage. Once-glorious kings are dragged by, hands pinioned; chariots, carriages, wagons, ships hurry on, carrying looted ivory and models of captured Corinth. If Democritus were alive he'd laugh at the way the hybrid camelopard or the white elephant keeps the crowds riveted; he'd watch the populace more attentively than the actual spectacle,

> as being more worthy of his gaze. As for the writers, he'd imagine they were telling their tale to a deaf ass.[5]

In an extraordinary variation on *ut pictura poesis*, Horace highlights spectatorship literally, in a context in which the "shifting and empty delights" of the visual tableau outvoice spoken words.

The stock notion that poetry has a slower and therefore more diluted effect than painting has been complicated by Leonard Barkan, who argues that the Horatian *ut pictura poesis* motto should be understood as giving primacy to mute poetry over speaking pictures, and that the visual image is always in service of literary art.[6] A critical step in his argument is to treat the theatre as a go-between – as both a spoken and a visual art. Barkan focuses on aspects of the theatre inscribed in portraits, still lifes, and other painted tableaux that quietly act out the spoken word and are altogether deficient in what poetry has. Both ancient and early modern visual artists understood their art by means of metaphors whose vehicle was a proscenium stage, but whose tenor was the human voice.

The above passage illustrates Barkan's point. Horace understands one medium (poetry) through another (theatre) with absence of voice as his concern. The theatre analogy combines a verbal element critical to the life of poetry with a visual element implicit in human ideation. But its first purpose is to draw attention to false spectacle and its adverse impact of drowning out lasting impression, which Horace conveys through the metaphor of sound – as if sound alone were the impress of the fictional reality of the work. The real-life effects Horace alludes to will play art false if it fails to resonate through them. Thus, Horace exhibits ambivalence about visual realism. He also highlights the vanity of poets, whose attention to surface values diminishes their achievement, and he reveals a social structure in which authority is undermined and knights' and poets' tastes equally suborned – in which popular opinion overrules the nobility of art and the imperial state alike.

The theatre antics conjured by Horace involve self-conscious acts of what today are called hyperrealism, including troupes of horses crossing the stage, and dazzling shows of surreal animal exoticism, such as the camelopard and the white elephant.[7] However styled, and real as they must be to be convincing, such effects ring false, catering merely to the public appetite for spectacle.

There is a macabre scene in the middle of Paolo Sorrentino's film *La Grande Bellezza* (2013), a Felliniesque take on the vain amusements of the idle upper classes in present-day Rome. Here the protagonist encounters a gigantic inflated giraffe in the middle of a vacant courtyard. The creator of this device says he can make it disappear, which he promptly does, and the scene changes without explanation. Sorrentino mines Horace's image of social vanity turned upside down: the giraffe, plainly not a real-life creature, is no less absurd in context than real ones were for Horace, but the sole witness of this spectacle is the bemused protagonist, a member of the cultural elite, whose values and grasp of reality are upset by the strangeness. If nothing else, the film's treatment of authority and reception of authority remind us that Horace's primary audience was the emperor: "But please spare a modicum of attention for those who devote themselves to a reader rather than put up with the haughty scorn of a spectator: if, that is, you want to fill your library … and spur on the poets to seek green Helicon more diligently."[8] The library, an organizing structure like the theatre in the analogy, is Augustus's to control, but with Horace and other writers pulling the strings. In the end, gently guiding the Emperor's authority, and so superseding it, Horace invites Augustus to satisfy poets' thirst for fame by feeding their no less vain diligence. His earlier allusion to a deaf ass picks up on an ancient theme of poetry falling on indiscriminate ears, while mocking the aspirations of the poet.

Drawing particular attention to the passage is the image of Democritus brought back from the dead to pass judgment on the audience and the writer, for the real spectacle is not what takes place on stage but in the seats and in the writer's consciousness. Democritus is the muse of such self-reflexivity, perhaps for no better reason than that he laughs at absurdity. Horace reveals that the philosopher was already the subject of exotic interest in Rome, and his reputation already sealed in the annals of fame. One might say that transporting Democritus from ancient Greece to Rome or from antiquity to the present is no less a caprice than transporting giraffes and elephants from Africa to Rome, and that it does nothing to allay concerns about Roman or other artists labouring under the shadow of the Greeks.

Taking his cue from Horace, and likewise musing ambivalently on the perils of democracy, Erasmus remarks that the folly of the plebs is so manifest that it goes without saying. But then he says it anyway:

> Besides, what would be the point of reminding you of the common herd, all of whom without any controversy belong to my camp. They riot in so many different forms of folly, and every day bring forth so many new ones, that not even a thousand Democrituses would suffice to laugh at them; and then you'd need one extra Democritus to laugh at the thousand laughers.[9]

The supernumerary Democrituses referred to by Folly are discerning theatre audiences, those in a position to disdain the lower classes. Notice, however, how Erasmus upends these elites through a single, objective Democritus mocking them in return.[10] In one sense there is no point in reminding anyone of anything, for, like suspension of disbelief in the theatre, people maintain their illusions to support their senses of reality, or their precarious self-esteem.[11] Thus, a brief throwaway fantasy girds the entire project of *The Praise of Folly*.

In context, Erasmus makes no mention of Heraclitus, and neither does Horace. Burton makes the connection, in an epigram added to the 1632 edition of *The Anatomy of Melancholy*:

> Now (for alas! how foolish the world has become),
> A thousand Heraclitus', a thousand Democritus' are required.
> Now (so much does madness prevail), all the world must be
> Sent to Anticyra, to graze on Hellebore.[12]

As with the thousand Democrituses in Erasmus, Burton's Heraclituses are both a typical theatre audience and the wider world. So as to bring this type of humanity into clearer focus, however, let me turn to a passage in the *Ars Poetica*, where, as Barkan remarks, Horace "most particularly fixes the triune relations of poet, painter, and actor."[13]

> It is not enough for poetry to be beautiful; it must also be pleasing and lead the hearer's mind wherever it will. The human face smiles

> in sympathy with smilers and comes to the help of those that weep. If you want me to cry, mourn first yourself; then your misfortunes will hurt me, Telephus and Peleus. If your words are given you ineptly, I shall fall asleep or laugh. Sad words suit a mournful countenance, threatening words an angry one; sportive words are for the playful, serious for the grave.[14]

As in the passage I cited earlier, here there is confusion between the visually displayed and the spoken, and the countenance and the chosen words. Barkan says that the poet carries this "almost to the point of incomprehensibility." Although a theatre context is implied, in which the full range of human emotions and how to enact them is at stake, there is lurking concern with how to *paint* emotions. The attraction of these lines for the early modern period, Barkan says, lay in "their reference to facial expression, so that they seem to be offering practical advice to painters." More to the point, they promote artistic devices making the viewer believe in the reality of images of reality. Barkan mentions a parallel passage in Leon Battista Alberti's *De pictura*:

> A "historia" will move spectators when the men painted in the picture outwardly demonstrate their own feelings as clearly as possible. Nature provides … that we mourn with the mourners, laugh with those who laugh, and grieve with the grief-stricken. Yet these feelings are known from the movements of the body.[15]

Alberti shows how the drama of history may be captured by the show of historical characters and their associated emotions, and how historical portraits might become sympathetic expressions of reality, able to "move spectators" through their attention to visual detail. But he also underlines how attention to detail might be carried beyond the history genre, as a practical consideration for artists seeking to address audiences.

Underlying Horace's concern with the theatre in the two epistles I have cited is a visual impression created by Democritus and Heraclitus taken together: as philosophical ambassadors for the array of human attitudes and emotions, as symbols of the dynamic range of the theatre in representing attitudes and emotions, and as representatives of the Greek *historia* manifest in Roman culture. Whether or not Horace intended such an impression, this was how it was taken by painters after Alberti. Moreover, the presence of the philosophers in portraits served to link visual perspective to the theatre in respect of the painting of emotions and the distribution of shades of meaning, for it gave the work multiple foci – visual expressions of voiced dialogue or debate – separate appeals for sympathy, which the spectator must judge. Nevertheless, since Horace's Democritus gestures to Heraclitus in his absence, marking comedy and tragedy as interdependent genres, it is clear that there was no need for portraits to represent them both to suggest their mutual affections. When Portia speaks of the Count Palatine in *The Merchant of Venice* (1.2.41–3) – "He hears merry tales and smiles not. I fear he will prove the weeping philosopher when he grows old, being so full of unmannerly sadness in his youth" – she foregrounds Heraclitus but turns Democritus into an absent signifier through the "merry tales" and "smiles" the Count has rejected. For the most part, in *The Anatomy of Melancholy*, Heraclitus is the elephant not in the room. His tears are provocatively ignored.

Blind Spectatorship in Raphael's The School of Athens

In 1509, Raphael's ambitious allegory of philosophy, *The School of Athens*, addressed the idea of sixteenth-century Rome as the "new Athens" – a bulwark of humanism, but, as we have noted, also an important theme for ancient Romans.[16] Raphael's fresco was a group portrait such as never could have come from a seating of real philosophers, not simply because philosophers are reluctant to hold positions on command, or because Raphael painted the work two millennia after the fact, but because the men belonged to different places and times and so could never have been assembled. In short, Raphael's was a fictionalized construction of ancient philosophy, and his purpose in monumentalizing the philosophers was in no small part to understand them as artists might understand them. He was intent, moreover, on exploring the fame of ancient philosophers in relation to anyone's claim to fame. Thus, Raphael embodied in them the physical characteristics of artists in his own circle in a setting evoking

Donato Bramante's design for St Peter's Basilica, and he used ancient Greek philosophy to advance his preferred but superficially unrelated topic, contemporary Italian visual arts.

It is often unclear who the ancient philosophers in the painting were intended to be, or which contemporary artists were intended for their roles and why. Heraclitus, looming large in the foreground and seriously commanding the viewer's attention, is a counterweight to the upward- and outward-tending aspects of the painting. Christian Kleinbub sees this as part of a strategy to highlight different attitudes to perspective, drawing attention to "another way of seeing, not the 'philosophical eye,' but something like the inner eye of the imagination."[17] His argument relies on the iconographic significance of Heraclitus's blindness.[18] Heraclitus may serve as a metaphorical complement to the transcendent sky glimpsed behind the framework of the school, but he seems more preoccupied with struggling to imagine than transcending; Ingrid Rowland says he "glowers."[19] What about Democritus? Scholars have failed to identify him, and yet the painting creates conditions in which the recognition of the one philosopher cannot help but summon thought of the other.

Group portraits like this documented dispute as a consequence of bringing different people together in the same work, even when they depicted nothing more than implacable faces. This is the case even in the peaceable, neatly organized realm of *The School of Athens*. The philosophical disputation was formalized as an academic genre by Marsilio Ficino and other humanists in the second half of the fifteenth century with the goal of putting on display the philosophies of the academies, though the measure of academic discourse remained the *viva voce*. If, as has been suggested, *The School of Athens* was meant to visibly reconcile divergent philosophies, it just as visibly embodied intellectual conflict, and it stood opposite a work in the Stanza della Segnatura that foregrounded religious dispute.[20] It is possible that such portraits as Raphael's offer new, alternative, heroic subjects for history painting – ancient philosophers in turn evoking early modern artists – and the greatness to which they might stake a claim.

Ficino had a portrait of Democritus and Heraclitus in his study, which was known to have sacred status for his academy.[21] Donato Bramante's 1487 fresco of the philosophers, now in the Pinocoteca di Brera in Milan, is likely a copy of this. Carlo Pedretti once speculated that the Heraclitus in Bramante's painting was a portrait of Leonardo and that the Democritus was a self-portrait.[22] This, alongside Raphael's representation of Heraclitus in the guise of Michelangelo in *The School of Athens*, has led to unresolved speculation about the significance of such characterizations. The philosophers may have signalled disputes about painterly values every bit as charged as the philosophical disputes of the academies. What we can say with certainty is that role-playing was central to the function of representations of Democritus and Heraclitus, and that the philosophers were able to accommodate allegories that made them stand for anyone and everyone. As such, portraits on this theme added to an effect of constantly shifting perspective. They were much more than acts of dressing up and representing people as other people; they were studies of the implications of doing so; and they were studies of the manipulation of visual effects to compensate for the absence of a truer voice. They were *trompe l'oeils*, illusions serving to destabilize the viewer through images of far-from-resolved disputes about values with social and political implications that extended into the politics of art and artistic genre. Above all, they were exercises in spectatorship – in seeing and hearing as a live audience might see and hear, and in imagining as a live audience might imagine.

Striking a Pose: History Painting Meets Still Life

The visual-arts legacy of Democritus and Heraclitus was deeply involved with changing attitudes to history painting, as is reflected in portraits of other historical figures. Nevertheless, inspired by Horace's reference to real-world creatures removed from their natural habitats and set on a theatre stage, I want to assert a departure from the often static narratives and values of history painting through a relationship with still-life painting – a "lower" genre whose liveliness is belied by the fixity of its subjects and by its lack of narrative. In this connection, Harry Berger stresses what may be called the theatricality of still-life art.[23] Berger argues that the iconographic images in Dutch *vanitas* paintings are visual red herrings, distractions from the real purposes of the art: to create dramatic tension in settings full of natural vitality. The drama unfolds on a table, in a window, or in a niche, as if in a theatre tableau, and the iconography cannot be read without regard to the ironic posturing of the figures in the scene. Berger documents wide-ranging topics of concern: in addition to the vanity of human wishes, compounded by imperfect, predatory aspects of the natural world, he sees topics related to the patterns of domestic life, national and international economies, and political relations among competing commercial interests. It all goes to say that, far from modelling fixed moral positions, Dutch still life provokes ambiguity, and an ever-changing relationship with its viewers, who are expected to discover more the more they scrutinize. The relationship begins with the hyperrealist art that Berger regards as the stock-in-trade of still life. The ruse of perfect representation of three-dimensional reality is nothing more than a "pretext" for showing off the skills of the artist, from which viewers must ultimately break in the realization that they are not viewing reality.

The unnatural contrivances of still life – blooming flowers crowded together without regard to the seasons in which they bloom, the fact that they are situated in artificial biomes and are removed from natural processes of time – ally it with portraits of historical figures, whose art fictionalizes real people while making fictional subjects real. Pretend figures are depicted on the painted surface with uncanny realism, an arbitrariness forcing the past into the present, and the present into the past, perhaps even turning the work into a *nature morte*. There is an accompanying loss of identity, like that of the fleshless skull in a *vanitas* painting, and an erosion of history and fame. Of paramount importance is the destabilization occasioned by the work, the confusion of roles in a process multiplying viewers' choices and undermining authorities – the powers of emperors, the pre-eminence of the Church, the monumentalizing capabilities of art, and the reality of reality itself. In an illuminating discussion of rhopography, or the depiction of trivial things, Norman Bryson notes that the art in Caravaggio's performance in the higher genres is subordinated to the narrative it illustrates. When what is displayed lacks such baggage, "art can display *itself*."[24] This is the freedom of low art, whether to all appearances self-effacing or not. And it was the freedom Democritus and Heraclitus would display as mockers of pretension, even within the confines of high art.

It should not be surprising, then, to find in the portrait history of Democritus and Heraclitus an overlap with the general preoccupations of still-life traditions. Given how basic the iconography was, what is sur-

Fig. 11.2 Donato Bramante, *Democritus and Heraclitus* (1487), Pinacoteca di Brera, Milan.

prising is how varied artists' perspectives on them were. In this respect, they were like the oft-painted vases of flowers, table settings, hanging meats, and other raw materials of still life. The artistic achievement scarcely depended on the uniqueness of the subject or the greatness of the narrative, but rather on the distinctive composition and the exactitude of the painterly performance. The social and political economies that Berger identifies with Dutch still life are in play here, for the good reason that the portraits serve to hold up for careful scrutiny and critique the hierarchical values identified with history painting.

While the subject of Democritus and Heraclitus had currency in Italy near the end of the fifteenth century, inspired by the academies, there are not many works to show for it. Bramante's *all'antica* fresco is the oldest extant portrait (fig. 11.2).[25] This crude, monochromatic painting, flat in appearance, provides the iconographic basis for later portraits. Note especially the books, which express their status as philosophers, and the globe, which floats fantastically in the space between them. The globe is a surreal presence in the work, detached, and set off by light and shadow. It evokes the universality found in many paintings of Christ with a globe. But the physical detail depicted on the globe conveys such a high degree of specificity as to counteract such a theme. The globe is usually identified with the encompassing nature of the men's philosophies and their expression of the miseries of the world, but I view it as an allusion to the universal theatre of laughter and tears in all its particular manifestations.[26]

The dark shadows on Heraclitus's face and costume are characteristic humoral features, as are the pronounced differences between the hair and facial expressions of the men. The hair is perhaps the most striking differentiating feature, as it is for people in real life, and as subsequent artists would reveal. Heraclitus's tears are unnaturally accentuated by contrast with his almost expressionless mouth.[27] Far from laughing, Democritus grins. The gestures of the men are understated: Heraclitus's hands are folded; Democritus's right hand is lifted, pointing to the globe. These became significant markers in the tradition, especially in paintings identifying the philosophers with religious piety or sanctimony.

Bramante's painting is recalled in an emblem in Andrea Alciato's *Emblemata* (1531), which brought familiarity to the philosophers in the centuries to come (fig. 11.3). The emblem uses stylized effects to evoke three-dimensionality, something Bramante gestures at but fails to capture. In the absence of a globe, the arc of the philosophers' bodies frames a sphere. The men are seated above and in front of a prospect scene, and their folded robes reveal the play of light and shadow. The prospect scene is revealed in few lines, but, as Bryson says (to describe the background in an Ambrosius Boschaert still life), the landscape provides "the idea of a space that is expansive and limitless, yet can be mastered by a prospect; and the further idea of a sudden leap from far to near. The space is centripetal."[28] Imparting just such a sense of movement, Democritus gestures upward and Heraclitus downward. At their feet lies an open book, which mirrors the scene – as if to say that the men and the prospect are open books to be read.

As with the Bramante painting, the iconography of the emblem is so understated that it is hard to say whether it points to social or artistic concerns. Raphael's *The School of Athens* appears indifferent to such matters,

Fig. 11.3 Democritus and Heraclitus, from Andrea Alciato's *Emblemata* (1531).

its attention lying in the sphere of idealized high art. The politics of perspective that made the philosophers so important in painting a century later had little place in Italian art before the Reformation, perhaps only surfacing during the Counter-Reformation. While Alciato's emblem contents itself with an epigram on the follies of the present time as taken from an ancient work, the *Greek Anthology*, the epigram in Geffrey Whitney's *A Choice of Emblemes* (1586) identifies sin as its primary concern.

> What if they lived, and shoulde behoulde this age,
> Which overflowes, with swelling seas of sinne:
> Where fooles, by swarmes, doe presse upon the stage,
> With hellish Impes, that like have never binne:
> I thinke this fighte, should hasten their decaye
> Then help us God, and Sathans furie staie.[29]

Whitney moves the generic and historical character of the original emblem into the domain of contemporary religion. The image of the masses pressing onto the stage suggests a theatre not unlike Erasmus's *The Praise of Folly*, which turns its gaze on the spectators and the world.

The idea of the philosophers inhabiting the real world of the present became a favourite theme, particularly in the Netherlands, where more than eighty works on the philosophers were painted in the seventeenth century alone.[30] The paintings engaged in a spirited debate about what to paint and how to paint it, and what it meant to do so. The value they attached to accurate depictions of reality countered the more abstract and moralistic aspects of history painting in favour of objective assessments of the here and now, promoting the independent judgments of spectators. The artists focused on what viewers might see in a work of art and how they might understand it in a realm of fluid possibilities. Thus, they sought to complicate the interpretative process, making spectators, briefly, kings and emperors in the act of interpretation, but also painfully subject to the burden of uncertainty.

Jacob Jordaens's impressionistic portrait (c. 1640), for example, disrupts conventions by depicting Democritus as a middle-aged Antwerp burgher and Heraclitus as a balding, heavily bearded ancient sage. The men are huddled together, their arms clustered over the globe, their postures and the shape of their hands defining a spherical motion. The darkness encircling them is a whirlwind of colours and shades, whose characteristics merge with Heraclitus's half-naked, formless body.[31] The painting suggests vagueness, forestalling fixed conclusions, for everything is in flux. Jan van Bijlert's portrait (1640), by contrast, uses more precisely realized shapes and colours revolving around an alarmingly white globe, echoed by Heraclitus's bald head and Democritus's exposed torso and illuminated face.[32] Heraclitus, wearing a brown cassock, rests his hands on the globe in prayer. Democritus's thick hair would be lost in the darkness were it not for an umbra around his head. Gesturing and pointing are important aspects of the imagery, and in van Bijlert's work Democritus points across the painting with his right hand while grasping a conical wine glass in the left. He is not laughing.[33] His left eye looks intently across the picture. A dying vine branch grazes the globe. Erika Langmuir suggests that the terrestrial globe became a "symbol of transience" in seventeenth-century art. Perhaps that is indicated by the branch, whose leaves replicate the triangular design of the three principal subjects of the work.[34]

The globe is of interest in most paintings on the theme. In one of a number of works Hendrick ter Brugghen painted depicting the philosophers, this one from 1628, Democritus leans on a celestial globe, pointing across the painting towards Heraclitus in the companion portrait (both works are in the Rijksmuseum). Half naked, half draped in a yellow-red robe, he is younger than his counterpart, and he wears a nautical cap on his moustachioed and lightly bearded face. He is at once a mocker and a wharf rat.[35] In the companion painting, Heraclitus leans on a terrestrial globe, glaring and looking suspiciously like Vladimir Lenin, his bald head reflecting the light. In a double portrait from 1618–19, ter Brugghen depicts men so ancient that one is clearly senile and the other subdued by melancholy (fig. 11.4). They wear black cassocks and have grey beards. Democritus's hands are folded. The tour de force of this painting is the globe, which rests on an open book propped on a fleshless leg bone.[36] It is composed of a mass of people jostling with one another for space in a social vacuum.[37]

An early portrait by Peter Paul Rubens (1603) imagines Democritus as a type of Christ and Heraclitus as a pious man of religion. Democritus's feminine hands are complemented by the lushness of his beard. By contrast, the musculature of Heraclitus's arms, his five o'clock shadow, and his general demeanour suggest masculine aggression. Conflicting values are conveyed by contrasting colours, a device imitated by later artists. While Rubens's Heraclitus looks nothing short of a villain (and a hypocrite), other paintings show the provocative side of Democritus's character. Agostino Carracci's mannerist *Democritus* (1598) displays an impish humour, notably expressed by the philosopher's hands. In this category, most striking are two portraits by Johannes Moreelse (c. 1630), in which Democritus is a young rascal (with a jaunty cap) making faces and mocking gestures with his hands.[38]

In keeping with tradition, many painters saw the philosophers as an inseparable pair; others laboured to disambiguate them. Many created complementary single portraits, such as those by ter Brugghen, Moreelse, Rubens, and Jusepe de Ribera. Perhaps best known among single portraits is Diego Velázquez's *Democritus* (1628; fig. 11.5). Aside from the globe, and

Fig. 11.4 *Above* Hendrick ter Brugghen, *Democritus and Heraclitus* (1618–19), private collection.

Fig. 11.5 *Opposite* Diego Velázquez, *Democritus* (1629), Musée des Beaux Arts, Rouen.

the philosopher's act of pointing to it, one might not judge this painting to be a Democritus at all.[39] Indeed, it prompts consideration of still more ambiguous pronouncements on the theme, such as early and late self-portraits in the guise of Democritus by Rembrandt (1628 and 1668), which confirm that the type was expressive of moods discernible in any human being, not least the artist.[40] Such works differed from those imposing the artist's features on either of the philosophers, which sometimes occurred (for example, in a 1646 painting by Salvator Rosa), for they skipped over the phantom narrative, turning the self-portrait into a theatre of personal identity and the self.

As can be seen from the paintings that turn the philosophers into religious figures, or into types of Christ, it was natural for the portraits to broach religious subjects, in part so as to challenge one form of dogmatism or another. Usually Democritus was thought to be open-minded and

agreeable, and Heraclitus closed-minded and disagreeable. Among moderate Christians, Heraclitus was a Puritan; among Protestants, he was a monk.[41] Above all, however, the philosophers triggered awareness that the human condition is refracted in perspectives that extend beyond those of nominal authority figures and into the realm of all people – actors in and spectators of the human scene – new authority figures who, in watching the drama unfold, impose their own judgments, and to whom even artists must cede authority. The artwork is a public artifact, which anyone may possess and over which anyone may assert authority. The artist derides but cannot deny such authority, for he is caught up in a universal comedy of ambition, mitigated success, and ultimate failure wholly dependent on the spectator – who, in turn, is just like the artist. Along the way, the artist illustrates how human nature exhibits limitless shades of mood, genre, and gender. The painting might allude to Jacob and Esau, for example – to hairless men and bearded men, to tricksters and plain dealers – indicating types of people, social posturing, and religion, and touching on what in England would serve to distinguish the Cavalier and the Roundhead. Or it might juxtapose voiced identity and silence (raucous laughter and visible tears), youth and age, femininity and masculinity, or all of these together. In sum, the artist evokes a world marked by competing aspects of life, and so one ruled by none – or by nothing more than the grave.

For me, this is illustrated by a painting that brings Democritus and Heraclitus squarely into the realm of still life. Jacques De Gheyn's *Vanitas* (1603), one of the earliest Dutch *vanitas* still lifes, situates its subject in an architectural niche (fig. 11.6). In addition to the characteristic skull, there is a soap bubble, which evokes the impermanence of human life and the vanity of pipe dreams while doubling as a globe.[42] The surface of the bubble reflects the "real" setting, the room in which the painting was painted, catching the painter and the viewer in the act of painting and viewing.[43] On either side of the niche are single flowers in vases. Beneath is the monetary currency of a sad social enterprise. That this is a performance space is revealed by the figures of Democritus and Heraclitus, on either side and above, who make jibes at the scene. Although they are imagined as statuary adornments, their gestures are so animated as to render them a living audience as well as static features of the genre. They can barely hold the pose.[44]

Portraiture and Dialogue in English Literary Culture

Taking up the theme of Whitney's emblem epigram on Democritus and Heraclitus, Joshua Sylvester's "A Dialogue upon the Troubles Past; Between Heraclitus and Democritus, the Weeping and Laughing Philosophers"

Fig. 11.6 Jacques De Gheyn, *Vanitas* (1603), Metropolitan Museum, New York.

(1598) recalls the religious wars in France near the end of the sixteenth century.[45] However, since it makes no specific reference to them, its preoccupation with "treasons, murders, massacres, / Sacks, sacrileges, losses and alarmes" is also broad and generic.[46] It can afford to be generic, for, as Democritus says, "I take this world to be but as a Stage, / Where netmaskt men do play their personage: /'Tis but a mummerie, and a pleasant show; / Sith over all, strange vanities do flow" (21–4). As has been noted from time to time, these lines resemble Jaques's "All the world's a stage" speech in *As You Like It*. In much the same way, they complicate fixed personality by stressing that all people have the theatre metaphor in common – that their parts in this world are played by "net-maskt men." Even so, the poem's sense of personality is driven by ever-changing mood rather than time of life, and so it distributes personality types in distinctive ways. In the end, Heraclitus vows to live in the desert, far from the madding crowd, and Democritus among people in the city. These gestures reveal opposed private and public aspects of human personality not unlike those registered in John Milton's *Il Penseroso* and *L'Allegro*, which were to exert so strong an influence on Henry More's poetic monologue *Democritus Platonissans* (1646). There are other refractions, such as Heraclitus's tearful rejection of rebellion against authority and Democritus's scornful laughter at social and political levelling – porters who "prate of State-designes, / And make al common, as in new-found *Indes*" (55–6), or Heraclitus's complaint about religious hypocrisy and Democritus's mockery of people who alter their beliefs to conform with prevailing forms of atheism. In short, the poem reveals many ways in which people are incapable of playing their parts consistently or well at any juncture of their lives. Needless to say, the import of the discussion is not lost on its auditors, who may be imagined entering into it themselves. In the course of developing these ideas, the poem uses fragmented dialogue, such as might be experienced by a listening theatre audience, to evoke the coloration of mood.

That Democritus and Heraclitus should be employed to decide on Christian religious wars is a mask of violent forces at work in colossal struggles for authority. Bringing unique critical distance to such struggles, the philosophers turn them into ludicrous comedies, and as such they play into Democritus's hands. As if in explanation, Henri Bergson once observed, "Now step aside, look upon life as a disinterested spectator: many a drama will turn into a comedy."[47] Sylvester's poem ends with laughter – "Such plenteous store of laughing-stuffe to fill me, / That still Ile laugh, un-lesse that laughing kill me" (79–80) – and similar dynamics are at work in painted portraits of the philosophers, whose comic or melodramatic exchanges demonstrate the enormity of the task involved in painted art to voice both the majesty of human ambition and its ultimate collapse in the arms of a low genre.

Conclusion

In discussing the conflict of styles when Velázquez's court paintings come up against his still life art, Bryson says,

> This is not simply a formal choice between genres, but a genuine crisis in which painting is forced to contemplate two utterly different conceptions of human life: one that describes what is important in existence as the unique event, the drama of great individuals, the disruptions of creaturely repetition that precipitate as narrative; and one which protests that the drama of greatness is an epiphenomenon, a movement only on the surface of earthly life, whose greater mass is made up of things entirely unexceptional and creaturely, born of need on a poor planet.[48]

By contrast with the mildly derisory pose of Carracci's Democritus, or the insouciance of Rembrandt's laughing self-portraits, Velázquez's rather stiff Democritus seems to reflect this dilemma, as if the painting were both a history painting and a still life of the nobility; and the dilemma is further reflected to an audience who must look at the courtly figure and see an image of Democritus and, of course, themselves. Velázquez, self-conscious artist that he was, must have seen his ambivalence embedded in the knowledge that the hyper-attuned lens of low art finds cracks in the stiff postures of the elites.[49]

Near the end of his celebration of still-life painting, by way of measuring the stakes involved in a genre focused on trivial detail, and by way of assessing the crisis identified above, Bryson provides an apt comparison.

> It is the same opposition which, in Greek theatre, is projected as the masks of tragedy and comedy. Their perspectives are complementary and intertwined, equally true and untrue, and between them, by exaggeration, they were perhaps able to give some structure and intelligibility to the mass of human experience that lies between their extremes.[50]

Bryson's analysis of still-life painting thus signals how Democritus and Heraclitus functioned in the portrait tradition. The philosophers suggested a dispute between high (tragic) and low (comic) genres, which undermined stable social hierarchies, but which also imparted some dignity to the low – not least that of mocking the dispute. At heart, however, portraits of the philosophers were less concerned with high and low than with voicing "real" art through the canvas, in all its shifting, malleable tones and shades.

If Democritus and Heraclitus are still-life subjects, it is because they have been transposed from their native settings and positioned by the artist for contemporary effect. As we have seen, Horace employed Democritus in just such a way in his epistles, as did Erasmus in *The Praise of Folly* – both sharing an acute sense of the philosopher as a critic of artistic practice in the present time, catching out the pretentions of the artist above all. Burton's Democritus is a distinctly contemporary object of curiosity, who devotes the last two paragraphs of the preface to apologizing for his abrasiveness – "I have anatomized mine own folly" – before endeavouring to put himself in the "good favour" and "gracious acceptance" of his readers.[51] This is a rhetorical gesture, to be sure, but it is fraught with significance.

The Anatomy of Melancholy tries to escape the shackles of genre by hiding in the guise of an academic treatise absurdly heaped with scholarship. In a sense, it is both fiction and non-fiction, for, though many real-life effects of human nature enter into its field of vision, they seem on the whole like *trompe l'oeils* – like footnotes in a Flann O'Brien novel. Despite its success in Burton's lifetime, *The Anatomy of Melancholy* is a curiosity, a bauble tossed before a distracted audience, for whom all it amounts to is "Allicholy and musing," as Mistress Quickly says in *The Merry Wives of Windsor* (1.4.142). But Democritus Junior's is an enfranchising voice for anyone who cares to listen. Burton could hardly imagine what would transpire in English society a scarce two decades after the publication of his work: the division of his country along the lines of elites, levellers, and the common people who had nothing like his intellectual or aesthetic concerns. Nevertheless, he expressed a bond with the people, voiced by a lone actor on the stage who was able to put himself in the place of his spectators. It is precisely this sense of spectatorship that prevails from beginning to end in the story of Democritus and Heraclitus – that the theatre represents the realm of human ambition, that the artist is perennially teased by such ambition, and that, like kings and emperors, and indeed the common people, the artist must yield, without prospect of personal gain, to the judgment of his audience and time.

NOTES

1 Burton, *Anatomy of Melancholy*, 1:1.

2 See, for example, Quiring, ed., *"If Then the World a Theatre Present"*; West, "Knowledge and Performance," 1–20; Christian, "*Theatrum Mundi.*"

3 For discussion of these philosophers, see Lepage, *The Revival of Antique Philosophy in the Renaissance*, 81–135.

4 West remarks "regular attribution to the theater – metaphorical and actual – of a division between what it represents and the means used to represent it. Because of this, the theater metaphor includes the possibility that whatever hierarchy it seems to establish may suddenly find itself subverted by the working-through of the metaphor" ("Knowledge and Performance," 5).

5 Russell and Winterbottom, *Ancient Literary Criticism: The Principal Texts in New Translations*, 277.

6 Barkan, *Mute Poetry, Speaking Pictures.*

7 The cameleopard and the white elephant are not merely exoticisms, but illustrations of how reality can seem stranger than human contrivance – like creatures designed by a committee. For hyperrealism, see Baudrillard, *Simulacra and Simulation*; and Eco, *Travels in Hyperreality: Essays*. Berger, Jr., *Caterpillage: Reflections on Seventeenth-Century Dutch Still-Life Painting*, 4–5, passim, takes the hyperreality of Dutch still-life painting to be an indicator of its fictionality – the marvel that the viewer experiences when he or she realizes that it is all made up; see Bryson, *Looking at the Overlooked*, 140–5, for hyperreality and still-life *trompe-l'oeil.*

8 Russell and Winterbottom, *Ancient Literary Criticism*, 277. Francis Bacon mentions an emperor too distracted to spare attention for the writer: "An emperor of Rome, to show the certainty of his hand, did shoot a great forked arrow at an ostrich, as she ran swiftly upon the stage, and struck off her head; and yet she continued the race a little way with her head off" (cited in West, "Knowledge and Performance," 15).

9 Erasmus, *The Praise of Folly and Other Writings*, 49.

10 Erasmus perhaps entertains philosophical ideas: de Fontenay, "Rire et larmes

présocratiques," in *Les curieux philosophes de Velázquez et de Ribera*, cites a La Fontaine fable in which the concept of infinite worlds evokes "Démocrites infinis" (17).

11 Folly says: "If someone in a theater should try to strip the masks off the actors in the middle of the play … wouldn't he be destroying the entire illusion … ?" (28).

12 Burton, *Anatomy of Melancholy*, 1:115. The reference to Anticyra and hellebore (a cure for madness) echoes a relevant passage on Democritus in Horace's *Ars poetica* (298ff.).

13 Barkan, *Mute Poetry, Speaking Pictures*, 135–6.

14 Russell and Winterbottom, *Ancient Literary Criticism*, 282.

15 Cited in Barkan, *Mute Poetry, Speaking Pictures*, 136.

16 Rowland, "The Vatican Stanze," *The Cambridge Companion to Raphael*, 103.

17 Kleinbub, *Vision and the Visionary in Raphael*, 69.

18 Both philosophers were blind, Democritus by his own hand and Heraclitus from an edema, which made his eyes water.

19 Rowland, "The Vatican Stanze," 107. Bryson refers to the "Albertian window" of Italian art opening onto "sacred spaces and transcendental truth" but distinguishes a blocked transcendent in northern, Protestant art (*Looking at the Overlooked*, 150). Here, Raphael has placed similar tendencies at loggerheads.

20 For the *disputà* genre and for the *School of Athens* resolving doctrinal disputes, see Cutler, "The Disputà Plate in the J. Paul Getty Museum and Its Cinquecento Context," 21. For discussion of the Segnatura, see Gombrich, *Symbolic Images*, 85–101.

21 See Wind, "The Christian Democritus," 180–2.

22 Pedretti, "The Sforza Sepulchre," Part I, 121–31. See also Nicholl, *Leonardo Da Vinci*, 310–12.

23 Berger, *Caterpillage*; cf. Berger's *Fictions of the Pose*, for e.g.: "the portrait's primary 'object of representation' is not the 'human subject' or 'human original' *tout court* but its (his, her) act of posing" (7).

24 Bryson, *Looking at the Overlooked*, 81.

25 Blankert, "Heraclitus en Democritus Bij Marcilio Ficino," 133–4, discusses other early Italian depictions of the subject, a woodcut in Antonio Fregoso's *Opera Nova* (1505), and a painting from the 1520s attributed to Bernardino Luini.

26 Berzal de Dios ("Velázquez's *Democritus*: Global Disillusion and the Critical Hermeneutics of a Smile") says that the globe in Velázquez's *Democritus* is the kind of artifact a philosopher might have in his study (50). The contrast with Bramante's globe, which is less an object and more a concept, is marked. Berzal de Dios finds "a readable (though abstruse) geography" in Velázquez's globe, likewise a departure from the known-world focus of the Bramante, creating a mix of the concrete and the abstract.

27 Nicholl, *Leonardo Da Vinci*, 312, says that Heraclitus's tears conform to Leonardo's understanding of the effects of weeping and laughing on the eyes and lips (thus supporting the identification of Heraclitus with Leonardo).

28 Bryson, *Looking at the Overlooked*, 105.

29 Whitney, *A Choice of Emblemes*, 14.

30 Blankert, "Heraclitus en Domicritus, in het bijzonder in de Nederlandse Kunst van de 17de eeuw," 44. This work is a comprehensive survey of Dutch paintings on the theme; the four essays in *Les curieux philosophes* provide invaluable additional context.

31 Paintings of the philosophers often explored the relationship between colour and the humours. At a rudimentary level, some painters drew on ancient associations of melancholy with black and yellow bile.

32 Artistic naturalism was especially favoured by the Caravaggists in Utrecht, who used lighting and other effects like those demonstrated by van Bijlert.

33 The philosophers are often depicted without laughter and tears; in this respect, artists sought Albertian emotional realism, heightened by fastidious attention to detail. Blankert ("General Introduction," in *Gods, Saints, and Heroes*) quotes Van Mander to illustrate concern among artists for correct depiction of emotion: "People rightly reproach us, the artists, because it cannot be determined if the heads we depict are laughing or crying" (27).

34 Langmuir, *Imagining Childhood*, 165. Coudert ("Velazquez, peintre philosophe," 90) links the vine branch to Pliny's observation that Democritus had unparalleled knowledge of the vines of Greece.

35 *The Encyclopedia of Comparative Iconography*, 493, links this characterization to peasant traditions associated with laughter.

36 This work is partially reproduced in another painting by ter Brugghen (1621), whose human skull replaces the globe. Lurie ("The Weeping Heraclitus by Hendrick Terbrugghen in the Cleveland Museum of Art," 279) assumes it is a

Heraclitus, but Slatkes and Franits (*The Paintings of Hendrick ter Brugghen: Catalogue Raisonné*, 119) identify it as a Saint Jerome.

37 Lurie calls them "carousing couples" and "revellers" ("The Weeping Heraclitus," 279, 280).

38 Langmuir imagines Democritus evoking "fickle *Pueritia*" (*Imagining Childhood*, 165).

39 De Fontenay ("Rire et larmes présocratiques," 19) observes that this painting has often been misidentified. The likeness of the philosophers to melancholic Christian saints such as Jerome has led to periodic misreadings, as with ter Brugghen's aforementioned painting.

40 The later self-portrait has been linked more recently to Zeuxis, who laughed himself to death while painting an old woman; see van de Wetering, *A Corpus of Rembrandt Paintings IV*, 556. Given Zeuxis's status as an exemplar of realism, the symmetry of his story with the function of Democritus in seventeenth-century portraiture is striking.

41 Artists expressed both Catholic and Protestant leanings, particularly, as Lurie says, "moralists in the north" ("The Weeping Heraclitus," 279), but more often they highlighted public dispute without taking positions.

42 For similar *vanitas* effect, compare ter Brugghen's 1621 painting, whose skull replaces the globe; or Salvator Rosa's *Democritus in Meditation* (1650), a huge canvas strewn with bones and assorted detritus.

43 The reflection is indistinct, but in Pieter Claesz's similar *Vanitas* (1628) the artist is clearly reflected in the bubble. See Grootenboek, *The Rhetoric of Perspective*, plates 22 and 23. Groetenboek, 137–42, uses De Gheyn's painting to highlight perspective as "allegorical form."

44 Barnes ("Bowls with Souls," 4) reports that Cézanne once angrily said to a sitter, "You've ruined the pose! I tell you in all seriousness you must hold it like an apple. Does an apple move?"

45 Some scholars have taken the poem as a translation from Du Bartas, Sylvester's usual source, but Snyder (*The Divine Works of Guillaume de Saluste Sieur Du Bartas*, 1:34) says that no source has been identified.

46 *The Complete Works of Joshua Sylvester*, 2:45–6.

47 Bergson, *Laughter*, 222.

48 Bryson, *Looking at the Overlooked*, 54.

49 Berzal de Dios stresses the critical and ethical role of the painting in the context of Spain's troubled politics. He observes that the value of Democritus's

laughter is "pedagogical and therapeutic, and it is the viewers' actions that will determine the potential outcome, and with it, the genre of the performance" (57).

50 Bryson, *Looking at the Overlooked*, 178.

51 Burton, *Anatomy of Melancholy*, 1:112–13.

12

Spectacle and the Chronotope of Progress in William Hogarth's London

ALLISON MURI

Hogarth's London, a Society of Spectacle

On 28 February 1730, *The Universal Spectator, and Weekly Journal* reported that Colonel Francis Charteris had been convicted capitally at the Old Bailey for the rape of his servant Ann Bond. The trial was a media sensation, and the paper, founded by Daniel Defoe and his son-in-law Henry Baker a little over a year before to "restore" its readers' "Taste to Things truly Superior and Sublime," was as heavily invested in capitalizing on the scandal and titillating events as were the others that reported on them. Charteris had "brought several Witnesses in his Defence, who were his Servants," the *Universal Spectator* related,

> but their Depositions contain'd many Contradictions and Inconsistencies; several Persons appear'd in Behalf of the young Woman, who gave her the Character of a very honest and virtuous Person. It appear'd, among other Things, that to prevent her crying out he cramm'd his Handkerchief down her Throat, and almost choak'd her. His chief Defence was a sham Letter, sworn to by his Footman to come from her, which was prov'd to be a Forgery.

Although "Persons of Distinction" were present on his behalf, Charteris was found guilty and was "carry'd up to Newgate" prison, "greatly dispirited" as all his property had been forfeited by the verdict, the report concluded.[1] In the same issue, readers would have seen that a scheme was being circulated by two hundred eminent merchants who proposed to advance £3.2 million to the East India Company in exchange for the right for all subjects to purchase a licence to trade to the East Indies. The paper also reported that highwayman Francis Hackabout had been capitally convicted, and another notorious highwayman, James Dalton, had been indicted for robbery. The spectacle of early eighteenth-century London in the newspapers, broadsheets, and weeklies was a narrative of progress, industry, justice, and prosperity – largely reporting on the city's trade and commerce, the property and wealth of its valued citizens, and the criminal acts of its disenfranchised. Indeed, these reports presaged Guy Debord's suggestion that the "whole life of those societies in which modern conditions of production prevail presents itself as an immense accumulation of *spectacles*," where everything "that once was directly lived has become mere representation."[2]

Ultimately, Hackabout and Dalton would be hanged at Tyburn, both proclaiming innocence of the crimes for which they had been condemned, while Charteris would effectively purchase his release while availing himself of all the influence his powerful friends and allies could provide. Charteris was almost universally reviled, but the highwaymen evoked contrary reactions. These two were not presented as folk heroes comparable to the romanticized figures of Jack Sheppard (1702–1724) or Dick Turpin (1705–1739); like many others, they served the pro-government papers as spectacles of terror and as evidence of rampant crime being curtailed through the justice of the gallows. The Ordinary of Newgate's account of Dalton's death, for example, justified his punishment by claiming he "was a Thief from his Cradle, and imbib'd the Principles of Art from his Mothers Milk … and as he himself said was one of the most impudent irreclaimable Thieves that ever was in England." Indeed, "for twenty Years past he never rose out of his Bed, but he deserv'd the Gallows." The account also offered a rationale for such executions in the potential redemption of the sinner: "He profess'd himself Penitent, that he believ'd in Christ, and died in Peace with all the World."[3]

It is my contention here that William Hogarth's series *A Harlot's Progress* (1731) subverted such progress narratives with a critique of London's politics

Fig. 12.1 Detail from *A New Plan of the City of London, Westminster, and Southwark*, in *A Survey of the Cities of London and Westminster* by John Strype (1720).

and rapacity, its government, and its people, of criminality and justice, and of their representations in print. His scenes of distinct, often readily identifiable, locations within London and Westminster functioned as sequential episodes in a moralized spatial narrative. My discussion will focus on reading the events depicted in *A Harlot's Progress* through the city's representations in news and pamphlets, and through contemporary maps. Graphic representations as provided by the eighteenth-century maps, which offer glimpses into the built topography of the city, however, are inadequate to fully understand the spatialization of power that Hogarth draws upon and critiques in his own representations. To this end, Mikhail Bakhtin's concept of the *chronotope* (time-space) is particularly useful. Bakhtin defined the chronotope as "the intrinsic connectedness of temporal and spatial relationships that are artistically expressed," where "spatial and temporal indicators are fused into one carefully thought-out, concrete whole." In this mode of expression, he argued, time "becomes artistically visible; likewise, space becomes charged and responsive to the movements of time, plot and history. This intersection of axes and fusion of indicators characterizes the artistic chronotope."[4] The satiric caricatures in Hogarth's progresses effectively re-mediated *spectacle* through the chronotope that his images of London deliberately evoked. I have suggested elsewhere that Bakhtin's chronotope of the road as a path-of-life metaphor can be applied to Hogarth's progress narrative in *Industry and Idleness* (1747), where significant turning points in the course of events are fused with the characters' spatial courses on streets, roads, and waterways.[5] In the chronotope of the road, Bakhtin suggests, the hero might be defined by the sequence of guilt→retribution→redemption→blessedness, but might also be defined by an ironic or didactic denial of the sequence leading to redemption: Tom Idle in *Industry and Idleness* highlights the latter. I argue here that the paths Moll Hackabout follows through and around the spaces of London reflect a temporal progress of spectacle in the papers, and similarly serve to ironically undermine the redemptive possibility that the prints might at first seem to suggest.

London's Spaces

What do London's spaces mean when they are represented in art? The cities of London and Westminster by the eighteenth century had been joined into a continuous entity by urban sprawl along the Strand and into the northward expanse of streets and buildings, but the spaces of wealth and power (the Court and Parliament in Westminster and the Corporation of the City of London) and the area between customarily called "the Town" (the locale of the theatre and prostitution, of fairs catering to the "lower" tastes of the city, and of a variety of low markets and commodities) remained distinct. Early in the century, the City Wall still represented a physical barrier surrounding the City of London (visible in John Strype's map of 1720, fig. 12.1). Though it experienced gradual decay and demolition through later years (it is not identified in Rocque's map based on surveys done from 1741–45, fig. 12.2), it continued to present a formidable barrier in the psyche of the city's inhabitants. Thus, as I have shown elsewhere,[6] though the Wall itself was crumbling away to barely visible traces in the lines of remaining streets and building foundations, the space that had once been circumscribed by the great barricade remains as a virtual citadel in narratives of the City's commerce and industry.

One reading of Hogarth's series *Industry and Idleness* (1747) is that it shows a chronotope of progress and prosperity with a clear pattern of good, industrious citizens moving on a path to wealth and prestige, and idle ne'er-do-wells to justified banishment and punishment. While the

Fig 12.2 From John Rocque's *An Exact Survey of the City's of London Westminster, ye Borough of Southwark and the Country Near Ten Miles Round* (1746).

plates seem to provide a simple moral tale of two apprentice weavers embarking on their careers in London, I suggest that a more complicated irony is implicit in Hogarth's chronotope. The extreme poverty for many weavers amidst the affluent silk merchants, master weavers, and related business owners and retailers in the industry contributed to riots and other criminal acts, and a long history of disputes between apprentices, journeymen, and the prosperous members of the trade. Whether Tom Idle truly has the same opportunity as Francis Goodchild in this series is certainly questionable. Francis Goodchild's centripetal gravitation toward wealth and prestige within the City Wall (fig. 12.3), explicitly contrasting the centrifugal passage of Tom Idle propelled to corporeal punishment and death far beyond the bounds of the greater city (fig. 12.4), shows a subtly ironic view of prosperity and industry in eighteenth-century London. This later series showed a distinct contrast between the places of wealth and affluence: the affluent districts of Westminster and the City of London, versus the areas without the Wall, "the Town" and especially the larger city's perimeter. *A Harlot's Progress*, completed more than ten years previously, shows a similar narrative of progress through London's spaces of poverty, wealth, and criminality (fig. 12.5). Unlike Tom Idle, whose progress is almost entirely outside the locales of power in London and Westminster (with the exception of his trial at Guildhall), Moll's progress is from the unattainable potentials implied by her traversal through the two centres of wealth and power in London and Westminster to the squalor, scandal, and avaricious markets of the Town.

The Chronotope of A Harlot's Progress

A Harlot's Progress is a moral tale of a youthful maid in a corrupt city.[7] It is also a sustained critique of the contradictory justice administered to the city's residents high and low under Robert Walpole's government:[8] inhabiting the locales of power and vulnerability in London, Moll characterizes the unattainability of progress in light of the city's corruption. Targeting particular people and specific events, Hogarth incorporated details from a number of sensational newspaper reports and pamphlets from the 1720s through to the completion of the prints in 1731/2. Key characters in the series and in the news were Charteris – thought to be one of Walpole's runners[9] – convicted of raping Ann Bond in 1730; highwayman John Dalton and first-time thief Abraham Israel, two of ten malefactors who received a sentence of death at the Old Bailey trials in 1730; the nameless "Hundreds of Drury" (the prostitutes who made their living in the area around Drury Lane) who were regularly arrested and sentenced by several magistrates including Sir John Gonson in the campaign against disorderly houses and prostitution; the Covent Garden prostitute Kate Hackabout, whom Gonson arrested in 1730; and the procuress Elizabeth Needham, who had been in the news frequently since the early 1720s for arrests associated with keeping a bawdy house, was sentenced to stand twice in the pillory in 1731, and died after rough treatment by the crowd of spectators.

Charteris had a reputation as a notorious card sharp, fraudster, and libertine who had made a fortune through gambling and usury and reputedly through investments in the South Sea Company. He had, as Pat Rogers puts it, "made a not very heroic stand against the Jacobite army at Preston in 1715."[10] Charteris's contemporaries were less circumspect: Jonathan Swift famously described him as "a most infamous, vile Scoundrel … He had a Way of insinuating himself into all Ministers under every Change, either as Pimp, Flatterer, or Informer."[11] Charteris was sentenced to death 28 February 1730 in the sessions of the Old Bailey for the rape of Ann Bond. During Charteris's incarceration in Newgate the newspapers diligently reported on his ill health and the confiscation of his property. A

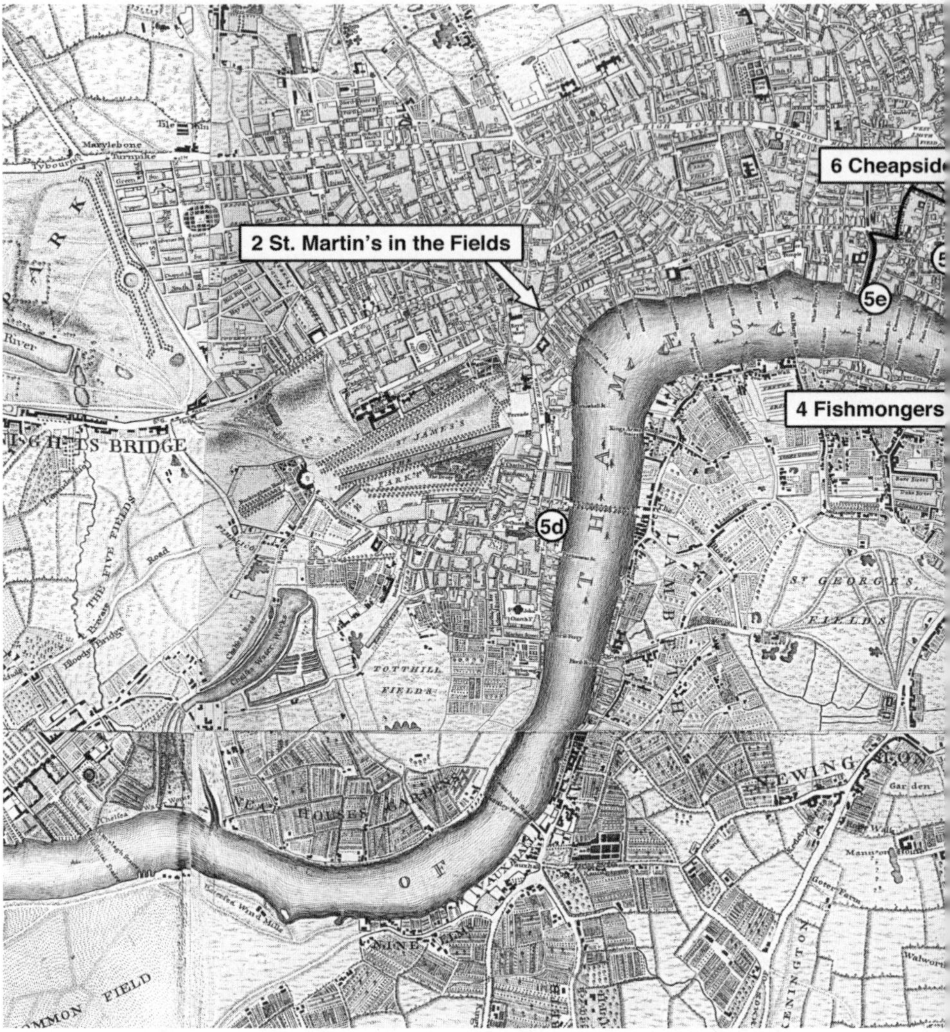

Fig. 12.3 "Francis Goodchild" Chronotope and City Wall overlay on Rocque's *Exact Survey*.

1. Plate 1: "The Fellow 'Prentices at their Looms" in Spitalfields.
2. Plate 2: "The Industrious 'Prentice Performing the Duty of a Christian," at St Martin's in the Fields, Westminster.
3. Plate 6: "The Industrious 'Prentice Out of his Time, & Married to his Master's Daughter," at Fish Street Hill in the City of London.
4. Plate 8: "The Industrious 'Prentice Grown Rich & Sheriff of London," at Fishmongers' Hall in the City of London.
5. Plate 10: "The Industrious 'Prentice Alderman of London, the Idle One Brought Before Him & Impeach'd by his Accomplice," in Guildhall in the City of London; and the Lord Mayor's Procession at the inauguration of the Industrious 'Prentice as new Lord Mayor.

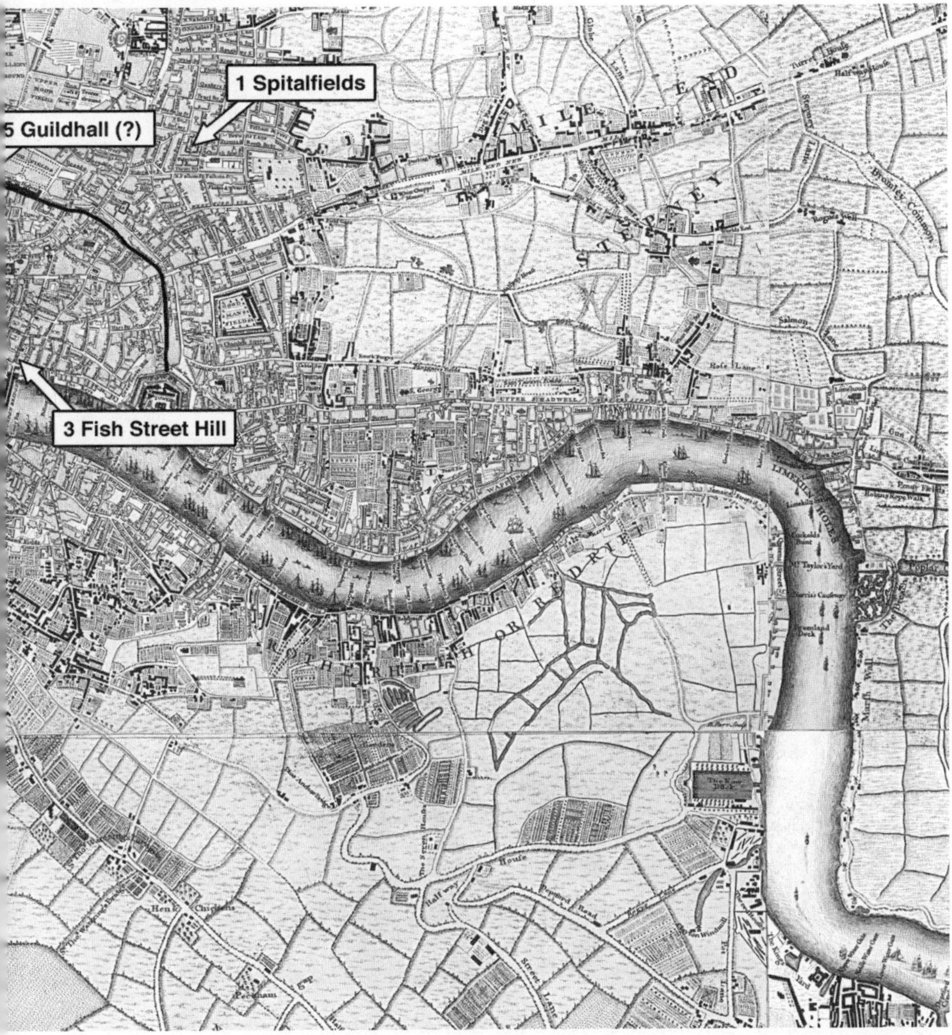

5a: The new and previous Lord Mayor embarked from Guildhall and proceeded down King Street and 5b. Queen Street (formerly Soper Lane) to 5c. Three Crane Wharf; from there, the Mayor and his party travelled by barge to 5d. Westminster Hall or the Exchequer to receive the oath of office, and returned by barge to 5e. Blackfriars Landing, from which the procession progressed to 5f. St Paul's Churchyard, east along Cheapside.
6. Plate 12: "The Industrious 'Prentice Lord-Mayor of London" in Cheapside, showing the Lord Mayor, with the eastern side of the cathedral visible on the right; the procession then returned to Guildhall, where the Lord Mayor and two Sheriffs hosted a feast, after which they returned to St Paul's Cathedral for a service to pay tribute to the inauguration. (See also fig. 9.4.)

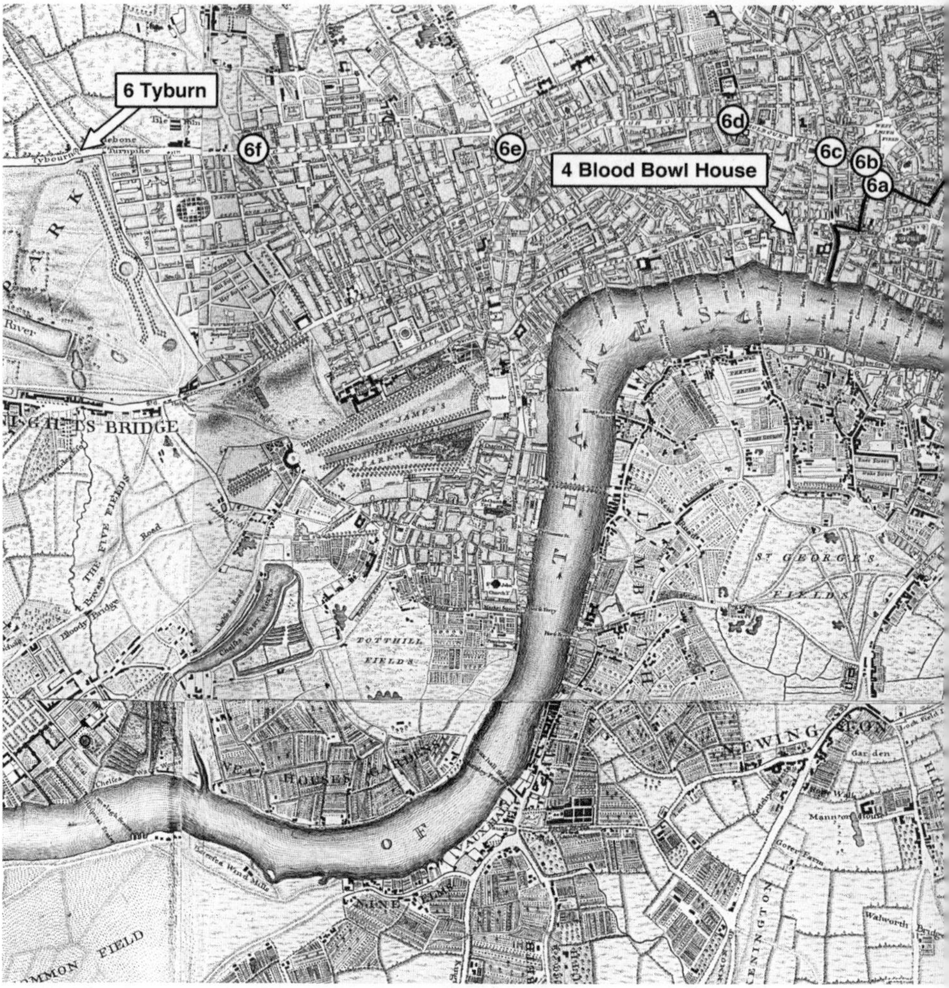

Fig. 12.4 "Tom Idle." Chronotope and City Wall overlay on Rocque's *Exact Survey*.

1. Plate 1: "The Fellow 'Prentices at their Looms" in Spitalfields.
2. Plate 3: "The Idle 'Prentice at Play in the Church Yard During Divine Service," likely at St Paul's, Shadwell.
3. Plate 5: "The Idle 'Prentice Turn'd Away, and Sent to Sea," at the Isle of Dogs near the pirate's gibbet.
4. Plate 9: "The Idle 'Prentice Betray'd by his Whore & Taken in a Night Cellar with his Accomplice," at the Blood Bowl House in Hanging Sword Alley.
5. Plate 10: "The Industrious 'Prentice Alderman of London, the Idle One Brought Before Him & Impeach'd by his Accomplice," in Guildhall in the City of London.

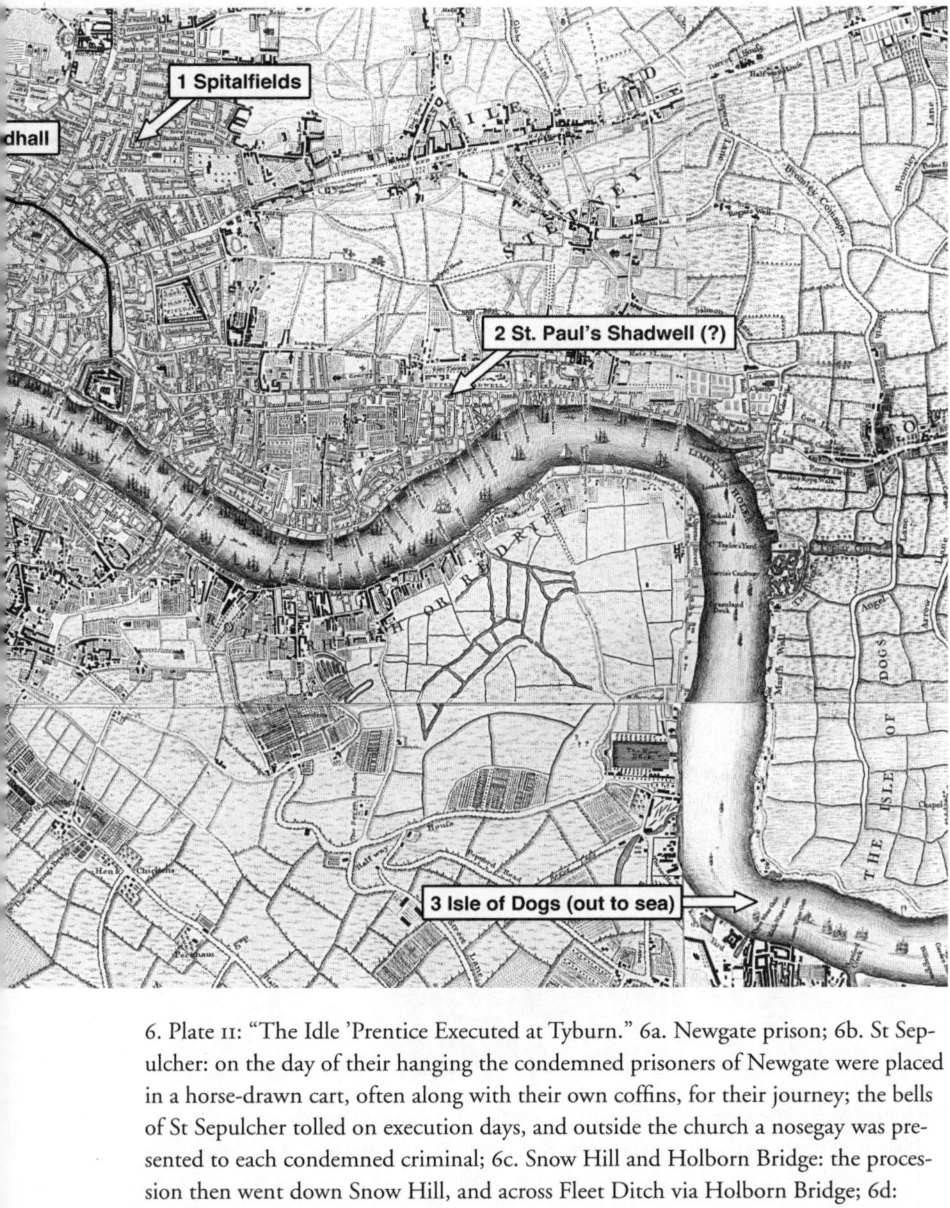

6. Plate 11: "The Idle 'Prentice Executed at Tyburn." 6a. Newgate prison; 6b. St Sepulcher: on the day of their hanging the condemned prisoners of Newgate were placed in a horse-drawn cart, often along with their own coffins, for their journey; the bells of St Sepulcher tolled on execution days, and outside the church a nosegay was presented to each condemned criminal; 6c. Snow Hill and Holborn Bridge: the procession then went down Snow Hill, and across Fleet Ditch via Holborn Bridge; 6d: Holborn Street: from there they proceeded along Holborn Street; 6e. past St Giles, where prisoners historically stopped to drink their last bowl of ale; 6f. along Tyburn Road. (See also chapter 6, 137–8 and note 166n33.)

Fig. 12.5 "Mary Hackabout." Chronotype overlay on Strype's *New Plan*.
Plate 1: Mary Hackabout arrives at the Bell Inn in Wood Street, in the City of London; she is destined to visit, or join, her cousin in the prosperous area of Thames Street in the City of London; she is seduced, however, to the employment of Colonel Charteris who lived in Great George Street in Westminster (in 1729), the neighbourhood of the notorious Mother Needham who had houses of ill repute in Great Pulteney Street (1723), Conduit Street (1724), Union Street (1725), and Park Place (1731). Plate 2: Moll Hackabout is now in the keeping of a wealthy Jew, possibly stockjobber John Mendes da Costa, in Winchester Street near to the exchanges for stocks in the East India Company and Sword Blade Company at Exchange Alley in the City of London.

Plate 3: Moll is now a streetwalker in Drury Lane in "the Town" close to Covent Garden, the stroll of Kate Hackabout in Bridges Street, and the one-time residence of James Dalton in Lewknor's Lane.
Plate 4: Moll, arrested and tried in her finery, is at Tothill Fields Bridewell at the outskirts of Westminster.
Plates 5 and 6: Moll's short life comes to an end, probably at her old haunts in Drury Lane, despite or perhaps due to the ineffectual medicine purchased from The Anodyne Necklace at the border between the cities of London and Westminster.

campaign to have him pardoned ensued, ultimately joined by Bond herself. On 12 March, the pseudonymous Bavius sarcastically remarked in *The Grub Street Journal* that the process of prosecuting "Persons of considerable fortune, or quality" involved too many inconveniences and expenses, "it being more difficult to get a rich man hanged, than to save a poor fellow from the gallows."[12] Reportedly through the influence of Walpole, George II pardoned Charteris on 10 April.[13] The papers continued to report on his health, property, and whereabouts until his death on 4 March 1732. It was not a leap in the various satiric treatments of the events to connect Walpole, the Screen-Master General, with Charteris, dubbed the Rape-Master General. Paulson suggests that it is possible *A Harlot's Progress* "is serving, in a secondary way, as part of the *Craftsman*'s campaign against Walpole."[14] A reading of Hogarth's *Progress* as a response to and participant in the spectacle of London suggests this is likely to have been the case.

While the papers were reporting on Charteris's trial, they also followed Francis Hackabout (brother of Kate), who had been sentenced to death on 26 February for highway robbery.[15] From December 1729, the highwayman James Dalton (whose wig box makes an appearance in Plate 3 of the *Progress*) had also been also making regular appearances in the paper after his arrest for robbing the physician Richard Mead. Dalton had been sentenced to three years in Newgate and while serving his time there was accused by John Waller of assault and robbery. Although he confessed to other crimes, Dalton denied this accusation, and at his trial on 8 April 1730 he pointed out that Waller was known to commit perjury for payment. Nevertheless, and despite having two witnesses swear on his behalf against Waller's story,[16] on 10 April (the same day that Charteris was pardoned) Dalton was one of ten malefactors who received a sentence of death at the sessions of the Old Bailey, along with Abraham Israel (alias Jonas) for robbing his master John Mendes da Costa. Francis Hackabout was hanged at Tyburn on 17 April, aged twenty-eight; Dalton, aged thirty, and Israel, aged twenty-two, were hanged there on 12 May. The value of young Abraham Israel's theft – and thus ultimately his life – was estimated in the newspapers to be around £300;[17] meanwhile Charteris's son-in-law the Earl of Wemyss and friend James Bruce had posted £500 in bail each, and Charteris himself £1,000, whereupon he was released and "carried in his Chair from Newgate to his Lady's Lodgings in Warwick-Lane."[18]

The crackdown on disorderly houses and the "Hundreds of Drury" by the Westminster justices began the following summer, led by Gonson. Reports appeared regularly in the news, and Gonson, known for his zeal in leading the raids and in prosecuting the malefactors, became a key protagonist in the drama that the newspapers presented. By the end of July, the papers reported that the justices had committed "above 40 lewd Women to Tothill Fields Bridewell in the past fortnight."[19] One of those was Kate Hackabout, who was taken into custody on 31 July for keeping a disorderly house, and sentenced the next day by Gonson to hard labour in Bridewell.[20] On this occasion, the "famous Kate Hackabout (whose Brother was lately hang'd at Tyburn)" was arrested, a woman noted "for being a very Termagant, and a Terror, not only to the Civil Part of the Neighbourhood by her frequent Fighting, Noise, and Swearing in the Streets in the Night-Time, but also to other Women of her own Profession, who presume to ply or pick up Men in her District, which is half one Side of the Way in Bridges-street."[21] This side of Kate Hackabout Hogarth chooses not to portray in Moll, a character who seems deliberately drawn to stir viewers' sympathies, and probably their desires, too. Her silliness and vulnerability will ultimately make her powerlessness all the more deadly.

Ann Bond was reported to have "met several Persons of Distinction and eminent Lawyers at the Horn Tavern in the New Palace Yard, Westminster" on 6 April,[22] and ended up receiving £800 in "Consideration of her having joined in the Petition" [23] for Charteris's pardon, which was "paid to her by a Gentleman of St. Margaret's at Westminster."[24] Immediately following these comments in some papers was the announcement of the execution of five malefactors at Tyburn, one of whom was Francis Hackabout. Bond seems to have done much better for herself than the fictitious Moll: she was said to be marrying Charles Heather, a Drawer at a tavern at Westminster, and setting up a tavern in Bloomsbury.[25] In August there were reports of her setting up a coffee shop in Lombard Street,[26] later identified as Daniel's Coffee House.[27]

On 19 March 1731, while Hogarth was nearing completion of his paintings, Mother Needham reappeared in the papers, having been committed to the Gatehouse.[28] On 23 April, she was brought before the court at the Sessions of Peace for the City and Liberty of Westminster chaired by Gonson and was sentenced to stand in the pillory at New Palace Yard in

Westminster and in St James Street, across from Park Place where she kept her disorderly house.[29] The final spectacle in Mother Needham's life was the theatre of her death, witnessed in part by the crowds at the pillory on 30 April and related afterwards in all the major papers of London. One striking aspect of the spectacle is that a key inspiration for Moll (or Mary) Hackabout – Kate – is utterly lost. After her arrest and sentence by Gonson, described alongside reports of Ann Bond's coffee house, she seems to disappear from the news completely. Hogarth's *Progress,* then, might also be understood as redress to the only story with a conclusion untold, of the person who is perhaps lowest in the hierarchy of power delineated by these spectacles in the news.

Plate 1: From the Bell Inn in Wood Street in the City, to Mayfair in Westminster

Moll Hackabout's progress begins outside the Bell Inn on Wood Street in the City of London. Just arrived on the York Wagon, Moll stands dumb among her packages, which include a gift of a fine goose "For my Lofing Cosen in Tems Stret in London." The note suggests that she originally intends to remain in, or at least maintain connections with, the prosperous and industrious folk in the City. The tie around the goose's neck reflects the bow around Moll's throat, however, and foreshadows her early death. "Goose," a euphemism for prostitute or for a desirable sexually inexperienced woman, also indicates her imminent downfall within London's vicious society. A clergyman turns his back on the young woman on the verge of ruination, absorbed instead in a pamphlet addressed to Bishop Edmund Gibson, "To the Right Reverend Father in God." The anonymous pamphlet had been occasioned by the order of the bishop (Walpole's close ally) to remove an altarpiece from St Clement Danes Church in the Strand, painted by William Kent. Kent's depiction of Saint Cecilia had generated a great deal of interest because of its likeness to Maria Clementina Stuart (née Sobieska), wife of Jacobite pretender to the throne James II. The "*Sons of* Belial" went to the church to "*decypher* the *dumb Libel,* and sneer at the *pictur'd Lampoon,* which tacitly *mocks the Church,* and openly *affronts the State,*" the pamphlet reads. "No *Wonder* our Church has been throng'd with Spectators, to the great Hindrance of *Divine Worship.*"[30] The pamphlet praises Bishop Gibson's protection of his flock: "Nor have you watch'd the *Sheep only, but the Shepherds likewise*; *redressing* and *preventing* all Abuses in the Church."[31] The irony was that the intolerant bishop, infamous for numerous appointments of clergymen supportive of the Whig administration to influential positions in the Church of England, attended more diligently to the reigning government than to the needs of the lesser members of his flock such as Moll.

The allusion to the pamphlet establishes Hackabout's Jacobite sympathies: her imminent profession as a prostitute links her explicitly to the painting above the altar, "the *known Resemblance* of a Person, who is the Wife of [the king's] *utter Enemy*, and *Pensioner* to the *Whore of* Babylon," according to the pamphlet. The pamphlet attacks the Roman Catholics – "our *inveterate Enemies* the *Papists*"[32] – and to a lesser extent the Jews. The clergyman's indifference to the vulnerable young woman standing behind him is occasioned by his absorption in the hyperbolic spectacle of print. That such biased representations supersede ethical engagement with real harms in society is a repeated theme throughout Moll's progress.

At the centre of Hogarth's image stands Mother Needham, procuring for her friend Charteris, who is pictured in the doorway of the Bell Inn with his hand suggestively out of sight under his coat. Viewers would have recognized some similarity between the scene depicted and that described during Charteris's trial: Ann Bond had testified that around the middle of October 1729 a woman had asked whether she wanted a good service and had told her she would recommend her to "a very honourable Gentleman, and a good Master, that wants a Servant at this very Instant." Bond testified Charteris had stopped her mouth with a nightcap and raped her, then lashed her with a horsewhip and turned her out of his house on the afternoon of 10 November.[33]

The implication is that Hackabout will end up in similar circumstances, possibly in the same place. Thames Street, where one might find mansions and the great halls of the City livery companies – the Worshipful Company of Fishmongers and the Worshipful Company of Vintners – and the Custom House, centre of London's prosperity and worldwide trade, could have provided a young woman with a good placement. However, her progress from this point is a movement to, presumably, the wealthy district of Mayfair in the city's fashionable west end where Needham and Charteris – two of the most immoral and malevolent people referenced in this series – were neighbours. In a narrative that resonates with Ann Bond's, she might be imagined to find herself in the employ of Charteris at his home in Great George Street leading into the newly built Hanover Square – a street known for its strong base of military Whigs who had served in Marlborough's campaigns or against the Jacobite Rising of 1715.[34] If she joins the other harlots at Mother Needham's house, then she spends time in Park Place near St James's Square and Pall Mall, about four blocks away from Charteris. Needham had lived within a few blocks of this address since the early 1720s, and was reported to be keeping a bawdy house in Great Pulteney Street in 1723,[35] in Conduit Street in 1724,[36] and in Union Street in 1725.[37] Her presence had been a longstanding blight on the upscale community, with numerous raids and arrests of madams, their "nymphs," and diverse "Gentlemen, some of whom appeared to be Persons of considerable Distinction."[38]

In March 1724, self-styled "spectatress"[39] Mary Wortley Montagu described a new secret society of rakes and their mistresses in that neighbourhood. The involvement of Philip Wharton, Charteris's associate, suggests the colonel might have participated:

> They call themselves Schemers, and meet regularly 3 times a week to consult on Galant Schemes for the advancement of that branch of Happyness which the vulgar call Whoring. Viscount Hillsborrough … has turn'd his house, one of the handsomest in Hannover Square, into an Edifice appropriated to this use.
>
> The Schemers were all sworn to several Articles … 1st, every member should come at the hour of 6 mask'd in a Domine, leading in the then predominant Lady of his affections mask'd likewise; 2ndly, that no member should presume, by peeping, squeaking, staring or any other impertinence, to discover his brother's incognita, who should remain wholly and solely his, without any molestation soever, to his use for that night.[40]

The Universal Journal warned of the new "Nocturnal Society" of rakes called the "Galant Schemers" (derived from a story of the directors of a company or bank that traded in public funds endeavouring "to raise Stock to Two Thousand"), which aimed to be at least as frightening as the Mohock gang that had terrorized the city (with the help of the papers) in 1711–12.[41] Presumably it is within this area of the nobility and gentry, with its undercurrents of corrupt schemes and viciousness, that Moll experiences her unhappy introduction to London.

Plate 2: Winchester Street / the City of London's Financial District

Hogarth's second plate shows Moll, now kept by a wealthy Jew, in her luxurious boudoir. On the dressing table to the left is a mask; in a heap on the right is a mass of heavy dark cloth, suggesting the domino or loose cloak worn at masquerades. Moll has been having a liaison with a young lover who steals away as a serving woman holds the door open, ready to hand the gallant his shoes. Moll distracts her cuckolded protector by exposing her breast and surreptitiously kicking over an elaborately carved tea table. It is a scene of chaos: the Jew, who seems to have just arrived with his hat under his arm, attempts to steady the table, wide-eyed and mouth agape, as some of the china crashes to the floor and shatters. On the right a black servant boy in a feathered turban stares wide-eyed at the scene. The bed curtains are closed, suggesting that they have screened Moll's intrigue. On the left a monkey with a startled expression scampers away wearing Moll's laced cap. The harlot's disordered room is filled with the fashionable commodities that trade with the colonies had brought to London – tea, an exotic pet, a slave. If the scene of the first print is the result of a sordid financial exchange, this one might suggest another, but in far greater magnitude.

The scene establishes a link between the conspicuous consumption of wealth, the luxuries of foreign trade, and the corruption of values that Moll and her lovers represent. The negro attendant is commonly noted as a possession in vogue for women of wealth, an object of ostentation. Indeed, the "Black Boy" as a trade sign was an emblem associated with luxury trades, and the Black Boy in Lombard Street was the sign of goldsmith, entrepreneur, and trader Sir Stephen Evance, whose business interests included the Royal African and East India Companies, and who had founded what would become the Sword Blade Company, the bank of the South Sea Company. Moll's black servant boy and the gallant's sword, which appears through a trick of perspective to stab the Jew in the back, provide at best a tenuous connection to the sign of the Black Boy and to the slave trade that the South Sea Company had engaged in; at the least, they and the room's extravagant material goods provide a clear sign of the morally dubious exotic trades that had helped to fuel the South Sea Bubble.

The Jew is generally treated as a representation of a category rather than an identifiable individual – a socially marginal figure, or an anti-Semitic stereotype, a point vigorously debated by, among others, David Solkin and Ronald Paulson.[42] (See also chapter 9, 220, 223.) Certainly, with a framed portrait of controversial clergymen Thomas Woolston on the wall directly above the Jew's head,[43] one could read this plate as an indication of the Jew as an outsider in London society. Woolston was fined and imprisoned for blasphemy after publishing claims in his bestselling *Discourses on the Miracles of our Saviour* (1727) that biblical events were figurative rather than literal. Bishop Gibson had tried once previously to have him prosecuted for blasphemy; Woolston's first *Discourse* was prefaced by a sarcastic dedication to him:

> Whether your Prosecution of me … was just and reasonable, I'll not dispute here … Your *Lordship*'s persecuting (or if you will prosecuting) Humour is reputedly all pure Zeal for God's Glory … And what Pitty is it, that *Infidels* … are not to be quell'd with your Threats and Terrors?[44]

For his sixth and final *Discourse* Woolston had invented an "old Friend, the *Jewish Rabbi,* for his Thoughts on this grand Miracle of *Jesus*'s Resurrection."[45] Thus Uzzah being stabbed in the back by an Anglican bishop in the painting above Woolston's portrait creates an equation of Woolston and the Jew. Hogarth's targets are both Gibson, known derogatively as "Walpole's Pope," and Walpole's government, together engaging in the intolerant persecution of marginal people as a theatre of justice addressing the crisis of immorality, crime, and irreligion in the city.

The Jew, however, is not simply representative of a general category. As do all the other major figures in *A Harlot's Progress*, he designates a particular person representing a particular category of power under Walpole's government, and is likely to be the affluent merchant and stockjobber John (Abraham) Mendes da Costa, Jr (1683–1763), son-in-law of Alvaro (Jacob) da Costa (1646–1716) – so-called founding father of the Anglo-Sephardi community in London and one of its wealthiest and most powerful members.[46] John Mendes da Costa, with the others in his family, traded in diamonds and coral in the East Indies, along with other imported commodities. One of the earliest investors in the Bank of England, holding stock from 1705 to 1722, he was also a stockjobber for the bank from 1696 to 1725.[47] M.J. Landa speculates that John's son, the rake Philip Mendes da Costa (1708–1780), may have been the model for Hogarth's Jew, though he would have been only twenty-four years old in 1732 when the prints were published.

The principal evidence suggesting that John Mendes da Costa inspired Hogarth's Jew is found in the newspaper reports of spring 1730. In early March, the *London Evening Post* itemized jewels and plate that had been stolen "out of the House of John Mendes da Costa, in Winchester-Street," by his servant "Abraham Jones,"[48] that is, Abraham Israel/Jones or Jonas who would shortly be tried and executed for this crime. In a later report the victim of the robbery is identified as "Mr. Mendez da Costa, jun."[49] While Hogarth's Jew is arguably a sympathetic character, he is nevertheless a culpable player in London's vicious games of justice, finance and industry, poverty and wealth. A feasible location for Moll's luxurious chamber depicted in the second plate, then, is in or very close to Winchester Street, within a few minutes' walk of Exchange Alley in London's financial district. It seems unlikely that the actual Mendes da Costa would have a kept woman in his home (his wife Ester lived with him), but Hogarth's inclusion of two paintings featuring scenes from the Old Testament suggest that the apartment belongs to the Jew. Certainly, the theft of "things" owned by the wealthy Jew from his own home (jewels or plate in Mendes da Costa's case, or the Jew's mistress in Hogarth's representation) reinforces the proposition that Hogarth's series explicitly connects the ill-fated fictitious Moll to Kate and Francis Hackabout and Abraham Israel.

Jews were conspicuous among the investors and stockjobbers in London's financial realm. They held a smaller percentage of stock, but were among the wealthiest and most active traders,[50] and they were notably present in trading companies' governance. The Jewish presence in London's financial markets and among the stockjobbers in Exchange Alley, and especially their involvement in the South Sea Bubble, was routinely caricatured in popular print and drama. Satires of the Bubble frequently characterized Exchange Alley as the discomfiting mingling of men and women of all ranks along with Jewish traders. Popular representations added a sexualized undercurrent to emphasize the immorality embedded in such transactions, both social and financial. Ned Ward, for example, makes note of the promiscuous commingling of women, Jews, and high and low society gambling in Exchange Alley where "Stars and Garters" mingle with the "Rabble"

> To buy and sell, to see and hear
> The *Jews* and *Gentiles* squabble.
> Here "crafty Courtiers" do not trust Fortune:
> They see the Cheat with clearer Eyes,
> Who peep behind the curtain.

The "greatest Ladies" and "Young Harlots" from Drury Lane go there alike to pawn their jewels or gamble their ill-gotten money.[51] All the usual elements are here: the promiscuous intermingling of religions, sexes, and foreigners, the gambling and the cheating, and the screens.

Locating the scene of Plate 2 in the City close to Exchange Alley invites a reading of *A Harlot's Progress* as an allegory of the city's corruption and decay in its pursuit of wealth, also suggested by the two framed paintings of Old Testament stories that hang on the wall behind Moll. On the left is Jonah outside Nineveh after he has gone to preach in the city about its wickedness and to proclaim to its citizens that it will be overthrown; when God mercifully spares the city, Jonah, fearing that he will be perceived as a false prophet, retreats to a mountain a distance away. The painting on the right shows King David dancing before the Ark of the Covenant, while a well-meaning Uzzah puts his hand on it to prevent it falling as the cart is shaken by the ox that is drawing it. In the biblical story, God is angered at Uzzah's violation in touching the holy object and strikes him dead (2 Sam. 6); in Hogarth's version, an Anglican bishop stabs Uzzah in the back.

Comparisons of London with Nineveh were not altogether uncommon. *The Fatal Consequences of Gaming and Stock-jobbing*, a sermon preached by "a Presbyter of the Church of England" (1720), for example, compared London to the ancient "*bloody City*, delighting in Rapine and illegal Means of Oppression and Extortion" – "impoverishing *many* to make a *few* great and wealthy. She was full of *Lyes* and *Robberies*, the one being usually the effect of the other; a *Lye* either preparing a Snare of the Innocent, or defending the Guilt when committed."[52] Recalling the biblical judgment against Nineveh, Moll then takes on a larger role – the corrupted "bloody" city "full of lies *and* robbery" presents itself as "the well-favoured harlot, the mistress of witchcrafts, that selleth nations through her whoredoms" (Nah. 3:1–4). Possibly the stories of Uzzah and Jonah allude to circumstances concerning the Jewish involvement in London's finances, especially around the time of the Bubble. While pamphlets and ballads in popular literature suggested the Jews were unscrupulous cheaters in the London stocks trade, London's Sephardic community actually used its financial capital to stabilize the price of stock and slow its decline in 1720. When the price of South Sea stock plunged and investors hurried to liquidate their assets, Jews bought Bank of England stock and prevented its price being driven down further:[53] Anthony da Costa, also of Winchester Street, and son of Alvaro da Costa, ranked in the top fifteen most active jobbers. The Jew's hand steadying the table (its carved scallops and waves suggestive of the sea) could imply such activities; his hand mirroring Uzzah's hand on the Ark in the painting behind him insinuates that the ox causing the cart to fall is a pun on "bull market." Hogarth's scene might then speak to the Jewish financiers' warning of the impending crash (Jonah-like) and perhaps even helping to steady the teetering markets (Uzzah-like). In general terms, if Charteris represents the debauchery of the powers in Westminster – the peerage, the Whigs in support of William and Mary – then the Jew might represent the powerful moneyed interests in the City of London gambling with the lives of the citizens.

Plate 3: Drury Lane

Moll now lives in a squalid apartment. A beer tankard in the corner bears the inscription "in Drury Lane" and establishes Moll as one of the "Hundreds of Drury" – prostitutes who seemed to swarm around the area. Kate Hackabout's district was known to be in Bridges Street (along Drury Lane Theatre and a block over from Drury Lane). James Dalton lived for a period in Lewknor's Lane at the top of Drury Lane, a street also notorious for its lewd women and houses of ill repute. At the eastern edge of Westminster, Drury Lane was a resort of the city's two centres of power, and at the margins of both. In this plate Moll looks coquettishly into the viewer's eyes, her nightdress open to reveal her breast. In case the viewer is in doubt regarding her profession, beside the bed is a cat in heat, tail raised, back arched, and hindquarters elevated to signal her receptivity ("cat" was also slang for "a common Whore or Prostitute"[54]). Hanging above the headboard is a witch's hat and birch rod used for erotic flagellation. These details indicate Moll's connection to Nineveh, "the well-favoured harlot, the mistress of witchcrafts." Hanging on a line behind the bed is what appears to be a supply of condoms. Usually made of sheep bladders, these were said to protect against pregnancy and venereal disease. Dr Joseph Cam, who avidly promoted the use of mercury to increase salivation and thus expel and cure venereal disease,[55] had cautioned in 1729 against the use of condoms since, just as in "common Bladders," a pox might pass from the outside to the inside of the device and cause an infection. Moll – attended by her servant, whose nose is showing the ravages of syphilis – has clearly ignored the medical advice: her medicine bottles on the windowsill suggest she too is infected. Moll is rising late, not yet aware that the magistrate, John Gonson, and his bailiffs armed with cudgels, one of them brandishing a cane, are entering the room to arrest her. Her watch suggests the time is a quarter to twelve, and reinforces a connection with the real-life Kate, arrested at around twelve or one o'clock.

The print gestures to the events leading up to the Bubble, the rise of the Whig government under Walpole, and the ensuing social and financial outcomes of its policies. A poster of Macheath from *The Beggar's Opera* is pinned under the window, a reminder perhaps of Lucy Lockit singing of her seduction by the rogue who "Is lost in the arms / Of that jilt, that inveigling harlot!" to the tune of "The South-Sea Ballad."[56] Macheath, of whom Mrs Peachum comments "there is not a finer gentleman on the road than the Captain," represents an inversion of supposed gentlemen, upholders of the law, and the putatively villainous thieves that continued to defy it. Also pinned to the wall under the window is an icon of the Virgin Mary, indicating Moll's Jacobitism. Above it is a print of Dr Henry Sacheverell, who had briefly supported the Jacobite cause after the death of Queen Anne. These position Moll in opposition to Walpole's government: Sacheverell had delivered a sermon in 1709 before the mayor and aldermen of London that attacked Dissenters and, by implication, the Whig government, as false prophets who had made the "*House of God*, not only a *Den of Thieves*, but a Receptacle of *Legions of Devils*."[57] The published sermon had sold a staggering 100,000 copies and resulted in Sacheverell's impeachment in 1710.

Moll's disregard for the city's leaders is further illustrated by her use of Bishop Gibson's *Pastoral Letter* (1728) as a wrapper for her butter. Gibson's publication was a response to what he characterized as a crisis of "Profaneness and Impiety … grown bold and open" in London and Westminster. Among other wicked behaviours, he wrote, "in some late Writings, *Publick Stews* have been openly vindicated."[58] This was a reference to Bernard Mandeville's *A Modest Defence of Publick Stews: or, an Essay upon Whoring* published four years earlier. Mandeville's argument in favour of state-run brothels was prefaced by a scornful address to "the Gentlemen of the Societies," that is, the Societies for the Reformation of Manners of which Gonson was an enthusiastic proponent, noting, "Your Endeavours to suppress Lewdness, have only serv'd to promote it; … But however Your ill Success may grieve, it cannot astonish me: What else could we hope for, from Your persecuting of poor strolling Damsels?"[59]

The theme of persecution by the justice system carries through this plate. According to Bishop Gibson in the *Letter*, "great pains have been taken to make Men easy in their Vices, and to deliver them from the restraints of Conscience, by undermining all Religion, and promoting Atheism and Infidelity."[60] One of those, "under colour of great zeal for the Jewish Dispensation, and the *literal* meaning of Scripture, has been endeavouring to overthrow the Foundations of the Christian Religion."[61] The *Pastoral Letter* admonishes Woolston and "the Jews" at length, concluding: "I cannot but think it the Duty of the Civil Magistrate … to discourage such Books and Writings, as strike equally at the Foundation of all Religion, and of Truth, Virtue, Seriousness, and good Manners; and by consequence, at the Foundation of Civil Society."[62]

The various prints scattered throughout Moll's room underscore the terrible irony in any claim for a "civil society" that ineffectually imprisons its clergymen for expressing ideas, punishes the victims of rape instead of their rapists, sentences impoverished women turned to prostitution, and hangs its young men and women for minor thefts while the city's most powerful destroy one another's lives. If we accept that John Abraham Mendes da Costa might be in part the inspiration for the Jew in Plate 2, then the print of Abraham's sacrifice of Isaac on Moll's wall develops a new resonance. In the Old Testament story depicted in this scene, Abraham has bound his son and laid him on an altar in order to sacrifice him. The message seems to be of a society mad with slaughtering its own children in the name of virtuously upholding its codes of justice and religion.

Plate 4: Bridewell Prison, Tothill Fields

Moll, dressed in a splendid gown, is now imprisoned in Bridewell on the western outskirts of Westminster. She raises a mallet for beating hemp, while a cruel-looking keeper with cane ready to strike points threateningly at a leg iron on the floor. A man stands with his hands in a pillory under the sign "Better to Work than Stand thus," and a whipping post is labelled "The Wages of Idleness." The prison keeper has been linked by David Dabydeen to John Huggins (who appeared in the newspapers in December 1730 because of the case brought against him for the death of one of his prisoners after harsh treatment by the warder, and was found not guilty by the same Justice Raymond who had sentenced Charteris, Israel, and Dalton), and to Thomas Bambridge, who had been found not guilty (again, by Justice Raymond) for the murder of an inmate earlier in the year.[63] A woman, winking, fingers the fine fabric of Moll's clothing: she will either steal it or accept it as a high price in exchange for some favour or item. Moll's splendid clothing is likely inspired by a report in the papers.

The Grub Street Journal on 24 September 1730 had reported on two recent events in a thought-provoking juxtaposition:

> Some Days ago Mr. Major Smith, who marry'd Mrs. Anne Bond, who cast Col. Charteris, was arrested in some sort of actions by persons employed in that affair, viz., one action for 18 l. another for 1600 l. but the young man says, he owes them nothing, and hath given bail to the actions, being resolved to see them out. We are well assur'd that the Col. hath no hand in this affair. *D.P.* 4 *Ev.— I wonder at the assurances of my Brethren in vindicating the Colonel's reputation by such an Innuendo.*[64]

It seems likely that both "Mr. Major Smith" (who probably performed the ceremony) and Ann Bond had been well paid for their efforts against Charteris. Immediately following this paragraph is one describing how Mary Muffet, one of the "Hundreds of Drury," had been committed to hard labour in Tothill Fields Bridewell. Expecting to be discharged, she had appeared in her best clothes and was now beating hemp in a gown very richly laced with silver.

The other inmates include prostitutes and a card sharp. A torn playing card, the eight of spades, lies on the floor and might recall a set of South Sea Bubble playing cards printed for Carington Bowles (1721), in which the eight of spades shows a despondent woman holding a banner that reads "Oh fatal Blow to loose at once what through Artfull Charms I've got these many Years – Undone, Undone!" The verse underneath reads:

> A Broker went to let a Lady know,
> That South Sea Stock was falling very low;
> Says she, then what I gain in my good Calling –
> By rising things, I find I loose by falling.[65]

The gamble of finances is here again reinforced as a vice, a form of prostitution, and in Moll's case as the capricious and transitory nature of her calling with the "rising things" that had briefly afforded her some power and autonomy. A stick figure drawing on a window shutter of Gonson hanged on the gallows emphasizes once again the implied indistinguishability of London's high and low wrongdoers and the arbitrariness of its "justice."

Plate 5: Drury Lane?

The last two plates of this series might represent the return of Moll to Drury Lane after her incarceration, but just as her face and body become hidden from the viewer – first by the sweating blankets in Plate 5 and ultimately by her coffin in Plate 6 – Moll's whereabouts, like Kate's, fall into obscurity. She is in a dilapidated room, near death, suffering the ravages of both syphilis and its "cures" while two quacks argue over her treatment. A woman roots through her trunk looking for items to pilfer; along with an elegant pair of shoes, she has tossed Moll's mask, a closed fan thrust through the eyehole, to the floor – an indication that her anonymity is no longer playful, desirable, or beneficial. Other than her faithful servant, the only suggestion of a caring presence in the room is the Passover bread tacked to the wall: this, and that she can afford the care of two doctors, quacks though they may be, suggests her old protector is providing limited financial support. On top of a coal scuttle her teeth are scattered on a paper labelled "Dr Rock," their loss likely the outcome of taking mercury to increase salivation in an attempt to expel the disease; a clyster pipe used to inject medication hangs on the wall above the mantle; Moll is wrapped, suffering, in sweating blankets – all ineffectual and injurious attempts to draw the disease from her body. Moll's servant ineffectually gestures at the quacks to attend to their patient, who is close to death. Hogarth biographer John Nichols identified the tall, slender one leaping up and knocking over his chair and a small stool as the "foreign quack" Dr John Misaubin (actually a well-qualified member of the Royal College of Physicians). The larger one still seated he identified as either Dr Richard Rock or Dr Joshua (Spot) Ward.[66] Generally these have been accepted, with most commentators preferring Rock because of Hogarth's clearly labelled reference.

Dr Richard Rock had embarked on an aggressive print advertising campaign in 1731, promoting his cures for toothaches, hysteric diseases, ulcers, asthma, and consumptions in numerous papers. Rock's advertisement for his "never failing TINCTURE for curing the TEETH" appeared in the Ordinary's Account for 16 June 1731,[67] alongside an advertisement for

A Practical Treatise: Or, Second Thoughts on the Consequences of the Venereal Disease ... To which is annex'd, a Vindication of the Practice of Salivating &c. by the aforementioned Dr Joseph Cam (Cam's ad had also appeared in the 1730 Ordinary's account of the executions of Israel and Dalton). Mercury caused ulcerations of the gums, hence the loosening and loss of teeth: apparently Moll has tried Rock's tincture without success, or perhaps made use of his service to have "Teeth or Stumps taken out with a Touch." In the summer Dr Rock started advertising "A speedy and infallible Cure For the Venereal Distemper" through an "incomparable ELECTUARY," a bottle of which he holds in his hand. Almost immediately after the ad appeared in *The Daily Advertiser*, an announcement was placed in the adjacent column advertising the "famous Anodyne Necklace." The competing announcements appeared through July and August 1731.[68] The anodyne necklace was a "prepared" coral necklace sometimes used with "liquid Coral" rubbed on the gums to aid with alleviating children's teething pains. It was invented and first promoted by Dr Paul Chamberlen, a member of the celebrated family that practised medicine and midwifery in the city. Chamberlen had died in 1717, but an anonymous author continued to promote the necklace along with other medications. It could be purchased at a shop called The Anodyne Necklace located near Devereux Court, next to the Rose Tavern just outside of Temple Bar, where also might be had a free pamphlet detailing the cure for venereal disease. It seems to have been a surprisingly effective means of selling sensible family medications along with secretive treatments. Editions of the pamphlet had been given free of charge for years to advertise a variety of quack remedies, including a "chymical cleansing lotion" that would cure "the venereal distemper."[69] The lotion could be bought only at The Anodyne Necklace or at the house of the author's servant. The pamphlet was published under various titles, the 1728 version of which was *The Practical Scheme of the Secret Disease, a Gleet and a Broken Constitution, caused by Fast Living, Former Cures, Salivations, Taking of Mercury, Self-abuses, &c.* The lean quack, angrily pointing to a jar of ointment as he argues with the self-satisfied Dr Rock, has upset Moll's stool and knocked a version of this pamphlet, along with an ink bottle and writing quill, to the floor.

The situation echoes the upsetting of Moll's tea table in the Jew's apartment, and links the "schemers" of the South Sea stock and the da Costa family's exotic trade in coral with the schemer marketing the coral anodyne necklace. The pamphlet also suggests an intriguing possibility for the identity of the lean quack. Dr Misaubin is a somewhat unsatisfactory original for this character in that there is no clear reason for his appearance in this scene, given the close attention Hogarth was paying to the spectacle of the press in this series: Misaubin does not appear to be a controversial figure in the press leading up to 1732 when *A Harlot's Progress* was published. Most commentators have ignored the identification of the two quacks by an anonymous author in a key to *The Harlot's Progress* published in 1732, who says they are "Ta—r and C—-m."[70] The latter is surely meant to suggest the aforementioned Joseph Cam, who had published a scathing critique of *The Practical Scheme* in 1717. There is little information to be found about Francis Tanner, here identified as the "Scheme-Maker,"[71] but Tanner appears to have been an enterprising scribbler and quack. *The Plainest, Easiest, and Prettiest Method of Writing Short-Hand, ever yet Published. By F.T.* had appeared in 1712, followed by *A Short Discourse of the Canary Bird … By F.T.*, c. 1714, which contains an advertisement for the shorthand manual as well as remedies for several illnesses. Dr Cam suggests in his introduction that potential buyers should beware of Tanner's remedies:

> *this* Tanner *is, according to his own Account, the brightest Man of the Age … let him teach* Short-Hand *and breed up* Canary-Birds, *which are innocent Diversions and will do no harm … I have given what caution I can to my Readers to avoid for the future such* gilded Baits, *and duly consider with themselves before they trifle with so precious a thing as their* Lives *and* Health.[72]

Cam concludes: "Is it not a vile Imposition in these Men, to dispose of such common, useless, and dangerous Medicines at so extravagant a Rate?" Worse yet was that "Men of Sense and Worth should hazard their Lives and Fortunes by buying Medicines at such Places, and taking them, without knowing the *Author*."[73]

The questionable attribution in the above-mentioned key might explain why Hogarth added Dr Rock's name to the second state of the plate;[74] however, Francis Tanner would seem to be the original of the second quack. Tanner's tracts on shorthand writing were also advertised at the back of some versions of *The Practical Scheme*. Tanner's involvement in the business was, apparently, something of an open secret: a satirical work by the pseudonymous "Anodyne Tanner" published circa 1721 claimed that the sole executor of the last will and testament of the procuress Elizabeth Wisebourn (for whom the infamous Sally Salisbury had worked in her early career) was himself, Anodyne Tanner, "Author of the P-c-l Sch-e, &c. and One of her Physicians in Ordinary."[75] Notably, Wisebourn's will purportedly left "To his G— the D— of —— a Gross of *right Dutch C- — -ms,* newly imported from *Holland,* by Mr. *M— —ez* the *Jew*."[76] The broken inkwell and quill further indicate that Tanner is the second quack.

Plate 6: Drury Lane?

The final plate, like the previous one, depicts an impoverished room in an unidentified location. Moll's faithful servant, her prostitute acquaintances, a clergyman, and an undertaker have gathered around her open coffin; she is obscured from view. On the left, a beautiful young woman now captures the gaze of the spectator. Nichols identifies her as Elizabeth Adams.[77] Hogarth clearly indicates a cyclical, never-ending drama of whores progressing through London: he may have predicted such an outcome but he could not have known Adams would be executed in 1738 at twenty-six years of age. The clergyman seated beside her has been identified as "the famous Couple-Beggar in The Fleet," notorious for conducting irregular marriages on urgent occasions: his oddly pained and pleased expression, eyebrow arched, his and Elizabeth's hands hidden under their clothing behind a shielding hat, her knowing expression, and his wine spilling over into the cloth on his lap all suggest an activity not normally suited to mourning. Moll's servant gazes on them as she uses the coffin for a table for her own glass and bottle. On the right, the undertaker seems besotted with another harlot, and helps her pull on a glove (suggesting sexual activities) while she picks his pocket. The bawd crying on the right is identified as Mother Bentley, possibly lamenting a loss of income with Moll's death.[78] The other harlots are a study in disinterest and oblivion: one gazes at herself in a mirror; another, weeping, shows her friend her fingers, perhaps identifying the early symptoms of syphilis on her hands. Another stares absently into the coffin. In the forefront, Moll's well-appointed young son, dressed as a gentleman, plays with a spinning top that visually echoes the spigots on the harlot's coat of arms hanging on the wall in the rear (which suggest the facility to turn on and off the fluid running from the faucet). The top, while it could in other contexts suggest the innocence of child's play, here could predict a future of carelessness and indifference – games and toys trumping the seriousness of death, suffering, inequity – that will be the boy's lot. The casket, the funeral, and the elegant clothes for the boy all suggest again that the Jew might be financing in part Moll's final days and the child's future.

Debord argues that "the spectacle is both the outcome and the goal of the dominant mode of production" and in "news or propaganda, advertising or the actual consumption of entertainment – the spectacle epitomizes the prevailing model of social life." *A Harlot's Progress* surely confirms that Walpole's regime, at the nascence of the modern culture of "news" – so reliant on the support of government, legal, and consumer financing – "is the very heart of society's real unreality."[79] The screen in the background is a reminder of Walpole. That the profundity of Moll's death is acknowledged by no one suggests a recurrent narrative about the corruption of London, where "progress" is illusory, and the spectacle serves as justification for the conditions and aims of the existing system. There are no allusions to other works in this final plate – simply the recognition that, like the clergy and like the financiers, the army generals, and the justices of the city, and its doctors were little more than gallant schemers. If the chronotopic Moll represents the potential for "progress" through the spaces of wealth and power in London, Hogarth's message might well be that she had little hope of avoiding, escaping, or being cured of the corruption that was endemic throughout the rapacious city.

NOTES

1 *Universal Spectator, and Weekly Journal* 73 (28 February 1730).

2 Debord, *The Society of the Spectacle*, 12.

3 Guthrie, *The Ordinary of Newgate his Account*, 1730, n.p.

4 Bakhtin, "Forms of Time and of the Chronotope in the Novel," 84.

5 Muri, "Beyond GIS."

6 Ibid.

7 High-resolution images of *A Harlot's Progress* referred to here are available from the Lewis Walpole Library digital collections. http://findit.library.yale.edu/.

8 See Paulson, *Hogarth: High Art and Low*, 248–9.

9 On the connections of Charteris and Walpole, see Goldgar, *Walpole and the Wits*, 106–9.

10 Rogers, *The Alexander Pope Encyclopedia*, 59.

11 Swift, *Verses on the Death of Dr. S——*, 18.

12 *Grub Street Journal* 10 (12 March 1730).

13 *London Gazette* 6873 (11–14 April 1730); *Daily Journal* 2893 (15 April 1730); *Daily Post* 3298 (15 April 1730); *Weekly Journal or British Gazetteer* 265 (18 April 1730); *Craftsman* 198 (18 April 1730); *Grub Street Journal* 16 (23 April 1730); *Monthly Chronicle* (April 1730); etc.

14 Paulson, *Hogarth: High Art and Low*, 249–50.

15 *Daily Journal* 2851 (26 February 1730); *Fog's Weekly Journal* 75 (28 February 1730); *Grub Street Journal* 9 (5 March 1730).

16 Guthrie, *The Ordinary of Newgate, his Account*, 1730, n.p.

17 *Daily Courant* 8894 (11 April 1730); *Weekly Journal or British Gazetteer* 265.

18 *Daily Journal* 2890 (11 April 1730).

19 *London Journal* 574 (1 August 1730).

20 *Daily Journal* 2987 (3 August 1730); *Evening Post* 3283 (1–4 August 1730).

21 *Daily Post* 3392 (3 August 1730); *Grub Street Journal* 31 (6 August 1730).

22 *Daily Post* 3292 (8 April 1730); *London Evening Post* 364 (7–9 April 1730).

23 *London Journal* 559 (18 April 1730).

24 *Universal Spectator, and Weekly Journal* 80 (18 April 1730).

25 *Weekly Journal or British Gazetteer* 265 (18 April 1730); *Grub Street Journal* 16 (23 April 1730), citing *St James's Evening Post*.

26 *Daily Post* 3392 (3 August 1730); *Evening Post* 3283 (1–4 August 1730); *Grub Street Journal* 31 (6 August 1730).

27 *Select Trials for Murders*, 2:350.

28 *Daily Journal* 3184 (20 March 1731).

29 *Daily Advertiser* 70 (24 April 1731); *Daily Journal* 3215 (26 April 1731); *Daily Post* 3620 (26 April 1731); *London Evening Post* 532 (24–7 April 1731); *Grub Street Journal* 69 (29 April 1731).

30 *A Letter from a Parishioner*, 6.

31 Ibid., 3.

32 Ibid., 4–5.
33 "The Case of Col. Francis Chartres," 26–30.
34 Summerson, *Georgian London*, 81–2.
35 *Weekly Journal or British Gazetteer* (16 March 1723).
36 *Evening Post* 2356 (29 August –1 September 1724); *Weekly Journal or Saturday's Post* 306 (5 September 1724); *Post Boy* 5482 (5–8 September 1724).
37 *Parker's London News or the Impartial Intelligencer* 997 (7 April 1725); *Weekly Journal or British Gazetteer* 15 (10 April 1725).
38 *London Journal* 190 (16 March 1723).
39 Montagu, *Selected Letters*, 200, 270.
40 Ibid., 195.
41 *Universal Journal* 26 (6 June 1724).
42 Solkin, "The Excessive Jew in *A Harlot's Progress,*" 219–35, and Paulson, "Some Thoughts on Hogarth's Jew," 236–63.
43 Nichols, *The Genuine Works of William Hogarth*, 2:101.
44 Woolston, *A Discourse on the Miracles of our Saviour*, iv–vii.
45 Woolston, *A Sixth Discourse on the Miracles of our Saviour*, 3.
46 Landa, "Kitty Villareal, the Da Costas and Samson Gideon," 289–90.
47 Giuseppi, "Early Jewish Holders of Bank of England Stock," 149.
48 *London Evening Post* 349 (3–5 March 1730).
49 *Weekly Journal or British Gazetteer* 265 (18 April 1730).
50 Carruthers, *City of Capital*, 156–7.
51 Ward, "A South-Sea Ballad."
52 *The Fatal Consequences of Gaming*, 5.
53 Carlos, Maguire, and Neal, "'A knavish people …,'" 728–48.
54 *A New Canting Dictionary.*
55 Cam, *The Practice of Salivating Vindicated.*
56 Gay, *The Beggar's Opera*, 98.
57 Sacheverell, *The Perils of False Brethren*, 9.
58 Gibson, *The Bishop of London's Pastoral*, 2.
59 Mandeville, *A Modest Defence of Publick Stews*, ii.
60 Gibson, *The Bishop of London's Pastoral*, 2–3.
61 Ibid., 3.
62 Ibid., 35.
63 Dabydeen, *Hogarth, Walpole, and Commercial Britain*, 120–1.
64 *Grub Street Journal* 38 (24 September 1730).

65 Eight of Spades, South Sea Bubble Playing Cards, Kress Collection, Baker Library, Harvard Business School.
66 Nichols, *Anecdotes of William Hogarth*, 182.
67 Guthrie, *The Ordinary of Newgate*, 1731, 16.
68 See, e.g., *Daily Advertiser* 140 (15 July 1731).
69 *The Practical Scheme of the Secret Disease*, n.p.
70 *The Harlot's Progress … which is a key to the six prints*, 51.
71 Ibid., 6.
72 Cam, *A Short Account of the Venereal Disease*, n.p.
73 Ibid., 48–9.
74 Nichols, *Anecdotes of William Hogarth*, 184.
75 Tanner [pseud.], *The Life of the Late Celebrated Mrs. Elizabeth Wisebourn*, 54.
76 Ibid., 53.
77 Nichols, *Anecdotes of William Hogarth*, 101.
78 Ibid., 182.
79 Debord, *Society of the Spectacle*, 13.

13

Mural Painting and Spectatorship in Early Eighteenth-Century Britain

LYDIA HAMLETT

Mural painting is a visual genre particularly suggestive of affective intent. First, it is hard – nay, impossible – to ignore. Paintings that are integral to an architectural interior demand to be looked at, at every turn of the head, sideways to the walls or upwards to the ceiling: the viewer is surrounded. Secondly, the content of murals seeks to lure the viewer into an imaginary illusionistic space, the real architectural space through which they move – staircases and walls – metamorphosing into a narrative landscape, the ceiling into a heavenly vault where one might witness an apotheosis. Lastly, murals purposefully draw the viewer into them through the way they are composed, using techniques such as illusionistic perspective, mimesis, and wit. These features, already exploited in mural painting on the Continent, were brought into the domestic spaces of the British Isles mainly by migrant artists from Italy, France, and the Low Countries in a great flowering of the genre from the 1680s, beginning with the Restoration and lasting to the death of Queen Anne. Almost every major patron expended vast amounts of money, time, and effort on mural painting. Its status as a serious art form has since waned, and this essay explores the notion that part of the reason for this is that the genre of mural painting falls between artwork and spectacle, casting those who look upon it as something between disinterested viewer and involved spectator.[1] My plan is to interrogate preconceived ideas, and open up questions, about early modern British visual culture, and specifically mural painting. I examine the notion of spectatorship – both through the actual spectator, the ideal spectator, and the painted spectator – in relation to just three case studies from the 1710s, all by the French artist Louis Laguerre (1663–1721): the sites of the works studied are Marlborough House, Blenheim Palace (the town and country houses of the Duke of Marlborough), and Petworth House. In each case, the content of the murals and the way this content is represented can tell us something not only about the intended functions of the murals and how they were to be viewed but also about post-Restoration spectatorship in general.[2]

Murals were typically visual projections of power intended to impress, overwhelm, or persuade the viewer of a particular idea or stance. The catalyst for the flowering of murals in the great houses of British aristocrats was Charles II's first major artistic program at Windsor Castle, a grand sequence of illusionistic interiors painted around the same time as Charles Le Brun's murals for Louis XIV at Versailles.[3] England had an early taste of murals projecting images of power in Peter Paul Rubens's ceiling mural *The Apotheosis of James I*, painted for Charles I at Whitehall (c. 1629), which suggested the divinity of the monarch. But, as Roy Strong and Vaughan Hart have noted, this mural was intended to form part of a much wider spectacle, sharing in many of the aims and functions of the masques performed beneath it.[4] Increasingly, scholarship is demonstrating that later in the century, too, murals were part of a wider interest in effect and affect, both in relation to architecture (which has often since been modified) and to ephemeral events such as performance, public speaking, opera, and music, as well as more private activities including conversation.[5] Many of the artists employed as mural painters in houses and palaces were also involved in the design of stage scenery.[6] On the other hand, the mural is an artwork in itself, a fixed image: it does not move and, standing alone without accompanying music or drama, relies on its inherent forms to move and interact with us. Like many other monuments once integral to early modern festivities – think of Bernini's Four Rivers fountain in Rome's Piazza Navona – the murals endure long after the performance has ended.[7] The composition of Rubens's ceiling, for example, itself engaged the spectators, who had to crane their necks to see it from below, drawing them upwards into the heavens through the steep perspective, identifying them, perhaps, with the human, uncertain expression of the King as his limbs and drapes are pulled forcefully upwards by the surrounding allegorical figures.[8] We have some, albeit few, records of the effects of mural paintings on the early modern viewer, including Richard Steele's reaction to seeing Sir James Thornhill's painted ceiling at Greenwich, which left him at a loss for words.[9] In the context of the following three early-eighteenth-century case studies, this essay asks what visual effects and affects were created in the spectator by Laguerre's very different mural programs, and whether the intentionality of effect can properly be realized in retrospect, given our temporal and subjective distance.

Marlborough House, St James's, London, circa 1712–14

One mural commission that subverts the type of representations discussed above is situated at Marlborough House.[10] Here Laguerre's paintings of the bloody exploits of his patron, the superlative military leader John Churchill, Duke of Marlborough, saturate the walls – and yet there is neither an apotheosis nor an emblematic exposition of power. Laguerre was well aware of French courtly mural traditions, having studied under Charles Le Brun, the *Premier peintre du Roi* of Marlborough's enemy Louis XIV, and he consciously chose to reject these modes for his British patron.[11] To understand why, we have first to examine who was supposed to see the murals, and how they were to experience them *in situ*.

The years 1710 to 1712 saw what the Marlboroughs viewed as their rejection by an ungrateful Queen Anne within an anti-war climate that was gathering apace, factors that conspired to prompt their self-imposed exile. The Duchess frequently expressed her desire to jolt those who indulged in armchair politics into the world in which her husband was still fighting, and I have recently argued that both Marlborough House and its murals were designed to persuade the spectator of her husband's strength of character in the face of continuing sacrifice within this particular historical moment.[12] Given that it was built directly next to the heart of Queen Anne's court of St James, it can only be assumed that Marlborough House's intended spectators – the "ideal," as defined by Mieke Bal and Norman Bryson, and from hereon in called "the spectator" – were powerful individuals from the court and of all political persuasions who would pass through the house on a regular basis.[13]

The early-eighteenth-century visitor would enter Marlborough House and be introduced straight away to the murals of the Battle of Blenheim in the hall (the existing anteroom was added only later). Time spent here, perhaps waiting for one's host to arrive, would allow an opportunity to scan the upper register of the room where the different stages of the battle raged, as they had done in actuality only a few years before. In order to access other parts of the house, the spectator would subsequently be inducted to the even more recent battles of Ramillies and the notoriously bloody Malplaquet on the staircases flanking the hall (see figs. 13.1 and 13.2 respectively). The images in these spaces are not idealized but chaotic: Le Brun's *Histories of Alexander* series provides visual sources, but without the gravitas of classical historicism they here take on a contemporary urgency. These were the only murals of the period to depict contemporary events naturalistically, the battles of the Duke of Marlborough in the still ongoing War of the Spanish Succession. It cannot be underestimated how this temporal proximity of the events to the spectator, in whose minds the memories of the battles would still have been fresh, might have distracted or caused discomfort – not quite in the manner of rolling news today but nonetheless as close as one might get at the time to partaking in a war still ongoing, unresolved, and threatening. There is no juxtaposition of homeliness and ancient epic here (a common trope in both literature and the visual arts of the time); rather, at Marlborough House, the murals introduce contemporary chaos into the domestic sphere.[14] In this sense, as I have argued elsewhere, the murals' immediacy of purpose is suggestive of pamphlets rather than the distant "histories" more typical of mural painting as a genre.[15] Thus the murals represent a schism in mural painting in Britain up to this point, but they are just as, if not more, wedded to the transformative effects of the genre.

It is not just the chronological proximity of depicted events but every aspect of the composition of the Marlborough House murals that encourages a diminishing of distance between the spectator and the object, which, as described by Edward Bullough, increases the intensity of the experience and the spectator's level of discomfort.[16] The principal scenes reject allegory, which had been a commonplace feature of every mural commission in England since Rubens.[17] Whereas most murals relied on allegory in a bid to bridge the distance between the spectator and the grand "ideas" they

Fig. 13.1 *Top* Marlborough House, Ramillies Staircase.

Fig. 13.2 *Bottom* Marlborough House, Malplaquet Staircase.

portrayed, the Marlborough House murals omitted this bridge in favour of reaching the end point more quickly; that is, they express an urgent reality. They give the appearance of showing the battle as it happened, not with the patron unrealistically grandstanding – as he had been, for example, in the tapestries of the battles of the same subject for Blenheim Palace – but caught up in the onslaught. The tapestries mount the Duke and the main protagonists of the battle on imaginary *repoussoirs* at the forefront of the scene, whereas the murals place them in the less undulated, more realistic topography of the landscape. Neither are any of the gory details spared: the rears of careering horses, half-naked wounded soldiers, and anonymous acts of violence are all foregrounded into view. Distance between the spectator and the murals is also diminished through the lack of framing devices that, in contrast, are a feature of the two case studies discussed below. In contrast, too, to the tapestries, the principal mural scenes in the hall and on the Malplaquet staircase are designed to flow from one to another without interruption.[18] The heavily decorated borders that frame the tapestry battles only serve to emphasize their status as works of art, as opposed to the murals, the purpose of which is to affect through their realism, as described above. Illusionistic continuations of real to painted architecture are also abandoned within the principal scenes.[19] Crucially, the trope of the "painted spectator" – who often in murals provides an intercessory character between the actual viewer and the imagined scene, adding another layer of objectivity to the experience – is abandoned at Marlborough House. Leaving out the painted eyewitness spectator, we ourselves become the eyewitness.

Despite their similarity to printed pamphlets in terms of their purpose, the way that the image is communicated in mural paintings is of course entirely different, relying on the way that the images are experienced in partnership with the architecture of the house, and on a grand scale. Mural paintings exist solely within a relationship of codependent animation with architecture, in that the images are encountered only as one advances through the space. In this sense, the viewer is cast as protagonist: the full force of the spectacle cannot be realized unless she stands on a particular spot or advances along a particular route.[20] Key visual elements are revealed as this movement through the architectural space takes place, on landings or pressed up close to the staircase walls: a totally contrasting viewing experience to related artworks executed before or after the murals, where the entire composition is laid out on one portable plane, as in a sketch, print, or painting.[21] At Marlborough House the eye is drawn deliberately and without exception to images of human (and animal) suffering, while, as explored above, the image of the military leader, the owner of the house, is sidelined. Instead of being presented with glorious images of the Duke as war hero, spectators find themselves in the undergrowth, face to face with the debris of war, fallen soldiers, horses, spent and discarded weapons. The compositional imperative is to take the spotlight away from the Duke and instead direct it towards the reality of the horrors of war he was experiencing by encouraging the viewer to experience them too. The only figures that we see in the Marlborough House murals are those heavily engaged within the battle, not spectators of it. As we ascend the second flight of the Ramillies stairs, for example, we find ourselves walking alongside a life-sized, open-mouthed figure fleeing in fear (see again fig. 13.1). Details such as this, and many others, serve to accentuate the lack of allegory and artifice, forcing us into the position of witness rather than innocent bystander.

Moreover, the effects and affects of those images experienced as the spectacle unfolds serve to convey the very meaning of the building. The construction of Marlborough House is a prime example of the important relationship between painting and architecture, the mutual nature of which has gone largely unappreciated due to the subsequent raising of the profile of architecture and the simultaneous intellectual disparaging and physical deterioration of mural painting.[22] The ultimate importance of the relationship is clear, though, in the primary function of Marlborough House, where the time between the purchasing of the land for its construction – at the heart of the court of St James's – and the execution of the murals was a mere few years. The unusually plain architectural exterior can be explained only by the wall paintings for which it provided a platform: their images show us that the Duke is not a greedy, self-serving warmonger but a parsimonious leader, at war for the good of his Queen and Country. The murals cover the entire core of the house, the inevitable result of which is that any visitor to it – as described above – is obliged to navigate the transformation of house to battlefield.

In a sense, the Marlborough House murals form part of a double metamorphosis: from the pared down architectural house exterior to painting overwhelmed by detail, and from an interior domestic environment to a physical landscape embroiled in contemporary politics. There is no preparation of the spectator for this type of transformation. Instead of the Duke being presented to us straight away in the hall, we have to seek him out on the battlefield: realistic details supposedly lead us to a more credible representation of his character. These messages were similar to those in many pamphlets of the time that counteracted criticism of the Duke, but here the spectator is forced to participate, physically and psychologically, in a sort of reenactment.[23] Our own chronological distance from the events portrayed, as well as the unfashionable nature of the genre, the physical deterioration of the condition of the murals, and the modifications to the architecture on which they are painted, inevitably change and dull the effects and affects of this experience. But this should not stop us trying to understand where the murals fitted into the cultural life of the times, where they held just as much relevance as the pamphlets, plays, and literature in the tumult of the Marlboroughs' political jostling.

Blenheim Palace, Woodstock, Oxfordshire, circa 1719

At Blenheim Palace, Laguerre's murals were also part of an architecturally ordered sequence designed to persuade the spectator of a particular way of thinking. It has been argued that they were part of an iconographical axis running through the interior and beyond – from the saloon to a hilltop column – that celebrated the Duke's greatness.[24] It is true that the iconography of these different artistic elements broadly glorifies the Duke, but the mural-covered spaces require further interrogation in relation to the way that they are experienced as interiors. The hall would be the first room a palace visitor would see, its ceiling painted by Laguerre's British rival, mural painter Sir James Thornhill, with *Hero Entering the Temple of Fame* (1716).[25] The same artist was originally lined up to paint the saloon beyond, though he fell out with the Duchess and so she, presumably impressed by the Frenchman's work at Marlborough House, gave Laguerre the commission instead.[26] In Thornhill's hall ceiling mural, the elliptical arch of the temple occurs in the actual architecture of the hall below it. And it is clear that both anticipate the saloon as being the interior of this same temple, an idea reinforced by the fact that Thornhill includes the same arch in one of his designs for the saloon.[27] Originally the wall between the hall and saloon was more porous, with the balcony under the adjoining arch opening out onto both spaces.[28] It is also evident that Laguerre took up the idea of the saloon as a continuation of the architecture and themes of the hall. The painted temple's warm-hued, fluted, Corinthian columns are transformed by him on a grand scale into Composite columns with gilt capitals in the saloon. It is as if Laguerre has turned this room into the interior of Thornhill's painted temple, by including an illusionistic double colonnade around the walls, populated with painted spectators (fig. 13.3). Some of Laguerre's spectators look into the (real) space within – separated by an extended *die* – and others look to the outside, represented by a realistic cloudscape. The sense of the visitors inhabiting a sort of inner sanctum, or *cella*, is reinforced by the large swaths of drawn-back curtains that, if released, could separate them from the realm and gaze of the painted spectators. On the saloon's ceiling is an allegory of the progress of War (represented by the Duke) being arrested by the hand of Peace, with numerous classical gods and attendant figures.

The painted spectators in the saloon are taken by Laguerre directly from Charles Le Brun's grand staircase at Versailles (since destroyed), with similar architectural framing and large areas of sky above.[29] As figures from around the world, they are also a continuation of Thornhill's hall ceiling, where the continents are represented allegorically. Nonetheless, Laguerre employs the painted spectator more actively in his saloon, using them to induct the actual spectator into the very meaning of the space. At life-size and in contemporary dress, Laguerre's painted spectators contribute to the curious mix of the mimetic and allegorical, making the segue into another reality – the heavenly ceiling representing Peace – more palatable, perhaps more believable. Similar to intercessors in earlier religious art, the painted spectators here are available to the real, visiting spectators who can identify with them and are thus prepared for the complex ideas contained within the otherworldly narratives represented. The painted spectators occupy a liminal space, on the boundary between the real and the unreal, placed all around the walls where they are most acces-

Fig. 13.3 Blenheim Palace, Saloon.

sible to us in order that we might identify with them and be drawn into the mural, adding a sense of authenticity to our experience. Laguerre's painted spectators, engaged in conversation, acts of persuasion, or contemplation, appear as casual, and curiously uninterested, observers of the ceiling above them. The fantastical nature of the scene with its otherwordly cast is intended to emphasize and glorify the idea of a divine peace, placing the concept at the core of the Marlboroughs' new palace, and contrasting with the more fallible and familiar human activity below. (This is a trope that was also pursued by the Duchess of Marlborough, who, in 1711, moved the artwork created by Orazio Gentileschi showing an allegory of Peace from its original location at the Queen's House, in Greenwich, to Marlborough House, where it presented a heavenly contrast to the territorial wars being fought below.[30])

The original function of the painted spectators at Blenheim has been obscured by subsequent scholarship that has largely assumed them to be allegorical, on the basis that those at Versailles broadly represent the four continents (Asia, Europe, Africa, and America). But despite the fact that the costumes of the spectators at Blenheim show them to be generally from all parts of the globe, many of them are clearly portraits of specific individuals. While it is not within the scope of this essay to try to identify all the painted spectators, it is worth noting that such identifications would not only enhance our iconographic understanding but also add to our sense of how they were to be viewed. Many of them may have been known to the actual or ideal spectator, thus giving them a contemporary relevance that today is difficult to comprehend. To take one example, there is an individual – on the wall to the left of the window – whose strong profile and uncommon swarthiness (at least in a British context at that time) appear to be particularly suggestive of a portrait. He is cast in rather an ambiguous light, the emphasis on his exaggerated profile in keeping with contemporaneous racial typecasting of Jews and his hand gestures suggesting a certain irresistible persuasiveness. This may be the first Jew to be knighted, Solomon de Medina, whose testimonies over his dealings with the Duke may have catalyzed the military leader's downfall. If this is correct, it would be the only known portrait of de Medina, and would fit in with the allegory of Peace on the ceiling and the emphasis on the powerlessness of human politicking, which, ultimately, was not as responsible for halting the Duke's military progress as divine will. This would appear to shed new light on the iconography and persuasive message of the entire room, prompting us to look again at the other painted spectators and how they help us to understand the functions behind the artistic commissions of the Marlboroughs.[31] Mayu Fujikawa has recently identified many of the painted spectators in the frescos of the Sala Regia of the Palazzo del Quirinale, Rome, which provided inspiration for Le Brun's *escalier*, on which Laguerre's saloon was modelled.[32] She argues that the identifications are key to our understanding of the significance of the frescos as an exposition of papal power. Depicting key figures as evidence of the pope's influence across the globe, they would have been recognized by the many and important visitors to this principal room. This function is surely shared by the spectators in Laguerre's saloon, included as allusions to Marlborough's influence rather than as meaningless witticisms. It would appear that Laguerre, by depicting his allegory of Peace on the ceiling, has once again, as at Marlborough House, subverted contemporary criticisms

Fig. 13.4 Blenheim Palace, Saloon: detail with Louis Laguerre (left) and Dean Jones (right).

of the Marlboroughs as warmongers, converting the Palace – traditionally read as a paean to military glory – into a Temple of Peace, to be entered by all those who visited the house.

Two of the spectators have been identified and much discussed: one is Laguerre himself and the other the duke's chaplain, Dean Jones (see fig. 13.4). Laguerre's incorporation of Jones has often been viewed as act of wit, because he was a member of the household to whom the duke was close but of whom the duchess was dismissive. Humour is detected in the saloon, too, by a near-contemporary visitor to Blenheim, Thomas Hearne, who, upon visiting the palace in 1719, described finding in the saloon "Persons of different Countries, Atheists, Infidels, & Heathens, being mixt, on purpose to please Buffoons."[33] He goes on to lament the fact that the paintings are not "historical," nor do they depict "great Persons," as this "would have answered the Nobleness of the Room."[34] Reminiscent of the criticism levelled at Paolo Veronese by the Inquisition for incorporating extraneous figures into his Last Supper, Hearne's lament was that this room in a new palace should have been devoted to a subject historically pertinent to its old foundations, such as the story of Rosamund's Bower, said to have been built by Henry II on the site of the future Blenheim Palace as a place to protect his concubine.[35] Hearne contrasted the murals in the saloon with those in the hall, which did, in his estimation, possess sufficient gravitas. And yet his opinion is outweighed by the contrasting – albeit similarly biased – opinion of the Duchess, who claimed that the saloon was in fact nobler than the hall and, moreover, that prevailing critical opinion agreed with her.[36] In any event, the painted spectators are shown neither to indulge in, nor to react to, comedic activity, and there is no evidence to suggest that Laguerre intended them to amuse a buffoonish beholder.

The lack of willingness to properly understand the basic iconographical tenets of these mural paintings is perhaps due to the treatment of this genre as a whole, which has consistently failed to take into account their original functions, including an understanding of who was to view the murals, and how. In the case of the Blenheim saloon figures, this is evident from the persistent notion that these characters were meant to be humorous, which distorts the way they were intended to be viewed and reduces them to the frivolous.[37] As is so often the case in the critical reception of the genre, all that is needed is a single documented derogatory comment, contemporaneous to the murals' execution, to perpetuate the myth that somehow they were not "serious" art. But if we delve further into our spectator source here – the reaction of Thomas Hearne to the murals – we can in fact start to think about an apparent gap between the intended aesthetic experience and the actual one as recorded. Hearne was a local antiquarian and well-known pedant who, walking to Woodstock with a view to visiting the old site of Rosamund's Bower, dropped in on the off chance of seeing the new palace. He had not been the recipient of an invitation to a specific occasion there, such as a dinner, and the likelihood of him having had an audience with the Marlboroughs is negligible.[38] He clearly failed to make the connection between the hall and saloon and, not recognizing any of the spectators in the latter, assumed them to be generic representations. If he had been part of the courtly cabal to which the Marlboroughs had once belonged, he would perhaps have known the significance of the faces and their part in the meaning of the projection of the image of the Marlboroughs.

What we can infer from comments such as Hearne's is not that the murals did not have the desired effect on, or inspire the desired affect in the spectator *per se*, but rather that Hearne was not the ideal spectator. The murals were not only to be read as histories, as Hearne wished, but to be experienced on following a specific route through the architecture, conversing with fellow spectators taking part in an occasion or ceremony, complete with particular sounds – musical, certainly, and perhaps also spoken. The two principal mural spaces, the hall and the saloon, were, as mentioned above, originally joined architecturally. During the residence of the Marlboroughs, musical performances would have been enacted on the adjoining balcony by musicians imitating the statues of the musical cherubs.[39] The metamorphosis of architecture into art would have been complemented by one of sculpture into sound, creating a typically Baroque interplay between art and life to which the murals were central. Vaughan Hart has described the view of the architect of Blenheim Palace, John Vanbrugh, as unambiguously narrative, in the business of storytelling for effect.[40] Traditionally murals have been seen as a side issue to this, a frivolous, decorative addition to rooms that were "used only by a throng of people, whose mood and dress made them ready to accept the fairy tales on the walls."[41] But in fact, at Blenheim Palace, as at other buildings of the time, they are the *sine qua non* of architectural projects, serving to convey the very meaning of the building. In Laguerre's saloon, Vanbrugh's real architecture is transformed into an imagined fantasy, again recalling (but by no means faithful to) the architecture of the ancients.[42] The murals communicated that although the progress and terms of the Treaty of Utrecht (1713) had been carried out without due consultation, peace was, after all, the ideal to which the Marlboroughs aspired. While the palace, pledged to the Duke following his victory at the Battle of Blenheim (1704), was intended to express the gratitude of Queen and Country, the situation had changed dramatically by the time its murals were painted, due to its long, drawn out construction. All this is important: these are not merely paintings of architecture – even iconographically loaded architecture – but instead an attempt at a transformation of the actual architecture of the palace and the painted temple of Fame into a temple dedicated to Peace.

The murals at Marlborough House expressed the moment of the duke's falling out of favour and his continued bravery, while, even though Blenheim had been begun earlier, its murals reflected the peace that had come about soon after. The peace had been designed while the duke was still fighting, though he and the duchess had always argued that this was purely out of necessity rather than any desire for self-glorification or thirst for war. The saloon ceiling murals express the glorification of the idea, the principle, of peace, as separate to their involvement in human politics. The figure of War is steadied not through human, but divine, intervention, rendering the political machinations of the period futile. In this sense, it is important to examine the meaning of the pictures that remain extant. But it is also crucial to remember that they required a transformation of the spectator, and were intended to evoke a repositioning of their view of its patrons. Just as at Marlborough House, Laguerre created a complex program at Blenheim based on a nuanced idea of the meaning of war and communicating the views of its patrons in a way that was not often heard. To do this, the murals needed not only to be seen but to be experienced and can only, perhaps, be properly understood as site-specific but also as a time-based genre.

Petworth House, Petworth, West Sussex, circa 1719

I recently argued that the iconography of Laguerre's murals on the grand staircase at Petworth – which centres on the myths of Prometheus and Pandora – seeks to highlight female agency and virtue, and that this discrete project, completed later than the rest of the house, was likely to have been instigated by the Duchess of Somerset.[43] But further investigations as to how these "histories" are experienced in the domestic sphere are needed to make full sense of them. A number of diverse mythological and allegorical scenes, taken from various sources, are presented to us. They vary in scale and shape, depending on their physical location, with the major scenes covering whole first-floor walls and the entire ceiling. While contained by painted architectural boundaries, it is this very element that also unifies them, and links them sequentially. The result is that the spectator no longer experiences them as separate artworks but more as an installation in which, once again, they are the agent in a spectacle that opens up only as they move through the space. This is the antithesis of what had been recommended for history painting by the Earl of Shaftesbury a few years previously, in his *Tablature of the Judgment of Hercules* (published in 1714), containing instead those elements of the theatrical "wildness" (unpredictability, dislocated narratives, lack of compositional clarity) that he himself associated with mural painting.[44] But the murals at Petworth, similar to those in other houses, speak to a long-established, wider cultural fascination with the idea of metamorphosis, seen in the literature and drama of the time. Both the iconography and composition of the murals revolve around the idea of transformation, displaying their patron in various allegorical, emblematic, and mythic guises, and inviting a transformation – of sorts – in the mind of the spectator. Ultimately, as in the previous two case studies, the murals, experienced *in situ*, prompt the spectator to consider the house and its inhabitants in a different way.

On the ground floor, in the staircase hall, stories of Prometheus told in Ovid's *Metamorphoses* – from the creation of man, to the theft of fire, to his punishment and redemption – are displayed on the walls, under stairs, and under balconies. They are of varying sizes and shapes, and are even enacted within different illusionistic media, including painted landscapes, painted architecture, and painted sculptural reliefs. Moreover, they adhere to no discernible narrative order. The wall scenes on this ground-floor level also contain a painted architecture that serves to open out the real architecture into the illusionistic scenes beyond. A painted spectator – a woman with a child who, resting on a painted architectural ledge, watches the *Prometheia* within (see fig. 13.5) – prompts us to engage with these scenes as continuations of the house, once again providing a liminal link between the real and the fantastical. One of the illusionistic caryatids appears to abandon his entablature to engage in conversation with a putto. Both serve the purpose of catching the attention of us, the actual spectator, drawing our curiosity into the painted scenes beyond. Beyond this, whatever the desired effect of these paintings was is difficult decipher, but even with the uncertainty of subsequent modifications – of which there are certainly many – it is unlikely that the scenes were to be individually picked over, read, or understood pedagogically. Rather, they contribute to the idea of transformation, the real walls of the house extending into mythic landscapes, the stories of Prometheus preparing us for the development

Fig. 13.5 *Top* Petworth House, mother with children watching the *Prometheia*.

Fig. 13.6 *Bottom* Petworth House, detail showing female spectator through columns.

of the story of the female protagonist, Pandora. Spectators are not expected to read these histories as *tabulae* but to experience them unfolding before their eyes.

The first truly grand-scale narrative the spectator witnesses is of Pandora and Epimetheus, and it covers the entire first-floor north wall. Like many contemporary murals in Britain by a range of artists, this one appears to have been based on a book illustration by Sébastien Le Clerc, from Isaac de Benserade's Ovidian verse, *Les Métamorphoses d'Ovide en rondeaux*.[45] Turning to the left on the first staircase landing, the viewer sees that a palatial space opens up, with Pandora, to the left, reclining on a divan and Epimetheus, to the right, opening the jar given to her. Showing Epimetheus with the jar is rare in art, though it was a recognized trope within seventeenth-century literature.[46] Based on a tiny book illustration of a historical subject, the print is here translated on a grand scale. On the south wall opposite is a scene of Elizabeth, Duchess of Somerset, riding in a triumphal carriage through a fictive colonnade towards her house, Petworth, which is seen on the west wall. On the ceiling, the heavens open to show Pandora being offered gifts from the gods, also described in the *Metamorphoses*. An almost total lack of narrative logic continues from one level to the next, but, again, this does not detract from the strength of the message conveyed. Here are three depictions of good, wise women, while the men in the scenes – Jupiter offering Pandora the fateful jar and Epimetheus opening it – display destructiveness and ignorance.

Perhaps even more extraordinary than these rare iconographical juxtapositions is the order in which the spectator experiences them, for we are guided up the staircase alongside a series of painted spectators, all of whom are women. This is in contrast to Blenheim, where not a single woman is included except as allegories in the depictions on the ceiling. Below the stairs, a female figure sits with a child on an illusionistic ledge looking at the torch race (see again fig. 13.5). Upstairs, female figures stare out at the viewer: a lively young woman between two columns on the south wall, a woman gazing out at us from between two columns on the north wall (see fig. 13.6), as well as multiple female deities who engage us in the allegories of architecture and music to the west. There are other intriguing female characters, including the veiled figure following the procession and placed between two columns on the south wall. The preponderance of female spectators, and female figures in general, is rare, and surely relates to a thematic celebration of womankind within the principal murals that has has largely gone unnoticed.[47] An explanation of this can perhaps be found in a consideration of who the ideal and actual spectators of the Petworth murals were. Petworth was the family home of the Duchess of Somerset before she married the duke, Charles Seymour, and though the duke took it upon himself to rebuild and vastly alter the estate, she remained fondly attached to it. Indeed there is correspondence to suggest that, rather than spend her time at court with Queen Anne, the duchess was more often than not to be found in residence at Petworth.[48] Laguerre was of course engaged at the same time in the Blenheim Palace saloon for her courtly rival Sarah Churchill, and had also recently completed the mural program at Marlborough House. The Duchess of Somerset may very well have taken both these mural commissions into account to inform her own, as they would surely have been seen and discussed by visitors in the same social circles.

Unlike Sarah Churchill, who expressed herself as freely as an early-eighteenth-century woman could and who wrote a prodigious amount, the Duchess of Somerset appears to have left almost no discernible written legacy. It could be said that the Petworth murals allowed her to write her personal mythology into the fabric of her house. Having been married twice before her marriage at fifteen to the duke, the duchess was made a figure of fun by Jonathan Swift in *The Windsor Prophecy*, in which he accused her of being complicit in the death of her second husband and called her "Carrots" because of the colour of her hair.[49] In the murals, both the duchess and Pandora have strawberry-blond hair and also share a distinct facial likeness. This may seem an unlikely association, but Pandora here is a heroine; the myth retold by Benserade to a French seventeenth-century reader is once again reinterpreted through imagery on British walls.[50] Laguerre's murals at Petworth become the physical and symbolic core of the entire house, offering a memorable transition from the ground-floor state apartments to the bedrooms above, a metamorphosis of the actual house into fantasy, painted space. But perhaps more pertinent are the transformations that the lady of the house herself undergoes. Connected to themes of virtue and wisdom through her paralleling with Pandora and the choice of narratives that implicate male rather than female wrongdoing, the duchess is shown riding in triumph towards her house, a poignant reimaging of her role in the household and in the world only a couple of years before her death at fifty-five years old in 1722.

Conclusion

The three mural commissions discussed in this essay, all by Laguerre, fall somewhere between artwork and spectacle. In themselves, they can be considered as artworks of history and mythological subjects, albeit not presented in the ideal way recommended by commentators, including Shaftesbury. In some cases, they aim to relay the reality of actual events, in others to convey a fantasy space; in doing so, Laguerre often translates the histories of others, including French artists and book illustrators. He takes the courtly tropes of Le Brun and transforms them for the British viewer, or the book illustrations of Le Clerc and renders them on a grand scale. At the same time, these histories cannot be divorced from the architecture in which they are set. Fixed into a three-dimensional space, they present as a kind of stage set, where the performance can occur only as the spectator moves. They depict subjects common to other media – not just history painting but pamphlets, prints, illustrations, and architecture – but they also provide something more. Because of the way that they are encountered, murals add something unique to the way that visual messages are conveyed. While many would have been part of a wider time-based spectacle, part of an event or performance, even without these extra sensory additions, the spectator's experience of murals alone is often all that is required to experience the sense of transformation that each offers. The aim is – common to many early modern artistic schemes – to be persuaded of a different point of view about our patrons, an idea, or way of life. And so, while they were often animated by external sounds or ceremonies, they were fundamental to the very purpose of the building, a permanent fixture to be experienced at any time through their inherent element of display.

What is clear is that the ways of viewing murals in the early eighteenth century were quite different from the ways we view them today. Whereas now we experience them almost as wallpaper, unconvinced as we are by their illusionism, and accustomed as we are both to the experience of new landscape through travel and to sophisticated media such as film, at the time they were almost certainly intended to evoke visually the idea of transformation, then culturally prevalent through the rediscovery and translation of ancient texts. All of the patrons in this essay can be seen to take the idea of transformation and use it to their ends within their own domestic spheres. Painted onto the core of their houses, and integral to the original function of their architecture, the murals would have been just as important as the architecture when considering patronage and the image of themselves they wished to project. The result is a deliberately structured experience of transformation that, though reliant on being *in situ*, was perhaps a more powerful experience because of it: murals, while being a permanent fixture, allowed a certain sense of transience to the permanent built environment, and for the patrons' own mythologies to play out within. The onus is entirely on the spectator, as explorer and eyewitness, to discover it.

NOTES

1 This essay represents early thoughts on ways of viewing mural painting that are developed in an upcoming monograph by the author, *Murals in Britain 1630–1730: Experiencing Histories* (Routledge 2019). Calls for new scholarship on mural painting as a genre have come from recent publications including Dolman, "Antonio Verrio," 18–28; Johns, "'Those Wilder Sorts of Painting,'" 79–104; and Hamlett, "Rupture through Realism," 195–216.

2 The emphasis on the need for the presence of a spectator to activate the experience of such artworks is explored in relation to the Renaissance by Shearman in *Only Connect*.

3 On the Windsor Castle murals, see Gibson, "The Decoration of St George's Hall," 30–40; Johns, "Antonio Verrio and the Triumph of Painting," 153–76; Burchard, "Illusion and Involvement," 99–119.

4 Strong, *Britannia Triumphans*; Vaughan Hart, *Inigo Jones*, 193–201.

5 For example, Strong, *Britannia Triumphans*; Vaughan Hart, *Inigo Jones*; Hamlett, "The Longinian Sublime,"187–220; Pinnock, "*Deus ex machina*: A Royal Witness," 265–78; Geraghty, *The Sheldonian Theatre*, 75–81; Johns, "Antonio Verrio."

6 See, for example, Thornhill, Designs for Thomas Clayton's *Arsinoë* (performed 1705). Victoria and Albert Museum, nos. D.26–1891, D.27–1891, and D.28–1891. On the theatricality of domestic architecture see Vaughan Hart, *Sir John Vanbrugh*.

7 On Bernini and theatricality, see Warwick, *Bernini: Art as Theatre*.

8 The King's expression can be more easily viewed in the Tate's preliminary sketch for the ceiling, Tate no. T12919.

9 Steele, *The Lover*, 189–95. See also Hamlett, "The Longinian Sublime."

10 This section relies heavily on research into the Marlborough House murals presented at two conferences by this author (University of York, September 2012, and Paul Mellon Centre, September 2013) and then published in Hamlett, "Rupture through Realism." See also Solkin, *Art in Britain 1660–1815*, 57–60.

11 "The Notebooks of George Vertue II," *Walpole Society* 20 (1932), 124.

12 Hamlett, "Rupture through Realism."

13 Bal and Bryson, "Semiotics and Art History," 174–208.

14 To take just one example of homeliness and epic, see Raphael Lyne on Dryden's juxtaposition of Homer and Chaucer in "Dryden and the Complete Career," 253.

15 Hamlett, "Rupture through Realism."

16 See Bullough's seminal essay, "'Psychical Distance' as a Factor in Art," 87–118.

17 For example, in Rubens's apotheoses for the Duke of York at York House and Charles I at the Banqueting House, Whitehall.

18 On the Ramillies staircase, two extensive landscapes face each other.

19 All three spaces do, however, contain *trompe l'oeil* decoration elsewhere.

20 This was common to many early modern murals including, for example, Andrea dal Pozzo's Sant'Ignazio, Rome, where it was necessary to stand on a particular part of the nave floor to experience the full force of the painted ceiling. On Baroque rhetoric and aesthetics, see Minor, *The Death of the Baroque*, 4–25.

21 On the prints see Hamlett, "Rupture through Realism," 213, n8.

22 On the latter see John, "Those Wilder Sorts of Painting."

23 Contrast Elizabeth Eisenstein on printed materials that "address an invisible public from afar," discussed by Rick Bowers in chap. 3 of this volume. See Eisenstein, "Some Conjectures about the Impact of Printing," 42.

24 Girouard, *Life in the English Country House*, 156.

25 Its iconography is described in British Library MS Add.61354, 38–9.

26 On the falling out see David Brontë Green, *Blenheim Palace*, 159, and Croft-Murray, *Decorative Painting in England*, 1:75.

27 From an earlier design by Thornhill for the saloon, it appears that he, too, intended to make a link between the hall and saloon, by repeating the same elliptical arch with coffers. In the design, he projects an inner architectural courtyard beyond the arch. See David Brontë Green, *Blenheim Palace*, 123 and 58, and Appendix IX, 306–8.

28 Girouard, *Life in the English Country House*, 158. On the building of these rooms see James Legard, "Vanbrugh, Blenheim Palace," 1:167. I am very grateful to the author for his insightful comments on an early draft of this essay.

29 On the escalier see Burchard, *The Sovereign Artist*, 197–231.

30 Royal Collection Trust no. RCIN 408464; Hamlett, "Rapture through Realism," n. 22.

31 On the artistic patronage of the Marlboroughs see Johns, "'The British Caesar,' John Churchill," 341–6; Hamlett, "Rupture through Realism"; Hargraves, "The Public Image of John Churchill," 177–94; and Robert Wellington, "A Reflection of the Sun."

32 Fujikawa, "Pope Paul V's Global Design," 192–217.

33 Hearne, *Remarks*, 6:339.

34 Hearne's pedantry was satirized by Alexander Pope in *The Dunciad*, 3.185–94.

35 An anonymous poet adopted the folkloric tale in 1659 and wrote "A lamentable ballad of fair Rosamond"; it also inspired the operatic work *Rosamond* by Joseph Addison and Thomas Clayton, first performed in Drury Lane in March 1707. See Hart, *Sir John Vanbrugh*, 144.

36 Green, *Blenheim*, 249.

37 Green calls the caricatures a "deliberate joke" that become tedious to live with; see Green, *Blenheim*, 159. See also Lenygon, *Decoration in England*, 181.

38 On visitors to country houses see Arnold, "The Country House and its Publics," 20–42.

39 Girouard, *Life in the English Country House*, 158.

40 Hart, *Sir John Vanbrugh*, 138.

41 Lenygon, *Decoration in England*, 181.

42 On the architecture of Blenheim Palace see Green, *Blenheim*, and Hart, *Sir John Vanbrugh*, 136–45.

43 Hamlett, "Pandora at Petworth House," 950–5.

44 Cooper, *An Essay on Painting*, 4.

45 Benserade, *Les Métamorphoses*.

46 See, for example, Dora and Erwin Panofsky, *Pandora's Box*, 79–84.

47 Hamlett, "Pandora at Petworth House."

48 David Hamilton, *The Diary of Sir David Hamilton,* 45.

49 On "The Windsor Prophecy" see Karian, *Jonathan Swift*, 222, n50.

50 The main focus of Benserade's verse, while acknowledging Epimetheus as the opener of the box, still largely centres on Pandora's role as seductress. This is confirmed in Le Clerc's accompanying engraving through her close proximity to the jar, the fingertips of her left hand reaching out to touch it. Laguerre's mural, in all the ways it relates to the rest of the physical environment of the staircase, as discussed in this essay, resituates Pandora as being unambiguously virtuous. This is made clear even in the wall with the adaptation of the engraving, whereby Pandora, bathed in light, is placed as far away as possible from Epimetheus and the jar, both of which are surrounded by dark cloud.

Illustrations

Bibliography

This bibliography consists of four separate lists: 1) primary sources; 2) early periodicals; 3) commentary; 4) databases and reference. Almost all printed items may be found in list 1 or 3. Items written before 1800 in list 1 (primary sources); those written after 1800 in list 3 (commentary).

1 Primary Sources

An Account of what passed at the execution of the late Duke of Monmouth on Wednesday the 15th of July, 1685, on Tower-Hill. 1685. [Wing / A433].

Addison, Joseph. "No. 216. Saturday, August 26, 1710." In *The Tatler. By Isaac Bickerstaff Esq.* Vol. 1, 486–7. London: Addison and Steele, 1709–11. ECCO (CW3314815140).

– No. 69. In *The Spectator.* 5 vols. Edited by Donald Bond. Oxford: Clarendon Press, 1965.

Arthington, Henry. *The Seduction of Arthington by Hacket especiallie, with some tokens of his unfained repentance and Submission.* London: R.B. for Thomas Man, 1592.

Askew, Anne. *The Examinations of Anne Askew.* Edited by Elaine V. Beilen. New York: Oxford University Press, 1996.

Aubrey, John. *Brief Lives.* Edited by Oliver Lawson Dick. London: Secker and Warburg, 1958.

Augustine of Hippo. *The City of God against the Pagans.* Translated by George E. McCracken. Loeb Classical Library. London: William Heinemann, 1966.

Ba., Ro. *The Life of Syr Thomas More, Sometymes Lord Chancellor of England.* Edited by Elsie Vaughan Hitchcock, P.E. Hallett, and A.W. Reed. EETS. London: Oxford University Press, 1950.

Beaumont, Francis. *The Knight of the Burning Pestle.* Edited by Michael Hattaway. New Mermaids. London: A&C Black, 1986.

Becon, Thomas. *The new pollecye of warre,* 2nd ed. London: John Maylerre for John Gough, 1542.

Behn, Aphra. *The Works of Aphra Behn.* 7 vols. Edited by Janet Todd. Columbus: Ohio State University Press, 1993.

– *The Emperor of the Moon.* In *The Rover and Other Plays,* edited by Jane Spencer, 271–335. Oxford: Oxford University Press, 1995.

Benserade, Isaac de. *Les Métamorphoses d'Ovide en rondeaux.* Illustrated by S. Le Clerc, F. Chauveau, and C. Le Brun. Paris: D'Imprimerie Royale, 1676.

Berkeley, George. *Passive Obedience, or, the Christian Doctrine of not Resisting the Supreme Power.* Dublin: F. Dickson for J. Pepyat, 1712.

– *The Works of George Berkeley Bishop of Cloyne.* Edited by T.E. Jessop. 9 vols. London: Thomas Nelson and Sons, 1948–57.

Birch, Thomas. *The history of the Royal Society of London for improving of natural knowledge, from its first rise. In which the most considerable of those Papers communicated to the Society, which have hitherto not been published, are inserted in their proper order, as a Supplement to the Philosophical Transactions,* vol. 1. London: A. Millar, 1757. ECCO (CW3303765227).

British Library Add MS.61354, 38–9ff.

Britton. Translated and edited by Francis Morgan Nichols. 1865. Reprint, Holmes Beach, FL: Garret and Sons, 1983.

Brome, Richard. "Praeludium" to *The Careles Shepherdess* by Thomas Goffe. London: Richard Rogers and William Ley, 1656.

Burke, Edmund. *The Correspondence of Edmund Burke.* Edited by Thomas W. Copeland et al. 10 vols. Cambridge: Cambridge University Press, 1958–78.

– *The Writings and Speeches of Edmund Burke.* Edited by Paul Langford et al. 9 vols. Oxford: Clarendon Press, 1981–2015.

Burton, Robert. *The Anatomy of Melancholy.* Edited by Thomas C. Faulkner, Nicholas K. Kiessling, and Rhonda L. Blair. 3 vols. Oxford: Clarendon, 1989.

Cam, Joseph. *The Practice of Salivating Vindicated.* London: J. Peele, 1724.

– *A Short Account of the Venereal Disease: With Observations on the Nature,*

Symptoms, and Cure … Together with Some Hints on the Practical Scheme. London: G. Strahan, W. Mears, C. King, F. Norris, and J. Baker, 1717.

Camden, William. *Britain, or a chorographicall description of the most flourishing kingdomes, England, Scotland, and Ireland, and the ilands adjoining.* London: F.K., R.Y., and I.L. for George Latham, 1637.

Casanova, Giacomo. *The Memoirs of Casanova.* Translated by Arthur Machen. EPUB. Tribeca Press, 2013.

"The Case of Col. Francis Chartres, as it Appear'd at his Trial …," *Monthly Chronicle* Appendix no. 11 (December 1730): 26–30.

Chamberlayne, Edward. *Angliae Notitia; or, The Present State of England.* London: T.N. for John Martyn, 1671.

Chambers, Ephraim. *Cyclopædia: or, an universal dictionary of arts and sciences,* 4th ed., vol. 2. London: D. Midwinter et al., 1741. ECCO (CW106304119).

Clarke, James. *A Survey of the Lakes of Cumberland, Westmorland, and Lancashire: together with an Account, Historical, Topographical, and Descriptive, of the Adjacent Country. To Which is Added, a Sketch of the Border Laws and Customs.* London: Printed for the author, 1789.

Cooper, Anthony Ashley, third Earl of Shaftesbury. *An Essay on Painting: being A Notion of the Historical Draught or Tablature of the Judgment of Hercules.* London: John Darby, 1714.

The Country Gentleman's Vade Mecum. London: John Harris, 1699.

Cowper, William. *The Bishop of Galloway his Dikaiologie.* London: Thomas Snodham for John Budge, 1614.

Cowper, William. *The Poems of William Cowper: 1782–1785.* Edited by John D. Baird and Charles Ryskamp. Oxford: Oxford University Press, 1995.

Crowley, Robert. *The Confutation of XIII Articles, Whereunto Nicolas Shaxton, late bishop of Salisburye subscribed and caused to be set forthe in print in the yere of our Lorde MCxlvi whe[n] he recanted in Smithfielde at London at the burning of mestres Anne Askue, which is lively set forth in the figure following.* London: Jhon Day and William Seres, [1548].

de Coeffeteau, Nicolas. *A Table of the Humane Passions.* Translated by Edward Grimestone. London: Nicholas Okes, 1621.

Dekker, Thomas. *The guls horne-booke.* London: Nicholas Okes, 1609.

Denham, John. *Expans'd Hieroglyphicks: A Critical Edition of Sir John Denham's Coopers Hill.* Edited by Brendan O Hehir. Berkeley and Los Angeles: University of California Press, 1969.

Donne, John. *Devotions Upon Emergent Occasions*. Edited by Anthony Raspa. Montreal: McGill-Queen's University Press, 1975.

– *John Donne: The Major Works*. Edited by John Carey. Oxford World's Classics. Oxford: Oxford University Press, 2000.

– *Pseudo-Martyr*. Edited by Anthony Raspa. Montreal: McGill-Queen's University Press, 1993.

– *Selected Prose*. Edited by Evelyn Simpson, Helen Gardner, and Tomothy Healy. Oxford: Clarendon, 1967.

– *The Sermons of John Donne*. Edited by George R. Potter and Evelyn M. Simpson. 10 vols. Berkeley: University of California Press, 1953–62.

Dryden, John. *The Works of John Dryden: Poems 1693–1696*. Vol. 4. Berkeley: University of California Press, 1974.

Du Bartas, Guillaume de Saluste. *The Divine Works of Guillaume de Saluste Sieur Du Bartas*. 2 vols. Edited by Susan Snyder. Oxford: Oxford University Press, 1979.

Echard, Laurence. *The History of England*. 2nd ed. 3 vols. London: Jacob Tonson, 1718.

Eight of Spades, South Sea Bubble Playing Cards, Kress Collection, Baker Library, Harvard University Business School. https://www.library.hbs.edu/hc/collections/kress/kress_img/bubble_newspaper2.htm.

Eikon Basilike: The Pourtraicture of his Sacred Majestie in his Solitudes and Suffering. N.p., n.p., 1648.

Erasmus, Desiderius. *The Praise of Folly and Other Writings*. Translated and edited by Robert M. Adams. New York: Norton, 1989.

Evelyn, John. *The Diary of John Evelyn*. Edited by E.S. DeBeer, 6 vols. Oxford: Clarendon Press, 1955.

The Fatal Consequences of Gaming and Stock-jobbing. A Sermon Preach'd in the City of London, on Sunday, November 6. 1720. London: T. Jauncy, 1720.

Fielding, Henry. *The History of Tom Jones, a Foundling*. Edited by Martin Battestin and Fredson Bowers. Middletown, CT: Wesleyan University Press, 1975.

Fitzgeffrey, Henry. *Satyres: and Satyricall Epigrams: with Certaine Observations at Black- Fryers*. London: Edw[ard] Allde for Miles Patrich, 1617.

Flecknoe, Richard. *Love's Kingdom, A Pastoral Trage-comedy: not as it was acted at the theatre near Lincolns Inn, but as it was written, and since corrected … with a short treatise of the English Stage, &c., by the same author*. London: R. Wood, 1664.

Foxe, John. *The Seconde Volume of the Ecclesiastical Historie, Conteining the Acts and Monuments of Martyrs*. 2nd ed. London: John Day, 1583.

Gareth. "Armoury Images Hampton Court." Flickr, photos taken April 13, 2009. https://www.flickr.com/photos/30728992@N04/3455364801.

Gay, John. *The Beggar's Opera*. Edited by Bryan Loughrey and T.O. Treadwell. London: Penguin, 1986.

Gibson, Edmund. *The Bishop of London's Pastoral Letter to the People of His Diocese*. London: Samuel Buckley, 1728.

Gifford, George. *A Plaine Declaration that our Brownists be full Donatists*. London: Toby Cooke, 1590.

Goodwin, John. *Hybristodikai: The Obstructours of Justice, or a Defence of the Honourable Sentence Passed upon the Late King, by the High Court of Justice*. London: Henry Cripps, 1649.

Gorrie, John, dir. *Twelfth Night*. London: BBC and Time-Life Films, 1980.

Gosson, Stephen. *Playes confuted in five actions*. London: Thomas Gosson, 1582.

Greville, Fulke. *Works in Verse and Prose*. Vol 4. Edited by Alexander B. Grosart. 1870; reprint, New York: AMS Press, 1966.

Grose, Francis. *A Classical Dictionary of the Vulgar Tongue*. London: S. Hooper, 1785. ECCO (CB3331204754).

Guthrie, James. *The Ordinary of Newgate his Account, Of the Behaviour, Confession, and dying Words of the Malefactors, who were executed at Tyburn, on Tuesday the 12th, of this Instant May, 1730*. London: printed by John Applebee, 1730.

– *The Ordinary of Newgate his Account*. London: John Applebee, 1731.

Hall, Edward. *The Union of the Two Noble and Illustre Famelies of Lancastre and Yorke*. [London]: Rychard Grafton, 1550.

Hamilton, David. *The Diary of Sir David Hamilton, 1709–1714*. Edited by Philip Roberts. Oxford: Clarendon Press, 1975.

The Harlot's Progress: or, the Humours of Drury-Lane. … which is a key to the six prints lately publish'd by Mr. Hogarth. London: B. Dickinson, R. Mountague, J. Brotherton, R. Ware, A. Dodd, J. Brindly, J. Jolliff, and J. Stagg, 1732.

Harpsfield, Nicholas. *The Life and Death of Sr Thomas Moore, Knight, Sometymes Lord High Chancellor of England*. Edited by Elsie Vaughan Hitchcock. EETS 186. London: Oxford University Press, 1932.

Hawkins, Henry. *Partheneia sacra. Or the mysterious and delicious garden of the sacred Parthenes*. [Rouen]: John Cousturier, 1633.

Hearne, Thomas. *Remarks and Collections of Thomas Hearne*. Edited by C.E. Doble. 11 vols. Oxford: Oxford Historical Society, 1885–1921.

Herbert, Thomas. *Memoirs of the Last Two Years of the Reign of King Charles*. London: Nichol, 1813.

Heywood, Thomas. *An Apology for Actors*. London: N. Okes, 1612.

Hogarth, William. *A Harlot's Progress*. The Lewis Walpole Library. Digital Images Collection, Yale University, Digital Collections. http://findit.library.yale.edu/.

Howell, T.B. *Complete Collection of State Trials and Proceedings for High Treason and Other Crimes and Misdemeanors*. 33 vols. London: Hansard, 1816.

Huggarde, Myles. *The Displaying of the Protestantes*. Cum privilegio ad imprimem / dum solum, 1556.

Hume, David. *A Treatise of Human Nature*. Edited by L.A. Selby-Bigge and Peter H. Nidditch. Oxford: Clarendon Press, 1978.

I.G. *A Refutation of the Apology for Actors*. Edited by Richard H. Perkinson. New York: Scholars' Facsimiles and Reprints, 1941.

Ignatius, Saint. *The Spiritual Exercises of Saint Ignatius*. Translated by Thomas Corbishley, S.J. London: Burns & Oates, 1963.

Jago, Richard. *Edge-Hill, or, the Rural Prospect Delineated and Moralized*. London: J. Dodsley, 1767.

James I. *Basilikon doron Devided into three books*. Edinburgh: Robert Waldegrave, 1599.

– *Basilikon Doron*. Edited by James Craigie. Edinburgh and London: William Blackwood and Sons, 1944.

Johnson, Samuel. *A dictionary of the English language: in which the words are deduced from their originals, and illustrated in their different significations by examples from the best writers*. 2 vols. London: W. Strahan and P. Knapton, 1755.

– *Lives of the English Poets*. Edited by George Birkbeck Hill. 2 vols. Oxford: Clarendon, 1905.

– *The Lives of the Most Eminent English Poets: With Critical Observations on Their Works*. Edited by Roger Lonsdale. 4 vols. Oxford: Oxford University Press, 2006.

– *Prologue and Epilogue spoken at the Opening of the Theatre in Drury-Lane, 1747*. London: W. Webb, [1747].

Jonson, Ben. *Ben Jonson*. Edited by C.H. Herford, Percy Simpson, and Evelyn Simpson. 11 vols. Oxford: Oxford University Press, 1925–52.

– *The Complete Masques*. Edited by Stephen Orgel. New Haven: Yale University Press, 1975.

– *The Staple of News*. Edited by Anthony Parr. Revels Plays. Manchester: Manchester University Press, 2002.

Johnstone, James. *Memoirs of the Chevalier de Johnstone*. Translated and edited by Charles Winchester. 3 vols. Aberdeen: Wylie, 1870.

Kesselring, K.J., ed. *The Trial of Charles I*. Peterborough, ON: Broadview, 2016.

Lant, Thomas. *Sequitur celebritas et pompa funeris*. London: Theodor De Bry, 1587 (1588).

Lemnius, Levinus. *The Touchstone of Complexions*. Translated by Thomas Newton. London: Thomas Marsh, 1576.

A Letter from a Parishioner of St. Clement Danes, To the Right Reverend Father in God Edmund, Lord Bishop of London. London: J. Roberts, A. Dod, and E. Nut, 1725.

Locke, John. *An Essay Concerning Human Understanding*. Edited by Peter H. Nidditch. Oxford: Clarendon Press, 1975.

Louthe, John. "The Reminiscences of John Loude or Louthe, Archdeacon of Nottingham." In *Narratives of the Days of the Reformation*, edited by John Gough Nichols, 1–59. London: Camden Society, 1859.

Mandeville, Bernard. *A Modest Defence of Publick Stews: or, an Essay upon Whoring*. London: A. Moore, 1724.

Marlowe, Christopher. *Doctor Faustus: A 1604-Version Edition*. Edited by Michael Keefer. 2nd ed. Peterborough, ON: Broadview Editions, 2007.

Marvell, Andrew. *The Poems of Andrew Marvell*. Edited by Nigel Smith. London: Pearson Longman, 2003.

Merritt, J.F, General Editor. Strype, *Survey of London (1720)* [online] (hriOnline, Sheffield), available from: November 2007, accessed 4 May 2017. https://www.dhi.ac.uk/strype/index.jsp.

Miège, Guy. *The New State of England under Their Majesties K. William and Q. Mary*. London: H.C. for Jonathan Robinson, 1691.

Milton, John. *Complete Poems and Major Prose*. Edited by Merritt Y. Hughes. New York: Odyssey, 1957.

Montagu, Mary Wortley. *Lady Mary Wortley Montagu: Selected Letters*. Edited by Isobel Grundy. London: Penguin, 1997.

Morden, Robert. *The New Description and State of England, Containing the Mapps of the Counties of England and Wales*. London: 1701.

More, Thomas. *The Correspondence of Sir Thomas More*. Edited by Elizabeth Frances Rogers. Princeton, NJ: Princeton University Press, 1947.

Munday, Antony. *A Third blast of retrait from plaies and Theaters.* London: Henry Denham, 1580.

Nashe, Thomas. *Pierce Penniless his Supplication to the Divell.* London: Abell Jeffes for John Busbie, 1592.

A New Canting Dictionary. London: booksellers of London and Westminster, 1725.

The new pollecye of warre. 2nd ed. London: John Maylerre for John Gough, 1542.

North, Dudley, 3rd Baron North. *A Forest of Varieties*. London: Richard Cotes, 1645.

Nunn, Trevor, dir. *Twelfth Night*. London: Renaissance Films, 1996.

De Onthoofding vande Rebellige Lords op Groot Tower Hill, 1746.

Parker, Oliver, dir. *Othello*. Castle Rock Entertainment, 1995.

Pepys, Samuel. *The Diary of Samuel Pepys: A New and Complete Transcription.* Edited by Robert Latham and William Matthews. 11 vols. Berkeley: University of California Press, 1970–83.

Pix, Mary. *The Deceiver Deceived, A Comedy.* London: R. Basset, 1698.

Platter, Thomas. *Thomas Platter's Travels in England, 1599*. Edited by Clare Williams. London: Jonathan Cape, 1937.

Power, Henry. *Experimental philosophy, in three books containing new experiments microscopical, mercurial, magnetical.* London: T. Roycroft, 1664.

The Practical scheme of the secret disease, a gleet and a broken constitution, caused by fast living, former cures, salivations, taking of mercury, self-abuses, &c. shewing To those who want a Cure of either the Venereal Distemper, or a Gleet, what will Best do it. London: H. Parker, 1728.

Price, Richard. *A Discourse on the Love of Our Country*. London: George Stafford for T. Cadell, 1789.

Ralegh, Walter. *The History of the World.* London: 1614.

– *The Poems of Sir Walter Ralegh*. Edited by Agnes M.C. Latham. London: Constable, 1929.

Ray, James. *A compleat history of the rebellion, from its first rise in 1745, to its total suppression at the glorious Battle of Culloden*. Manchester: 1747.

Reeve, Richard. "Tower of London: Royal Armoury." Fine Art America. http://fineartamerica.com/featured/tower-of-london-royal-armoury-richard-reeve.html.

Roberts, Helen, ed. *The Encyclopedia of Comparative Iconography: Themes Depicted in Works of Art*. London: Routledge, 2013.

Roper, William. *The Lyfe of Sir Thomas Moore, Knight*. Edited by Elsie Vaughan Hitchcock. EETS 192. London: Oxford University Press, 1935.

Rubens, Peter Paul. Preliminary sketch for the ceiling, Whitehall, *Apotheosis of James I*. Tate Gallery, no. T12919.

Russell, D.A. and Winterbottom, M., eds. *Ancient Literary Criticism: The Principal Texts in New Translations*. Oxford: Clarendon, 1972.

Sacheverell, Henry. *The Perils of False Brethren, both in Church, and State*. London: Henry Clements, 1709.

Select Trials for Murders, Robberies, Rapes, Sodomy, Coining, Frauds, and Other Offences: at the Sessions-House in the Old-Bailey. Vol. 2. London: J. Wilford, 1734–35.

Seneca. *Ad Lucilium epistulae morales*. Translated by Richard M. Gummere. Loeb Classical Library. Cambridge, MA: Harvard University Press, 1967.

"September 1642: Order for Stage-plays to cease." In *Acts and Ordinances of the Interregnum, 1642–1660*, edited by C.H. Firth and R.S. Rait, 26–7. London: His Majesty's Stationery Office, 1911.

Settle, Elkannah. *Glory's Resurrection: Being the Triumph of London Revived, For the Inauguration of the Right Honourable Sir Francis Child, Kt. Lord Mayor of the City of London*. London: R. Barnham, 1698.

Shadwell, Thomas. *The Complete Works of Thomas Shadwell*. Edited by Montague Summers. 5 vols. 1927; reprint, New York: Benjamin Blom, 1968.

– *The Virtuoso*. Edited by Marjorie Hope Nicolson. Lincoln: University of Nebraska Press, 1966.

Shakespeare, William. *The Riverside Shakespeare*. Edited by G. Blakemore Evans, J.J.M. Tobin, Herschel Baker, Anne Barton, Frank Kermode, Harry Levin, Hallett Smith, and Marie Edel. 2nd ed. Boston: Houghton Mifflin, 1997.

– *As You Like It*. Edited by Alan Brissenden. Oxford: Oxford University Press, 1993.

– *Hamlet*. Eds. Ann Thompson and Neil Taylor, Arden Shakespeare. London: Methuen, 2006.

– *Henry V*. Edited by Andrew Gurr. Cambridge: Cambridge University Press, 2005.

– *The Merchant of Venice*. Edited by Jay L. Halio. Oxford: Oxford University Press, 1993.

– *A Midsummer Night's Dream*. Edited by R.A. Foakes. New York: Cambridge University Press, 2003.

– *Much Ado About Nothing*. Edited by Stephen Greenblatt. In *The Norton Shakespeare*, edited by Stephen Greenblatt, Walter Cohen, E. Howard, and Katharine Eisaman Maus, 1381–444. New York: Norton, 1997.

– *Much Ado About Nothing*. Edited by A.R. Humphreys. Arden Shakespeare. London: Methuen, 1981.

– *The Poems*. Edited by F.T. Prince. Arden Edition. London: Methuen, 1960.

– *The Tragedy of Coriolanus*. Edited by R.B. Parker. Oxford: Clarendon Press, 1994.

– *Twelfth Night*. Edited by Roger Warren and Stanley Wells. Oxford: Oxford University Press, 1994.

– *The Winter's Tale*. Edited by Stephen Orgel. Oxford: Clarendon Press, 1996.

Shirley, James. *Honoria and Mammon, Whereunto is Added the Contention of Ajax and Ulysses for the Armour of Achilles*. London: John Crook, 1659.

Stapleton, Thomas. *The Life and Illustrious Martyrdom of Sir Thomas More*. Translated by Philip P. Hallett. Edited by E.E. Reynolds. New York: Fordham University Press, 1966.

The Statutes of the Realm.

Steele, Richard. *The Lover*, no. 33, 189–95. London: 1715.

Swift, Jonathan. *Verses on the Death of Dr. S——, D.S.P.D. Occasioned by Reading a Maxim in Rochefoulcault. Written by Himself, November 1731*. London printed: Dublin: re-printed by George Faulkner, 1739.

Sylvester, Joshua. *The Complete Works of Joshua Sylvester*. 2 vols. Edited by Alexander Grosart. 1880. Reprint, New York: AMS Press, 1967.

Tanner, Anodyne [pseud.], *The Life of the Late Celebrated Mrs. Elizabeth Wisebourn, Vulgarly call'd Mother Wybourn*. London: A. Moore, c. 1721.

Thomson, James. *The Seasons*. Edited by James Sambrook. Oxford: Oxford University Press, 1981.

Thornhill, James. Designs for Thomas Clayton's *Arsinoë* (performed 1705). Victoria and Albert Museum, nos. D.26–1891, D.27–1891 and D.28–1891.

The Tragedy of Master Arden of Faversham. Edited by M.L. Wine. The Revels Plays. London: Methuen, 1973.

Tragicum Theatrum Actorum. Amsterdam: Jodocum Jansonium, 1649.

The Triumphs of London, for the Inauguration of the Right Honourable Sir Richard Levett, Kt. Lord Mayor of the City of London. London: A. Baldwin, 1699.

A True Representation of Tower Hill, as it Appeared from a rais'd point of View on the north side, Aug. 18th 1746. Published According to Act of Parliament. G. Budd, pinx. P. C. Canot, Sculp. 1747.

Tyndale, William. *The Obedience of a Christen man.* 1535.

Villette, John. *The Annals of Newgate; or, malefactors register.* London: 1776.

Walpole, Horace. *Horace Walpole's Correspondence with Sir Horace Mann.* Edited by W.S. Lewis, Warren Hunting Smith, and George L. Lam. 3 vols. New Haven: Yale University Press, 1954.

Ward, Ned. *The Humours of a Coffee-House, A Comedy.* In *A Collection of the Writings of Mr. Edward Ward.* Vol. 2, 274–345. London: 1717.

– *The London Spy Compleat.* Edited by Allison Muri and Ben Neudorf. The Grub Street Project, Digital Research Centre: University of Saskatchewan. http:/grubstreetproject.net/works/T119938?display=text&page=265.

– "A South-Sea Ballad, or, Merry Remarks upon Exchange-Alley Bubbles." London: 1720.

– *A Trip to Jamaica: With a True Character of the People and Island.* 7th ed. London: 1700.

Wetenhall, Edward. *Enter into thy Closet: Or, a Method and Order for Private Devotion.* 5th ed. London: John Martyn, 1676.

Whitney, Geffrey. *A Choice of Emblemes.* Leyden: C. Plantyn, 1586.

The Witch of Wapping. London: Th. Spring, 1652.

Woolston, Thomas. *A Discourse on the Miracles of our Saviour.* London: printed for the author, 1727.

– *A Sixth Discourse on the Miracles of our Saviour.* London: printed for the author, 1729.

Wordsworth, William. *The Poetical Works of William Wordsworth.* Edited by Ernest de Selincourt. 5 vols. Oxford: Clarendon Press, 1952.

– *The Prose Works of William Wordsworth.* Edited by W.J.B. Owen and Jane Worthington Smyser. 3 vols. Oxford: Clarendon Press, 1974.

Wright, James. *Historia Histrionica: An Account of the English Stage.* London: G. Croom for William Haws, 1699.

Wriothesley, Charles. *A Chronicle of England during the Reigns of the Tudors.* Edited by William Douglas Hamilton. London: Camden Society, 1875.

Wyatt, Thomas. *Collected Poems of Sir Thomas Wyatt.* Edited by Kenneth Muir and Patricia Thomson. Liverpool: Liverpool University Press, 1969.

2 Early Periodicals

Craftsman 198 (18 April 1730).

Daily Advertiser 70 (24 April 1731); 140 (15 July 1731).

Daily Courant 8894 (11 April 1730).

Daily Journal 2851 (26 February 1730); 2890 (11 April 1730); 2893 (15 April 1730); 2987 (3 August 1730); 3184 (20 March 1731); 3215 (26 April 1731).

Daily Post 3292 (8 April 1730); 3298 (15 April 1730); 3392 (3 August 1730); 3620 (26 April 1731).

Evening Post 2356 (29 August–1 September 1724); 3283 (1–4 August 1730).

Fog's Weekly Journal 75 (28 February 1730).

Gentleman's Magazine and Historical Chronicle (April 1747).

Grub Street Journal 9 (5 March 1730); 10 (12 March 1730); 16 (23 April 1730); 31 (6 August 1730); 38 (24 September 1730); 69 (29 April 1731).

London Evening Post 349 (3–5 March 1730); 364 (7–9 April 1730); 532 (24–7 April 1731).

London Gazette 6873 (11–14 April 1730).

London Journal 190 (16 March 1723); 559 (18 April 1730); 574 (1 August 1730).

Monthly Chronicle (April 1730).

Parker's London News or the Impartial Intelligencer 997 (7 April 1725).

Post Boy 5482 (5–8 September 1724).

The Spectator 69 (19 May 1711); 411 (21 June 1712).

The Tatler 216 (21 August 1710).

Universal Journal 26 (6 June 1724).

Universal Spectator, and Weekly Journal 73 (28 February 1730); 80 (18 April 1730).

Weekly Journal or British Gazetteer (16 March 1723); 15 (10 April 1725); 265 (18 April 1730).

Weekly Journal or Saturday's Post 306 (5 September 1724).

3 Commentary

"1683: Lord Russell, Whig Martyr." ExecutedToday.com. Posted 21 July 2014; accessed 13 October 2016. http://www.executedtoday.com/2014/07/21/1683-lord-russell-whig-martyr/.

"1685 [15 July]: James Scott, Duke of Monmouth." ExecutedToday.com. Posted 15 July 2008; accessed 14 November 2018. http://wwwexecutedtoday.com/2008/07/15/1685-james-scott-duke-of-monmouth/.

Abbott, Geoffrey. *Lords of the Scaffold: A History of the Executioner.* London: Robert Hale, 1991.

Ackroyd, Peter. *London: The Biography.* New York: Nan A. Talese, 2001.

Alexander, Gavin. *Writing After Sidney: The Literary Response to Sir Philip Sidney, 1586–1640.* Oxford: Oxford University Press, 2006.

Anderson, Benedict. *Imagined Communities: Reflections on the Origin and Spread of Nationalism.* Revised ed. London: Verso, 2006.

Arnold, Dana. "The Country House and its Publics." In *The Georgian Country House, Architecture, Landscape and Society*, edited by Dana Arnold, 20–42. Stroud: Sutton, 2003.

Ashton, John. *A History of English Lotteries: Now Written for the First Time.* London: Leadenhall Press, 1893.

Atkinson, P. "The Execution of Monmouth." A Theory of Civilisation, OurCivilisation.com. Accessed 13 October 2016. http://www.ourcivilisation.com/smartboard/shop/macaulay/england/monmouth.htm.

Aubin, Robert Arnold. *Topographical Poetry in XVIII-Century* England. New York: MLA, 1936.

Backscheider, Paula. *Spectacular Politics: Theatrical Power and Mass Culture in Early Modern England.* Baltimore: Johns Hopkins University Press, 1993.

Bakhtin, Mikhail. "Forms of Time and the Chronotope in the Novel." In *The Dialogic Imagination: Four Essays*, edited by Michael Holquist, translated by Caryl Emerson and Michael Holquist, 84–258. Austin: University of Texas Press, 1981.

Bakhuÿs, Diederik, Marie-Claude Coudert, Élisabeth de Fontenay, and Laurent Salomé, eds. *Les curieux philosophes de Velázquez et de Ribera.* Rouen: Fage, 2005.

Bal, Mieke. *The Art of Viewing.* Amsterdam: G+B Arts International, 2001.

Bal, Mieke, and Norman Bryson. "Semiotics and Art History." *The Art Bulletin* 73, no. 2 (June 1991): 174–208.

Bald, R.C. *Donne and the Drurys.* Cambridge: Cambridge University Press, 1959.

– *John Donne: A Life.* Oxford: Clarendon, 1970.

Bannerjee, Pompa. *Burning Women: Widows, Witches, and Early Modern European Travellers in India*. Houndmills, Basingstoke: Palgrave Macmillan, 2003.

Barish, Jonas A. *The Antitheatrical Prejudice.* Berkeley: University of California Press, 1981.

Barkan, Leonard. "Diana and Actaeon: The Myth as Synthesis." *English Literary Renaissance* 10 (1980): 317–59.

– *Mute Poetry, Speaking Pictures*. Princeton, NJ: Princeton University Press, 2013.

Barnes, Julian. "Bowls with Souls: The Secrets of Cézanne-world: Ancient Earthware, Heavy Apples and the Six of Hearts." *Times Literary Supplement*, 21/28, December 2012, 4.

Barrell, John. *English Literature in History 1730–80: An Equal, Wide Survey.* London: Hutchinson, 1983.

Barton, Anne. *Ben Jonson: Dramatist.* Cambridge: Cambridge University Press, 1984.

Baudrillard, Jean. *Simulacra and Simulation*. Translated by Sheila Faria Glaser. Ann Arbor: University of Michigan Press, 1995.

Baxter, John. "Perilous Stuff: Poems of Religious Meditation." *Renascence* 62, no. 2 (Winter 2010): 89–115.

Benedict, Barbara M. *Curiosity: A Cultural History of Early Modern Inquiry.* Chicago: University of Chicago Press, 2001.

Benhabib, Seyla. *Situating the Self: Gender, Community and Postmodernism in Contemporary Ethics*. New York: Routledge, 1992.

Berger, Harry, Jr. "Against the Sink-a-Pace: Sexual and Family Politics in *Much Ado About Nothing*." In *Making Trifles of Terrors: Redistributing Complicities in Shakespeare*, edited by Peter Erickson, 10–24. Stanford: Stanford University Press, 1997.

– *Caterpillage: Reflections on Seventeenth-Century Dutch Still-Life Painting.* New York: Fordham, 2011.

– *Fictions of the Pose: Rembrandt Against the Italian Renaissance.* Stanford, CA: Stanford University Press, 2000.

Bergson, Henri. *Laughter*. Edited and translated by Wylie Sypher. In *Reader in Comedy: An Anthology of Theory and Criticism*, edited by Magda Romanska and Alan Ackerman. London: Bloomsbury, 2017.

Berzal de Dios, Javier. "Velázquez's *Democritus*: Global Disillusion and the Critical Hermeneutics of a Smile." *Renaissance and Reformation* 39, no. 1 (Winter 2016): 35–62.

Bevington, David, and Peter Holbrook. Introduction to *The Politics of the Stuart Court Masque*, edited by David Bevington and Peter Holbrook, 1–19. Cambridge: Cambridge University Press, 1998.

Billings, Timothy. "Caterwauling Cataians: The Genealogy of a Gloss." *Shakespeare Quarterly* 54 (2003): 1–28.

Blankert, Albert. "Heraclitus en Democritus Bij Marcilio Ficino." *Simiolus: Netherlands Quarterly for the History of Art* 1, no. 3 (1966–67): 133–4.

– "Heraclitus en Domicritus, in het bijzonder in de Nederlandse Kunst van de 17de eeuw." *Nederlands Kunsthistorisch Jaarboek* 18 (1967): 31–124.

Blankert, Albert, Rijksmuseum (Netherlands), Detroit Institute of Arts, and National Gallery of Art (U.S.). *Gods, Saints, & Heroes: Dutch Painting in the Age of Rembrandt*. Washington: National Gallery of Art, 1980.

Bloom, Harold. "Freud: A Shakespearean Reading." *The Yale Review* 82, no. 2 (1994): 1–23.

Boose, Lynda. "'Let it be hid': The Pornographic Aesthetic of Shakespeare's *Othello*." In *New Casebooks: "Othello*," edited by Lena Cowen Orlin, 22–48. New York: Palgrave Macmillan, 2004.

Bos, Sander, Marianne Lange-Meyers, and Jeanine Six. "Sidney's Funeral Portrayed." In *Sir Philip Sidney: 1586 and the Creation of a Legend*, edited by Jan van Dorsten, Arthur F. Kinney, and Dominic Baker-Smith, 38–61. Leiden: Brill, 1986.

Bradshaw, C. "Miles Huggarde (fl. 1533–57), poet and religious polemicist," *Oxford Dictionary of National Biography*. Oxford University Press. Accessed online: http://www.oxforddnb.com/2004.

Briggs, Peter. "Satiric Strategy in Ned Ward's London Writings." *Eighteenth-Century Life* 35, no. 2 (2011): 76–101.

Brownlow, F.W. *Shakespeare, Harsnett, and the Devils of Denham*. Newark: University of Delaware Press, 1993.

Bryson, Norman. *Looking at the Overlooked: Four Essays on Still Life Painting*. London: Reaktion, 1990.

Bullough, Edward. "'Psychical Distance' as a Factor in Art and as an Aesthetic Principle." *British Journal of Psychology* 5 (1912): 87–117.

Burchard, Wolf. "Illusion and Involvement: The Lost Baroque Architecture of St. George's Hall at Windsor Castle." *Immediations* 2, no. 4 (2011): 99–119.

– *The Sovereign Artist: Charles Le Brun and the Image of Louis XIV*. London: Paul Holberton, 2016.

Buxton, John. "The Mourning for Sidney." *Renaissance Studies* 3 (1989): 46–56.

Carey, John. *John Donne: Life, Mind and Art*. London: Faber, 1981.

Carlos, Ann M., Karen Maguire, and Larry Neal. "'A knavish people …': London Jewry and the Stock Market during the South Sea Bubble." *Business History* 50.6 (2008): 728–48.

Carruthers, Bruce G. *City of Capital: Politics and Markets in the English Financial Revolution*. Princeton, NJ: Princeton University Press, 1999.

Cartwright, Kent. *Shakespearean Tragedy and Its Double: The Rhythms of Audience Response.* University Park: Pennsylvania State University Press, 1991.

Chalmers, Alexander. "The Life of Jago." In *Works of the English Poets*, edited by Alexander Chalmers, 17:283. London: J. Johnson, 1810.

Chambers, E.K. *The Elizabethan Stage.* Vol. 4. Oxford: Clarendon Press, 1974.

Chandler, James K. *1819: The Politics of Literary Culture and the Case of Romantic Historicism*. Chicago and London: University of Chicago Press, 1998.

Chico, Tita. "Gimcrack's Legacy: Sex, Wealth, and the Theatre of Experimental Philosophy." *Comparative Drama* 42, no.1 (2008): 29–49. http://www.jstor.org/stable/23038077.

Christian, Lynda. *"Theatrum Mundi": The History of an Idea*. New York: Garland, 1987.

Cohen, Ralph. "The Augustan Mode in English Poetry." *Eighteenth-Century Studies* 1 (1967): 3–32.

– *The Unfolding of* The Seasons. Baltimore: Johns Hopkins University Press, 1970.

Colaianne, A.J. and W.L. Godshalk, eds. *Elegies for Sir Philip Sidney (1587)*. Facsimiles and Reprints 345. Delmar, NY: Scholars' Facsimiles and Reprints, 1980.

Coldham, Peter Wilson. *Emigrants in Chains: A Social History of Forced Emigration to the Americas of Felons, Destitute Children, Political and Religious Non-Conformists, Vagabonds, Beggars and other Undesirables, 1607–1776*. Baltimore: Genealogical Publishing Co., 1992.

Coles, Kimberly Anne. *Religion, Reform, and Women's Writing in Early Modern England.* Cambridge: Cambridge University Press, 2008.

Collington, Philip D. "'Stuffed with all honourable virtues': *Much Ado About Nothing* and *The Book of the Courtier*." *Studies in Philology* 103 (2006): 281–312.

Cook, Carol. "'The Sign and Semblance of Her Honor': Reading Gender Difference in *Much Ado About Nothing*." *PMLA* 101 (1986): 186–202.

Cook, G.H. *Old St Paul's Cathedral: A Lost Glory of Medieval London*. London: Phoenix House, 1955.

Coppola, Al. *The Theater of Experiment: Staging Natural Philosophy in Eighteenth-Century Britain*. Oxford: Oxford University Press, 2016.

Coudert, Marie-Claude. "Velázquez, peintre philosophe." In *Les curieux philosophes de Velázquez et de Ribera*, edited by Diederik Bakhuÿs, Marie-Claude Coudert, Élisabeth de Fontenay, and Laurent Salomé, 81–95. Rouen: Fage, 2005.

Coverley, Melvin. *Psychogeography*. Haarpenden: Pocket Essentials, 2010.

Crary, Jonathan. *Techniques of the Observer: On Vision and Modernity in the Nineteenth Century*. Cambridge, MA: MIT Press, 1990.

Cressy, David. "Death and the Social Order: The Funerary Preferences of Elizabethan Gentlemen," *Continuity and Change* 5, no. 1 (1989): 99–119.

Croft-Murray, Edward. *Decorative Painting in England, 1537–1837*. 2 vols. London: Country Life, 1962–70.

Cummings, Brian. "Animal Passions and Human Sciences: Shame, Blushing and Nakedness in Early Modern Europe and the New World." In *At the Borders of the Human: Beasts, Bodies and Natural Philosophy in the Early Modern Period*, edited by Erica Fudge, Ruth Gilbert, and S.J. Wiseman, 26–50. New York: St Martin's Press, 1999.

Cutler, Anthony. "The Disputà Plate in the J. Paul Getty Museum and Its Cinquecento Context." *The J. Paul Getty Museum Journal* 18 (1990): 5–32.

Dabydeen, David. *Hogarth, Walpole, and Commercial Britain*. London: Hansib Publishing Limited, 1987.

Daniels, Stephen. *Fields of Vision: Landscape Imagery and National Identity in England and the United States*. Cambridge: Polity Press, 1993.

Daniels, Stephen, and Denis Cosgrove. "Spectacle and Text: Landscape Metaphors in Cultural Geography." In *Place/Culture/Representation*, edited by James Duncan and David Ley, 57–77. London: Routledge, 1993.

Daniels, Stephen, and Susanne Seymour. "Landscape Design and the Idea of Improvement 1730–1900." In *An Historical Geography of England and Wales*, 2nd ed., edited by R.A. Dodgshon and R.A. Butlin, 487–520. London: Academic Press, 1990.

Darwin, Charles. *The Expression of the Emotions in Man and Animals* [1872]. New York: D. Appleton, 1998.

Davies, Hunter. *The New London Spy*. London: Blond, 1966.

Davis, Colin. *After Poststructuralism: Reading, Stories and Theory*. London: Routledge, 2004.

Davis, Jim. "Spectatorship." In *The Cambridge Companion to British Theatre, 1730–1830*, edited by Jane Moody and Daniel O'Quinn, 57–69. Cambridge: Cambridge University Press, 2007.

Day, J.F.R. "Death be Very Proud: Sidney, Subversion, and Elizabethan Heraldic Funerals." In *Tudor Political Culture*, edited by Dale Hoak, 179–203. Cambridge: Cambridge University Press, 1995.

Dean, Paul. "'Nothing that is so is so': *Twelfth Night* and Transubstantiation." *Literature & Theology* 17, no. 3 (2003): 281–97.

Debord, Guy. *The Society of the Spectacle*. Translated by Donald Nicholson-Smith. New York: Zone Books, 1994.

De Bruyn, Frans. "From Georgic Poetry to Statistics and Graphs: Eighteenth-Century Representations and the 'State' of British Society." *Yale Journal of Criticism* 17 (2004): 107–39.

– *The Political Genres of Edmund Burke: The Political Uses of Literary Form*. Oxford: Clarendon Press, 1996.

De Fontenay, Élisabeth. "Rire et larmes présocratiques." In *Les curieux philosophes de Velázquez et de Ribera*, edited by Diederik Bakhuÿs, Marie-Claude Coudert, Élisabeth de Fontenay, and Laurent Salomé, 14–23. Rouen: Fage, 2005.

Delano-Smith, Catherine, and Roger J.P. Kain. *English Maps: A History*. London: British Library, 1999.

De Marly, Diana. "The Architect of Dorset Garden Theatre." *Theatre Notebook* 29 (1975): 119–24.

Diamond, Elin. "Gestus and Signature in Aphra Behn's *The Rover*." *ELH* 56, no. 3 (1989): 519–41. http://www.jstor.org/stable/2873196.

Dickson, Donald R. "The Text of Donne's Good Friday Meditation." *John Donne Journal* 32 (2013): 87–106.

Dickson, P.G.M. *The Financial Revolution in England: A Study in the Development of Public Credit, 1688–1756*. London: Macmillan, 1967.

Dolman, Brett. "Antonio Verrio (c. 1636–1707) and the Royal Image at Hampton Court." *The British Art Journal* 10, no. 3 (2010): 18–28.

Donohue, Joseph. "Introduction: The Theatre from 1660 to 1800." In *The Cambridge History of British Theatre*, edited by Joseph Donohue, 2:3–52. Cambridge: Cambridge University Press, 2004.

– "Theatres, Their Architecture and Their Audience." In *The Cambridge History of British Theatre*, edited by Joseph Donohue, 2:292–308. Cambridge: Cambridge University Press, 2004.

Dubrow, Heather. *Captive Victors: Shakespeare's Narrative Poems and Sonnets.* Ithaca, NY: Cornell University Press, 1987.

Duffy, Eamon. *The Stripping of the Altars: Traditional Religion in England c. 1400 – c. 1580.* New Haven: Yale University Press, 1992.

Eco, Umberto. *Travels in Hyperreality: Essays.* Translated by William Weaver. New York: Harcourt Brace, 1986.

Edney, Matthew H. "Reconsidering Enlightenment Geography and Map Making: Reconnaissance, Mapping, Archive." In *Geography and Enlightenment*, edited by David N. Livingstone and Charles W.J. Withers, 165–98. Chicago: University of Chicago Press, 1999.

Eisenstein, Elizabeth L. "Some Conjectures about the Impact of Printing on Western Society and Thought: A Preliminary Report." *Journal of Modern History* 40 (1968): 1–52.

Elam, Kier. *The Semiotics of Theatre and Drama.* London: Methuen, 1980.

Erne, Lukas. "Donne and Christ's Spouse." *Essays in Criticism* 51, no. 2 (2001): 208–29.

Evans, Catherine. "'The church is his Eccho'; Spaces and sounds of memory in Donne's *Sermons*." Paper presented at the John Donne Society Conference, University of Lausanne, June 2018.

Fabricant, Carole. "The Literature of Domestic Tourism and the Public Consumption of Private Property." In *The New Eighteenth Century: Theory, Politics, English Literature*, edited by Felicity Nussbaum and Laura Brown, 254–75. New York: Methuen, 1987.

Fagan, Garret G. *The Lure of the Arena: Social Psychology and the Crowd at the Roman Games.* Cambridge: Cambridge University Press, 2011.

Fernie, Ewan. *Shame in Shakespeare.* London: Routledge, 2002.

Fisch, Harold. "Shakespeare and the Puritan Dynamic." *Shakespeare Survey* 27 (1974): 81–92.

Fleck, Andrew. "The Ambivalent Blush: Figural and Structural Metonymy, Modesty, and *Much Ado About Nothing*." *ANQ* 19 (2006): 16–23.

Fletcher, John. *A Study of the Life and Works of Athanasius Kircher, 'Germanus Incredibilis,' with a Selection of his Unpublished Correspondence and an Annotated Translation of his Autobiography*. Edited by Elizabeth Fletcher. Leiden: Koninklijke Brill, 2011.

Flynn, Dennis. *John Donne and the Ancient Catholic Nobility.* Bloomington: Indiana University Press, 1995.

Ford, Alan. "Ussher, James (1581–1656), Church of Ireland archbishop of Armagh and scholar." *Oxford Dictionary of National Biography.* Oxford University Press. Accessed online: http://www.oxforddnb.com/ 2009.

Foster, John William. "The Measure of Paradise: Topography in Eighteenth-Century Poetry." *Eighteenth-Century Studies* 9 (1975): 232–56.

Foucault, Michel. *Discipline and Punish: The Birth of the Prison*. Translated by Alan Sheridan. New York: Vintage, 1979.

Fournier, Marian. *The Fabric of Life: Microscopy in the Seventeenth Century.* Baltimore: Johns Hopkins University Press, 1996.

Frances, John. *A History of the Bank of England: Its Times and Traditions*, 2nd ed. London: Willoughby & Co., 1847.

Fraser, Antonia. *Faith and Treason: The Story of the Gunpowder Plot*. New York: Doubleday, 1996.

Friedman, Donald M. "Memory and the Art of Salvation in Donne's Good Friday Poem." *English Literary Renaissance* 3 (1973): 418–42.

Fritz, Ronald H. "Herbert, Sir Thomas, first baronet (1606–82), traveller and government official." *Oxford Dictionary of National Biography*. Oxford University Press. Accessed online: http://www.oxforddnb.com/ 2009.

Fujikawa, Mayu. "Pope Paul V's Global Design: The Fresco Cycle in the Quirinal Palace." *Renaissance Studies* 30, no. 2 (2014): 192–217.

Fulford, Tim. *Landscape, Liberty, and Authority: Poetry, Criticism, and Politics from Thomson to Wordsworth*. Cambridge: Cambridge University Press, 1996.

Garrett, James M. "Surveying and Writing the Nation: Wordsworth's Black Comb and 1816 Commemorative Poems." In *Literature and the Nation*, edited by Brook Thomas, REAL: *Yearbook of Research in English and American Literature* 14. Tübingen: Gunter Narr Verlag, 1998.

Geraghty, Anthony. *The Sheldonian Theatre*. New Haven: Yale University Press, 2013.

Gibson, Katherine. "The Decoration of St George's Hall, Windsor, for Charles II: 'too resplendent bright for subjects' eyes.'" *Apollo* 147 (1998): 30–40.

Gil, Daniel Juan. "Before Intimacy: Modernity and Emotion in the Early Modern Discourse of Sexuality." *ELH* 69, no. 4 (2002): 861–87.

Girouard, M. *Life in the English Country House*. New Haven: Yale University Press, 1978.

Giuseppi, J.A. "Early Jewish Holders of Bank of England Stock (1694–1725)." *Miscellanies* 6, 143–74. Jewish Historical Society of England, 1962.

Goldgar, Bertrand A. *Walpole and the Wits: The Relation of Politics to Literature, 1722–1742*. Lincoln: University of Nebraska Press, 1976.

Goldring, Elizabeth, ed. "The Death [1586] and Funeral Procession [1587] of Sir Philip Sidney." In *John Nichols's The Progresses and Public Processions of Queen Elizabeth I: A New Edition of the Early Modern Sources, Volume III 1579–1595*, edited by Elizabeth Goldring, Faith Eales, Elizabeth Clarke, and Jayne Elisabeth Archer, 283–340. Oxford: Oxford University Press, 2014.

– "Sir Philip Sidney and the Politics of Elizabethan Festival." In *Court Festivals of the European Renaissance*, edited by J.R. Mulryne and Elizabeth Goldring, 199–224. Aldershot: Ashgate, 2002.

Gombrich, E.H. *Symbolic Images: Studies in the Art of the Renaissance*. London: Phaidon, 1972.

Gosse, Edmund. *The Life and Letters of John Donne*. 2 vols. London: Heinemann, 1899.

Green, David Brontë. *Blenheim Palace*. London: Country Life, 1951.

Green, Susan. "Semiotic Modalities of the Female Body in Aphra Behn's *The Dutch Lover*." In *Rereading Aphra Behn: History, Theory, and Criticism*, edited by Heidi Hutner, 121–47. Charlottesville: University Press of Virginia, 1993.

Greenblatt, Stephen. *Renaissance Self-Fashioning: From More to Shakespeare*. Chicago: University of Chicago Press, 1980.

– *Sir Walter Ralegh: The Renaissance Man and His Roles*. New Haven: Yale University Press, 1973.

Grootenboek, Hanneke. *The Rhetoric of Perspective: Realism and Illusionism in Seventeenth-Century Dutch Still-Life Painting*. Chicago: University of Chicago Press, 2005.

Guibbory, Achsah. "John Donne and Memory as 'the Art of Salvation.'" *Huntington Library Quarterly* 43, no. 2 (1980): 261–74.

Gundersheimer, Werner L. "Renaissance Concepts of Shame and Pocaterra's *Dialoghi Della Vergogna*." *Renaissance Quarterly* 47 (1994): 34–56.

Gurr, Andrew. "London's Blackfriars Playhouse and the Chamberlain's Men."

In *Inside Shakespeare: Essays on the Blackfriars Stage*, edited by Paul Manzer, 17–30. Selinsgrove, PA: Susquehana University Press, 2006.

– *Playgoing in Shakespeare's London.* Cambridge: Cambridge University Press, 1988.

– *The Shakespearean Stage.* 4th ed. Cambridge: Cambridge University Press, 2009.

Hadot, Pierre. *The Veil of Isis: An Essay on the History of the Idea of Nature.* Translated by Michael Chase. Cambridge, MA: Harvard University Press, 2006.

Halpern, Richard. *The Poetics of Primitive Accumulation.* Ithaca and London: Cornell University Press, 1991.

Hamilton, Donna B. *Shakespeare and the Politics of Protestant England.* Lexington: University of Kentucky Press, 1992.

Hamlett, Lydia. "The Longinian Sublime, Effect and Affect in 'Baroque' British Visual Culture." In *Translations of the Sublime: The Early Modern Reception and Dissemination of Longinus' Peri Hupsous in Rhetoric, the Visual Arts, Architecture and the Theatre*, edited by Caroline van Eck, Stijn Bussels, Maarten Delbeke, and Jürgen Pieters, 187–220. Leiden: Brill, 2012.

– "Pandora at Petworth House: New Light on the Oeuvre and Patronage of Louis Laguerre." *The Burlington Magazine* 158, no. 1365 (December 2016): 950–5.

– "Rupture through Realism: Sarah Churchill and Louis Laguerre's murals at Marlborough House." In *Court, Country, City: British Art and Architecture, 1660–1735*, edited by M. Hallett, N. Llewellyn, and M. Myrone, 195–216. New Haven and London: Yale Center for British Art and Paul Centre for Studies in British Art, 2016.

Hammond, Paul. "Flecknoe, Richard (*b. c.*1605, *d.* in or after 1677)." *Oxford Dictionary of National Biography*. Oxford University Press. Accessed online: http://www.oxforddnb.com/2004.

Hanson, Marilee. "The Execution & Death of Mary, Queen of Scots, 1587." English History. Posted 9 February 2015; accessed 13 October 2016. http://englishhistory.net/tudor/execution-mary-queen-of-scots/.

Hargraves, Matthew. "The Public Image of John Churchill, First Duke of Marlborough, 1702–1708." In *Court, Country, City: British Art and Architecture, 1660–1735*, edited by M. Hallett, N. Llewellyn and M. Myrone, 177–94.

New Haven and London: Yale Center for British Art and Paul Centre for Studies in British Art, 2016.

Harley, John. *William Byrd: Gentleman of the Chapel Royal.* Aldershot: Scolar, 1997.

Harrison, Michael, Greg Lord, and Mike Quilligan. "The Funerary Procession of Sir Philip Sidney: An Early Modern Multimedia Site and Pedagogical Venture" [Flash Presentation]. Transcriptions by Elizabeth Martin. Project Director Elizabeth Bearden. Department of English and Comparative Literature, University of Maryland. Accessed 17 September 2016. http://www.michaelharrison.ws/Sidney/.

Hart, Patrick. "The Badge of Shame: Blushing in Early Modern Literature." *Ecloga* 3 (2003): 1–11.

Hart, Vaughan. *Inigo Jones, The Architect of Kings.* New Haven: Yale University Press, 2011.

– *Sir John Vanbrugh: Storyteller in Stone*, New Haven: Yale University Press, 2008.

Helgerson, Richard. *Forms of Nationhood: The Elizabethan Writing of England.* Chicago: University of Chicago Press, 1992.

Hillyer, Richard. *Sir Philip Sidney, Cultural Icon.* New York: Palgrave Macmillan, 2010.

Hind, A.M. *Engraving in England in the Sixteenth and Seventeenth Centuries, Part I: The Tudor Period.* Cambridge: Cambridge University Press, 1952.

Hiscock, Andrew. *Reading Memory in Early Modern Literature.* Cambridge: Cambridge University Press, 2011.

Hoak, Dale. "Edward VI (1537–1553), king of England and Ireland." *Oxford Dictionary of National Biography.* Oxford University Press. Accessed online: http://www.oxforddnb.com/ 2004–14.

Hobgood, Allison P. "Twelfth Night's 'Notorious Abuse' of Malvolio: Shame, Humorality, and Early Modern Spectatorship." *Shakespeare Bulletin* 24 no. 3 (2006): 1–22.

Holland, Peter. "Farce." In *The Cambridge Companion to English Restoration Theatre*, edited by Deborah Payne Fisk, 107–26. Cambridge: Cambridge University Press, 2000.

– *The Ornament of Action: Text and Performance in Restoration Comedy.* Cambridge: Cambridge University Press, 1979.

Holmes, Richard. *Falling Upwards: How We Took to the Air.* New York: Harper Collins, 2013.

Hosley, Richard. "Blackfriars." In *The Revels History of Drama in English*, edited by J. Leeds Barroll, Alexander Leggatt, Richard Hosley, and Alvin Kernan, 3:197–226. London: Methuen, 1975.

Hotson, Leslie. *The Commonwealth and Restoration Stage*. Oxford: Oxford University Press, 1928.

Huebert, Ronald. "The Female Breast in Reformation Culture." *The Dalhousie Review* 87 (2007): 205–24.

– "Performing Anatomy." *Renaissance and Reformation / Renaissance et Réforme* 33, no. 3 (2010): 9–26.

– *Privacy in the Age of Shakespeare*. Toronto: University of Toronto Press, 2016.

– "'Study our Manuscripts': John Donne's Problems with Privacy." *The Seventeenth Century*, 26, no. 1 (2011): 1–22.

Hughes, Derek. "Aphra Behn and the Restoration Theatre." In *The Cambridge Companion to Aphra Behn,* edited by Derek Hughes, 29–45. Cambridge: Cambridge University Press, 2012.

– *The Theatre of Aphra Behn*. New York: Palgrave, 2001.

Hults, Linda C. "Dürer's *Lucretia*: Speaking the Silence." *Signs: Journal of Women in Culture and Society* 16 (1991): 205–37.

Hunter, Michael. *The Royal Society and its Fellows 1660–1700: The Morphology of an Early Scientific Institution*. London: British Society for the History of Science, 1994.

Jackson, Robert. *Airships: A Popular History of Dirigibles, Zeppelins, Blimps and Other Lighter-than-Air Craft*. Garden City, NY: Doubleday, 1973.

Jay, Martin. "In the Empire of the Gaze: Foucault and the Denigration of Vision in Twentieth-Century French Thought." In *Foucault: A Critical Reader*, edited by David Cousens Hoy, 175–203. Cambridge: Basil Blackwell, 1986.

Jha, Alok. "What Is Heisenberg's Uncertainty Principle?" *The Guardian*. International Online Edition. 10 November 2013. https://www.theguardian.com/science/2013/nov/10/what-is-heisenbergs-uncertainty-principle.

Johns, Richard. "Antonio Verrio and the Triumph of Painting at the Restoration Court." In *Court, Country, City: British Art and Architecture, 1660–1735*, edited by M. Hallett, N. Llewellyn, and M. Myrone, 153–76. New Haven and London: Yale Center for British Art and Paul Centre for Studies in British Art, 2016.

– "'The British Caesar': John Churchill, 1st Duke of Marlborough, and the Visual Arts." In *Marlborough: Soldier and Diplomat*, edited by John B.

Hattendorf, Augustus J. Veenendaal, Jr, and Rolof van Hövell tot Westerflier, 341–6. Rotterdam: Karwansaray Publishers, 2012.

– "'Those Wilder Sorts of Painting': The Painted Interior in the Age of Antonio Verrio." In *A Companion to British Art 1600 to the Present*, edited by Dana Arnold and David Peters Corbett, 79–104. Chichester: Wiley-Blackwell, 2013.

Johnson, Jeffrey. "Gold in the Washes: Donne's Last Going into Germany." *Renascence* 46, no. 3 (Spring 1994): 199–207.

Karian, Stephen E. *Jonathan Swift in Print and Manuscript*. Cambridge: Cambridge University Press, 2010.

Kelley, Theresa M. "The Economics of the Heart: Wordsworth's Sublime and Beautiful." *Romanticism Past and Present* 5 (1981): 15–32.

Kennedy, Dennis. *The Spectator and the Spectacle: Audiences in Modernity and Postmodernity*. Cambridge: Cambridge University Press, 2009.

Kernan, Alvin. "Shakespearean Comedy and Its Courtly Audience." In *Comedy from Shakespeare to Sheridan*, edited by A.R. Braunmuller and J.C. Bulman, 91–101. London: Associated University Presses, 1986.

Kett, Henry. *Elements of General Knowledge, Introductory to Useful Books in the Principal Branches of Literature and Science*. 2 vols. Oxford: Oxford University Press, 1802.

Kishlansky, Mark A., and John Morrill. "Charles I (1600–1649), King of England, Scotland, and Ireland." *Oxford Dictionary of National Biography*. Oxford University Press. Accessed online: http://www.oxforddnb.com/2008.

Kleinbub, Christian K. *Vision and the Visionary in Raphael*. University Park, PA: Pennsylvania State University Press, 2011.

Knapp, James A. "Visual and Ethical Truth in *The Winter's Tale*." *Shakespeare Quarterly* 55 (2004): 253–78.

Kneidel, Gregory. "Donne's 'Via Pauli.'" *Journal of English and Germanic Philology* 100 (2001): 224–46.

Knowles, Richard. "Myth and Type in *As You Like It*." *ELH* 33 (1966): 14–15.

Krier, Theresa M. *Gazing on Secret Sights: Spenser, Classical Imitation, and the Decorums of Vision*. Ithaca: Cornell University Press, 1990.

Lake, Peter, with Michael Questier. *The Antichrist's Lewd Hat: Protestants, Papists and Players in Post-Reformation England*. New Haven: Yale University Press, 2002.

Landa, M.J. "Kitty Villareal, the Da Costas and Samson Gideon." *Transactions* (Jewish Historical Society of England) 13 (1932–35): 271–91.

Lane, Robert. "'Foremost in Report': Social Identity and Masculinity in *Much Ado About Nothing.*" *Upstart Crow* 16 (1996): 31–47.

Langmuir, Erika. *Imagining Childhood.* New Haven: Yale University Press, 2006.

Laqueur, Thomas Walter. "Crowds, Carnival and the State in English Executions, 1604–1868." In *The First Modern Society: Essays in English History in Honour of Lawrence Stone*, edited by A.L. Beir, David Cannadine, and James M. Rosenheim, 305–55. Cambridge: Cambridge University Press, 1989.

Leahy, William. *Elizabethan Triumphal Processions.* Aldershot: Ashgate, 2005.

Leites, Edmund. *The Puritan Conscience and Modern Sexuality.* New Haven: Yale University Press, 1986.

Lenygon, Francis. *Decoration in England from 1640 to 1760.* London: Batsford, 1927.

Lepage, John. *The Revival of Antique Philosophy in the Renaissance.* New York: Palgrave Macmillan, 2012.

Levinas, Emmanuel. *The Levinas Reader.* Edited by Seán Hand. Oxford: Basil Blackwell, 1989.

– "Philosophy and Infinity." *Collected Philosophical Papers.* Translated by Alphonso Lingis. Dordrecht: Martinus Nijhoff, 1987. Originally published in *Revue de métaphysique et de morale* 62 (1957): 241–53.

– *Totality and Infinity: An Essay on Exteriority.* Translated by Alphonso Lingis. Pittsburgh: Duquesne University Press, 1969.

Levine, Laura. *Men in Women's Clothing: Anti-theatricality and Effeminization from 1579 to 1642.* Cambridge: Cambridge University Press, 1994.

Lewcock, Dawn. "More for Seeing than Hearing: Behn and the Use of the Theatre." In *Aphra Behn Studies*, edited by Janet Todd, 66–83. Cambridge: Cambridge University Press, 1996.

Lindheim, Nancy. "Rethinking Sexuality and Class in *Twelfth Night.*" *University of Toronto Quarterly* 76 (2007): 679–713.

Lindsey, Karen. *Divorced, Beheaded, Survived: A Feminist Reinterpretation of the Wives of Henry VIII.* Reading, MA: Addison-Wesley, 1995.

Linebaugh, Peter. *The London Hanged: Crime and Civil Society in the Eighteenth Century.* London: Penguin, 1991.

Liu, Alan. *Wordsworth: The Sense of History.* Stanford: Stanford University Press, 1989.

Llewellyn, Nigel. *The Art of Death: Visual Culture in the English Death Ritual, c.1500–c.1800*. London: Reaktion Books, 1991.

Loewenstein, David. "The King among the Radicals." In *The Royal Image: Representations of Charles I*, edited by Thomas N. Corns, 96–121. Cambridge: Cambridge University Press, 1999.

– *Treacherous Faith: The Specter of Heresy in Early Modern English Literature and Culture*. Oxford: Oxford University Press, 2013.

Löffler, Catharina. *Walking in the City: Urban Experience and Literary Psychogeography in Eighteenth-Century London.* Wiesbaden: J.B. Metzler, 2017.

Love, Harold. "Who Were the Restoration Audience?" *The Yearbook of English Studies* 10, no. 1 (1980): 21–44.

Luckyj, Christina. *'A Moving Rhetorike': Gender and Silence in Early Modern England.* Manchester: Manchester University Press, 2002.

Lurie, Ann Tzeutschler. "The Weeping Heraclitus by Hendrick Terbrugghen in the Cleveland Museum of Art." *The Burlington Magazine* 121, no. 914 (May 1979): 279–87.

Lyne, Raphael. "Dryden and the Complete Career." In *Classical Literary Careers and their Reception*, edited by Philip Hardie and Helen Moore, 253. Cambridge: Cambridge University Press, 2010.

MacAulay, Thomas. *The History of England from the Accession of James II.* London: Folio Press, 1985.

Mallipeddi, Ramesh. *Spectacular Suffering: Witnessing Slavery in the Eighteenth-Century British Atlantic.* Charlottesville: University of Virginia Press, 2016.

Marius, Richard. *Thomas More: A Biography*. New York: Knopf, 1985.

Marsden, Jean I. "Spectatorship, Jeremy Collier and the Anti-Theatrical Debate." *ELH* 65, no. 4 (2016): 877–98.

Maus, Katharine Eisaman. "Horns of Dilemma: Jealousy, Gender, and Spectatorship in English Renaissance Drama." *ELH* 54 (1987): 561–83.

McAdam, Ian. *Magic and Masculinity in Early Modern English Drama*. Pittsburgh: Duquesne University Press, 2009.

McLynn, Frank. *Crime & Punishment in Eighteenth-Century England.* London: Routledge, 1989.

McManus, Clare. *Women on the Renaissance Stage: Anna of Denmark and Female Masquing in the Stuart Court.* Manchester: Manchester University Press, 2002.

Melvin, Peter H. "Burke on Theatricality and Revolution." *Journal of the History of Ideas* 36 (1975): 447–68.

Menzer, Paul. "Crowd Control." In *Imagining the Audience in Early Modern Drama, 1558–1642*, edited by Jennifer A. Low and Nova Myhill, 19–36. New York: Palgrave, 2011.

Milhous, Judith. "The Multimedia Spectacular on the Restoration Stage." In *British Theatre and the Other Arts, 1660–1800*, edited by Shirley Strum Kenny, 44–66. Washington: Folger, 1984.

Minor, Vernon Hyde. *The Death of the Baroque and the Rhetoric of Good Taste.* Cambridge: Cambridge University Press. 2006.

Mitchell, Charles. *Shakespeare and Public Execution.* Studies in Renaissance Literature 26. Lewiston, NY: Edwin Mellen, 2004.

Moir, Esther. *The Discovery of Britain: The English Tourists: 1540–1840.* London: Routledge, 1964.

Morely, Henry, *Memoirs of Bartholomew Fair*. London: Chatto and Windus, 1880.

Moschovakis, Nicolas R. "Topicality and Conceptual Blending: *Titus Andronicus* and the Case of William Hacket." *College Literature* 33 (2006): 127–50.

Muller, Frans. "Flying Dragons and Dancing Chairs at Dorset Garden: Staging *Dioclesian*." *Theatre Notebook* 47, no. 2 (1993): 80–95.

Muller, Frans, and Julie Muller. "Completing the Picture: The Importance of Reconstructing Early Opera." *Early Music* 33, no. 4 (2005): 667–82. http://www.jstor.org/stable/3519588.

Munro, Lucy. *Children of the Queen's Revels: A Jacobean Theatre Repertory.* New York: Cambridge University Press, 2005.

Muri, Allison. "Alexander Pope's Dunciad (1728–9)." *The Grub Street Project.* http://grubstreetproject.net/london/#map=3/categories=13.

– "Beyond GIS: On Mapping Early Modern Narratives and the Chronotope." In *Beyond Accessibility: Textual Studies in the Twenty-First Century*, edited by Brent Nelson and Richard Cunningham. *Digital Studies* 6 (2015–16).

– "Graphs, Maps, and Digital Topographies: Visualizing *The Dunciad* as Heterotopia." *Lumen* 30 (2011): 79–98.

– "The Technology and Future of the Book: What a Digital 'Grub Street' Can Tell Us about Communications, Commerce, and Creativity." In *Producing the Eighteenth-Century Book: Writers and Publishers in England, 1650–1800*, edited by Laura Runge and Pat Rogers, 235–50. Newark, NJ: University of Delaware Press, 2009.

Murphy, Anne L. "Lotteries in the 1690s: Investment or Gamble?" *Financial History Review* 12, no. 2 (2005): 227–46.

Myhill, Nova. "Taking the Stage: Spectators as Spectacle in the Caroline Private Theaters." In *Imagining the Audience in Early Modern Drama, 1558–1642*, edited by Jennifer A. Low and Nova Myhill, 37–54. New York: Palgrave, 2011.

Nathanson, Donald L., ed. *The Many Faces of Shame.* New York: Guilford Press, 1987.

Needleman Armintor, Deborah. "The Sexual Politics of Microscopy in Brobdingnag." *Studies in English Literature 1500–1900* 47, no. 3 (2007): 619–40. http://www.jstor.org/stable/4625129.

Neill, Michael. "Wits Most Accomplish'd Senate: The Audience of the Caroline Private Theaters." *Studies in English Literature 1500–1900* 18 (1978): 341–60.

Neudorf, Benjamin. "The Satirical Topography of Ned Ward's *The London Spy*." Paper presented at the Canadian Society for Eighteenth-Century Studies, Montreal, October 2014.

Nicholl, Charles. *Leonardo Da Vinci: The Flights of the Mind.* London: Penguin, 2005.

Nichols, John. *Anecdotes of William Hogarth. Written by Himself.* London: J.B. Nichols and Son, 1833.

– *The Genuine Works of William Hogarth; Illustrated with Biographical Anecdotes* … Vol. 2. London: Longman, Hurst, Rees, and Orme, 1808–17.

Nussbaum, Martha C. *Upheavals of Thought: The Intelligence of Emotions.* Cambridge: Cambridge University Press, 2001.

O'Connell, Michael. "The Idolatrous Eye: Iconoclasm, Anti-Theatricalism, and the Image of the Elizabethan Theater." *ELH* 52 (1988): 279–310.

Ormerod, David. "Faith and Fashion in 'Much Ado About Nothing.'" *Shakespeare Survey* 25 (1972): 93–106.

Ornstein, Robert. *The Moral Vision of Jacobean Tragedy*. Madison: University of Wisconsin Press, 1960.

Pangallo, Matteo. "'Mayn't a Spectator Write a Comedy?' Playwriting Playgoers in Early Modern Drama." *Review of English Studies* 64 (2013): 39–59.

Panofsky, Dora, and Erwin Panofsky. *Pandora's Box: The Changing Aspects of a Mythical Symbol.* London: Routledge, 1956.

Panofsky, Erwin. *Perspective as Symbolic Form*. Translated by Christopher S. Wood. New York: Zone Books, 1991.

Paster, Gail Kern. *The Body Embarrassed: Drama and the Disciplines of Shame in Early Modern England*. Ithaca: Cornell University Press, 1993.

– "The Tragic Subject and Its Passions." In *The Cambridge Companion to Shakespearean Tragedy*, 2nd ed., edited by Claire McEachern, 152–70. Cambridge: Cambridge University Press, 2013.

Paulson, Ronald. *Hogarth: High Art and Low, 1732–1750*. New Brunswick, NJ: Rutgers University Press, 1992.

– *Hogarth: His Life, Art and Times*. 2 vols. New Haven: Yale University Press, 1971.

– "Some Thoughts on Hogarth's Jew: Issues in Current Hogarth Scholarship." In *Hogarth: Representing Nature's Machines*, edited by Frédéric Ogée, David Bindman, and Peter Wagner, 236–63. Manchester: Manchester University Press, 2001.

Payne, Deborah C. "Theatrical Spectatorship in Pepys's Diary." *Review of English Studies* 66 (2015): 87–108.

Pedretti, Carlo. "The Sforza Sepulchre," Part I. *Gazette des Beaux Arts* (April 1977): 121–31.

Pequigney, Joseph. "The Two Antonios and Same-Sex Love in *Twelfth Night* and *The Merchant of Venice*." *English Literary Renaissance* 22 (1992): 201–21.

Petrie, Charles. *The Jacobite Movement: The Last Phase, 1716–1807*. London: Eyre & Spottiswoode, 1950.

Pinnock, Anthony. "*Deus ex machina*: A Royal Witness to the Court Origin of Purcell's *Dido and Aeneas*." *Early Music* 40, no. 2 (May 2012): 265–78.

Pollock, Anthony. *Gender and the Fictions of the Public Sphere, 1690–1755*. London: Routledge, 2009.

Poole, Kristen. "Saints Alive! Falstaff, Martin Marprelate, and the Staging of Puritanism." *Shakespeare Quarterly* 46 (1995): 47–75.

Poovey, Mary. *A History of the Modern Fact: Problems of Knowledge in the Sciences of Wealth and Society*. Chicago and London: University of Chicago Press, 1998.

Porter, Chloe. *Making and Unmaking in Early Modern English Drama: Spectators, Aesthetics, and Incompletion*. Manchester: Manchester University Press, 2013.

Powell, Jocelyn. *Restoration Theatre Production*. London: Routledge and Kegan Paul, 1984.

Previté-Orton, C.W. *The Shorter Cambridge Medieval History*. Vol. 2. Cambridge: Cambridge University Press, 1960.

Pritchard, Will. *Outward Appearances: The Female Exterior in Restoration London*. Lewisburg: Bucknell University Press, 2008.

Probyn, Elspeth. *Blush: Faces of Shame*. Minneapolis: University of Minnesota Press, 2005.

Quiring, Björn, ed. *"If Then the World a Theatre Present ...": Revisions of the* Theatrum Mundi *Metaphor in Early Modern England*. Berlin and Boston: Walter de Gruyter, 2014.

Rancière, Jacques. *The Emancipated Spectator*. Translated by Gregory Elliott. London: Verso, 2009.

Riggs, David. *The World of Christopher Marlowe*. London: Faber, 2004.

Roach, Joseph. "The Artificial Eye: The Augustan Theatre and the Empire of the Visible." In *The Performance of Power: Theatrical Discourse and Politics*, edited by Sue-Ellen Case and Janelle G. Reinelt, 131–45. Iowa City: University of Iowa Press, 1991.

Roberts, Helen E., ed. *The Encyclopedia of Comparative Iconography: Themes Depicted in Works of Art*. London: Routledge, 2013.

Rogers, Pat. *The Alexander Pope Encyclopedia*. Westport, CT: Greenwood Publishing Group, 2004.

Rowland, Ingrid D. "The Vatican Stanze." In *The Cambridge Companion to Raphael*, edited by Marcia B. Hall, 95–119. Cambridge: Cambridge University Press, 2005.

Sawday, Jonathan. *The Body Emblazoned: Dissection and the Human Body in Renaissance Culture*. London: Routledge, 1995.

Schalkwyk, David. "Love and Service in *Twelfth Night* and the Sonnets." *Shakespeare Quarterly* 56 (2005): 76–100.

Scott, Mary Maxwell. *The Tragedy of Fotheringay: Founded on the Journal of D. Bourgoing, Physician to Mary Queen of Scots, and on Unpublished Ms. Documents*. London: Adam & Charles Black, 1895.

Scott, Walter. *The Life of Dryden*. Edited by Bernard Kreissman. Lincoln: University of Nebraska Press, 1963.

Shami, Jeanne. *John Donne and Conformity in Crisis in the Late Jacobean Pulpit*. Cambridge: D.S. Brewer, 2003.

– "Labels, Controversy, and the Language of Inclusion in Donne's Sermons." In *John Donne's Professional Lives*, edited by David Colclough, 135–57. Cambridge: D.S. Brewer, 2003.

– "'Trying to Walk on Logs in Water': John Donne, Religion, and the Critical Tradition." *Renaissance and Reformation / Renaissance et réforme*, n.s., 25, no. 4 (2001): 81–99.

Shapin, Steven, and Simon Schaffer. *Leviathan and the Air-Pump: Hobbes, Boyle, and the Experimental Life*. Princeton: Princeton University Press, 1985.

Shearman, John. *Only Connect … Art and the Spectator in the Italian Renaissance*. Princeton: Princeton University Press, 1992.

Shuger, Debora Kuller. Review of *Reading Between the Lines* by Annabel Patterson and *Shakespeare and the Politics of Protestant England* by Donna B. Hamilton. *Shakespeare Quarterly* 44 (1993): 488–93.

Shullenberger, William. "Love as a Spectator Sport in John Donne's Poetry." In *Renaissance Discourses of Desire*, edited by Claude J. Summers and Ted-Larry Pebworth, 46–62. Columbia, MO: University of Missouri Press, 1993.

Siebert, Donald T. "The Aesthetic Execution of Charles I: Clarendon to Hume." In *Executions and the British Experience from the 17th to the 20th Century: A Collection of Essays*, edited by William B. Thesing, 7–27. Jefferson, NC: McFarland, 1990.

Simmons, J.L. "A Source for Shakespeare's Malvolio: The Elizabethan Controversy with the Puritans." *Huntington Library Quarterly* 36 (1973): 181–201.

Sinfield, Alan. "How to Read *The Merchant of Venice* Without Being Heterosexist." In *Shakespeare, Authority, Sexuality*, 53–67. London and New York: Routledge, 2006.

Slatkes, Leonard J., and Wayne Franits. *The Paintings of Hendrick ter Brugghen: Catalogue Raisonné*. Amsterdam and Philadelphia: John Benjamins, 2007.

Slights, Camille Wells. *Shakespeare's Comic Commonwealths*. Toronto: University of Toronto Press, 1993.

Smith, Irwin. *Shakespeare's Blackfriars Playhouse: Its History and Its Design*. New York: New York University Press, 1964.

Smith, Joshua S. "Reading Between the Acts: Satire and the Interludes in *The Knight of the Burning Pestle*." *Studies in Philology* 109, no. 4 (2012): 474–95.

Smythe, Sara Lanier. "Woodcuts in English Books, 1536–1560." PhD diss., University of North Carolina, 1973.

Solkin, David. *Art in Britain 1660–1815*. New Haven: Yale University Press, 2015.

– "The Excessive Jew in *A Harlot's Progress*." In *Hogarth: Representing Nature's Machines*, edited by Frédéric Ogée, David Bindman, and Peter Wagner, 219–35. Manchester: Manchester University Press, 2001.

Southern, Richard. *Changeable Scenery: Its Origin and Development in the British Theatre*. London: Faber and Faber, 1951.

– "Theatres and Scenery." In *The Revels History of Drama in English, 1660–1750*, edited by John Loftis, Richard Southern, Marion Jones, and A.H. Scouten, 5:3–52. London: Methuen, 1976.

"South Sea Bubble Short History." Harvard Business School. https://www.library.hbs.edu/hc/ssb/history.html

Spencer, Charles. *Killers of the King: The Men Who Dared to Execute Charles I*. London: Bloomsbury, 2014.

Stern, Tiffany. "Taking Part: Actors and Audience on the Stage at Blackfriars." In *Inside Shakespeare: Essays on the Blackfriars Stage*, edited by Paul Menzer, 35–53. Selinsgrove, PA: Susquehana University Press, 2006.

Stevens, Paul. "Donne's Catholicism and the Innovation of the Modern Nation State." *John Donne Journal* 20 (2001): 153–70.

Stewart, Alan. *Philip Sidney: A Double Life*. New York: St Martin's Press, 2001.

Stewart, Larry. "Physics on Show: Entertainment, Demonstration, and Research in the Long Eighteenth Century." In *The Oxford Handbook to the History of Physics*, edited by Jed Buchwald and Robert Fox, 300–25. Oxford: Oxford University Press, 2013.

Storey, Neil. *London: Crime, Death and Debauchery*. London: Sutton, 2007.

Stretter, Robert. "Cicero on Stage: *Damon and Pithias* and the Fate of Classical Friendship in English Renaissance Drama." *Texas Studies in Literature and Language* 47 (2005): 345–65.

Strickland, Ronald. "Pageantry and Poetry as Discourse: The Production of Subjectivity in Sir Philip Sidney's Funeral." *ELH* 57, no. 1 (1990): 19–36.

Strong, Roy. *Britannia Triumphans: Inigo Jones, Rubens and Whitehall Palace*. London: Thames and Hudson, 1980.

Stubbs, John. *Donne: The Reformed Soul*. London: Viking, 2006.

Summerson, John. *Georgian London*. New York: Charles Scribner's Sons, 1946.

Sutton, John and Evelyn B. Tribble. "Cognitive Ecology as a Framework for Shakespearean Studies." *Shakespeare Studies* 39 (2011): 94–103.

Taylor, Gabriele. *Pride, Shame, and Guilt: Emotions of Self-Assessment*. Oxford: Clarendon Press, 1985.

Thomas, David, and Arnold Hare, editors and compilers. *Restoration and Georgian England, 1660–1788*. Cambridge: Cambridge University Press, 1989.

Thompson, James Westfall. "Shakespeare and Puritanism." *The North American Review* 212, no. 777 (1920): 228–37.

Thompson, Judith. "Introduction." In *John Thelwall: The Peripatetic*, edited by Judith Thompson. Detroit: Wayne State University Press, 2001.

Thomson, Leslie. "Playgoers on the Outdoor Stage of Early Modern London." *Theatre Notebook* 64, no. 1 (2010): 3–44.

"Topographies of Literature & Culture in Eighteenth-Century London." The Grub Street Project. Director Allison Muri. Digital Research Centre, University of Saskatchewan. Accessed April 20, 2017. http://grubstreetproject.net/.

Tricomi, Albert H. *Reading Tudor-Stuart Texts Through Cultural Historicism*. Gainesville: University of Florida Press, 1996.

Troyer, Howard William. *Ned Ward of Grubstreet: A Study of Sub-Literary London in the Eighteenth Century.* Cambridge: Harvard University Press, 1946.

Turberville, A.S. *Mediaeval Heresy & the Inquisition*. London: Crosby Lockwood and Son, 1920.

Van de Wetering, Ernst. *A Corpus of Rembrandt's Paintings IV: Self-Portraits*. The Hague: Springer, 2005.

Waldron, Jennifer. "Gaping on Plays: Shakespeare, Gosson, and the Reformation of Vision." *Critical Matrix* 12 (2000): 48–77.

Walsh, Frederick H. Amazon review of *The New London Spy* by Hunter Davies. 6 March 2012. Accessed 24 May 2015. http://www.amazon.com/The-New-London-Spy-Pleasures/dp/0218514387.

Walter, John. *Crowds and Popular Politics in Early Modern England*. Manchester: Manchester University Press, 2006.

Ward, Charles E. *The Life of John Dryden.* Chapel Hill: University of North Carolina Press, 1961.

Warner, Marina. *Phantasmagoria: Spirit Visions, Metaphor, and Media*. Oxford: Oxford University Press, 2008.

Warwick, Genevieve. *Bernini: Art as Theatre*. New Haven: Yale University Press, 2012.

Watt, Diane. "Askew [married name Kyme], Anne (c. 1521–1546), writer and protestant martyr." *Oxford Dictionary of National Biography* . Oxford University Press. Accessed online: http://www.oxforddnb.com/ 2004.

Wellington, Robert. "A Reflection of the Sun: The First Duke of Marlborough in the Image of Louis XIV." *The Court Historian – The International Journal of Court Studies*, forthcoming.

Wells, Marion A. "'To find a face where all distress is stall'd': *Enargeia*, *Ekphrasis*, and Mourning in *The Rape of Lucrece* and the *Aeneid*." *Comparative Literature* 54 (2002): 97–126.

West, William N. "Knowledge and Performance in the Early Modern *Theatrum Mundi*." *Metaphorik* 14 (2008):1–20.

Wheeler, Elizabeth Skerpan. "*Eikon Basilike* and the Rhetoric of Self-Representation." In *The Royal Image: Representations of Charles I*, edited by Thomas N. Corns, 122–40. Cambridge: Cambridge University Press, 1999.

White, Matthew. "Public Executions and the Gordon Riots." In *The Gordon Riots: Politics, Culture and Insurrection in Late Eighteenth-Century Britain*, edited by Ian Haywood and John Seed, 204–25. Cambridge: Cambridge University Press, 2015.

Whitted, Brent. "Staging Exchange: Why *The Knight of the Burning Pestle* Flopped at Blackfriars in 1607." *Early Theatre* 15, no. 2 (2012): 111–30.

Wiley, Michael. *Romantic Geography: Wordsworth and Anglo-European Spaces*. Basingstoke: Palgrave, 1998.

Wilf, Steven. "Imagining Justice: Aesthetics and Public Executions in Late Eighteenth-Century England." *Yale Journal of Law and the Humanities* 5.51 (1993): 51–78.

Williams, Bernard. *Shame and Necessity*. Berkeley: University of California Press, 1993.

Williams, Owen. "Exorcising Madness in Late Elizabethan England: *The Seduction of Arthington* and the Criminal Culpability of Demoniacs." *Journal of British Studies* 47 (January 2008): 30–52.

Wilson, Catherine. *The Invisible World: Early Modern Philosophy and the Invention of the Microscope*. Princeton: Princeton University Press, 1997.

Wind, Edgar. "The Christian Democritus." *Journal of the Warburg Institute* 1 (1937): 180–2.

Wiseman, Susan. *Drama and Politics of the English Civil War*. Cambridge: Cambridge University Press, 1998.

Wittman, Laura. *The Tomb of the Unknown Soldier, Modern Mourning, and the Reinvention of the Mystical Body*. Toronto: University of Toronto Press, 2011.

Yachnin, Paul, and Anthony Dawson. *The Culture of Playgoing in Shakespeare's England: A Collaborative Debate*. Cambridge: Cambridge University Press, 2001.

Zaller, Robert. "Martin, Richard (1570–1618), *barrister and politician.*" *Oxford Dictionary of National Biography*. Oxford University Press. Accessed online: http://www.oxforddnb.com/2004–14.

Zamir. Tzachi. *Double Vision: Moral Philosophy and Shakespearean Drama.* Princeton: Princeton University Press, 2007.

Zuroski Jenkins, Eugenia. *A Taste for China: English Subjectivity and the Prehistory of Orientalism*. Oxford: Oxford University Press, 2013.

4 Databases and Reference

Early English Books Online.

Eighteenth Century Collection Online.

Oxford Dictionary of National Biography.

Oxford English Dictionary Online.

ProQuest Dissertations & Theses Global.

Web Gallery of Art.

Contributors

RICK BOWERS is professor emeritus, English, University of Alberta, and author of *Radical Comedy in Early Modern England* (2008). He has published on early modern English literature and culture in such journals as *English Studies, Early Theatre, Queen's Quarterly, Huntington Library Quarterly, Notes and Queries, Dalhousie Review, Parergon,* and *Shakespeare Bulletin.* He now divides his time between Southern California and Vancouver Island.

FRANS DE BRUYN is professor emeritus of English at the Faculty of Arts, University of Ottawa. He is co-editor (with Shaun Regan) of *Empire, Identity and the Arts in the Eighteenth-Century Atlantic World* (2014) and the author of *The Political Genres of Edmund Burke* (1996) along with many articles on Restoration and eighteenth-century culture and literature.

LYDIA HAMLETT is academic director in history of art at the Institute of Continuing Education, University of Cambridge, and a fellow and director of studies in history of art at Murray Edwards College. She has published on early modern Italian and British visual culture and is the author of a forthcoming book, *Mural Painting in Britain, 1630–1730: Experiencing Histories* (Routledge), researched and written while a Leverhulme Early Career Research Fellow.

RONALD HUEBERT is professor emeritus, Department of English, Dalhousie University, and Inglis Professor at the University of King's College. His first book, *John Ford: Baroque English Dramatist,* was published by McGill-Queen's University Press (1977). He has often been a spectator at productions of plays by early modern playwrights, a practice that led him to write *The Performance of Pleasure in English Renaissance Drama* (2003). He has served as Editor of *The Dalhousie Review* (1997–2004), and has also edited James Shirley's *The Lady of Pleasure* in the Revels Plays series (1986). He is a past recipient of both the Montaigne Prize (2004) and the Lifetime Achievement Award from the Canadian Society for Renaissance Studies / Société Canadienne d'Études de la Renaissance (2016), and a Life Member of Clare Hall, Cambridge. His most recent book is *Privacy in the Age of Shakespeare* (2016).

JOHN LEPAGE taught in the English Department at Vancouver Island University until his retirement at the end of 2018. His areas of expertise include Renaissance English and French literature, humanism, and encyclopedism. He has published articles and reviews in many journals, and his most recent publication is a full-length monograph, *The Revival of Antique Philosophy in the Renaissance* (2012). He is a former Dean of Arts at Vancouver Island University.

IAN MCADAM is professor of English at the University of Lethbridge. He is the author of two books, *The Irony of Identity: Self and Imagination in the Drama of Christopher Marlowe* (1999) and *Magic and Masculinity in Early Modern English Drama* (2009). He has published essays in collections from Greenwood Press, Bloomsbury, and Cambridge University Press, and has placed articles in the following journals: *Studies in Philology, English Literary Renaissance, Research Opportunities in Renaissance Drama, The Dalhousie Review, Texas Studies in Literature and Language, Pacific Coast Philology, Quidditas, Studies in English Literature, Philological Quarterly, Notes and Queries, Renaissance and Reformation, Marlowe Studies,* and *The University of Toronto Quarterly.*

DAVID MCNEIL has just retired from Dalhousie University where he taught from 1984. He has published *The Grotesque Depiction of War* (1990) and *In the Pressure of the Moment* (2016). He has done research on various subjects related to fiction, popular culture, and media studies. Currently, he is working on an edition of the *Memoirs of the Chevalier James Johnstone.*

ALLISON MURI is a professor in the English Department and the director of the Interdisciplinary Centre for Culture and Creativity at the University of Saskatchewan. She also serves as the director and editor of the SSHRC-supported The Grub Street Project, a digital edition currently in development, which comprises a database of maps, prints, works, and people of eighteenth-century London. She has published in *Lumen*, *Digital Studies*, and *Producing the Eighteenth-Century Book: Writers and Publishers in England, 1650–1800*.

NOVA MYHILL is a professor of English and theater and performance studies at New College of Florida, where she teaches British literature before 1700, drama from all periods, and performance theory. She is the co-editor (with Jennifer Low) of *Imagining the Audience in Early Modern Drama, 1558–1642* (2011) and has published numerous essays on audience and reception in the drama of Shakespeare and his contemporaries. She is currently working on projects on spectatorship at the Blackfriars and the relation between theatrical spectatorship and early modern public punishment.

WILLIAM W.E. SLIGHTS, emeritus professor of English at the University of Saskatchewan, is the author of *Ben Jonson and the Art of Secrecy* (1994), *Managing Readers: Printed Marginalia in English Renaissance Books* (2001), and *The Heart in the Age of Shakespeare* (2008). He has taught Shakespeare and his contemporaries at New York University, the University of Wisconsin-Madison, the University of Saskatchewan, and the University of Warsaw. He retired from full-time teaching in 2004. Since then he has completed his book on the Renaissance heart and has written essays on the reformed conscience (in *Stages of Engagement: Drama and Religion in Post-Reformation England* [2014]) and theories of the body (in *A Handbook of English Renaissance Studies* [2017]). In 2007 he received the Lifetime Achievement Award from the Canadian Society for Renaissance Studies / Société Canadienne d'Études de la Renaissance.

EMILY M. WEST, PhD McMaster University, was a visiting assistant professor at the University of Windsor, 2016–18. She has published on the British cotton industry (*Journal for Early Modern Cultural Studies*) and has forthcoming articles in *The Eighteenth Century: Theory and Interpretation* and *Eighteenth-Century Fiction*. Her research interests include eighteenth-century gender, material culture, technology, toys, and triviality.

Index

Page numbers in italics refer to illustrations.